Bat Chain Puller

BAT CHA

ROCK & ROLL IN TH

N **P**ULLER

GE OF CELEBRITY

KURT LODER

St. Martin's Press
New York

For George O. Loder of Ocean City, New Jersey,
and his wife, Anne.

CONTENTS

INTRODUCTION

The suspicion that rock & roll was entering a strange new phase first struck me one night in New York in the summer of 1978, while I was sitting on a shiny chintz sofa in a long, formal living room filled with Chinese antiques, talking to Vladimir Horowitz.

The great pianist, seventy-three years old at the time, had recently released a golden-jubilee recording of Rachmaninoff's Piano Concerto no. 3, and its appearance had been greeted with unbridled huzzahs in the classical-music community. Normally, this would have been a matter of little concern to me—having, as I did, an amateur appreciation of classical music at best, and being, as I was, employed as an editor at a relentlessly lowbrow metal-pop magazine called *Circus*. However, Horowitz's Rachmaninoff album was such a success that it crossed over to the pop chart—a commercial accomplishment rare for a classical record. So when I spotted it on the lower rungs of a trade-sheet listing one day, I figured: cute story. Rock mag interviews high-toned maestro. The title all but wrote itself: "Vlad All Over."

Horowitz found this concept amusing, too. His wife, the formidable Wanda, was out for the evening, and he was in an expansive mood. Over glasses of wine, he recounted his prodigy days in Kiev and Leningrad and a visit he'd made to a brothel in Dortmund in 1930 (playing piano in the parlor while his companions availed themselves of carnal ministrations on the floors above, he said). He recalled his friendships with George Gershwin, Duke Ellington, even Rachmaninoff himself. He admitted to a fondness for the Beatles (but not the Rolling Stones). And then he talked about Studio 54.

In that particular period of New York City nightlife, Studio 54 was the hottest discotheque in town, an all-night shrine to the champagne-and-cocaine lifestyle of that irrepressible tabloid tribe, the international jet set. (And of course, along with its craven coddling of the famed and the flamboyant, the club was also devoted, with equal obsession, to keeping the nonfabulous, in all their forlorn variety, well outside the velvet ropes at its entrance.) This cavernous disco—a onetime television studio located on West Fifty-fourth Street—was a crypto-psychedelic funhouse of neon and mirrors and room-strafing strobe lights. Faux spaceships intermittently blasted off toward the rafters, leaving the spotlit dance floor fogged with fake launch smoke. High above the dancing hordes hung an enormous, happily grinning man in the moon, with a huge coke spoon that ascended repeatedly—all through the loud, sleepless hours before dawn—toward his nose. Studio 54 was a roiling glitterpit in which the worlds of art and money and showbiz were blendered together into the rich stew of a new Celebrity.

I was surprised to learn that Horowitz loved Studio 54, that he was a regular there and had even sampled his first joint on its premises. I had imagined him gravitating more naturally toward the company of his fellow maestros and similarly cultivated art lions. At Studio 54, he was less likely to encounter Rostropovich or Zuckerman or even Leonard Bernstein than to find himself crammed onto a banquette between Liza Minnelli and Andy Warhol or scrunched in beside some fashionably starved society hag or dubious Bavarian princeling. In addition, there was the lively possibility of suddenly having to make small talk with, say, a 300-pound transvestite best known for eating dogshit on camera in a notorious John Waters movie. Not exactly an elevated scene.

But Horowitz enjoyed this new pop society of the late Seventies. Within its globe-girdling orbit, he was more than just a master of the traditionally reserved and faintly remote classical-music scene. He could be a player on the much larger, if less significant, stage of international media celebrity. The New Society (as some publishing wag eventually got around to naming it) genuflected before the traditional status altars of power, wealth and talent, but it seemed most deeply devoted to the concept of fame—of ubiquitous media renown, whether attended by talent or not. Somewhat disconcertingly, this new *haut monde* also included—for the first time on an equal footing—certain rock stars. People like Rod Stewart and Mick Jagger and Elton John—well-heeled veterans, walking institutions. Now moneyed and influential themselves, and famous beyond debate, they fit right in.

This commingling of rock and society wasn't new in itself: Swinging London in the mid-Sixties had drawn a certain number of rich and cotillioned hangers-on, as had the Warhol Factory in New York (home of the Velvet Underground) in that same period. But those wayward debs and trust-fund bohemians of yore were, essentially, slumming. Rock & roll was fun, but the thought of devoting one's life to it, or whatever . . . well, it was a thought that would know better than to arise. Rockworld was a kicky place to visit, but in the end, one generally remembered one's way back home—or had a driver who did.

The record boom of the late Seventies altered this social imbalance somewhat. With disco and New Wave rock and an international nightlife explosion all at full roar, the music industry was raking in unprecedented profits. Popular acts could sell multimillions of records around the world, and if they wrote their own songs—and those songs had any sort of enduring appeal—the resultant royalties could set them up for life. Performers who had been at it since the Sixties were way ahead of the game. Now, these onetime upstarts could afford the beach house on Mustique, the chalet near Montreux, tax exile in Jamaica or the south of France, and the discreet pleasures of banking in Nassau, of Netherlandic incorporation—just like the more ordinary rich, whom they now joined in the first-class cabins of getaway jets to Rio and Cannes, Tangier and Gstaad. Validated at last by their accumulated money and fame, the rock elite merged with barely a flutter into the continent-vaulting jet stream of the gypsy rich.

All of which was entirely their right, of course. People like Jagger and Stewart and Elton John—not to single them out, but they were emblematic of the period—had done enormously popular work and gotten well paid for it. There was no point to be proved by vacationing in St. Louis. They'd earned their elaborately elegant lifestyles, and most atoned for their success with occasional charitable works. No, what was dismaying about this embrace of the rock elite by international disco society—and, of course, vice versa—was that it diluted rock's cultural power (a phrase that already seems faintly quaint). This may have been inevitable, a function of advancing years and ever-compounding capital accumulation. In some ways, rock had become a business like any other, an industry whose captains might naturally prefer to consort with their social equals in other areas, rather than feign any continuing fascination with the art and import of the music that had so transformed their lives. Did we ever expect otherwise?

Well, yes, I think we did. Making it big was always a part of the rock & roll dream—consider Elvis Presley and his gold tuxedos and pink Cadillacs. But rock itself was always more than just a business. I won't tire you with a ritual deployment of such words as *passion* and *attitude,* but those qualities did initially distinguish rock from official American culture. It was transporting music, rudely made, ecstatic in spirit, and fundamentally irreverent. And while no one should expect a rock performer to remain a perpetual teen rebel—that would be ludicrous—one had always hoped that the music's most gifted practitioners would manage to maintain some vestigial commitment to its spirit and its basic nose-thumbing stance. But this proved a difficult act to carry off for rockers who were suddenly spending their nights tooting up with obscurely titled Euriff-raff in places like Studio 54. And as they ascended into the upper atmosphere of pure, moneyed celebrity and their lives, too, became simpleminded fodder for the supermarket gossip rags, some serious damage was done. Mick Jagger's immersion in the international round of jet-set revels contributed to a feud with his partner, Keith Richards, that eventually led to a three-year breakup of the Rolling Stones toward the end of the Eighties. Rod Stewart's career survived all of his wenching and disco excess, but his rock & roll credibility never quite recovered.

Fortunately, punk came along in the late Seventies to breathe some youthful fire back into rock. But, as I soon discovered, even punks weren't immune to the seductions of the New Society.

By 1980, like a number of other writers from such magazines as *Circus* (Paul Nelson, Daisann McLane, later David Fricke) and the recently defunct *Crawdaddy* (Timothy White, Jon Pareles), I had finally made my way to *Rolling Stone,* where I wound up staying for nearly nine years. For the first two of those years, I mainly wrote the magazine's "Random Notes" column. This was a job that consisted of going out to parties and rock clubs virtually every night, and then—big downside here—coming in the next morning to spend the day on the phone tracking down the tips and checking out the overheard rumors and whispered slanders one had managed to scribble onto the back of a cocktail napkin the night before. That I survived two years of this with my health intact is a marvel to me now.

Anyway, I discovered that punks were also susceptible to the siren call of celebrity one night in the spring of 1980, when I attended a performance by a particularly loud and fast combo called Shrapnel at the Brooklyn home of . . . Norman Mailer. Yes. It was a party, and the place was packed. Our host was knocking back Scotch, as you'd pretty much expect, and interacting heartily with such guests as Woody Allen and Kurt Vonnegut and Jose Torres, the boxer. The band had set up in a small loft above the partiers, and—with amps set for earbleed—was blasting out a barrage of songs with titles like "I Lost My Baby on the Siegfried Line." Allen seemed puzzled, maybe even frightened, and quickly disappeared. Vonnegut, on the other hand, appeared to enjoy it all immensely. *How clever of Norman,* he might well have been thinking, *I must get one of these punk bands for my next party.* Only a few years earlier, punk had been the new barbarian at the gates of "good music," a focus of intense loathing on the part of most record buyers and, indeed, most of the established music industry. Now, it seemed, punk too had become just another showbiz commodity, available for nightly rental.

In retrospect, I see that that night at Mailer's—like the very few evenings I had spent watching rock stars cavort at Studio 54 around the same time—was a portent of the decade to come. In the Eighties, the rock scene and the art scene and even the literary scene became cheap feeding grounds for a new and voracious celebrity industry. A new breed of magazines and TV shows clamored for star interviews, star sound bites, star tidbits, however trivial. Some rockers were rightfully wary. Prince, for one, wisely clammed up and thus cultivated his mystique. Bruce Springsteen ventured forth to engage the great media beast only when the release of a new record or the start of a new tour made such encounters unavoidable, and he did so only with the utmost reluctance.

A number of rock performers, however, perceived tantalizing possibilities in this new "Lifestyles of the Rich and Famous" form of celebrity. True, it did tend to reduce sometimes talented people to run-of-the-mill brand names, but those names—and the now-familiar music that had established their initial renown—could suddenly be used to sell other things: beer, cars, barbecue sauce, you name it. The money was amazing. Major corporations with a proprietary eye on the always profitable youth market would dispatch whole truckloads of cash to your doorstep in return for the privilege of printing their names on your concert tickets and maybe sticking an inflatable beer can up onstage with you. And for those still squeamish about being turned into corporate shills on their native shores, there were also lucrative deals for ad campaigns that would run only in such faraway places as Japan.

This is actually a murky area. If Eric Clapton does a beer ad, does it make him any less gifted a guitarist? If David Bowie and Tina Turner do cola commercials, does that in any way diminish their past musical achievements? Have these people not paid their dues? Are the names and the images and the music they exploit not their own? Is exploitation not, in fact, the name of the showbiz game?

Well, yes. And Buddy Holly did commercials in the Fifties, as the Who and even the Beatles did in the Sixties, and the music they made in those years retains its stature. But in the Eighties, the celebrity boom changed everything. Rock stars were no longer looked upon as cultural prophets or youth spokesmen or any of those other tired Sixties concepts. Now they were merely famous—like Brooke Shields, like Ralph Lauren, like everybody else accepted for entry into Studio 54, and inundated with talk-show invitations, and written up in the pages of *People* and *Us* and *USA Today*. And over the course of the decade, a very clear message was sent: rock & roll—like everything else, it seemed—was for sale.

Not everybody has "sold out" (to use another dated and now fairly irrelevant term). But those musicians still committed to the idea that rock can and should mean something more than just a beach house in Malibu and a sleek new circle of friends— that it should stand in opposition to those forces in American culture that figure everything has its price—well, such musicians are now an endangered minority in a world obsessed with expanding income and the howling winds of fame.

The pieces in this book—all published in *Rolling Stone* magazine (except for both Frank Zappa stories and the Blondie article)—focus on people whose lives have been shaped by rock (or soul or blues, or whatever you want to call it) and how they dealt with celebrity (or the lack of it) and the exigencies of maintaining a career in the Eighties. Some, like Bob Dylan and Bruce Springsteen, remain paragons of integrity. Others are sometimes perceived as having "sold out," and a few might welcome the opportunity to do so, should it ever arise. Some of the subjects here—Sean Connery, Mel Gibson, the late Andy Warhol—are nonmusicians whose work has nevertheless become a part of rock culture, and who have (in the first two cases, at least) been as plagued by fame as any rock star. There are also some passing thoughts on the greater American political context of the Eighties and research notes on a few key albums.

As for the title: I lifted *Bat Chain Puller* from a song by Captain Beefheart (who assures me he doesn't mind). You can hear it on an album called *Shiny Beast (Bat Chain Puller),* and if you do, you may find that its somewhat disturbing subterranean rhythms put you in mind of the incessant heave and wheeze of celebrity interaction at virtually every level of American media over the past decade. Or maybe you won't. In any case, one has to call a book something, and *Bat Chain Puller,* I think, has the advantage of being unforgettable. (Although I guess we'll see about that.)

My main reason for putting this book together was to preserve between hard covers the slices of rock and rock cultural history that many of these pieces represent. I believe that good writing about music is always at least partly documentary in purpose, whether it appears in a mainstream magazine like *Rolling Stone,* well-done fanzines like *Forced Exposure,* or such specialist periodicals as *Option* magazine. Anyone who interviews musicians or other artists for a living is in a unique position to fill in some blanks in the history of their art and the culture from which it springs. I only wish that more such magazine work by other writers could be similarly compiled, rather than allowed to molder away in a warehouse somewhere.

All of these pieces were written on deadlines, of course, and the urge to tone down patches of overwriting and other stylistic tics was hugely tempting, but in the interest of historical authenticity (or whatever), I resisted it. What you read now is what you would have read then. And if this collection leads even a few people to look into the work of such artists as Captain Beefheart, Iggy Pop and Ted Hawkins—well, that's purpose enough for any book to have served.

Kurt Loder
New York City
April 1990

ACKNOWLEDGMENTS

Every piece in this book was originally written for *Rolling Stone* magazine, and all but three were first published in its pages (the delinquent trio having either bogged down in a slough of multiple drafts or withered on the vines of various publishing exigencies). When I tell people in the book business that Jann Wenner, *Rolling Stone*'s editor and publisher, gave me the rights to reprint this material free and clear, and even offered to help out with the project, they gape in amazement. But Jann has always been a good guy, in my experience—apart from occasional barely veiled threats of physical violence over the entirely understandable lateness of certain pieces—and for this latest instance of his generosity and support I can only offer, once again, grateful thanks.

   Rolling Stone has been a remarkable school for writers over the years, and some of the most instructive encounters a cocky young scribe is likely to have there are with the editors, who he soon learns are indefatigable in their quest for structure and relentless in their pursuit of nuance. Many a long, deadline-flouting hour have I spent hunkered down with the invaluable Susan Murcko or Jim Henke, hacking through thickets of overgrown prose. And many's the illuminating pointer I've picked up from Bob Wallace—a gifted magazine man—and Terry McDonell, whose gifts now grace his own magazine, *Smart*. Thanks are also due to the *Rolling Stone* research department, which, in the course of driving writers up walls with its nonpareil nit-picking, also spares them the embarrassment of egregious oversights, mistaken assumptions and potentially expensive libels.

Writers learn constantly from one another, of course, whether gabbing over beers or simply reading each other's work. For musical enlightenment of various kinds over the years I thank my good friend David Fricke (a walking ten-volume encyclopedia of modern musical history, and right in the next office!); the legendary Paul Nelson; Jon Pareles; Dave Marsh; Robert Christgau (rock's most acute critic); and the late and great Lester Bangs. An appreciative nod is also due to rock's many unsung archaeologists: the retro-activists at such specialty labels as Ace and Line and Bear Family, to name a scant few; the admirably obsessive reviewers of California's Down Home Records mail-order catalogs; and all the similarly fanatic archivists at obscure and wonderful fanzines too numerous, I'm afraid, to mention.

Special thanks to Mary Astadourian for photo supervision and sage counseling; to Kent Brownridge for liquidity assistance; to John Payson and Betsy Bryon at MTV for graphic realization; to Bob Weil, Bill Thomas and the exotic Barbara Andrews for their unnatural patience at St. Martin's Press; and to my equally stoic agents, Michael Carlisle, Jim Stein, and Michael Naso, at the William Morris Agency. Special thanks to Roger Davies, Lindsey Scott and Tina.

Apologies to Christine Hopfensperger and Brendan Kelly for a thousand lonely nights.

PART ONE

FAME

To be famous is to be perpetually importuned—on the street, in midmouthful at restaurants, even while taking a leak. There is little respite from the clamor of one's fans, without whom, of course, one wouldn't be famous in the first place (a gnawing irony). And so the more fame a person acquires, the more reclusive he or she appears to become. This is generally as much a matter of self-preservation as it is of mere mystique. Fame can take over one's life, making it very hard to get any work done. It can also seduce one into adopting the Famous Person's World View—a state of mind in which all things are perceived to revolve around the celebrated one's art and interests, in which the rest of the world is measured against one's own unusually cushy standards.

This attitude tends to distance a person from his or her roots and to disfigure any subsequent work. Fame is hardly the worst thing that could happen to a person, but as anyone will know who's ever followed a star act around on tour—through the endless succession of anonymous hotel rooms, chilly sound checks, dispirited postshow bottle fests, and early morning airport departures—it's not exactly a rest cure, either. People already renowned worry about hanging onto their gig. Those who've never made it—despite abundant talent and vision—tend to grow morose and dejected. And those who've tasted fame but failed to hold onto it can become almost suicidally embittered. Fame is a bed of roses, all right—thorns and all.

The fourteen pieces that follow focus on performers attempting to deal with fame or the lack of it (or, worse in some regards, the loss of it) the best way they know how. What does it mean for American music when a hip and enjoyable, but nevertheless very traditional, blues-based boogie band like ZZ Top can sell more records in a couple of months than Captain Beefheart—an American musical genius with some of the same roots—has ever sold in his whole career? Why is it that a likable TV star like Don Johnson can get a recording deal without even asking, while a complete American original like Iggy Pop has had to hustle constantly just to keep himself afloat? And what can be done about the growing number of young music fans whose only knowledge of American music comes from what they "see" (an ominous new usage born on the Eighties pop-video scene) on MTV or hear on cookie-cutter Top Forty radio stations, when the overwhelming body of American music (blues, gospel, vintage R&B, hard country, early rock, jazz, experimental, underground, modern classical) gets virtually no exposure in these media? Finally, why is it that the most lovingly detailed and exhaustively complete compilations of classic American music are, for the most part, put together by the British, the Germans and the Japanese and not the American companies that own and license the original masters?

I don't have all the answers to these questions, but I hope a few may suggest themselves to you as you read on.

Joe Bangay/London Features International

ONE

Mick Jagger

(1983)

Few groups have lasted long enough to confront
the conceptual difficulties that the Rolling Stones
have encountered in attempting to continue making
credible rock records as they settle into middle age.
No one has really ever done this before—which is
not to say it can't be done, only that it's bound to be
a little difficult.

After releasing a very fine LP in 1981 (Tattoo
You), the Stones seemed tormented throughout the
rest of the decade by what might usefully be
characterized as midlife crisis. Freshly signed to CBS
Records, the group proceeded to put out albums that
were perceived as falling short of their past triumphs.
Mick Jagger announced that he would begin
recording solo albums on the side. This no doubt
irritated his songwriting partner, the world's greatest
thrash guitarist, Keith Richards; by 1986, the two
men had ceased speaking to each other, leaving the
future of the Rolling Stones very much in question.

At the time of the interview that follows, the band
was about to release Undercover, an album that, in
retrospect, seems to fall somewhere in the middle
rankings of the Stones' canon. Jagger was, as always,
sharp and perceptive; inasmuch as we have

continued to maintain cordial relations even in the wake of the following hardly worshipful article, I think it may also be said that the man has a sense of humor as well.

"Say I'm enigmatic."

—*Mick Jagger, 1968*

There are these two guys named Mick Jagger. One of them, whose life is laid out in lurid little exploits in the tatty press, seems a perfect prancing ass. The other one, however, makes these lately great-again albums with the Rolling Stones, whom he also inveigles out onto the road every three years or so in order to dredge up a quick $40 million and thus finance further society wallows. One suspects these two are acquainted, but you never see them together. (Well, maybe onstage.)

Additionally, there is sometimes a third Mick Jagger. While the other two have all the fun, this one makes himself available for interviews each time an album is released. It is an occupation clouded by great, gray billows of boredom. This Mick Jagger has not been asked an interesting question since, oh, Altamont—and how interesting was *that?* Journalists are always pushing the same old piffle, it seems. Much of it pertains to Mick I. Is he doped up? Shacked up? Fucked up? Fed up? Can he really be forty years old?

As it happens, there is now a whole generation of pop-music enthusiasts out there for whom such questions no longer burn. Mick Jagger? Took a lot of drugs? Used to think he was the devil or something? Hung out with Andy Warhol? Ick. And you say he's still at it?

Yes, dear God, he is. In fact, because the Rolling Stones are about to unleash their latest release, an album called *Undercover,* he is sitting right here behind a desk in the modest mid-Manhattan offices of Rolling Stones Records, doing his Mick III routine. It is a balmy, sunny afternoon in early September, and Jagger is casually stylish in pale yellow pants, a drape-cut cord shirt and woven leather sandals, no socks. He looks good, rather softer and less chiseled than in photographs, and while he's a bit fidgety—and there's a lot of odd tug-and-snort action going on with his nose—one assumes these are probably mannerisms he's picked up from Mick I.

The material on *Undercover,* however—rough mixes of which I have audited in the customary interval between when Jagger says he'll arrive and when he actually appears—is very much the work of Mick II, the musician. There is no other singer like him, of course. But this time out, there is also an even more corrosive intensity to his lyrics, particularly in such songs as "She Was Hot," "All the Way Down," "Tie You Up (The Pain of Love)"—the titles tell it all—and in two bracing blasts at totalitarian political tyranny ("Undercover of the Night" and "It Must Be Hell") and one true-life tale of a man in Paris who hacked up his girlfriend and ate her ("Too Much Blood"). As Keith Richards says, "It's a very gory album."

And a very good one. The music, painstakingly put together over the past year by Jagger and the invaluable Richards, is harder and more deliriously guitar-lumbered than ever. Listening as it leaped out of the speakers, I marveled anew at the fact that, come January, the Rolling Stones will have been together for twenty-one years. Not only have they still got it, they've still got *all* of it.

So, long live Mick II, I say: his is a life distinctively and productively led. If only it were enough.

But of course it's not. Jagger may be a millionaire many times over, but there's still something faintly . . . *frivolous* about the way he makes his living. He yearns to branch out, to act, to produce films, though "no one ever asks me," he says. But here he is, forty years old and still best known as the lead singer for the Rolling Stones. As if that's really all he ever intends to do with his life. It's beginning to be an embarrassment. Even his friends are starting to talk. On the occasion of his birthday last July 26th, for instance, Pete Townshend—who's allegedly retired his own band, the Who—wrote a windy salute to his old pal in the *Times* of London. Jagger might have beat Pete to the punch in sampling sex and drugs and major rock success, trumpeted Townshend, who's two years younger than Mick, "but I have stopped living for rock & roll before he has."

"That," says Jagger with a snort and a tug, "presumes the fact that I ever *did* live for it. I mean, yeah, when I was like fourteen. But I think after the age of . . . certainly thirty, if not twenty-five, I had ceased merely living for rock & roll itself, you know. I mean, I love rock & roll; it's wonderful. I know what the feeling is: you wake up in the morning, run down to the record store, get the new record, put it on, can't wait for all your friends to come over. You sing it all day. You go down to the bar, you're still singing it, putting a nickel in the juke. Then you go out and see the band at night, you know? I can do that. I mean, tonight I'm gonna see Yellowman; that should be fun. But being really caught up in rock & roll . . . that's something you do when you're a *teenager*. It'd be stupid to do that all the time."

Jagger leans back with a big, cheek-creasing grin. "Pete Townshend is talking about himself," he says.

"Mick could have been a marvelous cricketer, but other things got in the way."
—*Joe Jagger, 1974*

Michael Phillip Jagger always had big ambitions, right from the beginning. As his father, Joe Jagger, a phys. ed. teacher in a South London suburb, once observed, "He was in business administration at the London School of Economics when he took two years' leave to start his group. He did it because he thought it was something pleasant, but he realized the possibilities of making money, and since he was in business administration, he felt it was a good idea to make money."

Need we note that money is no longer a pressing concern for Jagger? Already awash in nearly twenty years of songwriting royalties and record-breaking concert receipts (much of it safely sheltered in the Stones' Holland-based holding company, Promotone B.V., or otherwise administered by their London-based financial adviser, Prince Rupert Loewenstein), Jagger recently engineered a rather astounding new recording contract for the Stones with CBS Records. The deal marks the end of the band's twelve-year relationship with Atlantic Records and its chairman of the board, Ahmet Ertegun, with whom they've had a long-standing friendship. The reason, Jagger says simply, was that "CBS offered us substantially more money." Twenty-five million dollars, to be precise. In return, among other things, CBS will eventually acquire much of the Stones' back catalog. Both sides seem pleased with the deal.

"I think the CBS offer was based on the performance of our last three studio albums," says Jagger, whose group has been on a dramatic creative upswing since the *Some Girls* LP in 1978. "I think CBS figures they can sell more records than anybody, so if our next three sell the same as the last three, they're gonna make money."

The heart of the deal, of course, is that CBS will release the next four Rolling Stones albums. In addition, it will also release, for the first time ever, a solo album by Mick Jagger himself. Maybe two or three. This is an unexpected breach in Jagger and Richards' longstanding no-solos tradition, and Mick seems excited by it.

"I could do all kinds of things," he says enthusiastically. "I could go very commercial—very, *very* commercial American pop. Or I could go for just ordinary, straight rock & roll, in an English way. Or I could mix it up: some very . . . you know, some *hits,* and some things that are a bit more experimental."

Experimental?

"Outside of this kind of mainstream rock," he fairly burbles. "More like the stuff Material [a New York jazz-funk unit] does. Slightly left of the mainstream, you know what I mean? You could do some interesting things in that area."

Experimental?

"I have a lot of stuff," Jagger says. "I think I'm gonna do it relatively soon."

"*I* don't know whether you could call Mick a good
actor—but he *is* an entertainer."
                                        —*Anita Pallenberg, 1968*

In the musical sphere, of course, Mick Jagger can do whatever he wants. But what is there really left to do? "No one seems to be doing anything very innovative in stadium shows," he says. "I've seen David Bowie, I've seen Talking Heads and the Police, and I mean, is that really all there is? Keith thinks that rock & roll shows should just be a few lights and a good sound system and a square stage. That's his idea of what it should be. But I like to do more than that. I want to have more lights, a better stage. I want to be able to see 360 degrees. I want to give the people in the back something to look at, and I want it to look right."

Getting the Rolling Stones to actually roll out on tour, of course, is another headache entirely. "I don't know whether the Stones are gonna go on the road next year or not. We're gonna sit down and talk about that in the next few weeks. I mean, *Charlie* obviously doesn't want to go on tour," he says, referring to drummer Charlie Watts. "But yeah, I love it. It's kind of in my blood. It would be awful if I went on and tried to do things I couldn't do. But if the body is in good enough condition to be able to sing and have the breath and the legs . . . then there's no reason I shouldn't be able to do it for a few more years. But as soon as it starts to show . . . well, I'll see it on video. I'll see it straight away."

The dwindling of Jagger's high-voltage performance style may not be imminent, but it is inevitable. This may be one reason why he continues to yearn for a breakthrough in his long-simmering movie career: something dignified to fall back on.

The Stones acquired the screen rights to Anthony Burgess' *A Clockwork Orange* back in the Sixties, but because potential censorship problems seemed impassable, the production fell through. So did subsequent projects. Jagger finally made it to the movies in 1970, starring in two films. He played a noted Australian outlaw in the Tony Richardson film *Ned Kelly* ("He looks too sissy," said one crusty local after the movie's outback première). He also appeared as the retired rock star Turner in *Performance,* a movie codirected by Nicolas Roeg and Jagger's painter-turned-filmmaker friend, Donald Cammell ("Loathsome," John Simon called the pic in the *New York Times*).

Jagger's name was subsequently floated in connection with such screen projects as *The Rocky Horror Picture Show* and Ken Russell's bizarre film bio of Franz Liszt (which eventually starred Who vocalist Roger Daltrey). In 1981, Jagger actually spent several weeks in the steaming Peruvian jungle working on Werner Herzog's *Fitzcarraldo,* but that ill-fated film fell behind schedule, and when Jagger was unable to extend his stay because of the Stones' U.S. tour, his footage was scrapped.

"But I wouldn't have missed it for anything," he says, with perhaps an iota of irony. "There was a nice moment when I came out. After waiting three days for transportation at this log-ging camp in the middle of the jungle, sleeping twelve in a room in hammocks with these loggers—and my Spanish is really rudimentary—well, this seaplane arrived. I had done myself up: best suit of clothes; I'd cleaned up, even shaved. And I stood up on the float of the seaplane, and just as I was about to open the door, I lost my balance and fell into the Amazon." The response he recalls hearing as he flubbered about was "just fits of laughter."

He remains game, however. He has acquired a powerful new theatrical agent (Rick Nicita of the Creative Artists Agency in Los Angeles), and he continues to test for parts, like any aspiring actor. Recently, he auditioned for Milos Forman's production of the Broadway stage hit *Amadeus;* the part of Mozart didn't pan out, but Mick remains unfazed.

"You have to have your nose to the ground for what parts are going around the major studios, which are very few," he says sagely. "They're mostly written with some guy in mind, and you only get the part if he gets ill or something. Which may be how Sting got that part in *Dune,* for instance. I'm not saying he won't be good in it, but it was an opening that came up, I think."

Things are brightening a bit on the extramusical front, though. Not long ago, Jagger sold a screenplay he cowrote called *The Tin Soldier* ("and got paid pretty good for it," he says proudly). He'll probably also sell the screen rights he acquired some years ago to the Gore Vidal novel *Kalki* ("No one wants to make it into a picture"). But it looks as if he finally has found financing for a project that he's wanted to do for a decade, a movie whose working title has been *Ishtar*. It seems to concern a video director and some terrorists; Jagger will be in on the action and may even star. Michael Butler, the money man behind *Hair,* is reportedly a likely backer. "We have the money and everything," Jagger says. "We have the script and some of the main cast. We're just arguing a little bit about the deal."

> "*I* don't go out with housewives. I never have, I'm never going to."
> —*Mick Jagger, 1977*

Mick II's movie career may yet pan out, who knows? Certainly his thespian setbacks are nothing compared to the battered fortunes suffered by Mick I in the world's gossip columns over the last twelve years. You'll recall that Mick I assumed a life of his own back in 1971, when Jagger married Bianca Perez Morena de Macias, a Nicaraguan diplomat's daughter, in glittery St. Tropez. The well-connected Bianca opened up all sorts of new social possibilities for Jagger (she, of course, benefited equally by her marriage to Mick), and soon, the favored couple was partying at "21" with Yves St. Laurent, dining at La Grenouille with Andy Warhol and checking out the gay floor show at the Continental Baths (where Mick was recognized and, according to one report, "had to flee from an army of eager queens clad only in bath towels").

None of this flouncing about with the fashionable set made Mick appear to be a very serious person. And unfortunately, the Jaggers' mid-Seventies jet-setting coincided with (and perhaps contributed to) an unprecedented slump in the Rolling Stones' music (think back to *Goats Head Soup, It's Only Rock 'n' Roll, Black and Blue*). Nor did the marital glow last for long: Bianca, who had given birth to a daughter, Jade, a few months after the wedding, couldn't have been too pleased when Marsha Hunt, a black American singer, filed a paternity suit against Jagger in 1973, claiming—and ultimately proving—that he had fathered her daughter Karis, who was born in November 1970. Eventually, Bianca began to complain about Mick's randy habits, and in 1978, she sued for divorce on grounds of adultery—the particular object of her ire being Jerry Hall, a six-foot-tall, $2000-an-hour fashion model from Mesquite, Texas, whom Jagger had wooed away from singer Bryan Ferry.

The Jaggers' divorce was a noisy one, great fun for the gossips. It was finally settled—for $2.5 million out of Mick's pocket—in 1980, allowing Jagger and Hall to make like real lovebirds. Jerry was subsequently portrayed in the tabloids as uttering let's-make-it-legal noises, but no wedding ensued. Then, in 1982, she dumped Mick and took up with multi-millionaire racehorse owner Robert Sangster, a man who, in Jerry's deathless phrase, "can buy [Mick] out ten times over." *Quel scandale!* Mick was said to be keeping company with a young Venezuelan model named Victoria Vicuna. It was all terrifically silly.

How Mick got Jerry back is not entirely clear. According to the gossip sheets, Sangster claimed that "Mick broke down on the telephone and cried like a big baby, begging her to come back to him." According to Jagger, "We just broke up for a while." Whatever the case, Jerry returned, bliss reigned and, as if in confirmation of their reunion, it was reported that she was pregnant. The baby is due in early 1984. Mick III answers the unavoidable question with some ambivalence.

"I'm not gonna get married," he says. "Not right now! I *may* get married. But I'm not getting married right now."

Gotcha. He waffled just as much about acknowledging the impending tot—a piece of news unleashed upon the world by garrulous guitarist Ron Wood, much to Jagger's chagrin.

"She could have a miscarriage, that's why I don't like talking about it," Mick explains. "It's never good to crow about these things until they're a little bit further gone. It's actually happened to me before. I wanted to tell people the girl was having a baby, and it was really kind of a bring-down when the news came out a month later in *Rolling Stone* and she had had a miscarriage." (At press time, all was well, and Mick and Jerry had broken the news in person to his parents in England.)

Fatherhood apparently appeals to him. At least he seems to dote on his daughters, both hitting their teens now (and, as their dad is at pains to point out to potential swains, "both too young!"). He gets to talk to their friends. They keep him up on the trends, like synth pop. "Old hat to us, mate," he says with a grin. "I'm still waiting for something I haven't already heard. But, I mean, there's no stopping a record like Eurythmics'—it's just straight pop. Real good for what it is. Better than a lot of the bands earning money in arenas, I think, just for records.

"Image is becoming very important. So is the performing artist. A record may sell, but if a guy comes over as a good performer, or he makes good videos, it helps him. So you've gotta be capable in all those areas."

Jagger should know, playing the shill, as he does, for MTV commercials. He, too, it turns out, has noticed the rarely tainted whiteness of the MTV airwaves. "It *is* kind of odd," he says. "I don't know why, but they'll probably bring out some excuse. I think MTV has done something great—although quite by accident, I'd imagine. It's shaken up all the radio people and made 'em realize that there's more to life than all those bands that they were playing over and over and over. Like the Rolling Stones."

He stays on the scene, hits the clubs. When the rumor spread earlier this year that the Hell's Angels, still miffed by Mick's unsupportive attitude after the Angel-plagued Altamont concert in 1969, had put a murder contract out on him, a meeting was set up at the Ritz, a New York rock club, to work things out. He caught David Bowie twice on his latest tour ("His singing was much improved," Mick cackles), and he's also gotten down at the Roxy, a Manhattan funk mecca. "I went a couple of times on scratch-dance night, and I got a lot of letters from girls afterward saying, 'You danced with me.' Of course, nobody really dances with anyone; it's just twitching around and scratching and getting on the floor. I tried spinning on my head and got a terrible hangover the next day."

Although, in the wake of John Lennon's death three years ago, Jagger made it known that he sometimes carried a gun, he now tries not to be paranoid about his partying. "Sometimes I go out with bodyguards," he says, "but sometimes I go on my own. There's places I go that nobody gives a shit. But there's other places you go where you really have to organize. It's so boring, but you have to do it. Otherwise, you can't see the show for all the bits of paper."

As for the dreaded drug question, Mick says, "You've got to know your own limits. Obviously, I'm no paragon of virtue. I've often been carried home in the last thirty years. But if you see that happening, you've just got to stand off. If you take too much of anything, whether it's coke or alcohol, you start to get paranoid, to get funny ideas about other people. The decisions you make are not right." His friend John Phillips, erstwhile leader of the Mamas and the Papas, was a heroin addict for several years, and Mick remembers the torments he endured.

"He was pretty insane at one point," Jagger says. "Heroin is a very dangerous drug. People think they can take it for a day or two on the weekends and then just quit. But they can't. It's very hard."

No, he says, "I don't want to get caught up in that."

"*It's stupid to think that you can start a revolution with a record. I wish you could!*"
                                              —*Mick Jagger, 1970*

These days, Jagger observes the world with a relatively clear eye from a house in France, a town house in Manhattan or his official residence (for the usual tax purposes) on the Caribbean island of Mustique. He observes, and he does not particularly like what he sees.

"Professional politicians are the bane of the earth," he says. "They are people who've done nothing else all their lives. When you read history, and you see how some of them screw up so incredibly, it's hard to believe that they're well-educated people. I mean, you can be in politics without being a professional politician. Certain people have certain qualities. Mrs. Thatcher, for instance, has guts and all that, and she's pretty intelligent. Mr. Gromyko is a great survivor. I think it's a bit wrong, Reagan running for a second term. I think he's too old for America."

Does he see himself as a socialist? A Tory? An aging anarchist? "Well, I'm left of Reagan, I can tell you that. But one sort of questions Sixties American liberalism now, in retrospect. I think liberals made a lot of mistakes in foreign policy, and some of the right-wing people have scored major successes. The British Labour governments never *had* a foreign policy. Reagan never had one either, I don't think. That dictator we (sic) supported in Nicaragua was definitely . . . I mean, anyone could tell that guy had to go. So if the Americans had wanted to be in control of that—which they were paying these people to be—they should have said, okay, your time is up, we're gonna put somebody else in. A centrist government, a left-wing coalition, whatever. Same thing with the shah of Iran. We were supposed to be in control of events in those countries—and we just never really, in actual fact, were."

Jagger is amused, and perhaps a bit dismayed, by the new breed of pop political sloganeers—bands like the Clash, calling for unity with their working-class audience and then embarking on a big-bucks tour of stateside stadiums—"playing Philadelphia's JFK Stadium in Clash T-shirts," as he says. "Yeah, you have to be very careful. You dig pits that you fall into. You may have to eat your words more than once in your life."

"*Rock & roll's not over. I don't like to see one thing end until I see another beginning . . . do you know what I mean?"*

—Mick Jagger, 1971

The Rolling Stones have eaten very few words in the course of their career, and they admit to few regrets. They never hoped to die before they got old in the first place. Age will eventually take its toll on their stage show, but nobody cares how many jump splits Mick Jagger can do in the recording studio, and that is where the Stones' multifarious gifts—for songwriting, playing and *performing*—flower most fully. *Undercover* is all new material, not studio scraps, and it's so vibrantly crafted that some of the songs might pass as outtakes from *Between the Buttons* or some similar primordial classic. Twenty years on, the Stones are still at the top of their class (admittedly, it's a class of one), and there's no reason their records shouldn't continue to keep them there.

As for Jagger, the gossip years will probably never end for him, but he seems to be attempting to put the gossip decade behind him. He genuinely dislikes the sort of overheated press coverage that greeted him and the pregnant Jerry when they arrived in England recently, en route to a video shoot in Paris for the "Undercover of the Night" single. Maybe he's had enough. Maybe Mick I is ready for that long rest he deserves. That would certainly take some of the load off of Mick III. And then Mick II, the musician, can get back to doing what, it seems to me, he does best: fronting the longest-running, inspirational-quality rock act in history. The future, at this point in the Stones' career, can be only vaguely perceived; but whatever it holds, Mick Jagger, after more than twenty years on the case, sweating it out in miserable little pubs and the most spectacular stadiums, is ready for it.

"I talked to Prince on the phone once after he got two cans thrown at him in L.A.," Mick says. "He said he didn't want to do any more shows." Jagger bursts out in a blaze of big teeth and stuttery chuckles. "God, I got *thousands* of bottles and cans thrown at me! *Every* kind of debris. I told him, if you get to be a really big headliner, you have to be prepared for people to throw bottles at you in the night."

He leans back and screams: *"Prepared to die!"*

Paul Slattery/Retna Ltd.

Two

The Who

(1982)

The Who, in their prime, were one of the most electrifying acts in rock history. Unfortunately, if you didn't see them while drummer Keith Moon was still alive, then you missed them forever. By 1982, when the following story was done, the Who had become just another rock trademark, essentially dependent on hired sidemen to pull off a convincing show. Nobody I knew at the time really believed all the "final tour" hype, and we were right: the band returned (with even more sidemen) in 1989 to mount an enormously profitable "reunion" tour, with leader Pete Townshend grousing out loud that this time, he really was only in it for the money. This struck me as a sad—and, for Who fans, insulting—state of affairs, but by this point it doesn't really matter. The '89 reunion show I saw actually was pretty good, despite all the hired firepower; if the group wants to continue reassembling from now until the end of the century, well, there'll no doubt always be an audience for Living Rock Legends.

More discerning consumers can content themselves with all the great Who albums on which Keith Moon still lives, and Pete Townshend hasn't yet developed a hearing problem. They're the closest you're going to

*get to hearing this legendary band at the peak of its
powers. Their music changed the sound and the
instrumental structure of rock in the Sixties and
Seventies, and that's more than any other band still
(more or less) extant can say. I hope they've got
another great record in them, but even if they don't,
they've already given us a unique and powerful
legacy. God bless these guys, whatever may happen.*

For nearly three years, Roger Daltrey watched Pete Townshend slowly killing himself with drugs and alcohol. It was almost a parody of rock-star decadence: Pete moved out on his wife and children and started making the rounds of trendy London clubs, slugging back brandy all night till he was nearly comatose, snorting cocaine to keep up the pace, dabbling in heroin and God knows what else. After twenty years together in a band that ultimately attained the heights of rock celebrity as the Who, Daltrey saw Townshend throwing away a life that apparently had come to mean more to Who fans than it did to Townshend himself. Finally, late last year, the tormented guitarist hit bottom. After a night of furious dissipation at London's Club for Heroes, Townshend suddenly turned blue and collapsed and had to be rushed to the nearest hospital.

Daltrey couldn't take it anymore. Something drastic had to be done, and he knew, at last, what it was. One night during Townshend's extended convalescence, the Who held a meeting at their manager's house, and Daltrey dropped the bomb: "I don't want to tour anymore."

For a man who still loved the Who as passionately as he ever had in his teens—maybe more—those were the saddest words in the world. But if Townshend were to be stopped from following Who drummer Keith Moon into an early grave, Daltrey felt he had no other choice.

"See, Pete didn't want to tour for years there before Moonie died," he explains. "I was the instigator—I was responsible for getting him back on the road after 1978. And after three tours of America, he was a bloody junkie. I felt responsible for that. It was really hard to live with, and I just don't want to do it anymore. I mean, I think the world of that guy. I think enough of him to stop the Who."

Not stop it cold, of course. They could do one last world tour—as long as they *called* it that, and knew it was *finis,* they could deal with it. "I want to end the group in the right way," says Daltrey. "On top, before we become parodies of ourselves. Then we can give Pete some freedom, because he deserves it."

Townshend is still struck by Daltrey's selfless and loving gesture. The two have had many a well-publicized row over the years, and yet, says Pete, "Roger was the most vociferous member of the group in saying that he would do anything, give up anything—even give up the group—if it would make me happy, you know? If it would *get me happiness.*"

The question now, of course, is: will it?

One week into the Who's last full-scale tour, all is quiet. Frankly, it's a little weird. Fifteen years ago, when Keith Moon was alive and destroying drum kits and hotel rooms with equal abandon, the Who's celebrated road antics earned them a lifetime ban from the Holiday Inns of America. But this afternoon, up on the sixth floor of the Greentree Marriott, near downtown Pittsburgh, a librarial silence prevails—you can almost hear the twiddling of thumbs behind each closed door. Can this be the same crazed band that exploded out of London's heady Mod scene in 1965?

No, of course not. One understands. This is the Who that survived into the Eighties, and its members, dispersed in their various suites, are conserving their no-longer-boundless energy for tonight's show at the 17,500-seat Civic Arena. There are eight tough weeks to go on this farewell tour, and looning takes a low priority.

Townshend has already caught a cold, which may explain the two sweaters he's wearing, if not the faded pink handkerchief that's knotted around his wrist. A copy of *Nostromo,* the Joseph Conrad novel, lies on a table near the sofa where he's sitting, and a stack of portable recording equipment—an adjunct to on-the-road songwriting—stands against a far wall. One year after nearly cashing in his chips, Townshend looks a little ragged, but he's obviously sober and straight. His only remaining vice is a penchant for miniature Indian cigarettes, which he smokes steadily.

"I do miss a drink before going onstage," he admits, raking a hand through his disheveled hair. "Even just a small brandy would always stop me from feeling nervous. But once I get on the stage now, I'm okay. I don't miss it," he says, waving the bad old days away. "I don't miss any of it."

And the days of big tours, big money, big roaring crowds—will he miss any of that? He stubs out a tiny butt and sighs. "I think there's a certain amount of relief about the fact that it's the last tour. There's a tremendous amount of sadness, though, as well, because I know it's not what everybody wants." Bassist John Entwistle, for example, loves being on the road more than any other aspect of his involvement in the Who. Therefore, Pete says, "I think John is probably . . . *more* than sad. He's not at all vocal, and that makes it very difficult, because he's actually sittin' and tryin' to work out how he feels half the time. But I think I know him well enough to know that he will probably mourn the Who more than anybody in the world. He's losing a vehicle for his talent and *passion* that he knows he'll never be able to find anywhere else."

It would, of course, be possible to accommodate Entwistle—keep the band in shape, maybe perform on some sort of reduced but semiregular annual schedule. Townshend stares down at his sizable feet, which are nestled in black velvet slippers with inscrutable golden crests, and he cradles his famous nose in a clump of Kleenex. "I very much doubt that will happen," he says with a soft honk.

Rock & roll glamour is in similarly short supply in each of the other band members' rooms. Entwistle, the stolid bassist, is in the grip of a backache that won't give up. Kenny Jones, the drummer—who is weathering a divorce and has kicked a debilitating booze habit—fidgets away the offstage hours compulsively gulping Perrier. Daltrey, a fitness buff, has beaten back the gout that plagued him on previous tours but is still pained by a back injury he sustained while filming *Tommy* eight years ago. Only Tim Gorman, the affable, conservatory-trained Californian who's playing keyboards on this tour, seems unscarred by his calling, happily munching cheese and *crudités* from a vast room-service platter as he waits for showtime.

Is this how it all ends—in a whimper of cheese and Perrier? Not exactly; Who fans needn't wear out their arms waving goodbye. Because, although it's billed as their U.S. swan song, this latest excursion (which kicked off September 22nd near Washington, D.C.) is also the longest tour the Who have mounted in twelve years; given the group's well-known volatility, anything might happen between now and mid-December, when the tour concludes. And they do have a future, however ambiguous: the band will tour Britain and Europe in the new year, then Australia, and for the first time, Japan. And Bill Curbishley, the group's enterprising manager, is already talking about the possibility of playing a quick cluster of dates sometime in 1984 and perhaps fulfilling the Who's longstanding plan to play Eastern Europe—maybe even doing *Tommy* at Moscow's opera house. As Kenney Jones says: "Little and often is the word—one-off concerts, or three or four days somewhere."

So there *is* a master plan, of sorts: the Who will leave the road because it's killing them—or, more precisely, because it was killing Townshend—and in the future will congregate only to record albums and perhaps perform the occasional brief burst of concerts. They've had it all, and now the three original members—Townshend, Daltrey, and Entwistle—are crowding forty. Their generation—the pill-head Mods and flower kids of the Sixties—is just another blip in the cultural memory bank. Hanging on to traipse on stages for yet another new wave of fans, they would run an increasing risk of becoming ridiculous. Or worse, boring. As Daltrey says one evening, squinting into the setting sun outside his hotel-room window: "I can't see the Who without its energy. If *I* go downhill, and if Pete gets slower . . . well, like it or not, the arm swingin' and the mike twirlin' *are* important to the Who. I mean, could you see us just standin' onstage, just playin'?" Daltrey's brow bunches up over his pale blue eyes, twin reflections of Townshend's own azure orbs. "Do you really want to see the Who like that?" he asks.

On this tour, at least, no one has seen the Who like that. Buoyed by what they conceive as a sprint toward some sort of final curtain, they have been *burning* through their two-hour-plus sets, lashing out the songs from their new album, *It's Hard,* with all the fire of their great, anthemic hits. So far, it seems like a great way to go out—on top, as Roger says. Even Mick Jagger, who turned up with his daughter, Jade, for the Who's second concert, at John F. Kennedy Stadium in Philadelphia, was suitably impressed—and not just because his old pals had set a house ticket-sales record at the same stadium where the Rolling Stones had played one year earlier.

"Mick was up on the side of the stage," Daltrey recalls, "and afterward, I said, 'Are you waitin' to go out and do it again?' And I think, suddenly, he really might have looked out at that crowd and saw what we were doin', and thought, 'Maybe we should have called that *our* last tour, too.''

The Who and the Stones go way back, but Pete is still bemused by Mick's tough business head. They spoke briefly in Philadelphia. "He was saying to me, 'Well, we started off in Philly, and then we went to Buffalo—it's 400 miles, you know, a very heavy thing for the trucks.''' Pete cackles appreciatively. "I don't give a shit how far it is for the *trucks*. I just *play*.''

Which is not to say that Townshend is a complete dummy about the mechanics of taking a rock band on the road. There are several levels of touring, and the Who have been through them all. They started, of course, at the penniless-unknown level, in which aspiring rockers commandeer a friendly automobile, pile their pathetic equipment into it and drive off to spend the night in some forlorn pub, playing for free beer and change. If they're *really* penniless—as Townshend, Daltrey and Entwistle were when they first came together as teenagers in a West London band called the Detours—they have to *build* their own instruments.

The next level is opening up for established acts. The Detours opened for the Rolling Stones before that band had even cut a record, and after Keith Moon joined the lineup in 1964, Townshend and company opened for the Beatles and the Kinks. In the days of package tours, they also played support for such briefly celebrated bands as Screaming Lord Sutch, and Johnny Kidd and the Pirates (whose guitarist, Mick Green, had developed a hybrid style of lead and rhythm playing that exerted a heavy influence on the young Townshend). Those shows were a lot of fun. Entwistle recalls a time the band played a package that included the Herd, a teen-pop band that featured Peter Frampton. For a laugh, he says, "I tied Frampton to a radiator by his scarf and wouldn't let him go onstage.'' No one took the music business too seriously in those days.

To attain the next rung on the ladder, a band needs a hit record. The Who's first single, "I'm the Face,'' released in 1964 during a period when they were briefly known as the High Numbers, was not a smash. But "I Can't Explain,'' released in January 1965 and credited to the Who, put them on a roll, and they had strong followups that same year with "Anyway, Anyhow, Anywhere'' and the epochal "My Generation.'' Hitmakers of such consistency become pop stars, and whole new worlds of indulgence open up: drugs (pills in the Who's case; pot, too, in Pete's), money, cars, girls. The Who rode their ever-cresting fame through the Sixties (*Happy Jack, The Who Sell Out, Tommy*) and into the Seventies (*Live at Leeds, Who's Next, Quadrophenia*).

Today, of course—despite the spottiness of such albums as *Who Are You,* their last with the doomed Moon, and the muddled 1981 LP *Face Dances,* which even the band didn't much like—the Who occupy a level of charismatic renown that's shared only by such survivors as the Rolling Stones. They've come out on the other end of the pipeline. Vulgar display is no longer necessary, but touring is still an enormously complex undertaking. In their early days, the Who would go on tour with two road managers and a light man; today, their traveling crew—swollen by ShowCo sound and Tasco Light technicians—numbers about ninety people. Ten trucks are required to cart their gear from gig to gig. And on the opening dates of their current tour, a 100-seat Boeing 707 was requisitioned—generally available at an estimated cost of about $5000 per hour—to fly the band and about a score of associates from city to city. When ninety people are eating and sleeping off a band's profits, some sort of compensation becomes essential. As the Rolling Stones did last year with Jovan fragrances, the Who have signed a lucrative sponsorship deal with Schlitz beer. In return for appearing in two thirty-second Schlitz commercials, allowing their music to be used in other Schlitz ads and permitting the Schlitz name to be used on concert tickets, the Who will receive a pot of money (described by a Schlitz spokesman as a seven-figure amount and "the biggest corporate-sponsored rock-music entertainment ever undertaken"). Then, there is merchandising—the sale of tour T-shirts and jerseys (ten to eighteen dollars apiece this year), tour programs (five dollars each) and, in an innovative move, an authorized biography called *The Who: Maximum R&B,* a four-color trade paperback that is being sold for fourteen dollars a copy. Every little bit helps.

So this is a big-money tour, but it is being carried off with a certain style. Townshend, a friend of the gentry back home in Twickenham, may take the stage in protopunk garb—black leather jacket and jeans—but when he steps off that chartered plane in the next city, he's likely as not to be wearing a tailored suit, silk tie and expensive two-toned wing tips. Meet the new boss.

*   *   *

Business smarts don't necessarily come with the bagfuls of money that accrue to *arriviste* rockers, however. One day not too long ago, Townshend went to draw some funds from a group of Who-related companies clustered under the name Eel Pie—and discovered not only that the coffers were bare, but that he was in debt to the tune of some $1 million. He's since sold off some of the companies—the Magic Bus Bookshop and a P.A.-equipment rental company that kept the Who's stage equipment profitable when the group wasn't using it—and he doesn't sound particularly worried.

"It's not like it's my money," he says. "It's company money, money that I invested. Personally, I have got financial security. I've got a home, a car—I've got everything that I need."

But as the Who say their long goodbye to the big-time concert grind, there's another fly in the ointment—a real threat to the master plan of turning the Who into essentially a stuido-only band. His name is John Entwistle.

Entwistle seems to be a stoic type. Although he's in the final stages of a divorce, he and his longtime American girlfriend, a striking brunette named Max, are demonstratively happy, and he says he loves his life at home in England, where he collects vintage guitars, stuffed fish, antique armor and pure-bred chickens. But this "last tour" business with the Who, well, it really honks him off. Of all the times for Roger and Pete to discover something they can agree on.

"You know," Entwistle says one night in his hotel room as a TV set drones soothingly in the background, "I don't intend to get off the road. At the moment, Roger and Pete are both agreein'—about this bein' the final tour and about the whole way they want to structure the Who's career. But I completely disagree. I think the way it's gonna be structured, we're gonna be still playing, but playing extremely badly, and rustily. I mean, to do one concert, you still need to do four weeks' rehearsal. And I don't think it's *worth* rehearsin' four weeks for one concert."

He lights a cigarette. "There's not much I can do about it except hope they change their minds. They frequently do, but in this case, I don't think they will."

So if the Who stop touring, he doesn't want to be involved in just making records with them? "Um, no," Entwistle says. "I mean, from my point of view, I'm not prepared to just carry on doing albums. If the touring isn't there, then I'd rather get my own thing together, which involves touring as well."

Interesting.

Very interesting, actually. Especially to Townshend and Daltrey, who have heard nothing about Entwistle's decision to bail out if the band really quits the road.

"He told you that?" says Daltrey the next day in Indianapolis. He's a bit taken aback, but after all these years, obviously nothing that happens within the Who really surprises him anymore. But could the Who bring in another bassist and still call themselves the Who?

"I don't know," says Daltrey carefully. "We'll have to cross that bridge when we come to it. I mean, I'm pretty ruthless about keepin' the Who together, and if John doesn't want to do it, then . . ." He's really thinking this one over now. "You see," he suddenly says, "John never *says* anything. We have meetings, and John actually says absolutely nothing—never has, never will. If we have a meetin', it'll be Pete and me talkin' and the other two just sittin' there. I mean, you never really get to know what John feels. So, in the end, it's just really what Pete and I want to do. . . . I'm sure if Pete and I wanted to do it and still call it the Who, we could do it successfully."

Strange news travels fast. At the concert that night in Indianapolis, the Who cranked up a rather emphatic version of "Long Live Rock," and as Townshend charged into the guitar solo, thrashing and flailing at his long-suffering Telecaster, he also started leaping across the stage to where Entwistle was standing and pumping out bass. When he reached Entwistle's ear, he shouted—the mouthing was unmistakable from the side of the stage—"Fuck you!" But then he broke into this big, goofy grin, rolled his eyes up in his head like the village spaz and bopped his way back to his amps. Lord knows. . . .

Backstage after the show, Townshend slumped on a dressing-room couch and considered Entwistle's dark mutterings. Was he serious?

"I think he's serious," Pete said. "I don't quite know. . . . It's one of the big question marks. You know, John's playin', the fulfillment he gets from the way that he plays, can only be experienced in a road situation—and *possibly* only with the Who. But I think when the band does stop workin', each member is gonna go through a different set of withdrawals, you know? If John feels that he couldn't even address himself to the prospect of doin' recording, then of course we've got a problem." Townshend cracks a sly grin. "He'll have to find about $1 million to give back to Warner Bros. He'll have to sell one of his 450 basses or something."

But if he leaves, could he be replaced? Would the resulting band still be the Who? After all, Roger thinks that as long as Daltrey and Townshend are up there, it still *is* the Who.

Pete shakes his head. "That is so mistaken," he says. "I mean, it would be Townshend and Daltrey—or Daltrey and Townshend." Another grin. "But, oh, it would *not* be the Who."

Well, what's the story with this band, then? This is the last U.S. tour because Pete Townshend is tired of the road—but then, according to the master plan, the group's apparently going to spend most of next year on the road. Will Entwistle leave the band? Will Townshend find a way to keep this show together?

Pete has a definite *que será* look in his eye. "I think the Who's relationships are more about need than desire," he says. "We don't necessarily *want* to be dependent on one another, but we *are*. So it doesn't matter whether you walk away from this relationship. . . ." He spreads his palms, all-explaining. "It still remains."

*T*HREE

Ronnie Lane

(1982)

*R*onnie Lane was a founding member of the
*Small Faces, a London Mod group of the early
Sixties, and he stayed on to live the rock & roll high
life after Rod Stewart and Ron Wood joined the band
and shortened its name to the Faces. Stewart went on
to solo renown, Wood joined the Rolling Stones, and
Ronnie Lane—a sweet, brave and selfless man—
came down with multiple sclerosis. I wish I could say
there was a happy ending to this story; to the extent
that Lane seems to have been helped in subsequent
years by hyperbaric therapy, and the fact that he's
still alive, maybe there is. On the other hand, his sad
story is a reminder—a constant one, to me—that
there are worse things in rock & roll than dying
before you get old. Count your blessings, kids.*

Ronnie Lane remembers the day, about five years ago, when
doctors first told him he had multiple sclerosis. How could he
ever forget? "They just looked at me with an awful, pitiful, sort
of helpless expression. It was scary—*really* scary. When they
look at you like that, you know they can't bleedin' do anything,
and *oh*, do you feel alone." Lane stares silently at the hands he

can no longer control, the legs that hardly work, the once happy-go-lucky life that now lies in ruins. "I can be in a crowded football stadium," he says, "completely alone."

Multiple sclerosis (MS) is incurable. That's what the English doctors told Ronnie Lane. But then late last year, Fred Sessler reentered his life. A longtime business associate of the Rolling Stones, Sessler knew Lane from his glory days with the Faces. Sessler had left the music business, taken his rock & roll money and invested it in a controversial MS therapy that involves daily injections of diluted poisonous snake venom. Basing himself in Florida, he opened the Miami Venom Institute. Keith Richards' aunt, who has a severe case of MS, was a patient there, and by last November, so was Ronnie Lane, the former, now penniless rock star. Sessler paid for everything, and Lane slowly started getting better. The venom injections, combined with a rigorous program of therapy, can't cure MS, but Lane says they did arrest the physical deterioration associated with the disease. Suddenly, he had hope.

But then earlier this year, the U.S. Food and Drug Administration intervened. The FDA did not approve of Sessler's venom treatments and closed down the Miami Venom Institute, forcing him to move his operation to Jamaica—and to put a heartbroken Ronnie Lane on a plane back to London.

Outside the small, tidy apartment in the London suburb of Kentish Town, a daylong drizzle drips through the trees. Inside, a small electric heater struggles to take some of the chill off the afternoon. A battered Hammond organ, a souvenir of happier times, stands against a wall in the living room. Lane bought it years ago from Faces keyboardist Ian McLagan. His hands can't finger the keys anymore, but music still fills his head, and with the assistance of Boo Oldfield, he still composes songs. Boo is a dark, pretty, determined woman, and this is her flat. She took Lane in when his life was at a low ebb—a bottomed-out chronicle of two failed marriages, a pair of sons (now three and nine years old) he was rarely able to see and, finally and most devastatingly, this cruel, crippling disease.

"Do you know about MS?" Boo asks from the kitchen, where she's brewing a pot of tea. "It's where the outer layer of the nerves breaks down. It's like a short circuit." She brings the tea into the living room, and Lane, who's sitting quietly on a couch, asks her for a packet of Sweet 'n Low. He's confined to a stringent diet—no sugar, no fat, no gluten. "Bread's out," he explains. "Anything to do with wheat flour is out."

"Rice flour you can use to make lots of things," Boo cheerily interjects. "It's not that bad."

"She's baked a few cakes with rice flour," says Ronnie, slowly stirring his tea, "and I think I like it better." He's trying to be optimistic, but suddenly his smile turns into a bitter, twisted grin. "That's just looking on the bright side of things," he says. "Let's look on the really dull side—it's *awful!*"

So are the snake-venom injections. (Before he left the States, Sessler provided Lane with a year's worth of the venom for home treatment.) "How can I describe it?" Ronnie says wearily. "Can you imagine the strands of your hair hurting? That's what happens. And when you blink—like that—it's like your eyelids are made of sandpaper. I was quite prepared to feel bad, like with the flu or mumps. But I've never had anything like this. This is like hell itself."

(According to a National Multiple Sclerosis Society spokeswoman, venom therapy is "an entirely unproven form of treatment." And while MS is not fatal itself, complications can lead to death.)

To make matters worse, Lane is broke. What money he had from his days of fame went to doctors. Now he can't even afford a record player, and British tax collectors constantly hound him for thousands of pounds they claim he owes in back taxes. He agrees that it might be a wise idea to check on the royalties accrued by sales of the old Faces albums and *Rough Mix,* the lovely LP he recorded with Pete Townshend in 1977, but he's unable to pay for an audit. Nor can he afford a security guard to watch over his last significant asset, a mobile studio, which he bought with his earnings from the Faces. The sixteen-track recording van is now parked in another part of London, where local punks—convinced that Lane was just another over-privileged rock star—stripped it of equipment. Ronnie was powerless to stop them.

All he has left, really, are his memories. They stretch back thirty-six years to the East End of London, where he was born. His father was a truck driver—"a saint," Ronnie says—who'd work all day and then spend his nights caring for his two sons and their mother, who also suffered from MS. (As a child, Lane was assured that the disease was not hereditary; when he later contracted it, doctors allowed as how it did tend to "cluster in families.") It was Ronnie's father who urged him to take up the guitar as a child.

"In his own kind of truck-driver way, he was very wise,"

Lane says. "He said, 'If you learn to play an instrument, son, learn to play a guitar. You'll always have a friend.' It's a great way of puttin' it."

His first band was called the Outcasts. Ronnie was the guitarist and lead singer, and a little kid named Kenney Jones played drums. When they couldn't find a steady bass player, Ronnie decied to switch instruments and got his father to accompany him to a music store to pick out a bass.

"I'd seen the bass I wanted, a Harmony, and it was only forty-five pounds [about $100]. We went to the shop, and this little fellow came up and said, 'Oh, yeah, that's a great bass,' and he showed it to us. I liked this little fellow a lot, and I ended up goin' home with him. He had a stack of records as high as that table over there—really early Sun records and Ray Charles. I'd never come across that kind of music before, but he had it all."

The "little fellow," whose name was Steve Marriott, was also a musician, so Lane invited him down to a local pub one night to sit in with the Outcasts. Unfortunately, Marriott destroyed the house piano, the band got fired, and Ronnie was chucked out of the group. Kenney Jones loyally followed him, and together with the incorrigible Marriott they started a new group. Since they were all rather diminutive, they called themselves the Small Faces.

With Ian McLagan on organ, the band acquired a following, a manager and a recording deal. They charted in 1965 with their first single, "Whatcha Gonna Do About It?" and had hits the following year with "Sha La La La Lee," "Hey Girl" and "All or Nothing" (which went to Number One). They smoked a lot of dope, dropped acid and generally lived it up. They were in it for love and fun, and they never knew where the money went. At one point, with three singles in the charts, they were sleeping on top of cars parked in the street.

Even though the hits kept coming—"Itchycoo Park" in 1967, "Lazy Sunday" in 1968—the group stayed poor. In 1969, Marriott left to form Humble Pie, and the remaining Small Faces looked for a replacement. Eventually, they found two: singer Rod Stewart and bassist-turned-guitarist Ron Wood, late of the Jeff Beck Group. This new combination was a hit, and life soon got better. The Faces liked only the best hotels, the biggest limousines. There was lots of drinking, and, of course, drugs. Lane happily consumed everything available, and when he'd occasionally notice a numbness in his fingers or a certain lack of coordination, he put it down to simple excess. After a few years, though, the extravagant lifestyle started getting to him.

"The thing that upset me was, like, to get a bloody private jet just to fly thirty-five miles. I thought, 'Come on, who are you tryin' to impress?' And then Rod Stewart got so big-headed I couldn't take it anymore. I don't know what he wanted. I don't think he knew what he wanted, either. He was just bein' stupid."

Lane left the Faces in 1973 and started a traveling rock circus—complete with jugglers and fire-eaters—called the Passing Show. He also put together a band, Slim Chance, and recorded four low-key, folksy albums. His physical coordination continued worsening, and after cutting *Rough Mix* with Townshend (with whom he shared a longstanding interest in the Sufi-based teachings of Meher Baba), he sought medical help. It was then that the doctors told him there was none.

Lane puts part of the blame for his condition on drugs and alcohol and the rock & roll lifestyle he knew with the Faces. "I did a lot of really unreasonable things in those days," he says softly. "I'm ashamed of myself for the way I've gone on, very ashamed."

He finds solace in the Bible and in Boo and, of course, in music. Last year, he even reunited with Steve Marriott, and they recorded a low-budget album called *The Midgets Strike Back*. No record company has yet expressed interest in releasing the record, however, and Lane is not in any position to promote it.

Outside, the rain has ceased and the sun is shining. A visiting journalist, taking his leave, asks Lane if there's any way in which people might help him—thinking he might appreciate charitable contributions from old Faces fans or something.

"How could they help out?" he says. "I'll tell you how your readers could help me out, if they want to: don't take dope. If you listen to me, that'll help me out." Then he cites the Book of Proverbs, chapter seven, verse seven: "And . . . I discerned among the youths, a young man void of understanding."

"I've been there and back," says Ronnie Lane, "and I know how far it is."

*F*OUR

Iggy Pop
(1986)

With the Stooges, Jimmy Osterberg—or Iggy Pop, as he'll be forever known to rock history—pretty much invented punk rock. Iggy would take anything, say anything, and do anything to get a response from the crowd. His records with the Stooges are essential artifacts, and his late-Seventies albums, The Idiot *and* Lust for Life, *are among the most richly conceived and musically stirring LPs of that decade. You and I know this, of course, but I notice we're alone. There hasn't been much of a market for raw, challenging music in this country lately, which just goes to show . . . well, something pathetic and depressing, I suppose. Iggy's still looking for a hit, but he has branched out into movies a bit (he was featured in John Waters' 1990 film* Cry Baby) *and of course he can never be counted out—which is what we love about him, right?*

Backstage one night at Manhattan's Westside Arts Theatre—home of the New Wave magic act Penn and Teller—excited staffers were conducting a celebrity inventory. Among the eve-

ning's attendees: one singer-songwriter, one film director and a
Broadway nabob. Not bad.

But Penn Jillette, the burlier half of the headlining illu-
sionist duo, was unimpressed. To his mind these were bush cel-
ebs, mere terrestrials. Penn and his partner, the mononomial
Teller—alone among Philistines, apparently—had sighted God
in the audience.

"It was like he had spotlights on him," Jillette recalls,
"like no one else was there. The box-office people were saying,
'Do you know who you had in the audience?' Paul Simon, Martin Scorsese, also all these theater creeps. But I never saw any of
them. I said, '*Iggy* was in the audience, man. We had fuckin'
Iggy!'"

Jillette, a closet rock scholar, still treasures the memory
of a concert in San Francisco several years ago, at which he
fought his way to a front-row seat. "I was sitting there, and
there was Iggy up onstage with his dick hanging out. He leaned
down, grabbed me by the collar, pulled me up hard and said,
'*You eat dog food!*' To which I responded, 'Yes, I do, Mr.
Pop.'" Jillette sighs. "I really have no understanding that the
masses don't know Iggy. He's been the number-one superstar
for me, and for everybody I know, for ten, fifteen years."

And so, sensing incomprehension among his colleagues
backstage that night, Jillette was dismayed. Soulless soft-rock
zombies—what did they know? Had they ever sucked at the
white-hot nozzles of the Great Fuzz Mother? Had they coupled
with the red-eyed Frenzy Demon in his bottle-and-bone-strewn
lair? Hapless radioheads—how could they even begin to understand?

"Iggy Pop," Jillette exlained, in his gentlest bellow, "is
God."

Jim Osterberg is inured to this sort of demented veneration. It
comes with the cult territory he's inhabited for the last two decades. But at age thirty-nine, the polite and bespectacled pro-
prietor of "Iggy Pop Inc."—as he half-laughingly refers to his
newly rehabilitated alter ego—is itching for change. Osterberg's
mission is to bust Iggy out of the punk-art ghetto—a prison he
practically built with his own hands—and put him on the charts,
a place he's only read about in other people's bios. And *Blah-
Blah-Blah*, Iggy's ninth and already fastest-selling solo album,
may well do the trick. Produced by David Bowie—a recurring

figure in the Iggy saga—and Queen engineer David Richards, the new LP is an unabashed attempt to launch Iggy, at last, into the musical mainstream. Punk purists may cringe at the sleek production, but it's getting him serious radio play for the first time in his career. *Blah-Blah-Blah* is no wholesale sellout: Iggy still sings like a lion, and "Cry for Love," the first single, illuminates his existential stance as clearly as anything on *Raw Power* did thirteen years ago. But in its sonic details, the album is frankly designed as a crossover move—one for which Iggy has never been readier.

"Yeah, it's the new regime," says Osterberg, flashing a great big Iggy smile, his hands reaching out to frame an unseen banner. "Iggy Pop: Under New Management!"

It is true that lately the Iggy Pop lifestyle—once a tent show of decadence pitched amid vast puddles of befuddlement—has taken on a zingy new sheen. Not long ago, for example, the Ig spent an entire evening hanging out with Raquel Welch, of all people. They were on call to do a wordless walk-on in *Sid & Nancy,* the film about the dead Sex Pistol Sid Vicious and his girlfriend, Nancy Spungen. Iggy hadn't planned on being involved in this project. He'd met Sid and Nancy once, and he dug Sid's music. ("His version of 'Somethin' Else' was *masterful!*"), but after reading the script, he decided that Sid and Nancy's story—two determined dead-enders meet their inevitable dead end—lacked uplift. So Iggy had turned down director Alex Cox's request that he contribute a theme song to the soundtrack (as he'd done for Cox's cult hit *Repo Man*). When Cox offered him a cameo opposite La Rocky, though, playing upscale tourists in a Chelsea Hotel sequence, Iggy figured there were less pleasant ways to hone his acting skills.

But it turned out to be weird. Raquel radiated Hollywoodness. "She's really intense," says Iggy, ever the diplomat. "It was like talkin' to Hitler."

Maybe it was just him—the king-of-punk-rock thing. Serious showbizzers must find it hard to relate to an art form that involves waving one's weenie in public. Iggy got the same vibe from Paul Newman, whom he encountered recently on the set of the new Scorsese film, *The Color of Money*. Scorsese had cast Iggy as a pool player in a scene with the movie's costar, Tom Cruise. It was another lineless bit part, but Iggy played it with his customary relish.

"I don't think Newman appreciated my scene at all," he says. "In one take, my character had to proffer a joint to the young hero, so I think he didn't like it on those grounds. He kind of sat in the background and harrumph-harrumphed a lot."

To tell the truth, Iggy's been having second thoughts about this acting enterprise lately. He's been at it for two years now, and the results have been meager. His most significant score—an actual speaking part in a "Miami Vice" episode (typecast as usual, he played the manager of an S&M bar)—was edited out of the final footage. And the round of casting calls and auditions has yielded little in the way of work. When his acting coach suggested that he stop dyeing his hair black ("She said it was too rock & roll") and maybe start seeing an analyst ("She was very Method"), he decided to can the lessons and devote himself more fully to his true calling.

But Iggy Pop hadn't had a record deal since 1982, when Chris Stein of Blondie produced *Zombie Birdhouse*. Maybe he was still the king of punk rock, but he was crowding forty now, and he had *never* had a major hit. To most record execs, he seemed just another fabled flameout, a freak act from rock's unruly past. Times had changed. Troublemakers and crazies were out of fashion in the music business. Eccentricity impeded the flow of product. This was the Eighties—and Iggy Pop, in effect, was out of a job.

To some, Iggy's plight—like Sid and Nancy's demise—might have seemed poetically appropriate. Weren't punks always nattering on about "no fun" and "no future"? Iggy contends he was never a nihilist, but his nut-case legend has plagued him. Ever since Halloween of 1967, when Iggy and the Stooges, his legendarily depraved band, played their maiden gig in Ann Arbor, Michigan, he has been perceived as rock's baddest boy. Who could ever forget Iggy onstage in his prime—ducking bottles, sputtering ethnic epithets, occasionally flinging himself out into the audience in search of a kick or a kiss, his face a whirling blur of smeared blood and cheap mascara? The Beatles, just a few years earlier, had only wanted to hold your hand; Iggy sang "I Wanna Be Your Dog." And "Gimme Danger." And "Death Trip." He stirred up dark and hard-to-handle urges that had lain hidden near the heart of rock & roll, and he was unforgettable.

But by 1975, the Stooges—whose three protopunk albums had dropped like swatted flies into the discount bins, and thence into oblivion—were only a memory. And Iggy himself was just emerging from a Los Angeles sanitarium, newly cured of addictions to heroin, booze and barbiturates.

At the same time, a fresh generation of punk rockers was arising, and it adopted Iggy as a kamikaze icon—these kids covered his songs, aped what they took to be his kill-me-please stage stance and eventually, in some cases, even managed to off themselves. Looking back, Iggy now sees these angry young apostles as sadly misguided.

"I never felt like a self-destructive sort of person when I started out," he says, munching from a healthful deli plate of buckwheat *varnishkes* one drizzly New York afternoon. "I admit I may have been the first performer to vent his immediate angers in this format—if I was pissed off, I sang about it. But that was only a part of what I did. I dealt with the subject of love from the viewpoint of someone who hadn't experienced it. So I was capable of writing a song like 'Cock in My Pocket,' because everybody's been through that—everybody's gone out one night or another with the subjunctive possibility of a hard-on, and they wanna put it to some girl. This is a common part of the human condition. I was just the first one to come out and actually *spill it* in a rock song. That was my experience at the time. And I didn't see any reason to chicken out and hide that experience to try to get a commercial hit."

So he didn't, and the rest is hitless history.

"I always felt that Stooge music could have attracted a larger audience had it been presented in a straightforward way," he says, draining a cup of black coffee and lighting a cigarette (his last remaining vice). "But there always had to be some gimmick—somebody writing my name in dripping blood across the album cover or something. Of course, *I* made numerous mistakes, too—I *was* a bit of a flake at the time. But I never felt dogmatic about inflicting pain as a way of life, you know? Not like some of the groups coming along now. I never called myself Iggy Crush, or Iggy Squeeze-Vomit. It was always just Iggy Pop, just a part of what was goin' on. There's not a total commitment to tragedy here."

Indeed, Iggy was feeling anything but tragic when he turned up at a Manhattan hotel suite one night late last year to pay a call on his pal David Bowie. Bowie was in town to work on a film soundtrack, and he had naturally rung Iggy up. They'd been buddies since the dawn of the Seventies and occasional partners ever since Bowie had pitched in to mix the chaotically recorded tapes for 1973's *Raw Power,* the final Stooges album. Back then, it was widely believed that Bowie's breakthrough persona, Ziggy Stardust, around whom he'd built his best-selling 1972 LP, was in fact an image of Iggy—the rock star as debauched primitive. Bowie denies that this was ever the case. Ziggy, he says, was "loosely woven around" an obscure figure named Vince Taylor, an American rocker who arrived in London in the late Fifties, formed a band called the Playboys and, after cutting a few marginal British singles, disappeared into the ozone. As for the character's name, Bowie says that "Stardust" was lifted from one of his Mercury Records label mates at the time, the Legendary Stardust Cowboy; "Ziggy," he contends, "was one of the few Christian names I could find beginning with the letter *Z.*"

Be all that as it may, Bowie stuck by Iggy through the years. They lived in Berlin together in the late Seventies, both winding down from past excesses, and it was there that Bowie, determined to rekindle his friend's career, recorded tracks for two of Iggy's finest solo albums, 1977's *The Idiot* and *Lust for Life.* They toured together, with Bowie, unbilled, playing piano in Iggy's band. Unfortunately, neither album yielded a hit single, and Iggy returned to square one. He continued touring, and he recorded six more albums with other producers. But Iggy was still Iggy: a primal talent, too raw for the masses, too real for radio.

Then, in 1983, Bowie scored a worldwide hit with his version of "China Girl," a song he and Iggy had cowritten for *The Idiot.* Several more of their collaborations were included on Bowie's 1984 LP, *Tonight.* Suddenly, Iggy, by now resident in New York's Greenwich Village, found himself the recipient of significant songwriting royalties. He opened a bank account, learned to balance a checkbook. And it occurred to him that this money might be his last stake—his last chance to shed the past, to come in out of the cold. He decided the time had come to finally get organized.

By this point, Iggy's life had taken on a few recognizably human dimensions. He was, for one thing, married to a Japanese woman, fourteen years his junior, named Suchi. He'd spotted her in the audience at one of his concerts in Tokyo in 1983 and had fallen in love with her at first sight. That she was young and still living at home—and that her father was a Tokyo policeman—complicated things a bit, but not crucially.

"There was no way I could've gone to her house and sort of said, 'Hello, I'm the king of punk rock, the guy who pulled his willy out onstage last night at the Sun Plaza. I hope you don't mind if I borrow your daughter-*san* for a few months of rock & roll slave labor.'" Iggy laughs even now at the thought. "So what I did was, I just took her. I said, 'I really like you. Why don't you come along and keep me company and try to keep me from drinking so much?'—which I was doing a great deal on the road. I said, 'We can start a new life.' And she was keen, so we did."

In October 1984, Iggy and Suchi married, and together they began renovating the family business, Iggy Pop Inc. Iggy took up jogging, got back into painting (a pastime he'd picked up from Bowie back in their Berlin days) and began offering himself as an actor. (In fact, when Raquel Welch got tired of waiting around for that *Sid & Nancy* walk-on and bowed out, Iggy even got Suchi to take her place.) By 1985, with song royalties streaming in from the Bowie recordings, he felt confident enough to attempt another album—and this one, he knew, had to sell.

He decided not to seek a record deal first because "at the time, I would have been perceived in the industry as basically a broken-down rock star. So instead, Suchi and I saved our pennies and dimes. We took subways, we kept all our receipts, we ate inexpensively and did our own housework—still do. I *enjoy* vacuuming. We bought our furniture at junk shops and carried it home. And by living on the cheap, we were able to save a big chunk of cash—about $40,000."

With money in hand, Iggy started scouting around for a collaborator. He huddled with Ric Ocasek of the Cars and Steve Stevens, the guitarist with Billy Idol's band, but neither seemed quite right for the sort of streamlined project he had in mind. Then Iggy placed a call to Steve Jones, the former Sex Pistols guitarist, who was living, as Iggy puts it, "in reduced circumstances" in Los Angeles. Although Jones had made his name as a thrash master with the Pistols, Iggy—who had employed his services to record the *Repo Man* theme—knew that Jones was capable of subtler stylings, too. Iggy ran down the plan to Jones: rent a house in L.A., meet there daily for a period of three to four months and endeavor, in a very workmanlike way, to write some songs.

"I told Steve one thing was important," Iggy says. "I was

gonna ask him to come up with some things that were softer in attack than what he'd done in the past. He said, 'Aw, I'm an old softy, always have been. People just don't know me.'"

Iggy and Jones worked through the summer of 1985, putting together about a dozen songs, three of which Iggy was completely happy with. They found a local eight-track studio that had great sound, rented it for a rock-bottom fifteen dollars an hour and began cutting demo tapes of the new tunes. They finished in October, right on schedule. Iggy, nearly broke again, returned to New York, and when he turned up at Bowie's hotel room to visit, he had with him a tape of his new material.

Iggy had no intention of asking Bowie to produce another album for him; he was simply proud of how much he'd been able to accomplish, for the first time, on his own. But Bowie was excited by what he heard—there was about half of a good LP on Iggy's tape—and he volunteered to help whip together additional songs and to produce the finished product. Iggy wanted a commercial record? "I can make this commercial as hell," Bowie told him.

It would be simple: Iggy and Suchi would join him for a pre-Christmas cruise in the Caribbean, during which Iggy and David would come up with the songs. Then Mr. and Mrs. Pop would fly, as they usually did each year, to Bowie's home near Montreux, Switzerland, for the holidays. There they could get in some skiing in nearby Gstaad and write more songs. In May, they would record at Mountain Studios in Montreux, where David could get a preferential rate.

Iggy told Bowie he'd have to think this offer over. His demo tape had already drawn nibbles from two record labels, one of which advised against bringing Bowie into the project. "They hated the idea," Iggy recalls. "They said, 'If you do get a hit with him, everybody'll say it was just his doing.'

"So I sat around and thought, 'God, would everybody think it was just a David Bowie album, and I was a fuckin' puppet?' Then I thought, 'No. The stuff's down on tape already. I'm singing it, I'm writing the lyrics, it's mostly my melodies. I might just as well get the most commercial producer I possibly can, someone who'll bring it in at cost—and that's Bowie.'"

Steve Jones was unavailable for the Montreux sessions, so Kevin Armstrong, a British guitarist who'd worked with Thomas Dolby, was signed on in his stead, as was Bowie's own current collaborator, a classically trained Turkish multi-instrumentalist named Erdal Kizilcay. The recording pace was brisk: basic tracks were cut at the rate of one song per day, and the entire album was completed within a month. All very businesslike.

The result is surely Iggy Pop's most professional performance. Bowie's contribution was significant—a connoisseur of rock oldies, he had the idea to cover an old Albert Lee version of an ancient Buddy Holly production of a Fifties Australian tune called "Real Wild Child." And it was Bowie who came up with the idea for "Shades," a moving ballad, based on his observation of Iggy's relationship with Suchi.

But the centerpiece of *Blah-Blah-Blah* is the new Iggy Pop—a singer who's determined to stick around. He thinks this album is his snazziest to date. "And I know it's gonna be heard this time, too," he says. "So I'm happy."

At last.

Simon Fowler/Retna Ltd.

*F*IVE

The Pretenders

(1980)

On 1980, the Pretenders—a very English band
fronted by a very American singer and songwriter
and rhythm guitarist named Chrissie Hynde—
released what may have been the most exhilarating
debut album of the decade. They were great drinkers
and carriers-on, and I remember returning from the
road trip that produced this piece in a very torn-
down state. I also remember bassist Pete Farndon
and angelic guitarist Jim Honeyman-Scott snorting
cocaine off a knife blade one rainy night in the
band's tour bus. Before the Eighties were over, both
men were dead.

Chrissie Hynde outlasted her demons, had a child
with Kinks leader Ray Davies and has since become
more and more preoccupied, apparently, with
nonmusical matters. Or at least we don't hear from
her as much these days as we'd like to. Back in 1980,
though, she was bursting with import.

Chrissie Hynde, the Pretenders' singer and songwriter, unzips
her trademark black leather pants and pushes them uncer-
emoniously down around her ankles. She is wearing what ap-

pear to be old-fashioned white cotton underpants. I try not to gawk. The silence here in the quilt-walled living compartment of the Pretenders' comfortably appointed tour bus is broken only by the clatter of a relentless March rainstorm playing popcorn rhythms on the metal roof, and by occasional shouts and soggy laughter from a nearby group of about a hundred Pretenders fans lined up outside an already-packed club called Detroit, in Port Chester, New York. Chrissie reaches into a capacious handbag, pulls out the elastic support band she has nearly forgotten, slips it over her foot and up her leg, and positions it around her right knee, which—she informs me—she recently strained.

"Ten minutes left," says Dave Hill, the Pretenders' manager, who is alertly perched on the edge of a chair near the bus door. "Ten minutes?" Chrissie responds. "That suits me. It's just ten minutes less of me boozin' before we go on." She flashes Hill a reassuring grin as she hitches up her britches. "But I haven't had a drink," she quickly adds. Hill, shiny-cheeked and boyish at twenty-six, is businesslike in a low-key, British way, and he casts an appraising glance at his chief charge. The pale, mercurial Hynde, who's twenty-eight, looks tired. Nine days into the Pretenders' two-month maiden tour of North America—with the group's self-titled debut album already bulleting toward the U.S. Top Twenty—the booze, the boredom, the incessant rain and general dankness of life on the road already are taking a toll on her.

"You've got those black lines under your eyes," Hill says solicitously. Chrissie's forehead—what can be seen of it through her long, raven bangs—crinkles in mock dismay. "It took me five minutes to *put* 'em there," she protests with a wounded whine. "I don't feel quite like a woman until I've got my eyes drawn on," she tells me, turning to assess her reflection in a full-length mirror. "I've got a technique that doesn't take any time, and you can do it when you're drunk."

Not quite happy with her somber ensemble of black leather and dark blue denim, she reaches over to the sofa for her favorite hat—a screaming pink, fake-fur coonskin cap, complete with a tawdry little tail. "Got it in London," she says a bit defensively, positioning the hat on her head. "I don't *try* to be tacky and out of fashion, but somehow I can never get it right. If I put on something pretty, it would be a joke, you know? I can't help it."

After a last, semisatisfied look in the mirror, Chrissie

sweeps up her red leather motorcycle jacket ("It's got my perfume in it"), and we both follow Hill out the door and into the teeming rain. It's showtime again.

There's a pronounced buzz in the air about the Pretenders: this is only the group's seventh American gig, and the saga of their whirlwind British success (three hit singles and a subtly startling debut LP that reached the top of the charts) has whetted Anglophile appetites here for months. The Pretenders arrived out of nowhere in January 1979 with a billowing, Nick Lowe–produced revamp of an obscure 1964 Kinks track called "Stop Your Sobbing." It was a breath of classic pop freshness for a musical scene that had bogged down in postpunk predictability. But "Sobbing" gave no hint of the band's range or originality, qualities confirmed by the self-penned follow-up singles: "Kid," with its wistful melody and alluringly ambiguous lyrics, and "Brass in Pocket," a near-Motownish declaration of female sexual assertiveness.

The clincher was the LP *Pretenders,* released last January, on which American expatriate Chrissie Hynde proved herself one of the most completely convincing female rock & rollers in recent memory. A stingingly effective rhythm guitarist whose voice combines the fluidity of jazz singing with the rawness of rock, Hynde wrote or cowrote ten of the album's twelve tracks, imbuing many of them with a psychosexual candor that goes beyond even the bounds recently set by Marianne Faithfull. Add to this a rhythm section that can rock out ferociously in seven-four time, if necessary, and a lead guitarist whose combination of precision and flamboyance sometimes recalls the young Jeff Beck, and you've got an album that—as Pete Townshend recently described it on a British radio show—is "like a drug."

But the question that hangs in the air here at Detroit is: can they deliver?

Backstage, mountains of empty equipment crates tower above scattered clumps of thick black cable and heavy-duty power plugs, and groups of old friends, new women and local notables wander the central corridor, swigging beers and swapping news. Mick Ronson, the ex–Bowie guitarist who now works with Ian Hunter, has driven up from New York, and so has Lenny Kaye, the rock writer and Patti Smith Group guitarist, who met Chrissie during one of her down-and-out phases in London not so long ago.

There's a row of small, brightly lit rooms in the rear, each stocked with platters of fresh fruit and tubs of iced beer and Pepsi. Chrissie stops at the first door to trade a few warmup wisecracks with Pete Farndon, twenty-seven, the Pretenders' bassist, and Martin Chambers, twenty-eight, their drummer. A gleaming, matched set of metal-faced Zemaitis guitars ($1300 a pop on custom order) stand ready in a corner, but lead guitarist James Honeyman-Scott—at twenty-three, the youngest and most fun-loving Pretender—is nowhere to be seen, having sequestered himself in one of the back rooms.

Chrissie listens attentively as Chambers, a heavy hitter, bemoans the condition of his drum kit, which was specially built to withstand his onslaughts. Last night he had to secure the snare drum with guitar strings, and tonight he's reduced to trying bootlaces. Farndon, a tall, dark and classically handsome sort, grunts sympathetically. Chrissie drifts off to greet an old girlfriend, and he watches as her jiggling pink coon's tail disappears into the crowd. "It's not easy to be in her position," he says, earnestly affectionate. "You know—locked up with four or five guys who are talkin' about tits and ass all the time. On the road, you've got nothing that most women would want. Chris isn't like most women." He upends the Johnny Walker Red in his hand and takes a bracing gulp, grimacing as the liquor goes down.

Out front, in Detroit's main room, the last pummeling power chords of the Ramones' "I Wanna Be Sedated" have receded into the house speakers. Suddenly, the air shivers with the bombastic strains of Wagner's "Ride of the Valkyries," which Dave Hill has nicked off the *Apocalypse Now* soundtrack for use as a fanfare. The Pretenders scurry onstage, the now-accounted-for Honeyman-Scott looking aroused and resplendent in a sparkling white Nudie-style cowboy jacket. Hynde, primed and nearly bouncing, jacks in her white Telecaster, and before the capacity crowd even has time to cheer, she's shouted out the raggedy count for "The Wait." For the next hour, the Pretenders' music—much of it composed in treacherously eccentric meters—explodes off the stage. Chambers churns up a brutal Bo Diddley beat for the jaunty "Cuba Slide" (the B side of their latest British single, "Talk of the Town") and then downshifts into a walloping, primordial thud for "Stop Your Sobbing." Farndon's fat, fluid bass slides through the tricky rhythms like an oiled snake, coiling up in unexpected grace notes and quirky arpeggios, then slipping back into the dense sonic mix to await another opening. The radiant "Kid" stirs some of the crowd to sing along, and Chrissie's full, uncaged alto soars.

After "Porcelain"—a raw, as-yet-unrecorded guitar wrangle, Chrissie, sweat-soaked and smiling, grabs a microphone and announces "Tattooed Love Boys," her bike-club gang-bang epic. "This song is not about bikers," she says. "It's about girls who get beaten up by the same guy more than once." The song erupts at a neck-cracking seven-four pace, with Hynde slashing at her guitar and spitting out the cold, pitiless words like razor blades: "I shot my mouth off and you showed me what that *hole* was *for!*"

The set is capped with a stirring reprise of "Stop Your Sobbing." When it's done, the band, dazed and breathless, looks out over a sea of clenched fists, all punching upward like the pistons of some strange new engine. "Don't think we're used to this reception," Chrissie yells, "'cause we're *not!*"

Later, after an hour of backstage boozing and congratulatory blather, Honeyman-Scott announces that he's being tucked in tonight by some local seductress, and departs in a Cadillac. Dave Hill and I clamber onboard the bus with the rest of the band for the long, rain-whipped ride back to their Manhattan hotel. As the numbing rumble of the road sets in, Pete Farndon slips a homemade cassette into the tape system and turns the volume way up. A postpunk pounder, "Real Fun" by Ten Pole Tudor, leaps from the overhead speakers like a raucous toad. The bus takes a curve and Farndon sways (is it the bus?) toward the table where Chambers and I are huddled. The bassist slides his half-full bottle of Johnny Walker onto the table, where we fumble it around for the next half hour.

Chrissie Hynde, beaming and lovely after the evening's success—and jovially befuddled on the better part of a fifth of Montezuma tequila—holds aloft a small bouquet of roses from an unknown backstage admirer. "Someone must want to marry me," she announces. "'Cause any man who sends me roses is a man I *might* marry." The bus rounds another bend and she tumbles onto the sofa, giggling and kicking her feet out in time to the slithery rhythms of Iggy Pop's "New Values," which is blasting out overhead. Hoisting the tequila up to squint level, she contemplates the few remaining slugs. "I've made quite an impression on this bottle," she says with a burp.

*   *   *

Christine Ellen Hynde was born and raised in Akron, Ohio, where her father, Bud, works for the telephone company and her mother, Dee, is a part-time secretary. "I was Joe Normal," Chrissie says, sitting in her hotel room later. "But I was never too interested in high school. I mean, I never went to a dance, I never went out on a date, I never went steady. It became pretty awful for me. Except, of course, I could go see bands, and that was the kick. I used to go to Cleveland just to see any band. So I was in love a lot of the time, but mostly with guys in bands that I had never met. For me, knowing that Brian Jones was out there, and later that Iggy Pop was out there, made it kind of hard for me to get too interested in the guys that were around me. I had, uh, bigger things in mind."

Chrissie's brother, Terry, played the saxophone, and when Chrissie was sixteen, she took up the baritone ukulele. Too shy to get involved with any of the local all-male garage bands, she kept to herself and started writing songs. "I never had that kind of experience most guys in bands do," she says. "I think that probably determined a lot of my style of playing. I still go by the dots on the guitar, you know? I have a very rudimentary knowledge of it."

At about this time, Chrissie had her first peek behind the scenes of big-time rock & roll—an experience that still causes her to cackle with dismay. After a concert in Cleveland by the Jeff Beck Group, she and an older girlfriend were taken back to the band's hotel and introduced to the bassist, Ron Wood, and the singer, Rod Stewart.

"We sat there all night—I was sixteen—and we smoked dope and got really out of our trees. At the end of the evening, the arrangement looked like my girlfriend would go with Rod Stewart and I would be left with Ron Wood. And . . . I'm not kidding, I'm not trying to put this on, but I seriously didn't know what was goin' on. I was a real virgin, man. I didn't even know what it *was*. And I just looked, and I said, 'I can't stay here tonight! I've gotta take my driver's training course in the morning! Let's go!' And I insisted on leaving, 'cause I wanted to get my driver's license. It never occurred to me until years later what could have transpired that night, you know? Just think— Ronnie Wood would've been my first big one."

After a one-gig alliance with a band called Sat. Sun. Mat. (which included Mark Mothersbaugh, later of Devo) and three listless years of art studies at Kent State University (where she got caught up in the 1970 National Guard riot), Hynde knew she needed a change. "I just wanted to get the hell out of Ohio," she says. "I always knew that, since I was in junior high school and this train used to go by. I know it sounds romantic, but it made me cry when I saw it. I just knew that I had to be on that train someday."

Working as a waitress, and at various other odd jobs, she put together a thousand dollars and, in early 1973, flew off to swinging London—a place she'd read all about in the British rock tabloid *New Musical Express*. With her art background, she landed a lowly position with an architectural firm. The job ended after eight months, but by then she'd met *New Musical Express* writer Nick Kent. Through his auspices she secured an assignment to review a new Neil Diamond album.

"I just took the piss out of it," Chrissie says, lapsing into British slang. "I was very sarcastic. I said, 'This song sounds like an ad for an American small car.' I just completely demolished this guy, you know? I ended it up saying, 'Hey, wait a minute, hand me those binoculars—I think I just saw Rod McKuen walking out of a bake shop.' And that was it!"

To Hynde's utter amazement—and despite the subsequent arrival in the *NME*'s mailbox of outraged letters from "all four Neil Diamond fans in Britain"—her editor liked the review, and next assigned her to interview Brian Eno. They wound up discussing pornography, and Chrissie posed for an accompanying photo dressed in bondage gear, complete with high heels and black leather miniskirt. "It was the cover story," she remembers. "Of course, we started gettin' letters sayin', 'Who *is* this woman, and why is she wearing that *tacky* miniskirt?' So I would reply in the paper: 'I still wear white cotton briefs, too,' and they'd *print* all this, you know? For some reason they went for it. And here I was, a zero hillbilly from Ohio."

England was going through a musical lull at the time, though, and after a year Chrissie lost interest in her budding journalistic career. She worked for a few weeks in a strange little clothing store in the King's Road run by Malcolm McLaren, the soon-to-be Svengali of punk. Then, after a disastrous period trying to start a rock band in France, she returned in 1975 to Cleveland.

"I had a terrible time," she says. "I was hitchhiking around, and I'd forgotten how dangerous it was. I had a few bad experiences, but the way I look at it now is, for every sort of act of sodomy I was forced to perform, I'm gettin' paid 10,000 pounds now." She laughs bitterly. "That's how I try to look at it, anyway."

After another abortive attempt to put a band together in France, Hynde returned to London in 1976. She sensed something new in the air, and she was right. It was punk. She tried to put a group together with a young guitarist named Mick Jones, "but it didn't work. He was really young and fresh, and here I was, already spent. I didn't have his sort of fresh innocence. I wasn't like the young punk who had just gotten out of school."

Next, she fell back in with Malcolm McLaren, who wanted her to play guitar in a band he was putting together to be called Masters of the Backside. They rehearsed a lot, but eventually Chrissie was dumped and the group evolved into the Damned, who became the first punk band to make a record. After being similarly ejected by another outfit, Chrissie started wondering if she'd *ever* make it. The low point came when Mick Jones and his new group, the Clash, invited her to join them on their riotous first tour of Britain.

"It was great," she says, "but my heart was breaking. I wanted to be in a band so *bad*. And to go to all the gigs, to see it so close up, to be living in it and not to have a band was devastating to me. When I left, I said, 'Thanks a lot for lettin' me come along,' and I went back and went weeping on the Underground throughout London. All the people I knew in town, they were all in bands. And there I was, like the real loser, you know? Really the loser."

But she didn't give up, and eventually a demo tape she had made wound up in the hands of Dave Hill, a former promo man who was looking for talent for his new label, Real Records. He liked Chrissie's material and was taken with her feisty determination. Hill stepped in to manage her career, which had yet to reach square one, and began by paying off the $140 back rent she owed on her rehearsal room in Covent Garden. He told her to take her time and get a band together.

Pete Farndon met Hynde in the spring of 1978, as she was making her umpteenth attempt to organize a group. Farndon had lately split from Sydney after a two-year stint with a popular Australian folk-rock band called the Bushwackers. Following an extended layover in Hong Kong—doing "drugs, mainly" and watching his teeth rot out—he returned to his mother's home in Hereford, a drowsy municipality near the Welsh border, to await the arrival of a new set of choppers, and, he hoped, some action. Through a drummer friend, he heard about an American singer, a girl, who had some good original tunes and was trying to build a group around them. Farndon, gigless and ichy, expressed interest, and a meeting was arranged at a bar in London's Portobello Road. It was not a cordial encounter.

"I walked into the pub and there was this American with a big mouth across the other side of the bar," he recalls. "She said hi, and turned around and ignored me for about an hour. I thought, 'Am I gonna be in a band with this *cunt?*'"

As it turned out, he was. "As soon as we got down to her rehearsal room, which was the scummiest basement I'd ever been in in my life, the first thing we played was 'Groove Me,' by King Floyd. The second thing we played was this *great* country & western song of hers called 'Tequila.' I was lookin' at this woman like . . . you know? Fuck, man, I'll never forget it: we go in, we do a soul number, we do a country & western number and then we did 'The Phone Call,' which is like the heaviest fuckin' punk-rocker you could do in five-four time. Impressed? I was *very* impressed."

Like Farndon, James Honeyman-Scott and Martin Chambers both hail from Hereford, home base of the once-mighty Mott the Hoople, and a place otherwise noted chiefly for its hobbitlike pastoral pleasures. "Dull," as Jimmy puts it. "Totally uneventful." Farndon had managed to escape, though, and Honeyman-Scott (who left school and home at fifteen) and Chambers (who'd been honing his chops with a fourteen-piece dance orchestra) finally scored their passage out with Cheeks, a band led by ex–Mott keyboardist Verden Allen. The group toured a lot but never recorded, and after three years it folded. Jimmy went back on the road with a straight-ahead rock band modeled after Bad Company, and Martin scrounged for studio gigs around London. Neither of them was going anywhere particularly quickly.

By the summer of 1978, Honeyman-Scott was back in Hereford, working in a music shop and raising vegetables in his considerable spare time. When local legend Pete Farndon rang him up one day to ask if he'd like to join a group with this terrific American girl he'd been working with the past four months, Jimmy was mildly intrigued. "I thought, 'Money first,'" he insists. "They had to pay me in money and drugs to come down and work with 'em." Initially, he recalls, the band was "too bloody loud. But as soon as I cranked some powders up me nose I became interested, of course."

With an Irishman named Jerry Mcleduff on drums, Honeyman-Scott, Farndon and Hynde did some quick rehearsing and then went to a small demo studio to cut a tape that included Hynde's "Precious" and "The Wait," plus their cover of "Stop Your Sobbing," a Hynde favorite since 1964. Chrissie had been rattling around London for some time by then and knew everybody. She took the tape to her old drinking buddy, Nick Lowe. He thought that "Sobbing" was a potential hit and agreed to produce a single for them, with "The Wait" on the flip side. It took one day. The next day, the Pretenders traveled to Paris to play a six-night stand at a club called Gibus—their very first gigs.

Mcleduff had been about the fortieth drummer Hynde auditioned, and he was good. But he couldn't quite put out the kind of visceral, Charlie Watts–style slam that Chrissie heard in her head. At the time, Martin Chambers was working as a driving instructor in London and "trying to sort out my life." Since both Honeyman-Scott and Farndon had been hanging out with him, they decided to bring him along one day to audition. The chemistry clicked immediately, and Chambers was in. The previously recorded "Stop Your Sobbing" was released in January 1979 and quickly climbed into the Top Thirty. The group played its first British gigs, and the press raved. By the time they'd played half a dozen shows, the London music papers were running front-page features on this hot new band with the tough Yank up front. For a brand-new group, the pressure was intense.

By spring, the Pretenders were ready to record again, but Lowe had lost interest. Chris Thomas, producer of the Sex Pistols and Roxy Music, agreed to give the project a week-long try. The week stretched out to six painstaking months. Last January the completed *Pretenders* album was released to choruses of acclaim, and the group's been going full-tilt ever since.

The exhaustion is beginning to show. It's the day after the show at Detroit, and everyone feels like dogshit as we set off from Manhattan for the next gig, a club called Emerald City in Cherry Hill, New Jersey. It's at least a two-hour bus trip in the ongoing monsoon. Honeyman-Scott, back on board again, tries to brighten things up with highlights of his carnal encounter of the previous evening. "I played 'Let Him Run Wild' seven times in a row last night," he says, citing his all-time favorite Beach Boys track. "With the sea goin' outside the window—*oh!*—and the Cad in the driveway!" He hugs himself with delight.

Ebullient as he seems, Honeyman-Scott has had his problems adapting to success. "I went through a bad patch," he admits. "Well, a couple of 'em. I was addicted to speed for God knows how many years—had to have treatment to get off that crap. Now I've got cirrhosis—burned my liver out. I'm under doctor's orders, and it's on the way to being cured, but I'm still gettin' the old withdrawal attacks. I've gotta take it easy, stop spacin' out."

I suggest that cocaine is not exactly a balm for burned-out livers. "Yeah, I've been doin' that again," he says sheepishly. "I don't know, maybe I expect too much of life," he muses. "When you're a kid and you see a group like the Beatles on TV, you say, 'I wanna be that.' But when you're there, everything's exactly the same, nothing changes. You think, 'Ah, a Number One album,' like the fucking skies are gonna open up or something—and *nothing happens*. When our album was Number One, I went right down into the depths."

Chambers, sitting across the table, pulls aside a thick curtain and peers glumly out the window at the gusting rain. Hynde is curled quietly in a corner, her hair pulled up into a careless pineapple topknot. She is perusing a book on palmistry. The bus rolls noisily on.

After checking into a nearby hotel, Honeyman-Scott and I stroll through the gaudy innards of Emerald City—a club that seems to have sprung full-blown from a Ricky Ricardo wet dream. Six-foot-tall corn plants imitate palm trees back among the rear tables, and a big, samba-size dance floor stretches out toward the broad stage. The guitarist says he loves it, and wanders off to join the sound check, which is already in progress. Hynde has just arrived, and now that we're both feeling a bit less bilious, I steer her off to a secluded lounge on the second floor. Chrissie turns her back to the looming picture windows and settles on a couch, pulling her coat—a chaotic assemblage of mismatched fake-fur pelts—tightly around her. The pink hat adds an almost poignant touch.

"The only time it's really hard," she sighs, "is like one week before I get my period. And then it really *is* hard." She nods at my tape recorder. "You should mention this, because this is reality, you know? This is life. Not just for women, but for men, because men have to deal with women, and they have to understand what a woman goes through. One night you can tease your woman, and you can make fun of her and joke around with her, and it's fine. Another night, you can't tease her, she can't handle it. She'll break down and cry, or throw something. You're supposed to be very kind and gentle at that time."

She pauses to light a Marlboro. "I have my mental breakdowns," she says with a weary half-smile, "but I try to do it back in my hotel room." She seems depressed. We agree to meet at the Holiday Inn after the sound check.

> Mystery achievement
> Where's my sandy beach?
> I had my dreams like everybody else
> But they're out of reach
> I could ignore you
> Your demands are unending
> I got no tears on my ice cream, but you know me
> I love pretending*

After seven years of banging her head against a wall of music industry indifference, Chrissie Hynde has finally found her sandy beach. She's got a band, a good one, and they're making it big on the strength of *her* songs—songs that are mainly about love (and sex) in all its variegated, sometimes violent forms, from the selfless kind ("Kid," "Lovers of Today") to playful randiness ("Precious," "Brass in Pocket"), lust-driven punch-outs ("Up the Neck") and quasi-rape ("Tattooed Love Boys"). She doesn't like to discuss the specific content of her lyrics ("Once a song's recorded, I kind of lose ownership of it"), but her amatory experiences have had an obvious and profound influence on her songwriting.

"I think we were very misled in the pill generation," she says. "The pill turned women into men. Men can afford to go around and fuck every night, but women can't. Women have to

* "Mystery Achievement" by Chrissie Hynde, © 1979 by Modern Publishing Ltd./Hynde House of Hits.

go by their own cycle, you know? I'm *very* governed by my cycle. And I think that to take a pill, and to turn yourself into a robot, and fuck every night like a man, it's . . . it's what it does to your intuitive psyche. A woman's gotta stay home some nights. If she doesn't want to get pregnant, she doesn't fuck, period. And if a guy that she loves wants to fuck someone, he's gonna have to go off and fuck someone else that night, and she's gonna have to put up with it."

Chrissie leans back on her Holiday Inn bed and takes a sip from a large glass of whiskey, chasing it down with a slug of Budweiser. She says she sees nothing unusual about a girl (as she still refers to herself) leading a hard-edged rock & roll band. "You've always had women playing instruments in the modern world. There's nothing butch about me. See, that's the big myth, you know—the 'loudmouthed American.' I *am* the loudmouthed American—no one can be meaner, and no one can be more of a *cunt* than I am. But I don't *want* to be. It's a front, you know? I just do what I do to get what I have to get."

Ironically, this single-minded pursuit has left her romantically unattached at the moment. "I don't have any one boyfriend," she says. "Boy*friends,* yeah, but I can't really have any distractions. I've got somethin' to do now. It's like all been laid out on a plate for me, and I'm gonna dedicate myself to doing the best I can. When the day comes that the band folds—because *all* bands fold eventually—then I can find . . . whatever is left to find."

There's a knock on the door. Dave Hill sticks his head in to tell Chrissie it's time to get ready for the gig. She climbs off the bed to collect her effects.

"Maybe I'll find someone who will just stay home and rub my feet at night," she says, walking toward the bathroom with hairbrush in hand. "That's the kind of man I'm lookin for myself. But, uh, I'll take what I can get."

Andrea Laubach/Retna Ltd.

SIX

Tina Turner

(1984)

$\mathcal{I}$ somehow doubt that a lot of her latter-day fans
are familiar with the amazing hard-R&B records she
did in the early Sixties with her ex-husband, Ike. But
just because Tina herself would rather forget about
them doesn't mean that you shouldn't go seek them
out right now. Similarly, you should find and pay
whatever is necessary to obtain their River Deep—
Mountain High *album*—half produced by Ike, and
not at all bad, and half produced by Phil Spector,
who showed her that there were other things in life
besides being a gutbucket R&B queen.

That said, the following piece—which led to my
writing the story of her life, which in turn changed
mine quite a bit—pretty much speaks for itself. I
would only add that, while Ike Turner may have
been an exceedingly unpleasant man to be married
to, his enormous contribution to the recording of
blues and R&B music (he scouted out and cut sides
with B. B. King, Elmore James and Howlin' Wolf,
among many others) cannot be overstated. And that
the reason the term force of nature *isn't* bandied
about as much as it might be these days is because it
has been reserved exclusively for all future references
to Tina Turner, an amazing and courageous woman.

At three o'clock in the morning, in a hotel room high above still-glimmering Montreal, Tina Turner is plugging into the universal buzz: *nam-myo-ho-renge-kyo, nam-myo-ho-renge-kyo, nam-myo-ho-renge-kyo.* The words are Japanese, but shaped by that dark, burnished voice, now pulsing with reined power, they sound like some plaintive Native American lament—an effect perhaps subliminally suggested by the dramatic sweep of Tina's high, part-Cherokee cheekbones. As the words gather speed, her voice rises slightly to a smoothly rippling alto drone, then winds down. The demonstration is done. She raises her head—wigless at the moment and casually wrapped in a white shower towel—and a smile crinkles her otherwise unlined features. The chant, she says, is a Buddhist invocation of "the mystical law of the universe. I'm saying a word, but it sounds like *hmmmnnn.* Is there anything that is without that? There's a hum in the motor of a car, in the windshield wipers, your refrigerator. An airplane goes *rowwmmmnnn.* Sometimes I just sit and listen to the sounds of the universe and to that hum that is just there."

This chanting—plugging into the universal buzz—has lent spiritual structure to Tina's life. These days, you might say, she is like an electric lamp, summoning power and illumination at the twist of a switch. Before, she suggests—back in the dark years—she was more like a candle, self-consuming and finally benighted. Not to mention trapped, battered and generally brutalized in one of the most famous marriages in R&B history. But that's all part of the very painful past. And the past is something Tina Turner has little time for anymore.

Two nights ago in Ottawa, Tina performed the last shit-can gig of her career. Another McDonald's convention. For seven weeks, McDonald's, the fast-food chain, had been rounding up its highest-grossing regional burger merchants for pat-on-the-back brain-fry junkets to centrally situated hotel ballrooms around North America. The Ottawa bash seemed typical: intensive hooch transfusions for the sales hotshots, a swank feed, some semihysterical corporate rah-rah from a presiding exec and then, with more than a few celebrants on the verge of 'facing out into their fruit sherbet, a show—the show being Tina Turner. One last time.

Many months ago, you see, when she really needed the

money—a common situation over the last seven lean years—
Tina contracted to play fourteen of these functions. At the time,
she hadn't the remotest inkling that her comeback single, "Let's
Stay Together," would become a Top Five hit in Britain or that
her startlingly strong comeback album, *Private Dancer,* would
top the charts in Australia and Canada and sell more than a
million copies in the U.S. Suddenly, Tina Turner found herself
the hottest female act on three continents. Yet in Ottawa, there
she was, headlining some fast-food fiesta on a stage framed by
two sets of glowing golden arches. *Eeesh.* She had attempted to
bow out of the McDonald's deal, but the burgerdomos were ad-
amant, and the shows went on. Ottawa was the fourteenth and
last of them, and the tech crew and the six-man band were audibly relieved. After hearing eerie massed chants of "beef-*steak!*
beef-*steak!*" and watching a fiery-eyed burger exec whip the assembled franchisees into a froth with the go-get-'em ethos of
"our leader"—the late McDonald's mastermind Ray Kroc, author of that tantalizingly titled memoir, *Grinding It Out: The
Making of McDonald's*—guitarist Paul Warren blinked his eyes
unbelievingly. "This is like Jonestown," he said.

Tina herself, however, remained uncomplaining. A total
pro, she knew the drill and accepted it. Taking the stage, she
noted the usual ocean of half-capsized banqueteers bobbling before her in ambiguous anticipation. What would *this* crowd be
expecting? How much might it remember? "Proud Mary"?
"Nutbush City Limits"? Maybe even "River Deep—Mountain
High"? Surely, these people wouldn't recall "A Fool in Love,"
the first record by Tina and her former husband, Ike Turner, an
epochal R&B hit in this same month of August exactly twenty-
four years ago. Perhaps they'd remember hearing about the glit-
terized solo show she'd taken to Vegas and Tahoe a few years
back—the one with the boy-and-girl dancers and the big-deal
disco interlude. In which case, maybe they were prepared to embrace the inevitable: for what else can one normally expect in
the ballrooms of American commerce but the last pathetic
flickerings of faded and irretrievable fame?

Imagine, then, the instant of lip-flibbering surprise when
Tina's band—which is a real rock & roll band, not some has-
been backup crew—whipped out the wild, synth-riddled riff to
"Let's Pretend We're Married," a song by Prince, and Tina
shimmied out onstage in tight black-leather pants and a punk
bouffant so bushed out you almost expected to see breadfruit

come tumbling down in mounds around her stomping, stiletto-heeled feet. Kick-stepping up to the microphone at center stage, she snapped the sucker off its stand, and with a smile on her face the size of a sweet new moon and a voice that could fuse polyester at fifty paces, she began to sing. To soar, actually. The effect was electrifying—this was no Vegas act. "What you've heard about me is true," Tina chanted. "I change the rules to do what *I* wanna do." She didn't write the words—she rarely has—but, as always, she made them her own.

And from that moment on, the whole potentially ho-hum gig took an entirely different tack. Because Tina in transit across a stage knows only one velocity—flat-out—and as she kicked, shimmied and soared through most of her album and into a withering rendition of ZZ Top's neoboogie hit "Legs," the burger folk first rose to their feet, then up onto their tables and finally into the very air, leaping and hooting and flapping their napkins overhead as this fabulous woman with the wraparound legs and the flatware-rattling voice proceeded to grind out an exhilarating hour-plus of artfully adult, but undiluted, rock & roll.

And Ottawa was it: the light at the end of the comeback tunnel. Tina Turner had outlasted her past. Now she could look strictly to the future: Her next single, "Better Be Good to Me," would be released as soon as her current hit, the reggae-spiked "What's Love Got to Do with It," could be pried out of the top spot on the U.S. singles chart, and several other tracks off the LP seemed likely candidates to follow. Six sold-out shows in Los Angeles were coming up, and after that she was off to Australia to confer with director George Miller, who's been waiting for two years to feature her in the third of his celebrated Mad Max movies (she'll play a kinkily costumed creature called Entity and may do a tune over the titles). Then it would be back to New York in September for the MTV Music Video Awards and the release of her pal David Bowie's new album—on which she harmonizes a haunting reggae track called "Tonight"—and then . . . well, who knows? If all of this could happen to a woman who didn't even have a U.S. record deal a year ago—who in fact not all that many years ago was feeling so slapped down by life that she almost bought out of it with a bottle of sleeping pills—well, then maybe there is a universal harmony. Whatever that buzz is, it's Tina Turner's theme song.

*   *   *

In her suite at Montreal's Le Quatre Saisons, Tina admits that
she thinks a crucial cosmic turnaround in her life occurred when
she began to let go of the past, allowing dribs and drabs of it to
float to the surface of occasional interviews. But to go back all
the way—back to the bad old days with Ike—was hard. "God,
you know, when I left Ike," she says, "I left all of those memories behind."

All the way back is a tiny town called Nutbush, Tennessee, which is located some fifty miles west of Memphis.
There, Tina (born Anna Mae Bullock on November 26th, 1939)
and her older sister, Eileen, grew up picking cotton and straw-
berries alongside their Baptist sharecropper father, Floyd Bullock, who managed farmland for a white plantation boss, and
their half-Cherokee mother, Zelma. The Bullocks weren't as
bad off as some of the people in Nutbush. "We always had nice
furniture, and our house was always nice," Tina recalls. "We
had our own separate bedroom and a dining room, and we had
pigs and animals. I knew the people who didn't, so I knew the
difference, and we weren't poor."

As a child, Tina attended a two-room grammar school—
not one of her favorite places—and in the summer there were
community picnics with big jugs of lemonade, fresh fruit pies,
hot barbecue and sometimes live music provided by such itiner-
ant musicians as Bootsey Whitelaw, who played jump-up good-
time tunes on his trombone accompanied by another man slugging a drum. And whenever "Mr. Bootsey" played, little Anna
Mae, who had inherited her mother's powerful voice, was always encouraged to get up and sing and dance along with him.
She sang in the Baptist church, too, of course, and heard secular
music on the family radio, both country and blues: Muddy Waters, Howlin' Wolf, the enormously popular B. B. King.

Tina's parents separated while she was still a teenager;
her mother moved to St. Louis and her father eventually wound
up in Chicago. When Tina was sixteen, she and Eileen joined
their mother in St. Louis, where school continued to be a bore,
but more interesting things soon started happening.

Eileen began frequenting an all-night R&B establishment
in East St. Louis called the Club Manhattan, and one night,
when Tina was about seventeen, she got to tag along. The Club
Manhattan was a wondrous place, full of flashy black men in
sharp suits and fine-looking women in their best dresses and

jewels. Anna Mae Bullock didn't know much about the actual making of music at that point, so the first real band she ever saw was the one standing onstage at the Club Manhattan that first night: Ike Turner and his Kings of Rhythm.

Born Izear Luster Turner on November 5th, 1931, in Clarksdale, Mississippi, Ike was a preacher's son who started out backing up such bluesmen as Sonny Boy Williamson and Robert Nighthawk in local clubs and formed the original Kings of Rhythm while he was still in high school. In 1951, with Kings saxophonist Jackie Brenston fronting the band on vocals, they cut a tune called "Rocket 88" at Sam Phillips' Sun Studios in Memphis—a track that's often cited as the first rock & roll record. In 1956, Ike and the Kings moved to East St. Louis, where he acquired a three-story brick house and moved the band in along with his common-law wife and two young sons.

Ever conscious of cash flow, Ike soon worked out a lucrative gigging routine for his group. From seven to nine they would play the Club Imperial in St. Louis, churning out Top Forty and rockabilly for an audience of white teenagers. Then they'd slide over to the Club D'Lisa—basically a black club, but with a smattering of Ike's white followers—from nine to one, finally ending up at the Club Manhattan, pumping out hard-edged blues and R&B—Little Willie John, B. B. King, Ray Charles—from one A.M. till dawn.

At the Club Manhattan, Ike was in his element—which is to say, among his many girlfriends. The situation sometimes became dicey: if too many of Ike's ladies showed up at the club at once, he wouldn't even come down off the stage between sets but instead hunker up there, noodling at the organ and pondering how best to extricate himself. "Oh, God," says Tina with a whoop. "I remember some nights when he would have maybe six girlfriends in the house, and he would stay *up* there and call his wife to come to the club that night—it was the only way they could save him."

Compared to the more generously fleshed beauties of that period, little Anna Mae Bullock was something of a scrawny kid, and so Ike didn't take much notice when she first approached him about getting up to sing with the Kings. Night after night she'd sit there waiting for the call, but it never came. Finally, one night, when Ike was up onstage playing the organ, Tina grabbed the mike and started to belt out a B. B. King tune.

"Everyone came running in to see who the girl was that

was singing," Tina remembers. "Then Ike came down. He was real shy. He said, 'I didn't know you could *really* sing.'" Slowly, Ike began working Anna Mae into his stage show.

"I became like a star," she says. "I felt real special. Ike went out and bought me stage clothes—a fur, gloves up to here, costume jewelry and bareback pumps, the glittery ones, long earrings and fancy form-fitting dresses. And I was wearing a padded bra. I thought I was so sharp. And riding in this Cadillac Ike had then—a pink Fleetwood with the fish fins. I swear, I felt like I was rich! And it felt good."

Soon, Anna Mae became a legitimate part of the group, returning with them to Ike's big brick house after gigs, where the band's attendant women would cook up steaks or chops and the musicians would continue to jam. "I guess they were parties," Tina says, "and I guess the girls went to bed with the guys, but I didn't really know."

At first, she looked upon Ike as a big brother, her mentor, and Ike reciprocated. She did, however, become romantically attached to one of the Kings' saxophonists, Raymond Hill, and just after her graduation from high school in 1958, she became pregnant with his son, whom she subsequently named Raymond Craig. Tina took little time out for maternity, though: she was making ten, sometimes fifteen dollars a night at gigs and could afford a baby-sitter.

After two years, Tina's relationship with Ike took a sudden, intimate turn. "Ike broke up with his common-law wife," Tina says, "and he said he was planning to go to California to do some recording. He asked me if I wanted to go. I said I didn't know what California looked like. He said it was a lot of pink houses and palm trees, and I tried to visualize it. All of a sudden, it became a little paradise.

"A couple nights later, we were working together, driving along, and it was the first time he touched me. I didn't want to touch. I liked him as a brother; I didn't want a relationship. But it just sort of grew on me." When Ike asked her again if she wanted to go to California with him, she said yes. "I would have gone anyplace with Ike, because I was very secure with him."

Before heading west, though, Ike wanted to complete another project he had cooking. This was a song, "A Fool in Love," that he'd written for one of the Kings' vocalists, Art Lassiter, to cut as a demo to shop around to record companies. When Ike had one of his not-infrequent falling-outs with

Lassiter, he asked his new sweetie to sing on the demo. The result—one of the most exhilaratingly primitive R&B records ever made—quickly caught the ear of Juggy Murray, head of Sue Records in New York, who signed the act under a new name the songwriter had just come up with: Ike and Tina Turner. "Tina" was not consulted about this name change (inspired by an old film-serial jungle queen) and didn't like it.

"A Fool in Love" became a Number Two R&B hit in 1960 and even went Top Thirty pop. As it began to break, though, Tina came down with jaundice—"I was totally yellow"—and was hospitalized. It was an inopportune moment to become ill, especially with such a lingering affliction. After six weeks, Ike—with an eye on the charts—decided she had recovered. "He came and said, 'The record is hitting, I've got some dates booked, and you've gotta sneak outta here.' I said, 'All right.'" Out she snuck.

The Ike and Tina Turner Revue—complete with three session girls Ike had hired to sing backup for Tina on "A Fool in Love," now billed as the Ikettes—hit the road in support of the record. Right away, Tina says, Ike established a pattern he'd rarely break again: driving from date to date, playing fill-in gigs wherever possible along the way, renting a studio as soon as they hit a new town and staying up night after night trying to concoct the next hit. The original Ikettes soon dropped out and were replaced by a series of postgig recruits from local talent along the way.

At this point, Tina became pregnant by Ike. Around the same time—about 1962, according to Tina—Ike decided to get back together with his common-law wife. The arrangement didn't last long, however, and when Ike returned to Tina, he asked her to marry him. "We went to Mexico," she says with a shudder. "Tijuana. It was horrible. When he asked me to marry him, I didn't want to, because I knew then what my life would be like. But I was afraid to say no. So we went to Tijuana and a man signed the paper, and he slid this paper across the table. And I just remember it was dirty and ugly, and I said to myself, "This is my wedding.'

"You see," says Tina, "I was still in love, but I was beginning to realize I was unhappy. I didn't want the relationship anymore—it started that early. We were two totally different people. When Ike got that record deal, I had already decided then that I didn't want to get involved. That was the first time he beat me up. And I thought, 'Okay, I'll do whatever it is.' Christ, I was afraid of Ike. I would do whatever he said. See, Ike was really very funny—he would joke and play—and I do remember good times and having some fun. But he was always so mixed up with confusion and anger that you could very easily forget the good times."

The hits, at least, kept happening. Ike and Tina followed "A Fool in Love" with the darkly funky "I Idolize You," the Mickey and Sylvia–styled "It's Gonna Work Out Fine," the familiar-sounding "Poor Fool," the primal "Tra La La La La" and, in the summer of 1962, a modified jump-band number called "You Should'a Treated Me Right."

But the situation with Ike was only getting worse. Still, Tina felt obligated to stay. "I felt very loyal to Ike, and I didn't want to hurt him. I knew if I left there'd be no one to sing, so I was caught up in guilt. I mean, sometimes, after he beat me up, I'd end up feeling sorry for him. I'd be sitting there all bruised and torn and feeling sorry for *him*. I was just . . . brainwashed? Maybe I was brainwashed."

Ike and Tina had settled in a Los Angeles suburb, but the act continued to work eleven months out of the year. When she wasn't onstage, Tina remained the perfect Little Woman. "Ike was like a king," she says. "When he woke up, I'd have to do his hair, do his nails, his feet. You know what I mean? I was a little slave girl."

In 1965, they were appearing at Cyrano's, a club on the Sunset Strip, when Phil Spector walked in. Spector was impressed. He approached Ike ("No one ever approached me," Tina notes) with a proposition to feature the Turners in a concert film he was involved with, *The Big T.N.T. Show*. That was just the opener, though. He was really interested in making a record with Tina—just Tina. Some sort of deal was cut—Tina's not sure exactly what it was. By that point, she was just going along with the program; after gigs, she would slip away and go home to provide the couple's four children (two of Ike's, one of Tina's, and Ronnie, the son they had together) a modicum of company.

In any case, Spector secured from Ike the right to use Tina, and he invited her to his house to hear the song he wanted her to sing, a composition he'd cowritten with Jeff Barry and Ellie Greenwich called "River Deep—Mountain High." Tina loved it. "For the first time in my life, it wasn't R&B. I finally had a chance to *sing*."

Spector and Tina recorded the song at Gold Star Studios. "He worked my butt off. Everything went fine except that opening line: 'When I was a little girl . . .' I did that 500,000 times. I don't know if I *ever* got that right. Nobody was there but Phil and me and the engineer. I was very comfortable with Phil. I remember taking off my shirt—it was drenched—and standing there in my bra singing. That's how *hard* I was singing. Phil was very patient. He would say, 'We're very close, that's very close. We'll try it again.' But I don't remember him saying, 'Got it!'"

Although credited as an Ike and Tina Turner performance on the record label, "River Deep" contained no input from Ike or anyone else in the Turner organization besides Tina. Released in 1966, the song was a sensation in England, where it went to Number Three. In America, though, it inexplicably bombed—a failure that so embittered Spector that he didn't produce another record for three years. Tina was hurt, too. "I felt I'd done something that I could be proud of," she says. "But that record had no home. It was too pop for black radio, and the white stations said, 'They're not a pop act; we can't touch it.'"

The Turners' career, however, was well served by "River Deep." The Rolling Stones loved it and invited Ike and Tina to open for them in Europe; they recruited the duo again as an opening act on the Stones' 1969 U.S. tour. Ike quickly realized he was hooked onto a happening scene and allowed Tina to persuade him to work up covers for her of the Beatles' "Come Together," the Stones' "Honky Tonk Women" and Creedence Clearwater Revival's "Proud Mary."

In hippie circles, Ike and Tina Turner became everyone's favorite gutbucket soul revue. Ike bought and decorated an elaborate house in Inglewood—orange carpet, green kitchen, mirror over the bed—and built a studio about five minutes away (with its own sort of playpen-apartment), to which he would summon Tina at all hours for recording work. She still didn't say much, but she was more miserable than ever. At one point, despairing about what her life had become, she procured a bottle of sleeping pills from a doctor and took them all before a show one night, hoping to pass out and die onstage.

"But I didn't make it to the stage," she says. "Ike walked in, and I was so scared, 'cause I knew that if he had to cancel before the show, he'd have to pay the musicians. And I did not make it to the stage, and I mean I was insanely afraid. I mean, he would *beat* me so, I cannot tell you, the choking and beating. And I was in the hospital, and I heard later from the doctors that they could not get a pulse. And apparently Ike came in and started talking to me. He said, 'You motherfucker, you better not die; I'll kill you'—and my pulse started!"

The Turners' long-sought success with white audiences—the real big time—only increased Ike's volatility. "The first time I remember seeing Ike do cocaine was in San Francisco," Tina says. "I think he was kind of doing it quietly for a while, and then he said, 'Oh, fuck, forget Tina. I'm just gonna let her know.' Then he started getting more bold.

"Ike never drank in St. Louis, just smoked and gambled. But when he came to L.A., he started the cocaine and the sherry, and then he moved to harder liquor, more and more, and he just slowly started getting crazy. He served cocaine like wine, and all of a sudden there were guns under the control board. It was like living in hell's domain."

According to Tina, Ike also moved one of his many mistresses into their home, leaving the two women to while away the hours while he and his cohorts pursued their own mysterious amusements out in his windowless studio. "She used to be with the Ikettes, this woman, and then she became pregnant and started handling wardrobe. And how I lived with that was . . . I lost my feelings for Ike as my husband. So it didn't really matter about the women, you know? The part that mattered was when I had to be intimate, because I didn't *want* to be intimate."

By 1975, the hits had dried up for Ike and Tina Turner, and so had a lot of the live work with which Ike had sustained his lifestyle over the years. And Tina, after nearly sixteen years of marriage, had finally reached the end of her rope. In the midst of what was to be their final tour, en route to the L.A. airport for a flight to Dallas, their whole tormented life together finally fell apart.

"He handed me this chocolate candy, and it was melting, you know? And I was wearing a white suit, and I went, 'Uh.' That's all—and he hit me. And this time, I was pissed. I said, 'I'm fightin' back.'"

When they arrived at the Dallas airport, the fight continued. "When I got in the car, he gave me a backhand, just like that. And I remember pointing my finger in his face and saying, 'I told you. You got the money, you got everything. I'm gonna try to stay—but I'm not gonna take your licks anymore.' And then the big fight started—and I started hitting back. I didn't cry once. I cursed back and I yelled, and he goes, 'You son of a bitch, you never talked to me like this before.' And I said, 'That's right, but I am *now*!'

"Because I knew I was gone. I was flying. I knew that that was it. By the time we got to the hotel, I'm not lying, my face was swollen out past my ear. Blood was everyplace. We walked upstairs, and Ike *knew*. So he went and laid across the bed. And I was still saying, 'Can I get you something?' And I started massaging him, as usual, massaging his head. And he started snoring. And I leaned over and I said . . . goodbye."

Ike was not all that easy to shake, according to Tina. There were a few bullets fired into one of the houses she moved to, and a car was burned. For a while, knowing Ike's own predilections, she took to carrying a gun herself. When she walked out on Ike, she had thirty-six cents and a single handbag to her name, and in the subsequent divorce action she asked for nothing more—no money, no property, no payoff on all the years she'd put into their career. It was the price of disengagement, she says—the price of finally buying her freedom.

For a year after the split, Tina did nothing. Through some women friends who put her up, she became interested in Buddhism and chanting. Eventually, she went back to work at the only job she knew. Unfortunately, since it had been she who had walked out on Ike in the midst of a tour, damages for all the resultant blown gigs were laid by the promoters at her door. A friend in the record business agreed to help, and realizing she needed immediate infusions of cash to begin paying off the hundreds of thousands of dollars of debts she'd suddenly fallen heir to, he steered her into cabaret—Vegas, Tahoe. Tina is not ashamed of those days: she had to work, and she was a pro.

Four years ago, Tina decided she needed management, so she approached Lee Kramer, who was then working with Olivia Newton-John. Kramer later dropped out of the picture, but when he first went to catch Tina's act, at the spiffy Fairmont Hotel in San Francisco, he brought along his Australian assistant, Roger Davies, and Davies was knocked out. Not by Tina's dancers and disco tunes, and not by her tuxedo-clad band, but by Tina herself—onstage, the woman was still dynamite.

Davies eventually wound up taking Tina on, persuaded her to chuck her supper-club show and aimed her back toward hard rock & roll. Then, two years ago, the members of B.E.F.—the independent production arm of the English synth-pop band Heaven 17—asked Tina to sing lead on their version of an old Temptations tune, "Ball of Confusion." The track, which appeared on B.E.F.'s *Music of Quality and Distinction* album, proved beyond any doubt that Tina could still raise a roof with the very best of them.

A buzz began. Tina regrouped with Heaven 17's Martyn Ware and Glenn Gregory last year to cut a hypnotic version of the Al Green classic, "Let's Stay Together," and it became a Top Five hit in Britain (and later a dance-floor smash in the States, too). Tina played the Ritz in New York City, and Keith Richards and David Bowie both came to cheer. Capitol Records, the American branch of her British label, became excited enough to put up $150,000 for an album—but only gave her two weeks to do it. Tina and Davies flew to London, and Davies began soliciting songs. Rupert Hine, producer of the Fixx and a songwriter himself, came up with "I Might Have Been Queen," a tune tailored specifically for Tina. Mark Knopfler turned over "Private Dancer," a number originally slated for Dire Straits' *Love over Gold* album. Terry Britten, an Australian friend of Davies', donated "What's Love Got to Do with It." Ware and Walsh produced a version of Bowie's "1984." Jeff Beck—a rabid fan—chipped in two guest guitar solos, and in two weeks, the record was done. And Tina Turner was back to stay.

Today, Tina looks better than ever, sings better than ever, and says she's now happier than ever, too. She has a new boyfriend—a younger man she'd rather not name—and is now attempting to find the "balance of equality between men and women." She sees herself performing till she's fifty, perhaps, and says she'd then like to become a teacher, a propagator of her beloved Buddhist beliefs. Apparently, it's preordained.

"I'm gonna focus on this," she says. "I think that's gonna be my message, that's why I'm here. And I think that's why I'm gonna be as powerful as I am. Because in order to get people to listen to you, you've got to be some kind of landmark, some kind of foundation. You don't listen to people that don't mean anything to you. You have to have something there to make people believe you. And so I think that's what's going on now. I'm getting their attention now, and then when I'm ready, they'll listen. And they'll hear."

Ben DeSoto/Retna Ltd.

SEVEN

Prince

(1984)

A lot of journalists are annoyed by the fact that
Prince doesn't do interviews. I cheer this
idiosyncrasy. Rock stars are all too accessible these
days—some of them won't go away. And stories can
be done without interviews; it's just a lot more
complicated. I was assisted in researching this
piece—invaluably—by writer Michael Shore, a
fellow Prince fanatic.

In the years since it appeared, Prince has gone on
to produce a lot of great tracks, a couple of spotty
albums and—in the summer of 1989—a massive hit
LP tied to the massive hit movie, Batman. Since
much of his really mind-bending work passed a lot
of people by, it was nice, in a fiscal sort of way, to
see him hit it really big again. Unfortunately,
Batman was one of his most run-of-the-funk-mill
albums. I only hope it doesn't give him wrong ideas
about his future direction.

I occasionally talk to Prince—off the record, of
course—and I have to say that I'm not sure you'd
learn much more about his life and times from
talking to the man himself for the normal length of a
media interview than you will from perusing what
follows.

P rince has come. It is a warm summer morning in the Minneapolis suburb of Eden Prairie, and a black-clad rider on a purple Honda has just pulled up to a nondescript modern warehouse on Flying Cloud Drive. Inside, a photographer is waiting. He has flown in from Toronto with an assistant and most of the contents of his studio to photograph Prince for the cover of *Rolling Stone* magazine. A standard rock-star shoot, he figures, scoping out the concert-size rehearsal stage, the costume room, the banks of musical equipment.

When Prince walks in, the first thing the photographer notices is how small he is: he seems slight even in his five-inch stiletto-heel boots. He is wearing a dramatic black hat, a skintight black shirt open to the navel and tight black trousers ringed with ruffles from the knees down. He is carefully unshaven—only his cheekbones have been scraped smooth, then caked with makeup—for that stylish New Wave–wino look. He seems to be saying something: Hi? He speaks so softly that the photographer actually has to lean down to within several inches of his face to hear him. He is making it quietly clear that, while he has agreed to pose for the cover, he will not pose for any photos for the magazine's inside pages. To be completely frank, he really doesn't even want to do the cover, but . . . The photographer presses ahead, flourishing concepts and asserting his magazine's insistence on a white backdrop for the photo. *Ach!* Prince had his heart set on hot pink. The session gets off to an uneasy start.

It is decided to wheel in the purple Honda, a perfect prop. The motorcycle is a central visual ornament of *Purple Rain,* Prince's custom-tailored movie debut—a picture with so much prerelease "top spin," as they say in Hollywood, that the media, anticipating a major sleeper, have been abasing themselves for weeks in the hope of wangling interviews with the recalcitrant star. But Prince does not do interviews anymore. He is, however, full of advice about camera angles and poses, and the photographer fights back a gathering urge to whack him with a light meter. Quickly, he snaps off some preliminary test shots with a Polaroid. Prince seems to approve of the results, then slips away while the photographer makes some final lighting adjustments. An assistant appears and carefully confiscates the seven Polaroids. When Prince returns, he seems restless and even more remote. He's decided he doesn't like the original setup, so they do another Polaroid, a full-length shot. Prince disappears again. The photographer hears the sound of drums and cymbals being bashed in another room. Then silence. After half an hour, the assistant reappears and announces that he's just driven his employer home. Prince, he says, is extremely sensitive: "He actually gets physically ill at having his picture taken."

On his way out, the photographer can't help but hurl a silent curse at the warehouse walls. They are lined with photographs—blowups, big ones. All studies of the same smooth, unsmiling features, the same inscrutable sensuality and unfathomable flamboyance. All of them dominated by those liquid, Keane-kid eyes. All of them pictures of Prince.

Just who is this self-enveloped star? How is it that he's outselling both Bruce Springsteen and the mighty Jacksons in the record racks? What sort of monumental chutzpah must it take to step away from rock videos and make a feature-length movie—one based on the hopes and deepest fears of your own brief life? How accurate is the portrait so exuberantly painted by *Purple Rain*? How much painful truth remains hidden beneath its often dazzling exterior?

The picture one acquires of this twenty-six-year-old wonderkid from scanning his songs and canvassing his colleagues and acquaintances is murky and uncertain—which is the way he wants it. As Owen Husney, his first manager, once advised him, "Controversy is press." And Prince, for all his vaunted reclusiveness, has certainly been controversial. Husney started the mystique ball rolling in 1977, trimming two years off his protégé's age and obscuring his full name. But Prince—Prince Rogers Nelson, actually, born in Minneapolis on June 7th, 1958—had his own ways of getting attention. Raised in an overwhelmingly white environment, he became as adept at playing hard, guitar-based rock & roll as he was at funkier black styles. (In early interviews, he also emphasized a multiracial background—half-Italian father, mixed-blood mother—even though, by most reports, both his parents are light-skinned blacks.) And then there was his frankly lubricious sexuality, relatively subtle at first, but later leading him to perform in heavy makeup, bikini briefs and thigh-hugging leg warmers, singing songs with such single-entendre titles as "Head."

These ploys got him noticed, all right. But to most of the record-buying public—even as he began spinning off such provocative satellite groups from his hometown as the Time (led by his favorite foil, Morris Day) and the all-girl Vanity 6—Prince was, and remains, essentially a mystery. In fact, about the only thing on which his friends—and even his foes—agree is that Prince appears to be the genuine article: a musical genius. And not since the Fifties, when that accolade was applied to Ray Charles, has the term seemed so attractively apt.

Signed by Warner Bros. Records in 1977 on the basis of an astonishing one-man-band demo tape, Prince was awarded what is said to be the most lucrative contract ever offered by the company to an unknown artist ("Well over a million dollars," claims Husney) and was granted near-total creative leeway in the recording studio. He wrote all the music, played practically every instrument, produced all nine tracks and delivered an album, *For You,* that kicked off with an ethereal, gospel-drenched mélange of a cappella voices (all Prince's), concluded with a screaming rock-guitar feature, touched down in between on a carnal classic called "Soft and Wet" and was dedicated to "God." But *For You* was not a commercial triumph: six years after its release, that first Prince LP has yet to sell 400,000 copies and remains his least-known album.

He's been riding a rocket to the top ever since, however. His next three records—*Prince,* the groundbreaking *Dirty Mind* and the even more successful *Controversy*—all went gold (sales of 500,000 copies). And then, late in 1982, came the dazzling *1999,* a double-record set that has sold nearly 3 million copies and is still on the pop charts more than ninety weeks after its release. The album fairly bristled with hits—the title track, "Delirious," the masterfully metaphorical "Little Red Corvette." In the view of Warner Bros., it marked the long-awaited point at which Prince's seamless fusion of white rock & roll and black dance-funk became commercially undeniable, and it was seen as setting the stage for Prince's next album to create the kind of cultural explosion that traditionally heralds the arrival of a true superstar.

But there was one unknown and slightly troubling factor in this commercial equation: along with his sixth album, to be titled *Purple Rain,* Prince would deliver a feature-length movie of the same name. Filming had begun in Minneapolis last November 1st, and details of the project were not such as to excite keen anticipation among music-biz moneymen. The director, Albert Magnoli, had never been in charge of a feature before. The cast, including all five members of Prince's band in key roles, had, with only two exceptions, no acting experience. The tight budget ($7 million) and rushed shooting schedule (seven weeks) did not augur well for stellar production values. And, of course, who ever heard of making a movie in Minneapolis? In the winter, yet? In addition, the script was said to be . . . autobiographical?

William Blinn knew nothing about Prince, really, when he was approached roughly two years ago about writing the script for a very vaguely conceived movie in which the singer would star. But Blinn, a mild, middle-aged man who'd written such Emmy-winning tube fare as "Brian's Song" and a "Roots" segment, had reason to be interested in the task, proffered by Prince's management company, Cavallo, Ruffalo and Fargnoli. At the time, Blinn was executive producer of the "Fame" series, and there was some doubt as to whether it would be renewed for a third season. A screenplay would be a handy diversion. What did the managers have in mind, exactly?

That was unclear. Prince had been jotting down ideas in a purple notebook for some time, and one night out on the road, he told Steve Fargnoli: This is great and all, but there must be something else. He wanted to do a movie. Unfortunately, Fargnoli knew little about the moviemaking business. With his partners, Bob Cavallo and Joe Ruffalo, he managed music acts, including such major attractions as Weather Report and Earth, Wind and Fire. But Prince was the one, they all knew it. Prince could do anything: why *not* a movie? Fargnoli shopped the pitch around to some major studios—got a black kid here who most ticket-buying citizens have never heard of who wants to make a movie about himself with some friends in Minneapolis—and got a lot of laughs. But he was unfazed. The managers would finance the film themselves. But they needed a script.

Blinn first met with Prince and Fargnoli at an Italian restaurant in Hollywood. He immediately knew there'd be strange days ahead. "I never met anyone in the world who ordered spaghetti with tomato sauce and orange juice to drink," he recalls. "He's definitely got his own drummer going." As they talked about the movie, Blinn found that Prince was "not conversationally accessible. He's not purposefully face-to-the-wall, but casual conversation is not what he's good at. It was as if I asked someone what they wanted for dinner, and they said they weren't sure, but they'd like it to have some tomatoes in it, and some beef, and some onions. And I'd say, 'I think we're talking about beef stew here.'"

During a meeting at Prince's home—a purple but otherwise unremarkable two-story affair situated on a lake in a well-to-do suburb several miles southwest of Minneapolis—Blinn realized that an important part of the story Prince was trying to formulate concerned his father, John L. Nelson, a piano player who had led a Minneapolis jazz trio in the Fifties under the name Prince Rogers. Nelson had separated from his wife, a singer, when Prince was seven, leaving a piano behind for his son to learn to play. The father, who reportedly still lived in Minneapolis, obviously remained a troubling figure.

"He was semicommunicative about his dad," says Blinn. "He played me some of his father's music on the piano, and when he played, and when he talked about his father's life, you could tell that his father is very key in what he's about. It was as if he were sorting out his own mystery—an honest quest to figure himself out. He saved all the money on shrinks and put it in the movie."

Blinn began pounding out a script called *Dreams,* a dark story in which the parents of the Kid—the character to be played by Prince—were both dead, the mother dispatched by the father, who in turn killed himself. Prince's Minneapolis music scene was in there, too, and so was the beautiful Vanity, lead crumpet with Vanity 6. Born in Ontario of Scottish and Eurasian parents (her original name was Denise Matthews), Vanity had been a model and sometime nudie actress who, under the name D. D. Winters, appeared in such Canadian-made films of the early Eighties as *Terror Train* and *Tanya's Island.* Vanity was also Prince's girlfriend—or one of them—and in *Dreams,* she was to play the stablizing influence in the Kid's otherwise chaotic life.

Blinn's story was beginning to sound very much like Prince's life. Following his parents' breakup, Prince had been bounced from mother to father to an aunt and finally, at age thirteen, of his own volition, into the home of Mrs. Bernadette Anderson, the mother of his best (and at the time, she says, only) friend. Prince and André Anderson had both attended a local Seventh-Day Adventist church as young children, and they shared a consuming interest in music. It was with André (and a young drummer named Morris Day) that Prince organized his first band, Grand Central. "Music is obviously a cloak and a shield and a whole bunch of things for him," says Blinn. "It's a womb."

Halfway through the second draft of *Dreams*, Prince told Blinn he wanted the word *purple* in the title. "At first, I thought it was a kind of strange request," Blinn says. "But he really identifies with purple. There's a whole dark, passionate, foreboding quality to the color and to what he does. Yet there's a certain royalty to it, too."

After finishing a second draft of the script, Blinn got word that "Fame" had been renewed for a third season, and so he returned to television-land, leaving the Prince management team with a script of sorts, but no director. After seeing a film called *Reckless,* they approached its young director, James Foley, and asked if he'd be interested in *Purple Rain.* He wasn't, but he recommended his friend, Al Magnoli, who had edited *Reckless.*

At first, the thirty-one-year-old Magnoli wasn't interested. Nevertheless, he agreed to meet with Bob Cavallo for breakfast one morning. Cavallo asked him what he thought the Prince team should do. Magnoli tried to be helpful. "I said, 'This is what I would do'—and right there I told him the entire story. It just came out. I knew they had this character Prince, the script had introduced me to this other character, Morris, and I knew that there was a girl in the middle. So it was like: where do you go with this? And I said Prince should do this, and Morris should do this, and Vanity should be this kind of girl and not this other thing in the script. And then the mother and father— and all of a sudden the world was shaped. And within ten minutes, I had convinced myself that this would be an extremely exciting film to make."

Cavallo liked what he heard, and Magnoli felt the stirrings of a buzz. He agreed to fly to Minneapolis. "The minute I met Prince, I realized that I hadn't gone far enough. That because of the nature of this person, I could go much further into the private sort of area. We had dinner, and he let me speak for about twenty-five minutes, and I began working off what was emanating from him. And I got very involved with the parents at that point: the father became a musician, the mother became sort of a woman wandering the streets, things like that. I was just basically watching the person in front of me, just feeling what that was all about. And at the end, he said okay, let's take a ride. So we took a ride, and he looked at me and he said, 'I don't get it. This is the first time I've met you, but you've told me more about what I've experienced than anybody in my life.'"

Magnoli told Prince that if he was willing to reveal the emotional truths of this material, of the character that they would create, then the movie could be made. Prince agreed, so Magnoli went to Minneapolis for a month and hung out with the people who would populate the film: Prince and his band (now to be called the Revolution), Morris Day and his group, the Time, the women in Vanity 6. Then he locked himself in a room for three weeks and completely rewrote Blinn's script.

In the completed *Purple Rain,* the Kid is an up-and-coming attraction at the First Avenue & 7th Street Entry Club, where he revels in his burgeoning musical powers despite the derision of the club's manager and the petty humiliations inflicted by a hilariously snide headliner played (to near perfection) by Morris Day. Offstage, though, the Kid is miserable, plagued by his parents' incessant domestic rows, increasingly alienated from his own band members (whose musical offerings he ignores) and awkward and inarticulate in his pursuit of a beautiful new arrival on the scene called Apollonia (the part originally intended for Vanity). When Apollonia announces her intention of joining a girl group being assembled by Day—for the express purpose of dislodging the Kid from his slot at the club—the Kid, like his bitterly abusive father, lashes out at the woman he loves. Meanwhile, Morris Day and Billy, the club manager, keep up a steady assault on the Kid's fragile ego, chorusing just the sort of criticisms that have been directed at Prince himself over the years. ("Nobody digs your music but yourself," says Billy. "Ya long-haired faggot!" screams Day.) Following an explosive encounter with his father, the Kid redeems himself with Apollonia and blows away all professional competition at a climactic concert at the club. It's not a happily-ever-after ending, exactly, but when Prince and his band dig into the luminous title tune at the end, a definite feeling of uplift is imparted.

"We are now in an era where films should in a sense have something uplifting going on," says Magnoli. "We've gotten away from the antihero of the Sixties and early Seventies, where films ended sort of with a thought and a dismal aspect, like: Okay, we're in the gutter. We wanted to say: Life's a bitch, but *wow,* if you can just get it together . . ."

Patty Kotero—or Patty Apollonia Kotero, as she currently calls herself—is kneeling on the floor of her immaculately tidy West Hollywood apartment, picking through a pile of tape cassettes. David Bowie, Eddie Murphy, Thomas Dolby—ah, there it is. She reaches up toward a small stack of stereo equipment arrayed against the wall, and suddenly the room is filled with the sound of cool, autumnal piano chords. It is "Father's Song," a haunting instrumental piece composed by Prince's father and performed by Prince. In Minneapolis, during the hectic shooting of *Purple Rain,* Patty had trouble getting to sleep each night. At five o'clock one morning, she remembers, Prince appeared at her door.

"He said, 'I've got something for you.' I said, 'Yeah?'" She pops her eyes in mock suspicion. "He said, 'You've been having trouble sleeping. Here.' And he gave me this tape. It's better than a glass of milk and honey."

As the tape plays, Patty's gaze drifts upward and fixes on a large, framed promotional portrait of Prince that's propped atop the stereo. It's enough to give one the feeling of having wandered into a private prayer grotto, a tiny temple to the Great Man.

Until last summer, Kotero was just another young L.A. photo model. Then, across the country, in Minneapolis one day, a woman named Vanity walked away from her projected part in *Purple Rain.* No one will say why she left—rumors range around money, ego and a faded relationship with the film's diminutive star—but it was Patty who was chosen as her replacement. A casting call had gone out for a woman who met certain requirements, some of them physical. Through her agent, Patty obtained an audition and quickly hied herself out to Minneapolis. Although her own personality is sweeter and considerably more wholesome than that projected by Vanity, the two women are obviously interchangeable within the cartoon context of the character. Vanity/Apollonia is a walking *Penthouse* wet dream of billowing breasts and plushly upholstered contours, her sultry face, framed by gleaming cascades of raven hair, a frank invitation to frolic.

One criticism of *Purple Rain* is that it's insufferably sexist. All of the young women in the picture are inexplicably addicted to décolleté and in many cases wear nothing but the skimpiest lingerie. In one scene, Apollonia is subjected to considerable humiliation in the course of a skinny-dipping interlude at a lake, and in another sequence, Morris Day has a troublesome girlfriend chucked into a trash dumpster by his fawning aide, Jerome.

Though Prince's female fantasies obviously run in the direction of impossibly pliant sex cookies, in *Purple Rain,* this attitude toward women is condemned through the character of Day, for whom the women in Apollonia 6 (né Vanity 6) are simply "the bitches," assumed to be sexually available after taking a few slugs from his silver hip flask. Since it was actually Prince who invented and produced Vanity 6, the film indicates that he is at least aware of his own worst concept of women.

There are also two women in Prince's band, and while they too tend to hang out of their dresses a lot (and Prince has concocted an oblique lesbian aura around their relationship), their main purpose is musical. Keyboardist Lisa Coleman and guitarist Wendy Melvoin are lifelong friends, the daughters of two veteran L.A. sessionmen (their fathers both played keyboards on the Beach Boys' "Good Vibrations"). Lisa is a classically trained pianist, and Wendy is a longtime jazz student who first attracted Prince's attention when she peeled off an elaborate jazz chord in his presence after a show one night and later won her funk wings during an extended jam with the man on James Brown's "Body Heat."

"The idea of integration is important to Prince," says Lisa. "To me and the rest of the band, too. It's just good fate that it's worked out as well as it has—you know, the perfect couple of black people, the perfect couple of white people, couple of girls, couple of Jews. Whatever. He's chosen the people in his band because of their musical abilities, but it does help to have two female musicians who *are competent.*"

In the past, Prince has used his band largely to flesh out onstage the music he wrote, played and produced on his own in the studio. Like the Kid in *Purple Rain,* though, Prince is now allowing other musicians to contribute to his music. Five of the nine songs on the new album were recorded by the full band, and Lisa and Wendy even get cowriting credit—the ultimate rarity, even though it's noted only in the film credits, not on the LP—for "Computer Blue."

"He loves those people," says Apollonia. "He cares for them, and they care for him." She crosses the room to a small couch. In her black slacks and plain white top she seems prettier, her face softer, than in the movie. But her dark beauty—both her parents were born in Mexico, but she describes herself as "a Latin-German Jew"—and extravagant figure would seem to suit Prince just fine. Has she also replaced Vanity in the little guy's affections?

"I don't kiss and tell," she says with practiced coyness. "He loves his women, but music comes first. He is *married* to his music. You can't compete with it."

With music, Prince seems to find his most perfect union. Apollonia remembers seeing him in the studio, her oblivious mentor, lost in sound. "It looks like he's in there in his own spaceship, his own capsule, just taking off, and the sky's the limit." She clasps a hand to her heart. "I still pinch myself every morning and say my prayers at night, and thank the good Lord someone's breathing in my direction."

Religious impulses in rock usually have taken the form either of woozy Easternalia or grating fundamentalist harangues. The musicians in Prince's orbit share an unlabored, though still deeply felt, faith in God. Prince himself has dedicated all six of his albums to the Deity, and out on the road, before each show, he joins hands with his musicians in prayer. There's an instrumental "love theme" in *Purple Rain* that's simply titled "God" (it's not on the LP), and the album itself is rife with messianic overtones, from the opening sermon of "Let's Go Crazy" to the suggestively titled "I Would Die 4 U," in which Prince sings, "I'm not a human/I am a dove/I am your conscious/I am love." When the album appeared, Bill Aiken, a production staffer at MTV in New York, noticed a snippet of backward dialogue tacked onto the end of the song "Darling Nikki"—the record's most brazenly salacious track. Reversing it on tape, Aiken discovered a message from Prince: "Hello. How are you? I'm fine. Because I know the Lord is coming soon, coming soon."

The strange dichotomy between Prince's compulsive carnality and his spiritual yearnings apparently isn't puzzling to those who've gotten close to him. "He's a man apart in many ways," says William Blinn. "But his whole sexual attitude is positive. It's: This is good, this represents growth, life."

Not everyone, however, is convinced that Prince is cognizant of his own contradictions. One New York actress who auditioned for the Apollonia role in *Purple Rain* (and who asked that her name not be used—a common request in the Prince orbit) expressed shock at the things she was asked to do. "I turned it down," she says. "It was way too pornographic for me. I mean, they had stuff in the script that I wouldn't even let my boyfriend do to me in my own bedroom."

Prince looked the actress up during a subsequent visit to Manhattan, and she found him alternately brilliant and pathetic. "He's got a *lot* of hang-ups," she says. "He means well, and he's genuinely talented, but he's got a lot of problems. He's really hung up on God, for one thing. I think he thinks he's *related* to God in some way."

One day, the woman says, she coerced Prince into accompanying her to the American Museum of Natural History to see a celebrated exhibition called *Ancestors*. "The show of the century," she says. "All these Neanderthal skulls, and how we evolved from apes and stuff, right? And he just wouldn't believe any of it. I said, 'Come on, you don't believe in that Adam and Eve crap, do you?' He just blankly stared back at me.

"There *is* a real dichotomy between his sexual hang-ups and God and the Bible," the woman concludes. "I mean, he's not leading a godly life. At least I don't *pretend* to lead one. But that *is* the most important thing in his life, God."

Even with God on his side, though, Prince seems a strangely solitary figure. In his pursuit of the success his talents so richly justify, he has ruptured a succession of once-important personal relationships. Bassist André Anderson, his closest boyhood friend, was the first to leave Prince's band, followed by guitarist Dez Dickerson. Prince fired bassist Terry Lewis and keyboardist Jimmy Jam from the Time, and keyboardist Monte Moir soon left of his own accord to join them. Recently it's been rumored that Morris Day—whose wild comic persona is more immediately charismatic than Prince's own—may be leaving the Time. (Inquisitive observers are told it's not true, but Day, for some reason, cannot be produced to confirm that contention.)

"I maintain we came out better in the end, for all we went through," says former Minneapolis studio owner Chris Moon, who started Prince off by giving the sixteen-year-old prodigy the keys to Moon Sound studio and getting a manager for him. On the other hand, Moon adds, "Prince may have come out worse off than us. He's gotta be one very lonely guy. I mean, he's left a long trail of broken hearts and broken egos behind him."

Unencumbered by his problematic past, Prince rises higher and higher in the pop-cultural firmament. Who's to say the trade-off hasn't made him happy? For the *Purple Rain* première at L.A.'s Chinese Theatre last month, he personally summoned a swarm of the superstars who are now his peers to come and pay homage. And another time, after both Prince and Michael Jackson joined James Brown for jams onstage at L.A.'s Beverly Theatre, the Godfather of Soul was heard to exclaim, "Look out, Michael!" This is what's called arriving. Whether or not that big limo in the sky he's pursued for so long has turned out to be otherwise empty is a matter for Prince to ponder in the splendid isolation to which he's now entitled.

"It's hard to have that much power and have close friends," William Blinn reflects. "It's tough for him. But if he does not have close friends, then neither do I feel that his solitude is threatening or harmful to him. Some people . . . well, you know, the four-in-the-morning phone call: 'I'm alone, what do I do?' I think Prince is perfectly capable of handling it. He might make that phone call, and he might be alone. But he knows what to do."

Eight

Bob Dylan

(1987)

As far as I'm aware, Bob Dylan has never made any concession to the extraordinary stardom that descended upon him in the early Sixties and has remained perched on his weary shoulder ever since. A man who detests all the traditional oppressions of showbiz celebrity—the autograph hounds, the interviews, the gossip about his private life—Dylan remains one of the most complex and mercurial of rock artists. That he has no interest in striking poses or dropping names, or in any way playing the media game, puts him in the very exclusive company of Phil Spector and Prince—the only other musical masters, to my knowledge, who simply do not give a shit.

Actually, strike that—Prince and Spector do care about the way they're perceived. Dylan, so far as I've been able to determine on the basis of firsthand encounters, genuinely feels that, on the great scale of life's important things, celebrity ranks somewhere slightly below kitty litter and colostomy bags. Who (besides most other celebrities) could disagree?

Has his music deteriorated? Is he only going through the motions all these years after his spectacular work in the Sixties? Maybe. But his love

*of American roots music—the country and blues
classics he came up on—remains genuine. And if his
personal obsessions seem far removed from the
transient concerns of making and selling records,
maybe he's learned something we'd do well to
discover for ourselves.*

Did you start out wanting to be a star?

Not really, because I always needed a song to get by. There's a lot of singers who don't need songs to get by. A lot of 'em are tall, good-lookin', you know? They don't *need* to say anything to grab people. Me, I had to make it on something other than my looks or my voice.

What was it that made you decide to become a rock & roll songwriter?

Well, now, Chuck *Berry* was a rock & roll songwriter. So I never tried to write rock & roll songs, 'cause I figured he had just done it. When I started writing songs, they had to be in a different mold. Because who wants to be a second-rate anybody? A new generation had come along, of which I was a part—the second generation of rock & roll people. To me, and to others like me, it was a way of life. It was an all-consuming way of life.

What was the rock scene like when you arrived in New York in the early Sixties?

What was happening was Joey Dee and the Starliters, which was, like, a twisting scene. There was a big twist craze. There were little pockets, I guess, all across the country where people were playin' rock & roll music. But it was awfully difficult. I knew some guys that played in the Village, and to make some extra money they would play in midtown clubs like the Metropole, which used to be a burlesque house on Seventh Avenue. Those were pretty funky places. You could play for six hours and make ten dollars, and there'd be some girl stripping all that time. Pretty degrading gig. But economics being what they are, you got to make *some* kinda money to exist with electric instruments. That's what got me out of it, actually. It was just too hard.

So you opted for folk music.

Folk music creates its own audience. Because you can take a guitar anywhere, anytime. Most of the places we played in the early days were all parties—house parties, rent parties. Any kind of reason to go play someplace and we'd be there.

Were you surprised by the public reaction to your early songs, or by your eventual mass acceptance?

Not really. 'Cause I paid my dues. It didn't happen overnight, you know. I came up one step at a time. And I knew when I'd come up with somethin' good. For instance, "Song to Woody," on my first record: I knew that no one had ever written anything like that before.

Still, given your unique style of writing and singing, you did seem an unlikely candidate for stardom on the pop scene in the mid-Sixties.

Well, I wasn't tryin' to get onto the radio. I wasn't singin' for Tin Pan Alley. I'd given up on all that stuff. I was downtown, you know? I wanted to make records, but I thought the furthest I could go was to make a folk-music record. It surprised the hell out of me when I was signed at Columbia Records. I was more surprised than anybody. But I never let that stop me [*laughs*].

Did you ever feel that you had tapped into the Zeitgeist in some special sort of way?

With the songs that I came up with?

Yeah.

As I look back on it now, I am surprised that I came up with so many of them. At the time it seemed like a natural thing to do. Now I can look back and see that I must have written those songs "in the spirit," you know? Like "Desolation Row"—I was just thinkin' about that the other night. There's no logical way that you can arrive at lyrics like that. I don't know how it was done.

It just came to you?

It just came *through* me.

By the time of "Desolation Row," in 1965, you had gone electric and had been more or less drummed out of the purist folk movement. Was that a painful experience?

No. I looked at that as an opportunity to get back into what I had been into a long time ago and to take it someplace further. Folk-music circles were very cold, anyway. Everybody was pretty strict and severe in their attitudes; it was kind of a stuffy scene. It didn't bother me that people didn't understand what I was doing, because I had been doing it long before they were around. And I knew, when I was doin' that stuff, that *that* hadn't been done before, either. Because I'd known all the stuff that had gone down before. I knew what the Beatles were doin', and that seemed to be real pop stuff. The Stones were doing blues things—just hard city blues. The Beach Boys, of course, were doin' stuff that I didn't think had ever been done before, either. But I also knew that *I* was doing stuff that hadn't ever been done before.

Did you have more of a drive to write back then? More of a drive to make it?

Well, yeah, you had all those feelings that had been bottled up for twenty-some years, and then you got 'em all out. And once they're out, then you gotta start up again.

Do you still get inspired the same way these days?

I don't know. It's been a while since, uh . . . What moves you to write is something that you care about deeply. You also have to have the time to write. You have to have the isolation to write. And the more demands that are put on you, the harder it is. I mean, it seems like everybody wants a piece of your time at a certain point. There was a time when nobody cared, and that was one of the most productive times, when nobody gave a shit who I was.

Life gets complex as the years go by.

Yeah. You get older; you start having to get more family oriented. You start having hopes for other people rather than for yourself. But I don't have nothin' to complain about. I *did* it, you know? I did what I wanted to do. And I'm still doing it.

A lot of fans would say that the Band, which was backing you up in the mid-Sixties, was the greatest group you ever had. Would you agree?

Well, there were different things I liked about every band I had. I liked the *Street Legal* band a lot. I thought it was a real tight sound. Usually it's the drummer and the bass player that make the band.

The Band had their own sound, that's for sure. When they were playin' behind me, they weren't the Band; they were called Levon and the Hawks. What came out on record as the Band—it was like night and day. Robbie [Robertson] started playing that real pinched, squeezed guitar sound—he had never played like that before in his life. They could cover songs great. They used to do Motown songs, and that, to me, is when I think of them as being at their best. Even more so than "King Harvest" and "The Weight" and all of that. When I think of them, I think of them singin' somethin' like "Baby Don't You Do It," covering Marvin Gaye and that kind of thing. Those were the golden days of the Band, even more so than when they played behind me.

What were some of the most memorable shows you guys did together?

Oh, man, I don't know. Just about every single one. Every night was like goin' for broke, like the end of the world.

It's funny, the music business was small back then, primitive. But the music that came out of it was really affecting. Now the business is enormous, yet it seems to have no real effect on anything. What do you think was lost back there along the way?

The *truth* of it all was covered up, buried, under the onslaught of money and that wolfish attitude—exploitation. Now it seems like the thing to do is exploit everything, you know?

A lot of people are happy to be exploited.

Yeah.

They stand in line.

Yeah, exactly.

Have you ever been approached to do a shoe ad or anything?

Oh, *yeah!* They'd like to use my tunes for different beer companies and perfumes and automobiles. I get approached on all that stuff. But, shit, I didn't write them for that reason. That's never been my scene.

Do you still listen to the artists you started out with?

The stuff that I grew up on never grows old. I was just fortunate enough to get it and understand it at that early age, and it still rings true for me. I'd still rather listen to Bill and Charlie Monroe than any current record. That's what America's all about to me. I mean, they don't have to make any more new records—there's enough old ones, you know? I went in a record store a couple of weeks ago—I wouldn't know what to buy. There's so many kinds of records out.

And CDs too.

CDs too. I don't know. I've heard CDs. I don't particularly think they sound a whole lot better than a record. Personally, I don't believe in separation of sound, anyway. I like to hear it all blended together.

The Phil Spector approach.

Well, the live approach. The world could *use* a new Phil Spector record, that's for sure. I'd like to hear him do Prince.

Do you think Prince is talented?

Prince? Yeah, he's a boy wonder.

Lately he's seemed to be a little trapped inside of it all.

Well, there must be a *giant* inside there just raving to get out. I mean, he certainly don't lack talent, that's for sure.

Who are some of the greatest live performers you've ever seen?

I like Charles Aznavour a lot. I saw him in Sixty-something, at Carnegie Hall, and he just blew my brains out. I went there with somebody who was French, not knowing what I was getting myself into.

Howlin' Wolf, to me, was the greatest live act, because he did not have to move a finger when he performed—if that's what you'd call it, "performing." I don't like people that jump around. When people think about Elvis moving around—he didn't jump around. He moved with *grace*.

Mick Jagger seems to jump around onstage a bit too much, don't you think?

I love Mick Jagger. I mean, I go back a long ways with him, and I always wish him the best. But to see him jumping around like he does—I don't give a shit in what age, from Altamont to RFK Stadium—you don't have to *do* that, man. It's still hipper and cooler to be Ray Charles, sittin' at the piano, not movin' shit. And still getting across, you know? Pushing rhythm and soul across. It's got nothin' to do with jumping around. I mean, what could it possibly have to *do* with jumping around?

Showbiz?

I don't know. Showbiz—well, I don't dig it. I don't go to see someone jump around. I hate to see chicks perform. *Hate* it.

Why?

Because they whore themselves. Especially the ones that don't wear anything. They fuckin' whore themselves.

Even someone like Joni Mitchell?

Well, no. But, then, Joni Mitchell is almost like a *man* [*laughs*]. I mean, I love Joni, too. But Joni's got a strange sense of rhythm that's all her own, and she lives on that timetable. Joni Mitchell is in her own world all by herself, so she has a right to keep any rhythm she wants. She's allowed to tell you what time it is.

Well, what about Chrissie Hynde?

Chrissie Hynde's a rock & roll singer who really should go back and study some country music. She should go deeply into the heart of that stuff and then come back out. Because

Chrissie Hynde is a good rhythm-guitar player. That's all you gotta be is a rhythm-guitar player and singer, and she writes good, and she's got good thoughts. She knows what's right and wrong.

So you're not saying women shouldn't be performers, are you?

No, absolutely not, man.

Do you see any bands of merit on the scene today? What about U2? They're friends of yours, aren't they?

Yeah, U2 will probably be around years from now. John Cougar Mellencamp, he'll be around as long as anybody will be. Sure, there's people. But, you know, as time goes on, it gets just a little more diluted. . . . In many ways, what's happening now in music is very corrupting. Especially European rock & roll—it's so weird. It all comes out of what America did, but it's so far from the early guys, like Little Richard and Chuck Berry. That was so pure, you know? But what's become of it? It's become degraded. . . . Like, I like U2 a lot, but . . . well, U2 are actually pretty original. But they're Irish; they're Celtic—they've got *that* thing goin'. You've gotta get away from America in order to make anything stick. America will just bombard you with too much shit. You have to make a conscious attempt to stay away from all the garbage. Whereas in the past, I don't remember ever having to make a *conscious* attempt to stay away from anything. You could just walk away, you know? Now, you walk away, it gets you no matter where you are.

Do you think there's any point today in people getting together—the way they did in the Sixties—to try to change things?

Well, people are still strivin' to do good. But they have to overcome the evil impulse. And as long as they're tryin' to do that, things can keep lookin' up. But there's so much evil. It spreads wider and wider, and it causes more and more confusion. In every area. It takes your breath away.

Because so many of the things that were scorned in the Sixties, like living your life just to make money, are accepted now?

Yeah. But it isn't really accepted. Maybe in America it is, but that's why America's gonna go down, you know? It's just gonna go *down*. It just can't exist. You can't just keep rippin' things off. Like, there's just a *law* that says you cannot keep rippin' things off.

Have you ever considered moving to another country? Where would you feel more at home?

I'm comfortable wherever people don't remind me of who I am. Anytime somebody reminds me of who I am, that kills it for me. If I wanted to wonder about who I am, I could start dissecting my own stuff. I don't have to go on other people's trips of who *they* think I am. A person doesn't like to feel self-conscious, you know? Now, Little Richard says if you don't want your picture taken, you got no business being a star. And he's right, he's absolutely right. But I don't like my picture being taken by people I don't know.

But you are a star. . . .

Yeah, well, I guess so. But, uh . . . I feel like I'm a star, but I can shine for who I want to shine for. You know what I mean?

Andy Freeberg/Retna Ltd.

NINE

Captain Beefheart

(1980)

*O*ne of the most astonishing musical
performances I ever witnessed was a concert by
Captain Beefheart and his two-bass version of the
Magic Band, back in 1972. It has broken my heart
ever since that—for the most part—it's mainly been
other musicians who have completely appreciated
what this man was up to.

Don Van Vliet—the Captain—is an often difficult,
sometimes cranky American musical genius who
exudes art and vision the way most of the rest of us
exude sweat. His music is grounded in the blues
(think Howlin' Wolf with a hellhound on his trail),
but Van Vliet took such primal influences and twisted
them into a whole new kind of American music—a
lurching and bearlike oeuvre that's unlike anything
else you or I or anyone tuning in from outer space
has ever heard. It's not pop music, but it makes your
body move in strange and funky ways.

There's a new generation of kid music consumers
who know nothing of Beefheart—but young
musicians continue to revere his groundbreaking
work. As is the case with many true originals, he has
no imitators (although Don himself would argue that
Ornette Coleman has lifted a few tips over the years).

His career is a case history of what can happen to a
gifted artist who refuses—either through
disinclination or incapability—to play the music-biz
game. The Beefheart saga is sad in this regard,
although the true sorrow, in the end, is mostly ours.

It's a dogshit day on West Forty-second Street, the neon-
choked main drag of Manhattan's cheap-thrills district. As the
daily midmorning traffic jam congeals into an unmoving mass,
Don Van Vliet peers out a drizzle-streaked car window at the
shuffling tribe of hookers, hustlers and head cases that clogs the
sidewalks, then squints up at the lewd movie marquees looming
above: SLAVES OF THE CANNIBAL GOD. SUGAR BRITCHES.
THAT'S PORNO! Reeling out into the street, a sputtering mad-
woman, dizzed-out and in full rant, does battle with her demons, flinging curses at the soggy September sky. Van Vliet
perks up, chuckling in appreciation. "Tell you what, I like her
style," he says, flipping to a fresh page in the squiggle-filled
sketch pad on his lap. "I don't pay attention to *periphera*. Only
noises pull me in."

Forty-eight hours ago, Van Vliet and his wife, Jan, were
puttering about anonymously in their tiny trailer out in the sun-
baked wastes of the High Mojave Desert. But now, in his capacity as Captain Beefheart—"The shingle that's given me
shingles," he grumps—Don has ventured back down into the
commercial lowlands to make yet another attempt at hustling art
in the East Coast rock & roll casbah. *Doc at the Radar Station,*
the eleventh Captain Beefheart album (twelfth, if you count
Bongo Fury, his 1975 collaboration with erstwhile pal Frank
Zappa; fourteenth, if you include two live bootlegs, *Easy Teeth*
and *What's All This Booga-Wooga Music?*), had critics baying in
adulation even before its official release. Not surprising: Beefheart has always been a critical icon and a commercial impos-
sibility, one of the sadder facts of contemporary American
music. But this time, after two years in eclipse, there's a feeling
of triumph in his return. Beefheart's spiritual children—bands
like Pere Ubu, XTC, Devo, the Contortions—have helped
create a more amenable context for the master's inimitable music. Now, his anarchic guitar wrangles, lurching rhythms, quirky,
animist poetry and seven-octave vocal swoops don't seem nearly

as weird as they once did. In fact, although *Doc at the Radar Station* must surely confirm Van Vliet's position as a major American composer, it could also lay claim to being the ultimate dance album—depending, of course, on how many dances your body is capable of doing at one time. In 1980, Captain Beefheart and his Magic Band sound utterly contemporary, even though Van Vliet hasn't altered his musical approach one iota in order to achieve that effect. "I'm not Chuck Berry or Pinky Lee or something," he says. "I'm right *now,* man. If I wanna do something, I do it right. Look how long I've been at this, my tenacity. It's horrible. It's like golf—that bad. But it's what I do."

Van Vliet had his own slant on things right from the start. Born thirty-nine years ago in Glendale, California, he taught himself to read at the age of three. At four, he dropped out of kindergarten ("They were playing with these gigantic blocks, and I never liked squares that much") and took up sculpture. At five, while visiting Griffith Park Zoo in Los Angeles, he met a noted Portuguese sculptor named Agostinho Rodriquez, and soon young Van Vliet was displaying his artistic talents on Rodriquez's weekly television show.

When he was thirteen, Don was offered a major scholarship to study sculpture in Europe. His parents, Glen and Sue Van Vliet, fearing that their only child might fall in with an evil—or possibly effeminate—crowd, decided instead to move him out to the desert, to the nice, safe town of Lancaster. There, Don met Frank Zappa, who was not a wholesome influence. The two spent much of their time auditing obscure R&B records. Sometimes they would sneak into the bakery truck that Don's father drove for a living and fill up on the fresh-baked goodies inside. (Although they were fast friends then, over the years Van Vliet has come to resent what he sees as Zappa's wholesale appropriation of his musical vocabulary: "He got a *lot* of goodies offa me," Don says glumly. "He never quit.")

The early Sixties found Zappa and Van Vliet in Cucamonga working on a concept for a band, the Soots, and a movie, *Captain Beefheart Meets the Grunt People.* Neither project panned out, and Zappa soon departed for L.A. to form the Mothers of Invention. Van Vliet returned to Lancaster with his new moniker ("I had a beef in my heart against the world") and started gathering musicians. By 1964, he was gigging locally, and before long, Captain Beefheart and the Magic Band were signed to A&M Records, which released a single—a version of Bo Diddley's "Diddy Wah Diddy"—that became a local hit in 1966. A&M, of course, wanted to follow up with an album, thinking it had a hot white blues-rock group on its hands. This was the first in a series of executive misperceptions that have plagued Van Vliet throughout his career.

A&M found Van Vliet's original material profoundly perplexing, and passed on putting out an LP. Buddah Records was willing to give Don a shot, though, and in 1967 released *Safe as Milk,* which contained such Beefheart classics as "Abba Zaba" and "Electricity." The next year's *Strictly Personal,* however, was grotesquely distorted by phasing—an obnoxious studio effect of the period—which was grafted onto the album without Van Vliet's approval. Fortunately, at that point, Frank Zappa reappeared and signed his old buddy to his new Straight label. Assured of complete artistic freedom, Van Vliet sat down at a piano and in eight and a half hours composed twenty-eight astounding songs, combining field hollers, fatback boogie and free-jazz blowing into a stupefying new sound that still seems exhilaratingly avant-garde thirteen years later. For those won over by *Trout Mask Replica,* run-of-the-mill rock & roll would never again seem quite sufficient.

Van Vliet's genius continued to flower on *Lick My Decals Off, Baby* (1970), *The Spotlight Kid* and *Clear Spot* (both 1972). Unfortunately, not many people *bought* those records. His career hit what is generally regarded as its nadir in 1974, when he signed with Mercury and released, in quick succession, *Unconditionally Guaranteed* and *Bluejeans and Moonbeams,* two unabashed bids for straight commercial success. (The former is an album of simple but engaging pleasures; the latter, a true turkey.) After the holding action of *Bongo Fury* in 1975, Van Vliet found himself labelless. Zappa helped him organize the sessions for what was to have been his next album, *Bat Chain Puller,* and eventually, most of this material appeared on 1978's *Shiny Beast (Bat Chain Puller),* which also introduced the nucleus of his current Magic Band. However, a legal dispute between Van Vliet's American and European record companies prevented the album from being released abroad until late last year—effectively scutting any major impact it might have had.

Given this chronicle of woe, it is remarkable that *Doc at the Radar Station* is one of the strongest and most uncompromising albums Van Vliet has ever made. "The people at Virgin Records told me that their favorite things were *Lick My Decals Off, Baby* and *Trout Mask,*" he says. "They said that it wouldn't bother them at all if I just went all out and did some things like that, and I said, 'No problem.'"

The album's twelve tracks were essentially cut live in the studio, with roaring performances by the Magic Band: Jeff Moris Tepper on guitars, Eric Drew Feldman on keyboards and bass, Robert Arthur Williams on drums, Bruce Lambourne Fowler on trombone and John "Drumbo" French—the original Magic Band drummer—on guitars, marimba, bass and drums. (Gary Lucas contributes French horn and fingerpicks a solo Stratocaster on the tricky neomadrigal, "Flavor Bud Living.") Produced by Van Vliet (who plays soprano sax, bass clarinet, Chinese gongs and harmonica), the album is a dizzying blast of pure, unadulterated Beefheart, from such (relatively) straight-forward stomp-alongs as "Hot Head" and "Run Paint Run Run" and the delicate, glimmering "A Carrot Is as Close as a Rabbit Gets to a Diamond" to the monumental flailings of "Sue Egypt" and especially "Sheriff of Hong Kong." Listening to the latter track, it's hard to comprehend how Van Vliet, an un-schooled musician, is able to compose each instrument's part—from crashing guitar chords to the tiniest sizzle of a cymbal—and then teach each musician how to play it. In effect, he's re-sponsible for every sound on the record, and he says it just comes to him naturally.

"'Sheriff of Hong Kong' was done on a grand piano," Don explains. "I played that damn thing exactly the way it is. I think guitar on one hand, bass on the thumb and the other guitar on the other hand. Pianos are great to compose on, man." He also wrote some songs on his latest acquisition, a Mellotron, the original, now-antiquated string synthesizer. "I heard them played so many horrible ways that I got interested in getting hold of one of them. The Mellotron's the only thing that can get that *Merthiolate* color, you know what I mean? Really abused-throat."

Although Van Vliet is only marginally aware of the many admirers he has among New Wave musicians ("I've heard a few things they've done that kind of annoyed me"), some of his new songs suggest that he resents the way certain of his techniques—usually the jangly slide guitars and discombobulated rhythms—have been adapted for fun and profit by some young bands, while he remains generally unheralded and basically poverty-stricken. In "Sue Egypt" he mentions "all those people that ride on my bones," and in "Ashtray Heart" he sings:

> You picked me out, brushed me off
> Crushed me while I was burning out
> . . . Hid behind the curtain
> Waited for me to go out
> . . . You used me like an ashtray heart

Don insisted that "Ashtray Heart" is "purely just a poem," which may well be. He couldn't be blamed for holding at least a slight grudge, though.

Bolstered by the clamorous reception accorded *Doc at the Radar Station*, Van Vliet is now itching to get out on the road. "Our sets will probably be an hour and thirty minutes, I think. That's too long, but after the Grateful Dead and Zappa, what can you do? I mean, if you don't *have it,* man, you have to play longer. It makes me feel funny. It's an insult to people to stay up there that long."

Long sets also mean more lyrics to be recommitted to memory—not an appealing prospect with a repertoire as complex and lengthy as Van Vliet's. "I have to learn all of that vomit, you know? It's like reaching back in a toilet, bringing it back up. God, that stuff is so far back to me at this point. I mean, Jesus Christ, I can't even remember where my keys are in my pocket."

Van Vliet and the Magic Band (with new guitarist Richard Snyder replacing the recently departed Drumbo) will kick off a major U.S. tour on the East Coast in late November, then head west after a brief holiday break. First, though, the group will embark on a two-week tour of Europe. Don likes visiting Europe.

"My favorite wine I ever had was in Brussels," he recalls, obviously relishing the memory. "This stuff was *old*—seventeenth century. There was a petrified spider in the cork. I thought it was about time we had some good wine, so I bought everybody in the band a bottle and charged it to the room. I did—charged it to Warner Bros. It was *good.* And it was snowing in Brussels, and the snowflakes were like white roses falling in slow motion. *Ooh,* it was wonderful—especially on that wine."

His enthusiasm is understandable—such conviviality is

hard to come by back in the High Mojave. "I split a bottle of wine in the desert with this black hobo," Don says. "Very hip fellow. He'd hitchhiked down from Oakland. He didn't take a train anymore. He said, 'I don't ride the rails because the young people, they kill tramps now, you know.' I said, 'That's disgusting.' He said, 'It isn't like it used to be, Don.'"

Breaking free from the Forty-second Street traffic impasse, we head north toward Central Park, where a photo session has been set up at the Children's Zoo. The photographer has decided to shoot Van Vliet with some dwarf goats, which sounds like a good idea. "I used to drink a lot of goat's milk when I was a child," Don explains. "Now they say you can get TB from it, but that's a bunch of hooey. Man already has TB, 'specially the government—Tired Butt."

The goats are nowhere to be seen, having retired inside their wooden shelter at the first sight of humans bearing photographic equipment—an entirely reasonable reaction. As soon as Don swings one leg into their pen, however, they come trotting out. One of them nuzzles his knee. Another chews lightly on his trouser cuff. Not only that, but a pair of squirrels come scampering up the walk to observe the scene, and as Don chats away, a totally unexpected banty rooster steps out from behind a nearby bush. It's really something to see: Doc and his radar.

Being around Don Van Vliet for any length of time, it's hard to repress the feeling that he's in direct contact with some benign but alien force. Or maybe he's just open to it. In "Dirty Blue Gene," a song on the new album, he mentions "The Shiny Beast of Thought/Standing there bubbling like an open cola in the sun." Where does it all come from—the poems, the paintings, the strange and wonderful music?

"Probably from a tortured only child," he says. "It just all comes right out of my . . . sometimes cesspool, sometimes not. It's always there. I just hope it doesn't stop. *And* I hope my water doesn't stop—wow, can you imagine that? I'm more afraid the water'll stop. God have mercy: all of a sudden you can't go to the bathroom. After all these years—what, thirty-nine years of goin' to the toilet. Wow. It certainly is comforting."

$\mathcal{T}$EN

Frank Zappa

(1988)

Frank Zappa is a very smart and funny man
who could still make it as a stand-up monologuist,
should he ever so choose. But Zappa has instead
chosen to pursue his musical inclinations into an area
of compositional sophistication that pretty much
eliminates any chance of scoring a Top Ten teen
single any time in the near future. So does he give
up, give in, reunite the Mothers of Invention for a
twenty-fifth-anniversary reunion tour? No way.
Zappa runs his own record label these days, catering
to his hard-core audience. He also does business
commentaries for the Financial News Network and
has audiences with the president of Czechoslovakia—
a newly liberated land in which, as this is written,
he's attempting to facilitate the installation of a Ben
& Jerry's ice cream outlet.

A self-taught musician and social theorist, Zappa
made challenging records with the Mothers of
Invention back in the Sixties (including the first
"concept" album, Freak Out, which predated the
Beatles' Sgt. Pepper opus by two years). Apart from
his generational fondness for Fifties doo-wop and
R&B music, he has little interest in commercial teen
pop, and if that precludes him from ever having a

megamassive multiplatinum monster chart hit . . .
well, okay. He'll find other things to do—such as
lambasting the hapless ladies of the Parents' Music
Resource Center (the rock-record rating group) and
lecturing the feckless music industry itself on the
importance of the First Amendment. The objects of
his ire rarely find much to laugh about in such
broadsides, but Zappa remains one of rock's
sharpest wits.

Were you a comedian as a kid?

I tried to be. It was a little rough, because I had a mustache when I was eleven, big pimples, and I weighed about 180 pounds. I first found out that I could make people laugh when I was forced to give a little speech about ferns in a class in school. I don't know what made them laugh, but they laughed, so I thought, "All right, not bad." So I tried to develop it into a . . . I won't say a *fern routine . . .*"

What was it that first attracted you to music in the early Fifties?

The first music that I heard that I liked was Arab music. But I can't imagine *where* I heard it, because my parents didn't even have a record player until I was fifteen. Then, finally, they got a record player, and I think the first rhythm & blues record that I got was "Riot in Cell Block #9," by the Robins. And shortly thereafter, I read an article about Edgard Varèse in *Look* magazine, and I found the Varèse album, and so that's what I had. I had the Robins and Varèse, and I think I got "Work with Me, Annie," by Hank Ballard and the Midnighters, too.

Did you see any sort of dichotomy between the Varèse and the R&B records?

No, not at all. I saw it as a totally unified field theory. What appealed to me in the Varèse album was that the writing was so direct. It was like, here's a guy who's writing dissonant music and he's not fucking around. And here's a group called the Robins, and they didn't seem like they were fucking around, either. They were havin' a good time. Certainly Hank Ballard and the Midnighters sounded like *they* were having a good time. And although harmonically, rhythmically and in many other superficial ways it was very different, the basic soul of the music seemed to me to be coming from the same universal source. You know: a guy who had the nerve to stand up and say, "This is my song, like it or lump it."

You taught yourself to read and compose music at an early age, but I gather you weren't otherwise a model student in high school.

I was getting thrown out all the time for various antisocial acts. My father was worried about keeping his security clearance.

One of your fellow students was Don Van Vliet, whom you later recorded as Captain Beefheart. What was he like then?

He drove a light-blue Oldsmobile with a hand-sculpted werewolf head that replaced the Olds emblem in the center of the steering wheel. His father was a Helms bread-truck driver. Don didn't spend a lot of time in school; most of the time I saw him was at his house. We would listen to rhythm & blues records in the afternoon, and then at night the most exciting thing to do in Lancaster would be go to Denny's and have a cup of coffee. 'Cause there was nothin'—I mean, places shut down at six o'clock. *Really* bad. So in order to afford this trip to Denny's, Don would have to acquire the finances by opening the back of his father's bread truck. See, the cab was locked, and the changemaker was hanging in the front. He had to undo the back door, pull out this bread drawer which was about from here to the wall, put it in a driveway and force Laurie, his girlfriend, to crawl through this slot like a squid to get in there and steal change. Then he'd pull her out by the ankles, and that's how we would finance our entertainment.

By the early Sixties, you'd moved to Cucamonga and started working in a small recording studio there. What kind of place was that?

It was built by a guy named Paul Buff. Paul is a genius, a great guy. Most places in those days were far-out if they had a three-track machine. Paul built his own five-track recording machine so he could do overdubs. He built this studio from scratch out of just garbage, using knowledge that he learned when he was in the Marines. And it was a great place. "Wipeout" was recorded in that studio, in *one session*. A little-known fact.

I was brought over there by Ronnie Williams, a musician I'd been jamming with in local bars. During that period of time, which was roughly '61, '62, there were these things called novelty records, you know? Like "Please, Mr. Custer." Radio still had a slight sense of humor. So if you could do a novelty record, the chances were you could lease it [to a record company]. I wrote one, and Paul and I leased the master to Capitol for the unheard-of sum of a $700 advance. I mean, that was a whopper. And the reason was because this record looked like it was gonna be unbelievably hot. You know why? It was called "The Big Surfer," and what it was, it was a guy—a San Bernardino disc jockey named Brian Lord—who could do Kennedy's voice better than Kennedy. It was like a take-off on the *First Family* album, where Kennedy is judging a surf contest. And totally produced—sound effects, the whole business, okay? The unfortunate part of the record was the punchline: the winner of the contest got an all-expense-paid trip as the first member of the Peace Corps to be sent to Alabama. Well, shortly after we signed the contract, Medgar Evers got killed, and Capitol refused to release the record.

You were expecting this to be your big breakthrough?

Yeah, well, it could've been. It was a cool record.

You also did the soundtrack for a movie called The World's Greatest Sinner *at that Cucamonga studio. What kind of movie was that?*

It was a feature film produced, directed by and starring Timothy Carey. . . . I did the score and the rock & roll theme song for it. The premise of the film was: a man believes he's God, doubts himself, breaks into a church, steals the communion bread, sticks a pin in it to find out whether or not it will in fact bleed, it bleeds, and he realizes he's not God. How's that for a great plot?

You almost made your own movie in Cucamonga, with Don Van Vliet in the title role. But then came your "porno" bust. What exactly was that all about?

Well, there's aspects of it that I still really don't understand. I was trying to make a science-fiction movie in a storefront building in Cucamonga, okay? I had the recording studio, and I had enough space in the back to actually put up sets and shoot the thing. I had gone to an auction at a place in Hollywood called the F.K. Rocket Studios. They were going out of business, and for fifty dollars I got a flatbed truck full of scenery. So I was ready to make a movie. And the name of the movie was *Captain Beefheart vs. the Grunt People*. I had also got, as part of this blob of scenery, a sign that said TV PICTURES—a nice red sign with gold lettering on it.

Now, my little place was directly across the street from the holy roller church and half a block away from a grammar school. In a town where, if I had hair half as long as yours, I would be considered a menace to society, and the approved dress code for men was white short-sleeved shirts—T-shirts were a mark of unusual behavior. That's Cucamonga. So here I am living in this studio, and living there with me were two white girls and a black baby.

How did they. . . ?

It's real complicated. They didn't have a place to stay, you know? I was helping them out. And in order for me to earn a living—since there weren't surf bands beating down my door to record yet another "Wipeout" there—I worked on weekends playing guitar at this barbecue joint in Sun Village, up near Lancaster, seventy-five miles away. I got seven dollars a weekend; only job I could get. Anyway, while I'm up there doing my gig, apparently, these two girls had gone out in front of the studio and were playing on the street with the black baby—which offended all parties concerned in this little village. So, the next thing I know, I got this guy knocking on my door saying he was a used-car salesman—saw the sign, they're having this party and can I make an entertaining movie for him? He starts talking nickles and dimes. I said, "You don't understand. Making movies is expensive. Tell you what—if you guys just want to have some laughs, let me make you a tape." So we agreed on the price of $100 to make this piece of entertainment material for used-car salesmen. *I* thought of this as a great entertainment challenge, myself. He was supposed to pick it up the following morning. I didn't realize that while he was in there, he was broadcasting our conversation by way of a wrist radio, out to a truck.

A wrist radio?

Yeah. It was total Dick Tracy. And while we're having this conversation, he is specifying in medical terms the activities that should be manifested on this tape. And, I mean, I'd never been near a policeman. I had no *idea* that this guy—Detective Willis, I think his name was—was an undercover anything. To me, it was a fuckin' joke, okay? I mean, the minute the man started talking about "oral copulation," I should've gone, "Huh?" But, no, I didn't. Because remember, I was making *seven dollars a weekend* up there in Sun Village.

So he leaves and I set up the recording equipment, and me and one of the girls go into this place I was using for my bedroom. There was absolutely no sex involved in this tape. It was just squeaking bedsprings and *grunt, grunt, ooh, ooh, ahh, ahh, ahh*. So I got this master tape of grunts. I had to cut all the laughter out of it, it was so absurd. Then I superimposed some background music onto it, so it was, like, produced. It was no more bizarre than side four of the *Freak Out!* album.

The guy comes in the next day, hands me fifty dollars. I said, "We agreed on $100. No deal." The tape never changed hands. Next thing I know, the door flies open—flashbulbs, handcuffs. It was like Nazi Germany. They snatched everything out of the place—reels of tape that had nothing to do with this; films, projectors, everything. I didn't have any money, so I had to plead nolo contendere. A twenty-six-year-old junior district attorney from San Bernardino County refused to let me go on probation, so I was given six months with all but ten days suspended, plus three years' probation. And as I was sitting in the holding tank waiting for the San Bernardino jail bus to pick me up, I'm visited by this Detective Willis, who says, "If you'll allow us to determine which of your other tapes are obscene, I'll give you back all the rest, erased." And I said, "It is not within my power to convert you from a policeman to a judge."

Your luck began improving in 1964, when you hooked up with the Soul Giants, the band that became the first Mothers of Invention. What were they like when you came upon them?

They were pretty good. I already knew that Ray [Collins] was a good singer; we'd recorded before that. But the thing that impressed me about the Soul Giants, being a rhythm & blues buff, was Jimmy Carl Black—the only drummer I'd ever seen who actually could sound like Jimmy Reed's drummer.

Really?

Yeah. Think about it: the absolute disregard for technique, know what I mean? The total dedication to going *boom-bap, boom-bap*. A *rare* talent.

So you convinced these guys you could make them rich?

No. I told 'em, "Let's learn more original songs and try and get a record contract." And the sax player, a guy named Davy Coronado—it was his group—he says, "You can't do that. The minute you start playing original music you'll get fired from these clubs." And he was right. We learned original music and we got fired . . . and fired and fired and fired.

You finally did land a record deal, though, and you've been at it ever since. Do you think the music business has changed at all since those days, for better or worse?

Oh, I can't imagine one instance in which the music business has changed for the better. Not one. Twenty-three years before the mast, me boy, and I can't think of one thing that is better about the business than when I started. The fact of the matter is, it's gotten to be more business and less music. Now, all the decisions about what is musical are made by accountants and fashion advisers. In the old days, they had these guys with cigars sticking out of the side of their mouths—this was before they had nonsmoking areas in the office buildings. A new act would come in, and these guys with the cigars would shrug their shoulders and go, "I don't know!" And because the signing fee was so cheap . . . I mean, our fee with MGM to make *Freak Out!* was $2500—yeah, split between four guys. And we were lucky to get it. And the reason we did was because somebody went, "I don't know! Who knows what these kids are listening to?"

Apparently, Tom Wilson, the young staff producer who signed the Mothers to MGM, did know.

Tom Wilson was a great guy. He had vision, you know? And he really stood by us. When we did that first album, he was definitely in a state of "I don't know!" by the time we did the second song. I remember the first thing that we recorded was "Any Way the Wind Blows," and that was okay. Then we did "Who Are the Brain Police?" and I saw him through the glass and he was on the phone immediately to New York going, "I don't know!" Trying to break it to 'em easy, I guess. Some things you just don't break easily, though.

What did MGM make of Freak Out! *when it was done?*

Well, they were violently opposed to it for several reasons. One, they were convinced that no radio station would ever play a record by a group called the Mothers—and by God, they were right! But not for the reason they thought. Anyway, they demanded that we either change the name of our group or not be recording artists. So, out of necessity, we became the Mothers of Invention.

And how did the album do?

According to their books, *Freak Out!* sold maybe 30,000 units when it first came out. But I think it sold a lot more, because that was during the time when they were having these problems with . . . how do I describe this? . . . "loose security at the pressing plant." It was something called pressing overruns. The company would send in a pressing order for 15,000 albums; the plant would press 15,000, and then they would leave the presses running for another 15,000. And the second 15,000 would not be reported to your royalty account. They would go into the back of somebody's car and be shipped across the state line and be traded for rooms full of furniture or favors or whatever. And they did it to us, they did it to . . . the biggest loser was the *Dr. Zhivago* soundtrack—I heard a quarter of a million units out the back door. Think of the publishing royalties on that for Maurice Jarre. MGM was a piquant company in those days. But people said, "I don't know!"

The Mothers became emblems of the L.A. "freak scene"—which was what, exactly?

It was a pretty short-lived phenomenon, actually. Because by the time it made the papers, it was dead. It was a thriving anthropological success for about a year and a half before any notice ever went into *Time* magazine. By the time they ran that first photograph—of a guy who used to be called Buffalo Bob; he had Prince Valiant hair, you know?—the cops were already chasing the kids out of Cantor's and off the street. They closed down every place where a band could work.

So you decided to move the Mothers to New York.

I believed that all the opportunities for performing were right here, even though the scene, as such, hadn't happened. There was no long hair here, there was nothin'. That's where that line came from: "Oh, my hair's getting good in the back." You used to hear these kids coming in from Long Island, with little rags around their heads; that's an actual quote from one of them.

And you perceived the possibility of a scene erupting?

Yeah. I figured, look: If it could happen in Los Angeles, where nobody really walks around, what could happen in a place where they had neighborhoods? Think of it: endless potential. So we set up in the Garrick Theater, on Bleecker Street. Four-walled our own show in there. And pretty soon the Fugs were four-walling theirs around the corner, and there was a lot of stuff goin' on. It was neat.

How were the Mothers received in New York?

We opened during Easter vacation of 1967. Freezing cold. It was snowing. But we had lines around the block for two shows a night. We thought: Oh, this is it, this is the big one. We're in New York City, and there's lines around the block.

As soon as school went back in, we had three, maybe five people a night. We played the shows anyway. When the place was empty, it gave us opportunities for a more personalized type of entertainment. Say there were three people in there. We'd go downstairs to the Café a Go-Go, put towels over our arms like waiters, come back up and serve them hot cider and stuff and sit and talk with them for the duration of the show. That *was* the show. Other times, there'd be five or six people come in, and we'd offer them our instruments—we sat in the audience and let them play. We'd do *anything*. Anything qualified as entertainment then. It was all in the spirit of it.

You also recorded two albums during that stay in New York: We're Only in It for the Money *and* Cruisin' with Ruben and the Jets—*the latter a tribute to the doo-wop and R&B music of your youth. How did the boys in the band respond to making that record?*

Well, some of them liked it and some of them didn't, you know? Every band I've ever had, there's been a few R&B buffs and a few guys that always scratched their heads because they couldn't understand why that was anything worth being excited about. Usually, the great musicians—guys who really have technical chops—don't know anything about rhythm & blues. That part of their musical life is completely missing. They have no comprehension of it. They were somewhere else when that took place.

I've always thought that Ruben and the Jets *contained some of your sweetest, most emotional music. Why haven't you done more along that line?*

Well, I don't know whether doing emotional music is a mark of excellence. That's been one of my downfalls with rock critics, 'cause they all seem to have this feeling that the more emotional it is, the better it is. And that's not my aesthetic at all. A little of each, you know? I like skill in music.

Is that why you've always been opposed to your musicians using drugs, and why you've been such an outspoken non-drug-user yourself?

I've smoked ten marijuana cigarettes in my life, and probably the last time I had one near my face was twelve, fifteen years ago. And the reason I did was because, since I do smoke, people would say, "Here, smoke this, you'll get high." So I smoked it, and it gave me a sore throat and made me sleepy. And I must either presume that that's what high means, or something was wrong. But I've never had a positive result from smoking marijuana. It just wasn't my cup of tea. And I never used LSD, never used cocaine, never used heroin or any of that other stuff.

What did you think, back in the hippie days, when you saw all those people getting stoned and purporting to play far-out music.

Well, basically, I saw assholes in action.

You and the Mothers once shared a stage with John Lennon and Yoko Ono and wound up on their Some Time in New York City *album. How did that gig come about?*

It was 1971, and we were working at the Fillmore East, and we had a recording truck set up out there, because we were doing an album. And we'd played one night until about three in the morning, and I was sound asleep the next afternoon when I heard this knock. I opened the door and here's this guy from *The Village Voice,* with John Lennon standing next to him and this microphone aimed at my face, waiting to record my first gasp of whatever. I said, "Come on in." And the first thing John said to me was, "You're not as ugly as you look in your pictures." I thanked him very much and offered him a chair. I told him we were working at the Fillmore East and, you know, "How'd you like to come down and sit in?" I thought it'd be good for a few laughs. So he said yeah, and they did.

Now the horrible part of the story. During our time onstage, a number of pieces were improvised, but a number of pieces that were played were absolutely written compositions that had already been on other albums—namely, a song of mine called "King Kong." The deal that I made with John and Yoko was that we were both to have access to the tapes and could deploy them any way we wanted. They got a duplicate copy of the master, and they mixed it their way. I had a copy of the master, and I was gonna mix it and put it out as part of this Mothers album. They put out this record and took "King Kong"—which obviously has a tune, and a rhythm, and chord changes—and they called it "Jam Rag," and accredited the writing and publishing to themselves. Take a look at the album.

What did you do?

I talked to Yoko last year, and I said, "By the way, you remember that 'Jam Rag'?" She said, "Well, we have a problem with Capitol Records. We are suing them, you know."

I can't imagine that album really sold a lot, anyway. It's the principle of the thing, you know? The other thing that was kind of sad was, there's a song on there called "Scumbag," but the way they mixed it, you can't hear what Mark and Howard are singing. There's a reason for that. They're singing, "Now Yoko's in the scumbag, we're putting Yoko in a scumbag."

Some critics would undoubtedly see that as part of your penchant for cheap smuttiness. Even today, you're still soliciting women's underwear from your audiences, and you keep a clothesline full of panties strung across your stage set. Do you have some sort of secret fetish for panties, or what?

Not on my part. But we used to have two guys in the band who were panty fetishists. It was a way to make them happy and to make the girls in the audience happy, too. I also think it's a good look for the stage. I think a stage with a clothesline full of women's underwear has a certain aroma to it, you know what I mean? We even have an underpants roadie—the same guy who takes care of the Synclavier. It's true.

As far as the smuttiness in the lyrics goes, a person can only be offended by smuttiness if they believe in smut as a concept and believe in the concept of dirty words—which I *don't*. It's always seemed to be something that bothered rock writers more than anybody else. I mean, who the fuck *are* these rock writers, anyway?

You finally decided to retire the Mothers of Invention in 1977. Why?

Well, for one thing, what the Mothers were famous for— this wild and woolly weirdness of the Sixties—had pretty much vanished from our stage show.

How come?

Because as you get musicians who can do certain musical things, you also find out that they sometimes lack a sense of humor. Or lack that particular aesthetic that makes it possible to take a toothbrush and a baby doll and a salami and a head of lettuce and a jar of mayonnaise and make entertainment out of it, you know? Not everyone can do that.

But you've soldiered on. Do you find that your audiences today come mainly to hear your new music—or to see a living legend from the fabled Sixties?

Look, the people at these concerts are literally fanatic. There's kids that have tickets to nineteen shows. They've taken off from work, they're living in the park—they're *way* into it. That's not living-legend time. I think the whole idea of a resurgence of interest in things from the Sixties is grossly over-estimated. There's a huge wishful-thinking factor attached to it on the part of *Sixties-age people* who wish that it were so. But younger kids don't give a rat's ass about the Sixties, and there's no reason why they should.

I did an interview with a guy from a paper, and he said, "What do you think of today's music?" I said, "*We are* today's music. We are *it*, like it or lump it. What do you mean? Do you think that what I'm doing is something imaginary? We're out there today. We're doing it. It's *alive*."

ℰLEVEN

ZZ Top

(1984)

America succumbed to boogie overload somewhere back in the primordial Seventies, but that didn't stop the Texas trio ZZ Top from turning themselves into amiable video cartoons and selling millions of records every few years throughout the Eighties.

The ZZs realized—apparently early on—that they weren't cut out to be heartthrobs. They built their postboogie success on big beards, sharp tunes and a very basic blues throb, and in effect created their own style of down-home, back-porch chic.

Which is nice, but only half the story. ZZ Top is also a walking repository of blues history, having worked, at various times and in various formations, with everyone from Muddy Waters to Jimmy Reed to Jimi Hendrix. No one can pump up a tall tale quite like Billy Gibbons, so it's sometimes difficult to discern where actual fact ends and endless elaboration begins. Fortunately, it's all so entertaining that, after a while, you don't really care.

Except for the fat, fleshy dildo sticking up from the center of its saddle at a salacious ninety-degree angle, the wooden hobby-

horse situated inside the door of the notorious Duty Hut in Tucson, Arizona, seems innocent enough: a sweet piece of salvage
from some long-gone kiddy carousel. There's nothing innocent
about the rest of the room, though, least of all the lascivious
chortle of its owner, a truly wild Westerner named Jim Anderson, as he details the potential delights of the big bondage wheel
on the wall, the sex chair nearby and, most eye-grabbing of all,
an imposing wooden pillory topped with the motto, "Don't
blow, suck"—this instruction pointedly appended to a woman's
name. "My ex-wife," Anderson jokes.

Behind his luxuriant beard, Billy Gibbons erects a smile
of polite amusement: He's taken this tour of Anderson's little
cowboy-porn museum before. Gibbons is passing through town
on a concert tour; this is a rare day off, and he's been on the
prowl for hours—cruising through funky South Tucson in his
long, white Lincoln limo, from taco stand to tortilla factory and
then on back up north toward the bars—in search of what he
likes to call "maximum input." After more than a year of mind-
fogging road blur, the man craves sharp sensations, emphatic
companionship. Gibbons is hardly a sex maniac, but he is an
inveterate collector of characters, and Jim Anderson is a longtime prize.

As Anderson prepares to lock up the Duty Hut for the
night, we step outside into a small, dusk-filled cactus garden,
pausing to savor the sweet Southwestern air. It's a short stroll
back out front to the main building—a college bar, not far from
the University of Arizona, called Some Place Else, which Anderson also owns. The decor here is equally arresting, the closest thing to a tasteful touch being a mounted deer head with a
brassiere draped across its antlers. The place is beyond vulgarity, of course—this is vulgarity with real esprit. Maximum
input. Or, as Billy might say, "Mighty *fahn.*"

In the midst of this grossorama sits a scattered handful of
early drinkers, quietly nursing their beers. One old geezer—
reputed to be a retired moneybags of the sort apparently drawn
to Tucson in their golden years—wears a crude tinfoil crown
on his head with a sticker pasted in front that says JIM ANDER-
SON FOR MAYOR. Gibbons, wearing a white ZZ Top tour cap
and ruby-rimmed shades, his long, faintly graying hair plaited
into a neat pigtail at the back of his neck and his trademark
beard wending down his chest, acknowledges this additional
flourish of eccentricity with an appreciative grin, then inquires

after the house specialty drinks. These are powerful potions, memorably named: Blow Job (Kahlúa, Amaretto and milk), Butt Fuck (liquor and fruit juices), that sort of thing. Billy orders a nice frosty Blow Job and pulls out a stool next to a kid who, it seems, is already deeply into the celebration of his twenty-first birthday. At the sight of the bearded superstar sitting next to him, the kid's jaw drops. *"Hahhh,"* says Billy, by way of greeting.

By now, Anderson has reappeared at Billy's side. A practiced raconteur, he launches into a jovial update of all his current exploits as a local character: his latest, legitimate campaign for mayor; his cars (the license plate on the BMW parked out front reads GOD); and the ongoing adventures of various cronies he and Gibbons cherish in common. Just then, the swinging doors behind us burst open, and in blows a burly, flush-faced figure with two obviously fun-loving women on his arms, one of whom has breasts the size of beach balls.

"Where's this Gibbons?" the man roars in a raucous croak. Billy swivels to scope out this noisy new arrival. Although the guy parked his car outside, he still seems to be going about eighty-five miles an hour. Billy smiles: another character for the collection. Turns out he's a locally celebrated hot-rod racer and—who isn't these days?—a big ZZ Top fan. He distractedly orders drinks for his little party—not their first of the day, it is apparent—and then grasps Gibbons' shoulder as if it were a tire he was hand-testing.

"I saw you at the Aragon Ballroom," he says, delving deep into the memory banks, "ten years ago! We were blasted! I had to carry my wife *into* the place!" The two cookies at his side titter appreciatively, and Billy mumbles something modest into his beard. The talk quickly turns to cars, one of Gibbons' main extramusical passions, and then to tales of ZZ and the band's lately renascent renown.

Soon, though, it's time to go. Billy slides off his stool, bestows a parting benediction upon his new pal, not to mention the babe with the balloons—*"Fahn,"* he says—then turns to the birthday kid by his side and enunciates the ZZ Top presidential promise: "A hot guitar on every table." And with that, he ambles out through the swinging doors, leaving the kid sitting there goggle-eyed beneath Anderson's ludicrous deer head.

"On my birthday," the kid keeps saying. "On my *birthday!"*

*   *   *

Well, imagine bearding Billy Gibbons on *your* birthday. Or any day. Lots of people apparently do. I first realized that ZZ Top had become the most famous rock & roll band in the land only a few nights before, after a sold-out concert in Albuquerque. Afterward, back at the hospitality suite at the band's hotel, a message arrived from New York to be sure to catch "Saturday Night Live," which, it was vaguely relayed, would feature some sort of skit concerning ZZ Top. At 11:30, Billy and his bandmates, bassist Dusty Hill and drummer Frank Beard, duly tuned in. But the first sketch they saw—a savage parody of singer Linda Ronstadt's current incarnation as a ballroom chanteuse—had Dusty moaning into *his* beard (which is blond and every bit as impressive a bush as Billy's). "Oh, no," he muttered. "What're they gonna do to *us*?"

As it happened, there was no need to worry. The show's central conceit was a nationwide phone-in asking viewers to pick a Democratic presidential candidate. All of the familiar stump-thumpers were enumerated: Mondale, Glenn, McGovern, Cranston, Hollings, Hart, Askew, Jackson. Then comic Don Novello (a.k.a. Father Guido Sarducci) tossed into the ring his own personal choice for the presidency: ZZ Top. He held up a picture of the boys, looking sharp in dung-colored slouch hats, cheap sunglasses and wall-to-wall whiskers. The studio audience loved it.

So did the viewers: more than 260,000 votes were called in, and when the balloting was tallied at show's end, the first runner-up was Jackson (with 66,968 votes), and the hands-down winner, with a total of 131,384 votes, was—who else?—a three-piece boogie band from Houston, Texas.

It was a pretty funny stunt, and Billy and the boys got a tremendous buzz off of it. But being president might seem a comedown for ZZ Top today. A no-frills rock & roll unit that's been blasting away since 1970, ZZ sold more records last year for its label, Warner Bros., than any of the company's other acts—and that includes such mainstream moneymakers as Rod Stewart, Christopher Cross, Paul Simon and Asia. The all-conquering album that turned this trick is ZZ's ninth, *Eliminator,* an LP boosted by a trio of slick, witty videos that have spawned two smash singles: "Gimme All Your Lovin" and "Sharp Dressed Man." *Eliminator* was released in March 1983, and nearly one year later, in February 1984—a month that marked the band's fourteenth anniversary—the record was *still* selling more than 100,000 copies a week.

Suddenly, beards are big news, Gibbons and Hill, the two hirsute Top members (drummer Beard is—heh-heh—the only ZZ without a beard), cannot step out into the street, walk through an airport, sit down in a restaurant or even stop by one of their beloved taco stands without being besieged by fans. From gurgling tots to good-time grannies, everybody, it seems, wants an autograph, a snapshot, a touch of the hairy ones' hem. It's ridiculous; ZZ isn't just massively popular—the band has actually become *hip*. Avant-garde star Laurie Anderson showed up at their postconcert party in New York last fall to talk tech with the ever-obliging Billy, and when ZZ played London's Wembley arena not long ago, who should turn up backstage but Pink Floyd figurehead Roger Waters, eager to gab with Gibbons about the blues. (So eager, in fact, that he invited Billy to his home to hear some newly recorded tracks, one of which featured Eric Clapton soloing all over a song that, according to Gibbons, "sounded like Pink Floyd on Mars—it took the blues back to Fifties sci-fi.")

This sort of heavy attention has taken some getting used to. "Yeah, we're hip now," says Frank Beard, the band's amiable drummer, golf nut and high-stakes gambling aficionado. "In England, they used to lump us in with the Southern rock bands—Lynyrd Skynyrd, the Allmans. Now they say we're like John Fogerty. It's weird."

'Twas not always thus. For years, ZZ Top was an all-purpose critics' punching bag, derided as a boorish boogie anachronism and castigated for their alleged sexism (particularly in the wake of the 1975 ass-man anthem, "Tush"). Touring as many as 300 days a year, the band built up an intensely loyal following among heartland record buyers (who've snapped up more than 13 million ZZ albums to date), but with their spangled Nudie stage suits and outsize cowboy hats, the Tops were always too off-the-wall, too unpretentiously populist, for the critical fraternity to get a fix on. Coolness eluded them. Frank Beard recalls an emblematic incident that occurred years ago, during the band's first Nudie-bedecked visit to New York City. They were staying at the Gramercy Park, a hotel that caters to English trendies and homegrown hipsters—in short, the heart of enemy territory.

"We were in the lobby, waitin' to go to the show," says

Beard in his seen-it-all drawl, "when the elevator opens and this
guy gets out. He's wearin' hot pants and black fishnet tights and
a feather boa and makeup, and he's got a bullwhip over his
shoulder and two *leatherette* women on his arms. He marches
through the lobby, and I'm elbowin' Dusty, goin', 'Goddamn,
look at *that*.' And we look around—and everybody in the whole
place is starin' at *us*."

ZZ Top has hardly changed at all since those days;
they've simply waited out an entire pop cycle—from early Seventies hard rock to soft rock to disco to punk and New Wave.
Never once did they compromise their sound—in fact, during
the disco boom, they took a three-year vacation. Now, with an
influx of pretty-boy synth-pop merchants upon us, ZZ still spe-
cializes in straight-from-the-hip hard rock (they've done only
one ballad in their entire career). It's music that's rooted in the
blues and rampant with Gibbons' endless supply of squalling
guitar riffs and Dusty Hill's paint-scraping vocals. And if such
single-entendre lyrics as "I got the six, give me your nine" sound
more than a little anachronistic in 1984—well, hey, this is rock
& roll, remember? Dusty concocted the lyrics to "Tush" during
a sound check in Florence, Alabama, in ten minutes flat—do
you really want to think about what that song means? It means
turn up the guitars. Maximum sonic input. Those in search of
philosophical disquisitions should go back to their Police records.

Given ZZ Top's musical stance, then, meeting Billy Gibbons
comes as something of a surprise. Although he sometimes en-
joys coming on like a king-size cornball, Gibbons is no simple
shitkicker. True, he was born in Texas thirty-four years ago, just
like Hill and Beard. But Billy's father was a New Yorker, a classically trained musician who moved to Texas in the Thirties,
spent time in Hollywood as a film-score arranger and later returned to Texas to conduct the Houston Philharmonic. Not your
standard redneck upbringing.

And so, Billy seems to straddle two worlds. When he's
with the boys in the band, for example, it's pure back-to-the-
Fifties locker-room regression. On the plane into Tucson, for
instance, a box of Milk-Bone dog biscuits was discovered among
the band's ever-present cache of tacky snacks.

"Don't throw them away," said Billy. "We may need
them if Dusty brings one of his girlfriends on board."

"I ain't never seen *you* with no pedigrees," said Frank.

"That's because they're all thoroughbreds, mother-fucker," said Billy.

"Well," said Dusty, "they're registered, anyway—I've checked their collars."

Like that. In private, on the other hand, Billy can be—dare we say—surprisingly reflective. When the opportunity for a second day off in Tucson arose, Billy decided to charter a plane and zip up over the Grand Canyon to Las Vegas. *Maximum* input. Upon arrival, a limo was waiting, and Billy directed the moonlighting thug behind the wheel to head straight for the MGM Grand. Action for sure. He was real excited. But the Grand was dead—a virtual desert of screaming psychedelic carpet overhung by crystal-blimp chandeliers. Billy dutifully bought $100 worth of chips, and within half an hour, he was up fifty—but bored. We adjourned to a dining room and ordered Mexican combo platters, heavy on the hot sauce, while Billy recalled the days, back in the Fifties, when he used to come to Vegas with his parents. Those were high times on the Strip. One day, Billy's father flew the family up for a birthday party at the Tropicana for Dick Powell. Being kids, Billy and his younger sister, Pam, were dispatched to the swimming pool to seek out their own amusement. The poolside was packed; not a seat in sight.

Then Pam spotted him—Bogey. Yes, it was Humphrey Bogart. And he was talking to *them.* "You need a chair, kids?" he said. "Here. Siddown." And he bought them a Coke. After a while, their father appeared, wondering where his children had gone. "These yours?" Bogart inquired, with that famous crooked smile. "They're nice kids."

There was something so touching, so long-ago-and-lost-forever about this little tale that . . . But the spell was suddenly broken. As Billy thoughtfully licked the last traces of a mediocre burrito off his fingers, a waitress appeared at his side and, with a lewd, knowing grin, leaned in real close. "I just *love* your beard," she purred.

And without missing a beat, Billy Gibbons, back again in ZZ world, looked up at her and said, "Honey, I'd like to show you more of it sometime."

So Billy grew up in Houston surrounded by classical music, which he never much related to. Nor was he particularly taken with the hard country sounds that abounded. One night, in the depths of the Fifties, he saw Elvis Presley on Ed Sullivan's TV show and immediately thought to himself: *"That's* the guy." Soon, he was tuning in local radio station KYOK, where DJs with names like Zing Zang and Hotsie Totsie were laying down roots-level black rock: Little Richard, Jimmy Reed, Larry Williams, the whole head-bending pantheon. His parents, of course, disapproved. But despite their upscale financial status, Billy was never deprived of rock & roll: when he wanted the records, he got the maid to smuggle them in.

On Christmas Day 1963, Billy's father finally gave him the guitar he'd been begging for. He immediately figured out two-finger versions of "Big Boss Man" and "What'd I Say," and after that, there was no turning back. He formed his first band, the Saints, at age fourteen, later moving on to an outfit called the Coachmen. Then, around 1966, came intimations of a new sound—psychedelia!—and a totally crazed new Texas band called the Thirteenth Floor Elevators. According to Texas legend, it was the Elevators who actually coined the term *psychedelic,* and who, on a pioneering visit to San Francisco, turned on a fledgling folk group called the Jefferson Airplane, thus instigating, for better or worse, West Coast acid rock.

In any case, the Elevators' 1966 hit, "You're Gonna Miss Me," blew young Billy Gibbons away. Inspired, he casually penned a song called "99th Floor" one day while sitting in math class. The Coachmen scraped together some cash and recorded the tune, and quickly decided to follow their new inspirations all the way.

"We made the jump from soul band to psychedelic band early in the summer of 1967," Billy recalls. "That's when the line was drawn. All of a sudden, nobody could understand what we were doing. We immediately changed our name to the Moving Sidewalks. We said, 'Hey, we're onto something—they hate us. Let's go for it!' "

A rerecorded version of "99th Floor" became a hit and garnered them the opening-act slot on one of the Jimi Hendrix Experience's first tours. Hendrix was using amplifier feedback to create a whole new sonic vocabulary for the electric guitar, and his playing was a revelation to Gibbons. "He had big hands," Billy remembers, "and he could just wrap around that neck and take it up into the stratosphere, easy as pie."

Hendrix was impressed by Gibbons, as well. He subsequently gave Billy one of his guitars—a vintage pink Stratocaster—and later, during an appearance on *The Tonight Show,* mentioned Billy's name as an up-and-coming guitar hotshot. Billy remembers all of this fondly. But the biggest favor Hendrix ever rendered, he says, was a piece of instrumental advice that's served him well ever since: "Jimi said, 'The best thing you can do, brother, is turn it up as loud as it'll go.'"

The army took its toll on the Moving Sidewalks, and in 1969, Gibbons and the group's drummer recruited a keyboard player named Billy Ethridge from a Dallas-based band. This early version of ZZ Top (a name inspired by such bluesmen as B. B. King) approached a manager named Bill Ham for guidance. Ham cut a record with them called "Salt Lick." Eventually, Ethridge suggested that another Dallas musician, Frank Beard, be brought in to play drums, and before long, Beard brought in bassist Dusty Hill, his longtime partner in a band called American Blues.

"The first time I ever heard Billy was when I played with him," Dusty says. "We did a shuffle in C, and it lasted forty-five minutes. One song. It was good, you know?"

And it's been good ever since. There was some resistance in the early days, according to Frank Beard, but Ham, a shrewd manager, overcame it. "When we were second on the bill," Beard says, "he would always get us on a tour with a band that was *through*—that was fixin' to break up and just doin' a money tour. And we'd get out there and just kick their ass. We did Mott the Hoople that way, Alice Cooper, Deep Purple. They were through, and they didn't care who knew it, so people would remember us."

All those years of accumulated fan loyalty tided ZZ over the rough spots, and lately, videos have been helping a lot, too. But as a few spins of *Eliminator* suggest, the group's songwriting seems sharper than ever. Where do the ideas come from? Well, the title of "Tush," to go back a bit, was taken from an old Roy Head B side called "Tush Hog" ("'Tush' is anything that's 'rico' or 'dino'—plush," Billy explains). "Sharp Dressed Man," on the other hand, was partially lifted from the credits of a long-forgotten late-night movie in which one peripheral character was identified as a "sharp-eyed man."

On our last night in Tucson, Billy Gibbons and I are sitting in the spacious, Southwestern-style lounge of the Tack Room, a very tush restaurant situated on an old estate called the Rancho

Del Rio. Dinner—duckling soup, veal *camarones,* vegetables *jardinière*—was mighty, mighty *fahn,* and now, already awash in the fine wines, we are blabbering at each other over iced Grand Marniers and cigars. Billy's enjoying it; he seems to have absorbed all the input he needed, and is now ready for one last stretch of road work before heading into the studio to whip up the tenth ZZ Top album.

Life is good, Billy agrees. Soon he may even take his first plunge into matrimony with his girlfriend, whom he describes as "Diane Taylor, the blues wailer." (Dusty's one marriage collapsed long ago, and Frank is embarked—quite happily—on his third.) Maybe Billy will even get to spend a little more time at his various houses: one in Santa Fe; one on South Padre Island, off the coast of Texas; and a dilapidated cabin on a mountaintop in Moab, Utah. Could be nice. Clearly, Billy is in his elegant, reflective mode.

But what about the music? That, too, he says, may change, but only subtly. He's fascinated by synthesizers and has, in fact, hours upon hours of Eno-like solo-synthesizer doodlings socked away in a vault somewhere. But synthesizers will never take over that bad ZZ Top sound. And how would he characterize that sound most succinctly? Billy Gibbons, the classical conductor's son, puts down his pricey cigar, sips delicately from his glass of Grand Marnier and says:

"Like four flat tires on a muddy road."

Nick Elgar/London Features International

TWELVE

Don Johnson

(1986)

This is the kind of assignment that sets music writers to weeping at their keyboards. A TV glamour boy making a "rock" album? Is God on vacation, or what?

I myself was brooding along similar lines when this job came down the pipeline. But Don Johnson turned out to be . . . well, pretty engaging. He'd hung around the New York and Hollywood rock scenes long enough to have amassed a backlog of illuminating tales. And he was far from the worst singer I'd ever heard (but let's leave Bruce Willis out of this). In addition—although it's sometimes forgotten at this late date—"Miami Vice," the weekly cop show of which Johnson was the star, changed the look and the sound of series TV in ways that are still apparent. He may not be a rock performer in any serious way, but that's not to say he won't be around for a good long while—or that he won't be pretty good company for as long as that may be.

It is high summer in Miami Beach, and the heat is Ethiopian. Down along the sweltering strand, off-season carcinoma fanciers sizzle under the fierce midday sun or baste listlessly in the souplike surf. But up here in the Hotel Alexander, far above the human barbecue, coolness reigns. The air is crisply conditioned, the decor *moderne*. Don Johnson fits right in.

He is wearing white suede deck shoes, off-white cotton slacks and—this being the season of "no more earth tones" on "Miami Vice"—a bright banana-yellow T-shirt. No socks, of course, and the celebrated chin stubble is perfect. A pair of Italian shades lies on the coffee table before him, and his eyes glint green and blue in the sunlight bouncing off a glass-top desk near the windows. Under the desk is a near life-size plastic replica of Elvis the alligator, Detective Sonny Crockett's eccentric pet; on a nearby wall are two gold keys awarded to Elvis and to Johnson, who plays Crockett on "Miami Vice," by the City of North Miami. Elsewhere on the walls are photos of Donnie with famous friends and acquaintances—Cybill Shepherd, Miles Davis, Ronald Reagan—and a swarm of framed magazine covers on which he is featured: *People, TV Guide* (three of them), *Tiger Beat,* the *Star,* even *Mad.* Also something called the *Gorgeous Guys Photo Album.* No mention of Don's recent pay raise—which reportedly put him over the $100,000-per-episode mark—but one look at the half pound or so of pricey Ebel wristwatch wrapped around his well-tanned arm or the sleek gray Mercedes that's parked out front, and you get the idea. Johnson is smiling. Let's face it, you'd be, too.

We are sitting in the Don Johnson Office, a suite of rooms of which the star's is the largest. In the others, office staffers—all female, mostly young: the Hen Squad, Don calls them—briskly administer his burgeoning empire. The Hotel Alexander is also home base for the "Miami Vice" production office, but that's on another floor and need not concern us. The action's all here. Don't misunderstand: Johnson appreciates what "Vice" has done for him. It's provided more than just fame and fortune and the attendant perks: the chauffeured Mercedes with the cellular phone and the top-drawer Alpine tape deck; the big silver Blue Bird mobile home stocked with the Sony A/V stack, a personal chef and a fridge full of Johnson's favorite coconut Popsicles; the thirty-eight-foot Scarab speedboat, with twin 420s in the stern, in which the off-duty Don likes to go for restless, postmidnight roars along Miami's moon-splashed canals, rattling the condo windows of all the less interestingly rich by whom he's now surrounded.

No, "Miami Vice" has meant much more than all that. The show has enabled Don Johnson, after eighteen years in showbiz—some of them truly grueling—finally to exercise all his options. "Vice" is nice: heading into its third season, the New Wave cop show that rewrote the rules for prime-time TV style is hotter than ever. But what it's mainly allowing him to do is branch out. And at thirty-six, looking back on a drug-addled youth merrily piddled away in bad B movies and worse, branching out is very much on Johnson's artistic agenda—however towering his current tube renown.

"This won't last forever," Don says, chastely sipping a Perrier. "It'll change. It'll become something else, maybe."

Strike that "maybe." In the last year, Johnson—who no longer drinks, smokes, dopes or even *sweats,* for all a casual observer can tell—has stepped out from under the "Vice" umbrella to star in a well-received TV remake of *The Long Hot Summer* and, with buddy Glenn Frey, to appear in a profitable and high-profile Pepsi commercial. Right now he's got at least three feature-film scripts in development, one of which—he hopes it's the one that has him playing the manager of a hot young rock band—will definitely start shooting next spring, during the "Vice" production break. That annual interlude is playtime for Johnson. This year he utilized it to whip up another project, and *that* is what really has him grinning now as the day dwindles down toward camera call for the third episode of the upcoming "Vice" season. Last spring, Johnson began working on some tracks at Miami's Criteria studios, and the resulting tracks, ten in all, are finally ready for release under the title *Heartbeat.* It is Don's debut album.

Yes, you heard that right: Don Johnson has made a record. Already you're thinking: Spare us, sweet Jesus. Not another TV-star pop move. Not another David-fucking-Hasselhoff, or some hideous New Age Jim Nabors. And not—please, dear God—*not* another Philip Michael Thomas turn.

Surely you remember? Perhaps not. Thomas, who plays Ricardo Tubbs to Don's Crockett on "Vice," released an album of his own last year, called *Living the Book of My Life.* It was a humongous bomb—the music a tepid gruel of treacly reggae, the lyrics a mind-puckering jambalaya of self-enthused psychobabble, the sound akin to something one might hear inside an industrial trash dumpster. Thomas took credits for almost all of it and fell flat on his profile. Nice voice. Musical taste: *nada.*

The vaunted "Vice" charisma did not carry over. *Living the Book of My Life* made a beeline for the cutout bins, and Philip Michael Thomas' hipness index dipped precipitously.

So why is Don Johnson, on the eve of offering up his own first disc for critical delectation, still smiling? Lame attempts by TV hotshots to rock out have been routinely savaged by reviewers over the years. Doesn't he fear backlash, a repeat of the P.M.T. debacle? A possible "Vice" wipeout?

"I was disappointed for Philip," he says, rubbing up against the subject with some reluctance. "Because Philip's got a beautiful, beautiful voice. But I think he would agree that he just tried to undertake too much, you know? Producing, writing everything. I know this sounds funny from a guy who is doing a television series, developing film projects, doin' a record and all this shit—but I know my limitations."

From the outset, he candidly assessed his musical assets as sparse—some at-home guitar slanging, desultory bouts of song scribbling. But he had been singing since his farm-boy days back in Missouri, when he'd soloed on Baptist choir anthems every Sunday. ("People'd pinch me on the cheek, give me a quarter, tell me how wonderful I was—that's where it all went bad!") And his light baritone, while limited—whose isn't in some way?—had a certain sinew to it, a discernible character. He really saw himself as a rocker, too, not just another hunk-puss imposter from the vast video wasteland, and he was determined not to make a hunk-puss record. As a kid, he'd frequently infuriated his father by dialing in black R&B stations out of Kansas City on the family radio. He was an original Beach Boys fanatic and later flipped for the Beatles and the Stones. Nothing radical, but Johnson felt that he, too, as much as anybody else, had lived the rock & roll life. There was a time, he remembered, when it was the life that everybody lived.

That time was the Sixties, of course. Following a mildly delinquent youth in the James Dean mode, Johnson had followed an acting muse to San Francisco in 1968, where he landed his first professional stage job—in an obscure rock musical—and on off nights immersed himself in flower power amid the hippie hordes at the Fillmore and Avalon ballrooms. By 1969, he'd relocated to L.A., hired by actor turned director Sal Mineo to appear in a homosexually explicit version of the prison play *Fortune and Men's Eyes*. Acting always remained primary—"I was less into music than perfecting my craft, so I could make a

living at it, you know?"—but before long Johnson was hitting
the clubs and catching every hip act from Tim Hardin to the
Mothers of Invention. At parties, he'd hang with members of
the Mamas and the Papas, or perhaps the Doors, knocking back
drinks, smoking dope, maybe snorting a little blow. L.A. was
wild then. "Stayin' loaded and fucked up all night long, hanging
out in the coffee shops, talking political trash with every idiot I
could find—that was pretty much what I was into," Don says.

He also met—and soon moved in with—a noted scene-
stress of the period named Miss Pamela, a member of the
GTO's ("Girls Together Outrageously"), a group signed to
Mothers leader Frank Zappa's record label. From time to time,
Miss Pamela also looked after Zappa's kids, Moon Unit and
Dweezil, and so Frank and Don quickly became acquainted.

"I remember Dweezil being diapered in my presence,"
Johnson says, chuckling. "Frank and I used to talk about doing
movies together, crazy videos, and I sang some stuff for him,
and we *talked* about recording, but it just never sort of worked
out. He'd be doing a record, or I'd be off in some other universe. But I used to enjoy just bullshitting with him. Frank's a
genius."

Don's first movie, *The Magic Garden of Stanley Sweet-
heart,* turned out to be a teen-junk abomination, but it took him
to New York in the summer of 1969, and there he fell in amid
the decadent denizens of Andy Warhol's Factory—Holly Wood-
lawn, Baby Jane Holzer, various members of the disintegrating
Velvet Underground. The Factory was also where he first laid
eyes on Patti D'Arbanville, the actress who, thirteen years later,
would become the mother of Don's son, Jesse, now three. Patti
was just seventeen when they met and at the time was posing
nude for a Warhol photo layout. It was the era of antic youth
and anything goes.

"We were all fairly fucked up," Don says, "and the reefer
took its toll on my memory. But I do remember we all knew
something was happening. We had come together from all over
the U.S.—me from Missouri, Holly from Florida, Lou Reed
from Long Island, Andy from Michigan or Minnesota or some-
fuckin'-where. And the one thing we all had in common was
that we hated boredom—I think that's why we gravitated to
each other. We were all young, and *completely* fuckin' crazy—
completely on the edge and pushin' the outside of the envelope.
It was just a constant ballet of debauchery."

Cocaine was definitely the hip drug by then, and Johnson dutifully dabbled. He remembers stuffing some up his nose one night in the men's room of a midtown disco called Hippopotamus. "I walked out of the bathroom with cocaine all over my upper lip, and I walked dead into this black guy. I looked up, and it was Jimi Hendrix. My jaw hit my chest. He smiles and goes, 'Man, you can't be walkin' around with shit on your face like this'—and he's like wiping the blow off my upper lip, you know? He was so charming. I might have given him some blow, I don't know what the fuck I did. I was thunderstruck."

Johnson's next film, *Zachariah,* released in 1971, considerably expanded his rock connections. Conceived by the Firesign Theatre, the conceptual-comedy troupe, it was an "electric western" that featured Country Joe and the Fish, Doug Kershaw and Joe Walsh's James Gang, among other acts. Don remembers its filming as being appropriately uproarious.

"We were all down in Mexico together, makin' this picture, and of course we were all fucked up and havin' a *wonderful* time. We made music constantly. And it occurred to me at the time that although I had spent the last few years concentrating on my acting, I really missed music. So back in L.A., I went down on Hollywood Boulevard, and I bought this twenty-dollar Crown guitar and started teachin' myself how to play. It didn't take long to realize that I was *not* going to play like Eric Clapton. But I found it therapeutic for between acting jobs—they weren't exactly beatin' my door down at the time— so I kept at it. I was never gonna be a virtuoso, but I *could play.*"

By the mid-Seventies, Johnson was embarked upon his fifth film: *Return to Macon County,* a drag-race epic in which he was paired with another semi-known actor named Nick Nolte. It was while filming this flick down in Georgia that Don made the sudden acquaintance of Allman Brothers guitarist Dickey Betts.

"We were doing a scene where I was in a yellow '57 Chevy with some guy, and we had blocked the driveway out to his farm. After a while, this crazy son of a bitch in a four-wheel-drive pulled down out of the driveway and started honkin' his horn and eventually drove right through the scene. I thought that was pretty fuckin' cool, not to be intimidated by a movie company, which most people are. Somebody said, 'Yeah, that was Dickey Betts.' And I went, 'What? No shit?' Later that week I was at the Bistro in Macon, and Dickey was there, and I bought him a beer. We started bullshitting, and we sat there and got drunk together. Just became instant friends. It's a friendship that's endured several road trips and a couple marriages each. Man, we had some big times together." (The two also cowrote "Blind Love" and "Can't Take It with You," which appeared on the band's 1979 LP *Enlightened Rogues*.)

The Allman Brothers, with whom Johnson was soon "roading it," were a group noted almost as much for their enthusiastic substance abuse as for their music, and they tended to attract similarly oriented interlopers. It was during an Allmans swing through New York one night that Don first encountered Rolling Stones guitarist Ron Wood. "We sort of got thrown out of a hotel together," Don recalls. "We were just practicing our art. Unfortunately, it was about four o'clock in the morning, and we were drunk or something and jumping up and down on a bed and playing guitars and stuff *real loud*."

All right, you get the picture—Johnson's been around the music scene. But he's never been *in* it, exactly, and he knew from the outset of the *Heartbeat* project that he'd need guidance. He wanted to make a saleable contemporary rock album, but he also wanted it to have spirit and at least some vestigial smidgen of spontaneity—no simple task even for those recording vets vaguely aware of how to go about doing it. He had no band, of course, so he knew he'd have to rely on session players to build his basic tracks. But he was also aware of how tired this strategy had become over the years—backup too seamless can put listeners to sleep. So instead of simply hiring the usual crew of practiced L.A. session aces, he recruited rock manager and record exec Danny Goldberg to monitor the project, and Goldberg brought in Chas Sandford, a guitarist and songwriter who'd recently penned hits for Stevie Nicks ("Talk to Me") and John Waite ("Missing You"). Johnson liked Sandford, who, like him, had been a hard-core Allman Brothers fan back in the carefree Seventies. So he named him producer and told him to put together a band.

Sandford enlisted bassist Mark Leonard and ex–Jo Jo Gunne drummer Curly Smith. Bill Champlin—frontman for the Sons of Champlin back in the Haight-Ashbury days, lately of the band Chicago—was brought in to play keyboards and sing backup vocals. Johnson and Goldberg iced this basic cake with contributions from celebrity pals—spare songs, guest vocals, hot guitar leads. Tom Petty turned over a tune called "Lost in Your

Eyes." Bob Seger contributed the oddly lilting "Star Tonight," and Don got Willie Nelson to drop in and add his trademark harmonies and a gut-string solo to the track. Ron Wood flew down to Florida to strum through a number called "Heartache Away" and was audibly impressed by *that* track's soloist, Stevie Ray Vaughan, another of Johnson's compadres.

"Stevie Ray's a trip," says Don. "I've never seen anybody attack a guitar like he does. He plays so loud that, I mean, I was in fear of not bein' able to have children. Ron Wood heard him and said, 'He plays louder than Keith—and believe me, *that's fuckin' loud!*'"

Another guitarist brought on board—for a rousing pop stomper called "Last Sound Love Makes"—was none other than Dweezil Zappa, now long out of diapers and heading his own band. "I had heard that Dweezil played like Eddie Van Halen," says Don, "and *that* interested me. But what most interested me was that he had a band named Fred Zeppelin—I laughed so hard when I heard that. So Dweezil came down and played his ass off. His solo on that track is one of my favorite things on the album."

Also chiming in on the sessions was singer Bonnie Raitt, whom Don had met last year at the annual New Orleans Jazz and Heritage Festival. "She was playing on this river boat, the *President,* and I was standing stage right when she came off. She went, 'Oh, my God! It's him!' I looked behind me to see who the fuck she was talkin' about. She said, 'No—*you,* you dummy!' Turned out she's a big fan of the show. And I just love her voice; she sings like an angel. So we went backstage, and there was this well-known rhythm & blues band back there. Bonnie went into their room and said, 'Guess who's here—the guy from "Vice."'" And the whole band took their drugs and threw 'em out the window of the boat! It's true! She said, 'No, you fuckin' idiots—the guy from "Miami Vice."'"

Finally, Whoopi Goldberg, yet another pal, came down to Criteria just to hang out, but Johnson inveigled her into teaming with him on a James Brown–style rap track called "Streetwise." It won't appear on the album—it's a little too horn charged and hard edged to fit in—but it will be featured on "Miami Vice" next season (as will "Star Tonight"), and there'll also be a separate "Streetwise" video.

In fact, a full-length conceptual video, made up of all the songs on the album, is being planned. Does the finished LP justify such lavish elaboration? CBS Records obviously thinks so—it's footing the many bills—and Johnson himself is not too modest to agree. The surprising thing is, both may well be right. *Heartbeat* is a shrewd and seductive record: an impeccably produced commercial rock album that ranges comfortably across several contemporary styles—from the sing-along, smart pop of "Last Sound Love Makes" and "Heartbeat" (the first single, an overhauled Eric Kaz–Wendy Waldman composition) to the Eagles-like "Lost in Your Eyes," the stark, Elton John–ish "Can't Take Your Memory" and the subtly haunting "Star Tonight," which sounds for all the world like just the kind of hit Neil Young could use right about now. Whatever the album's ultimate marketplace fate, Johnson says it's come out sounding exactly the way he wanted it, and that's enough. Of course, he *would* like to sell a few of the suckers, too.

"If it flies, great," he says. "If it doesn't," he adds with a laugh, "well, I hope it sells enough so they'll let me make another one."

We are wolfing down pasta in the kitchen of the big Bluebird trailer, parked somewhere in the affluent wilds of Coconut Grove. Johnson, between takes, is wearing one of his new "Vice" suits, a charcoal Gianni Versace number that he may well have acquired from the designer himself (Don was a houseguest not long ago at Versace's lakeside palace in Como, Italy). Even more decorative is the girl by his side, a young model named Donya (no lie) Fiorentino. Donya is from Florida, and first became aware of Don a few years ago when he moved in next door to her family. He was her first love. But she . . . well, she dumped him, it seems, to take up with an English musician named Andrew Ridgely, known to Brit teens as one-half—the lesser half, actually—of the rabidly adored pop duo Wham! Recently, with Ridgely's future in considerable question following Wham!'s demise, Donya dumped *him,* moved out of their Monte Carlo digs and returned to Johnson. She is now all of eighteen. So much for D.J.'s alleged lifelong attraction to older women. And so much for gossip.

Don is on to more substantial topics. His foray into the music biz has been educational. Like, what's with this PMRC—the group of Washington wives who want to rate records and, in general, remove from all kids' reach anything to the artistic left of, say, Howard Jones? Don's recording mentor, Danny Goldberg, founded a countergroup called the Musical Majority just to beat back the cultural incursions being made by such politically well-connnected fuds. Don finds their intermittent successes dismaying.

"I'm absolutely and completely against the PMRC," he says, in a tone that would not be inappropriate to the consideration of a bowlful of dead beetles. "It's bullshit. Either you have freedom of speech, or you don't. That's my feeling about censorship, pornography, all that stuff. Some people talk about pornography promoting violence, but violence is a result of repression, not liberalism.

"The sexual revolution brought free sex and all that, and it was prevalent for a long time, but now it seems to be waning. People are saying, 'Look, it doesn't work. You can't just have free sex, everybody fucking and sucking all over the place. You've gotta have some sort of code of morals, some integrity that works for you.' Okay, there was a gigantic explosion of pornography in the Seventies. But recently . . . well, look at *Playboy, Penthouse.* And *Playgirl*'s just gone bankrupt. Those magazines are not happening. So my feeling is, the less you regulate a society, the more it will regulate itself."

Of course, if there really is a sexual recession, the spread of AIDS may have more than a little to do with it. Don agrees— these are ominous times on the dating scene. But while he admits to having done some "major womanizing" in his day, he claims he was never as rapaciously promiscuous as some may have thought, even in pre-AIDS days.

"I don't like one-night stands," he says. "I mean, I've been there, it's happened, but my experience is that you're left empty and unsatisfied. There has to be some poetry."

Nor—despite rumors that he posed for youthful skin shots hawked in the back pages of gay-men's magazines—was he ever bisexual. He never posed nude, he says, but neither was he averse to baring a little flesh to hype his hunk quotient. "Some gay magazines probably got some pictures I had done with some photographer or another, and they published them. I don't really have an opinion about that. I made up my mind a long time ago that a person's sexuality doesn't make a difference. It's so hard to maintain relationships in this world anyway that what*ever* gets you off seems perfectly fine with me. I think I still have a large gay following—and I'm proud of 'em."

He is about to tear into the recent Supreme Court anti-sodomy decision ("That's what happens when you let the highest court in the land get too far to the right of center") when he catches himself and stops. He finds the idea of simple pop stars promoting their usually unremarkable political philosophies distasteful, not to mention tedious. Singers should sing, players should play. He's done his bit; now the public can decide whether he should press on or, in the future, just stick to doing prime-time designer shoot-outs on the tube. However the reviews may fall, Johnson is convinced he's delivered more than just another TV-star-goes-pop LP. But can that really be enough? Doesn't he, deep down, really hope that *Heartbeat* will make him the nation's newest musical sensation?

"Well," Don says, with appealing realism, "I'm not really new. I'm just sort of current."

Luciano Viti/Retna Ltd.

*T*HIRTEEN

Keith Richards

(1987)

*K*eith Richards is simply the most candid and
casually eloquent of all of rock's major stars—even
with the better part of a bottle of Rebel Yell under his
belt. The following interview, conducted at a time
when the Rolling Stones appeared to be on the verge
of calling it quits, exemplifies his offhand charm.
He's funny, he's bright, he fairly oozes music and
music lore—and you've heard all this, I know, I
know. So let's hear it from Keith himself.

*R*ock & roll has obviously been a major force in your life—
*you've been playing it with the Rolling Stones for a quarter of a
century now. Do you think rock & roll has as intense an effect on
kids today as it did when you were, say, fifteen?*

No, I don't see how it's possible, really. I mean, when I
was fifteen, rock & roll was a brand-new thing, and we were
very conscious that we were in, like, a new era. Totally. It was
almost like A.D. and B.C., and 1956 was year 1, you know? The
world was black-and-white, and then suddenly it went into living
color. Suddenly there was a reason to be around, besides just
knowing you were gonna have to work and draggin' your ass to
school every day. Suddenly everything went *zoom*—glorious

Technicolor. Kids now at that age, they've never known a world
without rock & roll. And I did, you know? That's the difference. I mean, it was an international explosion, man. Just a
few little goddamn records by some guys in Memphis and
Macon and places like that, but they really did have an effect.
It's absolutely amazing. It changed the world. It's reshaped the
way people think. I mean, goddamnit, now you've got rock &
roll concerts in *Moscow,* you know what I mean? 'Cause you
can't stop that shit. You can stop anything else. You can build a
wall to stop people, but eventually, the music, it'll cross that
wall. That's the beautiful thing about music—there's no defense
against it. I mean, look at Joshua and fuckin' Jericho—made
mincemeat of that joint. A few trumpets, you know?

*Do you think you're a much different person than you
were twenty years ago?*

Well, obviously. . .

Have you changed in essential ways?

Yeah. It's not that I *feel* that different. I mean, I've been
through twenty years of . . . I mean, my years are as long as
anybody else's. I mean, like, twenty years ago, let me think . . . In
'67, I was just learnin' how to get busted [*laughs*]. I was taking a lot
of acid and getting busted. Researching police cells, you know?

*Do you think that the Sixties changed things in significant
ways?*

Well, we all thought so at the time—at least the guys of
my age, doin' what we were doin'. It did look like there was a
possibility of it. But I'm sure all the guys that had to go and fight
in the Second World War thought the Forties were gonna do
that, and so did the guys in 1917, you know? It's a watershed in
everybody's life, that point in your late teens or early twenties
where you think you really know everything much more than
everybody else. Where everybody else is either an old fart or a
kid, and you're the only one who's got the balls to do anything,
you know? *But you'll find out, sucker* [*laughs*].

I mean, for me, the beginning of the Sixties was when I
got to be eighteen and nineteen, so in a way, it *was* a magical
time, because I actually managed to turn my little juvenile fantasies into a way of life. I mean, I never dreamt that I would be
able to do it, so it was magical in that sense, in that I'm still here

playin' rock & roll, and makin' a livin' at it, which is what I wanted to do. And I thought that would be impossible—that that was something that happened to stars. Even when we got our first record out, we all looked at each other with a little bit of dismay, you know? Because there was no precedent at that time; nobody lasted. You shot up there, and you were gone. There was no possible way you could believe that it was gonna last for anything more than another two years. So for us, it was like "Oh, man, this is great, makin' records—but that means it's the beginning of the end," you know? But of course, by the time a year or two had gone by, we realized that there was a whole different thing in the works, and we forgot about that. Because it became obvious that you could expand this thing. And what made that possible was that we managed to export it—which was the most *blinding* thing to any musician at that point. I mean, before that, you had to be the biggest dreamer in the world to think that you could export this stuff to America, you know?

Were you surprised by the reception you received in the States when you came over for your first tour?

Yeah, it was really weird. Because this is such a huge country, right? And you'd go into, like, New York or L.A., and it'd be *"Wow!"* Blown away, you know? But then you'd play, like, Omaha, and they'd be goin', "Who? What?" You'd do a gig in Chicago, and it'd be magnificent—all these kids goin', *"Yeahhh!"* And then you'd go off on a three-week slide through the South and the Midwest, and it would be like "What the fuck is *that?*" You know? "It's a buncha *chicks!*" And so you'd constantly be goin' through this thing of, like, one minute this sort of fanatical acclaim, and the next minute you'd go a few hundred miles and it'd be, like, "Scumbags!" You'd be nobody, the lowest, lower than the town bum—at least they *knew* him.

But the Stones prevailed in the end. What's kept you going all this time?

Well, mainly, I wouldn't know what else to do. I'm just personally very happy that I still enjoy doin' it. And I'm a lazy son of a bitch, you know? I mean, I *can* be. But at the same time, to me, that's the hardest work of all, bein' lazy. I mean, in a way, I enjoy it, lyin' around doin' nothing. But you can't just make a profession out of laziness—you have to work really hard at it, you know? It's easier to do some great music, to click off of a few other guys and get like "Yeah! Yeah! Yeah!" You may go eighteen hours without even takin' a pee, it's just such tremendous fun. Like "Yeah, man! That's *it,* man!" It might not even *be* it, you know? But at the time, it *was* it. And that's what I've always enjoyed. To me, to put four or five guys together and just sort of *boom,* let it go. When that happens, it's just the pinnacle. It's one of the purest pleasures that I know. I mean, it ain't gonna hurt nobody. It's not even gonna hurt *you.* It's just a pure pleasure.

Do you ever go back and listen to the Stones' old albums?

Well, funnily enough, this year I've listened to them more than ever, because they all came out on CD. That was the first time I listened to a whole series of Stones stuff for a long time.

Which of the albums emerged as your favorites?

Well, the ones that impressed me were the ones I always thought were superior—*Beggars Banquet, Let It Bleed.* And *Sticky Fingers.* And *Exile.* There's so much stuff on *Exile* that even I'm surprised. I can't even remember all of it: "Oh yeah. Did I write that?"

I quite liked *Black and Blue.* I hadn't listened to that for a long time, and some of that quite surprised me, especially as it was cut while we were auditioning guitar players [*laughs*].

What was your favorite edition of the Stones—with Brian Jones, Mick Taylor or Ronnie Wood?

The most fun is Ronnie. He's also the most open. However, I think some of our best work was probably with Mick Taylor. Ronnie's incredibly underrated in a lot of ways. He's got a lot more to him than you think, 'cause he's a very sort of superficially flippant character. But he's got a lot more depth to him than most people think. And I've always enjoyed working with him very much. I love his enthusiasm. And he's been with the Stones longer than any of the others. That was the amazing thing while we were doing *Dirty Work:* "Do you realize, Ronnie, that you've been in this band longer than Brian was? Longer than Mick Taylor? And you're still the new boy." [*Laughs.*]

How do you look upon some of the guitar players who were your peers—Eric Clapton, Jimi Hendrix, Jimmy Page?

Eric is a lovely player. Jimi, I would have loved to have heard what he was just startin' off to do. I saw him a few weeks or months before he died, and he was very eager to lay down some new stuff. He wanted to put the whole psychedelic thing behind him. He was almost embarrassed by some of his recorded work up to that point.

Did he play you any of his new material?

No. You see, he was just talking about it, and he was in the middle of putting a band together when he kicked it. If you could have hung on for another year, Jimi . . . I would have loved to have heard it, man.

Did you ever get to jam with him?

Dressing rooms a couple of times, just piddling about. In those days, everybody was always on the road, and you'd sit around maybe a couple of evenings here and there, and that would be it. And also you'd be out of it, you know? "I gotta call my dealer. . . ."

And Eric . . . I love to play with Eric. He came in for a number on the Chuck Berry movie. Did a lovely job. I hadn't heard him play so well. I have a feeling about Eric that when he's running his own show, there's nobody to kick him up the ass, you know? And in a way, I have a feeling that he does need that. Because he really pulled out some things in those couple of days in St. Louis that really knocked me out.

Going back to the Sixties again, were you ever seduced by "flower power" and all that?

Personally, no. I mean, you paid a fair amount of lip service to it at the time—peer pressure, et cetera. But I am quite proud that I never did go and kiss the maharishi's goddamn feet, you know?

Does it all seem pretty funny to you now?

Absolutely. I mean, it was like theater of the ridiculous. If it hadn't been promoted so hard—like, by the Beatles, especially—maybe it wouldn't have reached quite the insane proportions that it got to. The basic drive behind it, I suppose, one had to like. But the amount of people that were suckered into it . . .

Like "All you need is love"?

Yeah—try *livin'* off of it.

And yet the Stones had their hippie-trippy moment, too—with 'Their Satanic Majesties Request.' Was that really nothing more than a response to the Beatles' 'Sgt. Pepper'?

Really, yes. That was the bowing to the peer pressure. Suddenly everybody was stoned—all of us got this new stuff called LSD, man. And the Beatles were singin' about it, and Mick was goin' off to see the maharishi, and I'm thinkin', "Uhhh, I ain't too sure about this shit."

Back then, the Stones and the Beatles were always portrayed as polar opposites—they were the good guys, you were the bad guys. Was the reality ever anything like that?

No. I mean, we probably felt more of a kinship, because we were basically the same age, we liked basically the same kind of music, and we wanted to do what we were doin'. There probably weren't more than a few other groups of guys that had more in common, you know? There was a healthy bit of competition, but it was incredibly civilized. I guess from the outside, it seemed like they were the fresh-faced fab mop tops and we were totally the other end of the spectrum. But they were just as filthy as we were, really. And . . . I mean, Brian Jones used to wash his hair three times a *day*, man, you know?

One of the great rallying cries of the Sixties was "Sex and drugs and rock & roll." Given your own well-publicized problems with drugs over the years and the reported rise in heroin and cocaine addiction in the last two decades, do you think such proselytizing may have been a mistake?

Yeah. All of those rallying cries are. I mean, they're all slogans, and necessarily they're very simplistic. Obviously, there was drugs in rock & roll, and the sex wasn't too bad. But, I mean, I don't know anybody that actually *lives* like that all the time. I *used* to know a few guys that did, but they're not alive anymore, you know? And you kinda get the message after you've been to a few funerals.

There seems to have been a 180-degree shift in today's rock scene. A lot of young acts pride themselves on being drug free. They take part in antidrug campaigns and play benefit concerts for various worthy causes. Do you relate to this cleaned-up scene at all?

Yeah, but . . . I'm sure the principles may be sort of admi-rable, but I . . . I know this business too well. I have to doubt the motives in many, many cases, you know? I mean, I'm not gonna smear anybody, but this is one route to gettin' more exposure. It's a bandwagon to jump on. And also, it's a way for the so-called system, or the authorities or whatever, to sort of harness the music for their own purposes. I mean, in England now, every-body's leaping around with the prince and princess of Wales—"Come over the palace," you know? Jesus, I mean, it's ridicu-lous. Everybody's cozyin' up. To me, the only bright spot in all of that is that eventually it'll get so boring and sickening, a reac-tion'll set in the other way. Like disco: just hammer it in there until they get sick of it, and then something else'll come out.

It is sort of odd to see rock in the hands of so many goody-goody groups now.

Yeah, I know. It's basically against the whole idea of what always made rock & roll music interesting to me. I thought it was an unassailable outlet for some pure and natural expres-sions of rebellion. It was one channel you could take without havin' to kiss ass, you know? And right now it just seems like they're on a big daisy chain, each kissin' each other's asses.

This is the age of AIDS, and of drugs that are even worse than any that existed before. What do you tell your kids about stuff like that?

The kids I've got are old enough to worry about it. As far as I know, they've got a pretty good attitude toward that. I mean, Marlon's eighteen; Angela, she's fifteen. And they're in-credibly straightforward kids—especially considering when they were brought up and how. I mean, most people went, "Oh, my God, they'll . . ." [*Laughs.*] But I really never had any prob-lems with them. I mean, Marlon's more like a mate of mine. Now and again he puts me on the hot spot. Like, I have to go and see his *principal* at school. "How could you *do* this to me, Marlon? I haven't been in a principal's office for thirty years." And I hated it.

Do you think the music has lost a lot of its original spon-taneity today? Especially onstage, more and more acts seem tied down to lighting cues, timed effects, even choreography.

Well, yeah. But you see, it's big money now. And the more money's involved, the less spontaneity, the less fun, the less things are left to chance. It's always the same: the big budgets bring more pressure from the money people, the record companies, the promoters, to get it all together. And so you get these little groups, and they've got all this shit goin'—the video and the lights and all. But to me, the fun and the spirit of the thing shouldn't be just overawing people with slick productions, like they were in a Sensurround movie or something. It should come from the stage. I don't go to a show and look up and say, "Great lighting." To me, the most important thing about any musician is, can you walk in a bar and get a free drink with a song, you know?

With all the commercialism in rock now, it seems harder than ever for good, original bands to break through.

That's the thing. I don't really see that it's possible now the way it was for us. The whole business is just too big. Twenty-odd years ago, rock & roll was just peanuts to the money people, and therefore you could take chances, because they didn't really give a damn. But now, the price tag on puttin' out an album, and the videos and the stage show—there's so much investment in it that everybody's playin' safe. Somebody may come on with something really new to offer, but within a record or so, they're already toeing the line, playin' the game. I don't know if it's possible to be that free again, to get that amount of spontaneity. I don't know that it's gonna be allowed to exist. But you never know. I mean, that's another interesting thing about all this: there's music, and there's the music business. And there's always this weird balance as to who's holding the reins.

A lot of people have always seen you as the crucial member of the Rolling Stones—you know: "Keith Richards is the Stones." How do you respond to that notion?

It's far more subtle than that. I mean, there's no way you can say that any one person *is* the band and the rest are just padding. It is such a subtle mixture of characters and personalities and how you deal with each other. And if it works right, you never think about it yourself, because there's always the fear that if you analyze it, you'll blow it, you know? So you don't really wanna know. You'll just come up with something—a song or a riff—and you'll say, "I think we can nail this down." And you'll see a little look of mystification come over the rest of the band's faces. And if you feel strongly enough about it, you'll push it and push it, and they might be going, "Oh, no, not again." And then suddenly—if you were right—you'll look around and see that *boom, click,* and then it falls into place. And you say, "Oh, good, thank God—let's go, quick, before they lose it again."

I mean, it is the most difficult thing to talk about, because you feel that if you probe it too hard, it's just gonna collapse. You just go on this search for something, and *bang,* suddenly it happens. And then it infects everybody straight away—suddenly, everybody knows what it is they've gotta do. And those are the magic moments. Those are the ones where suddenly you sort of feel like you're ten feet tall and you're not touchin' the ground, you know? And that's what I've always lived for—that moment when a band just clicks in. For that little while you're playin' that thing, nobody can touch you.

Have you ever considered writing your autobiography?

No, I haven't, really. Because, I mean, I've only got to, like, Chapter 3, you know? I wouldn't know how to tie it all up. I gotta know the ending first—or at least be pretty *close* to it— before I can get a handle on what's gone down. Right now, I'm more interested in knowin' what the next half of the book is gonna be. Or the last third, or whatever.

Have you arrived at any spiritual conclusions after forty-four years?

No. I'm just more and more convinced that I'll find out when I'm supposed to find out. I mean, I've been closer to death a few more times than a lot of people. And what I've found out is that whatever it is, it's worth waiting for, you know?

Do you think you've mellowed over the years?

I guess everybody does, in a way, yeah. I mean, I enjoy doing things now that I would never have had the patience for twenty years ago. Like kids—I actually enjoy bouncing babies on my knee and shit, you know? And I enjoy goin' to see, like, me dad. We got together again in 1982, after twenty years of trepidation. 'Cause when the Stones started, it had been, like, him or me: "I'm leavin'! I gotta go!" And I moved to London. So after twenty years, we finally got it back together: me dad's comin' down to see me, and I'm sort of waitin' to get "Hi, son"—*bop!* But then this little guy came out, real sweet and . . .

aw, shit, you know? Now we sit around and play dominoes. And he can still drink more 'n me.

Back in the Seventies, the Stones seemed in danger of split-ting along the lines of your down-to-earth rock & roll instincts and Mick's jet-set lifestyle. What was really going on there?

Well, I would say that there you've got the seeds of why we're not together right now. I mean, Mick and I have different attitudes, and throughout most of the Seventies, I was living in another world from him. I didn't blame him—he'd earned the right to do what he wanted. It was just that I couldn't *relate* to that. And even if I could've related to it, I was too busy bein' busted—which, I mean, is equally as dumb, you know? Mick and I are incredibly diverse people. We've known each other forty years—ever since we were three or four years old. But while a certain part of our personalities is incredibly close, there's an awful lot which is very, very different. And so, yeah, it kind of got up my nose a bit, that jet-set shit and, like, the flaunting of it. But he's a lonely guy, too. He's got his own prob-lems, you know?

If you weren't so different in some ways, the musical chemistry probably wouldn't be the same.

No, precisely. So it doesn't rankle me. I'm his friend, and he knows it. It's just, like, "I love you, darling, but I can't live with you."

What is the Stones' future, then?

Everybody likes things cut and dried, and with the Stones, it never will be. Whether it's all over or not is really up to how everybody in the band feels. This particular period is basically, I think, a reaction to twenty-five years of being forced to work together whether we liked it or not. Luckily, we liked it. But, I mean, eventually, it's gotta get to a point where you say, "Hey, it's always been fun to work together, but now it's gettin' a little bitter here and there, and lines are bein' drawn." And you don't really know how to get out of it, or who's drawin' the lines, and there's a lot of interference from people who think they've gotta put themselves in one camp or another. So, better off, let's just give it a breather, and then we'll see how ridiculous it all is and work it out. I mean, I love working with those boys, and I don't see us not pullin' it back together. Just give us a break, and we'll come back for part two, you know? "We'll be right with you after these messages." [*Laughs.*] More to come, you know?

Whatever the group's future, the Stones have succeeded in removing age as an issue from the making of rock & roll.

Maybe that's because of what I was saying—that rock became a global thing just at that point where we started, and that enlarged all of the possibilities. That's really what rock & roll did, bless its old heart. It was—and still is, in a way—at the forefront of turning this little planet of ours on to the idea that it *is* a planet. It's managed to cross right through opposing countries and ideologies. I mean, you'll never get rid of nationalism and so-called patriotism and all that. But the important thing is to spread the idea that there's really this one planet—that's really what we've got to worry about. And all these little lines that were drawn by guys hundreds of years ago are really obsolete. And if we don't realize that, there won't be *anything* much in the world, you know? There's 5 billion of us now, man—in the Fifties there was only 2.5 billion. We managed to double it in thirty-some years. So in the long term, maybe that's the most important thing that rock & roll's done—it's opened up people's minds about these things.

Even if it hasn't taught us all how to love one another.

Yeah. Like "Now we're gonna give all 5 billion of you your daily drop of acid, and the maharishi's gonna come down and tell you how to deal with it." [*Laughs.*]

Maybe the true essence of rock & roll is simply that it was always great fun.

Oh, it still *is* great fun. You can take everything else, but don't take the fun out of it, man. I mean, if they take the fun out of this life—I'll *leave.*

Larry Busacca/Retna Ltd.

FOURTEEN

Bruce Springsteen

(1985)

I don't pretend to know Bruce Springsteen in any intimate way, but going by those encounters I have had with the man, I'd say he's very much the sort of hardworking, regular-but-gifted guy his low-key public persona might lead you to expect. Springsteen's colloquial art is deceptively simple—he strives for an Everyman effect in his music, but his talent is anything but ordinary. Some rock stars find it embarrassing to talk seriously about the power and importance of rock & roll when they're facing forty and feeling the beginnings of a midlife panic. Springsteen, however, still believes. And in sharing his belief in the nurturing power of rock & roll, he offers to his audience that rarest of pop benedictions: simple, heartfelt hope. Call it corny, but consider the alternatives.

One afternoon last fall, Bruce Springsteen sat sipping a beer in a room at the Sunset Marquis hotel in Los Angeles. He wore blue jeans, cowboy boots, a black-leather jacket and a news-boy's cap slouched down backward over the bandanna tied around his head. Not one of the great glamour-pusses, you

could say. At the peak of his twelve-year recording career, and
midway through his most clamorously acclaimed tour with the
precision-tooled E Street Band, Springsteen remained as wary
as ever of massive success and its attendant seductions. "I never
felt I was like an Elvis or a Dylan, or the Rolling Stones," he
said. "I don't see myself in that way. I see myself more like a
real good journeyman. And that's fine: You do your job real
good, you pass on some part of the flame . . . and you stir things
up a little bit if you can."

   Springsteen's diffidence is a well-known component of
what may now be called, with some justification, his legend: the
unassuming musical laureate of the working classes. Nevertheless, in 1984, as he began touring in support of *Born in the
U.S.A.*, his seventh and biggest-selling album (5 million copies
so far), the thirty-five-year-old Jersey flash found he had grown
from being the country's biggest cult artist—lionized on the East
Coast, more patchily appreciated elsewhere—into something
very like a national hero. There appeared to be several reasons
for this change. On a purely showbiz level, he is one of the most
uproariously exciting performers in rock history, and while an
ever-shrinking number of skeptics have sometimes found his
four-hour shows to be overblown endurance tests, there has
never been any doubt about the deep emotional connection he
makes with his audiences night after night. More than most major rock stars—Prince and Michael Jackson, the year's two
other musical phenoms, come most quickly to mind—Springsteen is publicly perceived as a real and complete person. There
is none of Jackson's ethereal remoteness or Prince's sexual
threat about him; he still lives in untrendy New Jersey, where he
was born and raised, still goes out unguarded to local bars and
clubs and still answers what fan mail he can with personal re-
sponses. He seems a regular guy. And yet the resonant social
vision set out in the best of his new songs—the working-class
despair of "Downbound Train"; the painful, betrayed patriotism
of his Vietnam-vets anthem, "Born in the U.S.A."; the sense of
small-town anomie so piercingly evoked in "My Hometown"—
marks Springsteen as a lyrical artist with a unique gift for popular expression. His concern for his characters, and by extension
their millions of counterparts in his audience, seems genuine—
seems, in fact, the wellspring of his art. As he toured the country, soliciting the realities of unemployment from local union
leaders, constantly promoting food banks and other community

groups from the stage (and often putting significant amounts of money where his mouth was), he appeared to be striving for a practical realization of the communitarian ideals of the Sixties in the more harshly pragmatic Eighties. Here was art once again stirring up social action, and in a year when the Jacksons were charging thirty dollars to witness their seventy-five-minute show (while Springsteen kept a sixteen-dollar lid on his four-hour spectacles), it proved anew that music can have meaning beyond mere entertainment.

"I want to find out what you can do with a rock & roll band," Springsteen said that afternoon in Los Angeles. "I'm trying to apply the original idea of our band, which was that the possibilities are vast. I first started to play because I wanted to do something good—I wanted to be proud of myself, to feel good about myself. And I found the guitar, and that gave it to me; it gave me my sense of purpose and a sense of pride in myself. And that is the gift of life. It was my lifeboat, my life-line—my line back into people. It was my connection to the rest of the human race, you know?

"Before that, it was a strange existence. I was a big daydreamer when I was in grammar school. Kids used to tease me, call me 'dreamer.' It's something that got worse as I got older, I think. Until I realized that I felt like I was dying, for some reason, and I really didn't know why. I think that's a feeling that a lot of people have. And so now I go out onstage and I feel like there's people dying out there, there's people really hurt—you know because you feel the same thing. And this is your chance to do something about it. So when I go out onstage at night, I feel like there's really something at stake, that it has some meaning. It's not just another night.

"When I sit down to write, I try to write something that feels real to me. Like, what does it feel like to be thirty-five or something right now, at this point in time, living in America? It's not much more conscious than that. I generally try to write songs that are about real life, not fantasy material. I try to reflect people's lives back to them in some fashion. And if the show is really good, your life should flash before your eyes in some way—the show's long enough, that's for sure! I think on a night when we're really good, you can come and hopefully you can see your relationships with your parents, brothers, sisters, your town, your country, your friends, everything—sexual, political, the whole social thing. It should be a combination of a circus, a political thing and a spiritual event. And hopefully you'll come and your life will flash before your eyes. That's kind of what I'm out there trying to do, you know?"

That he succeeds, and often brilliantly, is due in large part to his unusual empathy with his audience, his devotion to the otherwise unsung realities of their lives. "I never look out at my crowd and see a bunch of faces," he said. "It's never happened. Any night I've ever been onstage, I see people—individual people in individual seats out there. That's why, before the show, we go out and we check the sound in every section of the room. Because there's some guy sittin' back here, and he's got a girl with him, and, you know, it's like, this is their seat. And what you hope for is that the same thing goes the other way—that when they look up at you, they don't just see some person with a guitar."

That Springsteen is popularly perceived as much more than that is evidenced by his standing in *Rolling Stone*'s 1984 Readers' Poll, which he effectively swept. But along with his burgeoning success has come what would appear to be a personal paradox. With the money rolling in, this determinedly unpretentious chronicler of the working class has become a millionaire. Can he hold on to his soul, to his street-bred ideals, even as he moves into that mansion on the hill he once only dreamed about?

"I know this is idealistic," he said, taking a slug of beer, "but part of the idea our band had from the beginning was that you did not have to lose your connection to the people you write for. I don't believe that fame or success means that you lose that connection, and I don't believe that makin' more money means you lose it. Because that's not where the essence of what you are lies. That's not what separates people. What separates people are things that are in their heart. So I just can never surrender to that idea. Because I know that before I started playing, I was alone. And one of the reasons I picked up the guitar was that I wanted to be part of something. And I practiced and I studied and I worked real hard to do that, and I ain't about to give it up now."

SOME TIME I

PART TWO
NEW YORK CITY

There were, I realize, other interesting music scenes happening throughout the Eighties—in Los Angeles, in London, in Austin and Philadelphia and Sydney and Melbourne and Düsseldorf and Berlin, and even in Athens, Georgia, to name just a few. But, like you, perhaps, the one I know and love best is the one I got to observe on a daily basis.

New York City is the most intense and frantic of the world's major music-business cities—a lot of people can't stand it (and often can't stand the people who *can* stand it), but I've always found the constant frenzy to be a part of the scene's appeal.

In the Fifites, it was the home of Alan Freed and great, stomping studio bands and all-day rock & roll shows at the Paramount Theater and brilliantly produced Brill Building girl groups and about 10,000 heartbreaking doo-wop acts. Bill Haley recorded here; Buddy Holly moved here; the Shangri-Las were born here, as were the Ramones and—in the Eighties—the sound of rap. I'm happy to get out of New York once in a while, but I'm always relieved to get back.

"Night Creatures," the first piece that follows, isn't really about music at all (although its principal subjects are all avid connoisseurs of various obscure musical genres). It's mainly about certain areas of Manhattan that most people won't admit to liking at all, and as such, I think it offers a useful sense of the city's inimitable grit.

The story of the rise and sad fall of Blondie will, I hope, serve as a modest elegy for the late-Seventies New York punk scene—one of the most exciting and unforgettable explosions of creativity and experimentation I've ever had the good fortune to witness. The whole thrust of punk was essentially antinostalgic, but at a thirteen-year remove, nostalgia comes flooding back unbidden. (What we need now are some fresh punks to dispel such unseemly moping.)

The rest of this section focuses on one group and two women—Talking Heads, Cyndi Lauper, and Laurie Anderson—who were at the center of the downtown art-and-rock nexus of the early Eighties; it ends with a farewell to Andy Warhol, who taught a whole generation of young artists (for better or—more often—worse) how to be good little businessmen. But there was more to Warhol than that, as you'll see.

*F*IFTEEN

Night Creatures

(1984)

$\mathcal{S}$*ome of the scariest movies ever made don't
even have monsters in them. These flamboyantly bad
(or, alternatively, fabulous) films are the province of
a number of small cult publications devoted to the art
and the awfulness of the Z-grade movie in all its
many mutations. The first of these specialist
fanzines—as I learned only after writing the
following story—was* Fangoria, *a slasher mag. But
the "psychotronic" film research of Z-movie
archivist Michael Weldon continues to set the
standard for erudition in the field, and while Bill
Landis'* Sleazoid Express *is gone now, no one who
ever experienced its gripping mix of twisted laughs,
lurid sex and chronicles of human debasement is ever
likely to forget it. This is a story that asks the
question, "How could any decent person possibly be
interested in such hideous garbage?" . . . and
answers with a shrug.*

The theater is small, and packed with Popeyes. Even on a benign Sunday afternoon in late May, they are drawn in droves to
the dark, dingy innards of the Variety Photo Plays, a Z-movie

graveyard hard by the classic grime-ball intersection of Fourteenth Street and Third Avenue in Manhattan. They are men in
ill-fitting, strangely stained clothes, some wearing two and three
tattered coats at a time, most clutching plastic bags abulge with
their mysterious Popeye baggage. Those who aren't prowling
the aisles on some long-forgotten quest simply twitch and fidget
in their seats. It's a riveting spectacle: Popeyes on parade, their
stunned, stubble-encrusted faces gaping up at the flickering
screen, which is filled with the bare, bleeding back of actor
Ralph Meeker. The film is a 1975 drive-in bomb called *Johnny
Firecloud:* no sex, no good violence (despite Meeker's recent
horsewhipping) and, worst of all, too much talk—this crowd re-
lates visually, not verbally. The Popeyes are restless. They don't
get it.

Popeyes are "people created by pornography," according
to Bill Landis, the laconic publisher of *Sleazoid Express,* who
identified the archetype in his magazine. Their present incomprehension, he says, leaning back in his front-row seat and
lighting up a joint as Ralph Meeker flaunts his whip wounds
high above us, is due to the nonsalacious nature of this movie.
The Variety best pleases its Popeye clientele on Fridays and Saturdays, with day-long porn marathons. The rest of the week,
though, it unreels some of the world's strangest grade-Z features.

We're not talking *Attack of the Mayan Mummy* here, or
Zontar, the Thing from Venus, or any other sort of so-bad-it's-
great late-night tube fodder. No, we're talking truly subhuman
cinema, friends—movies with no buildup, no payoff, no reason
whatsoever to exist. True trash, unredeemed by even the fain-
test trace of talent. *Johnny Firecloud* is the opener of today's
double bill, an excruciatingly awful contemporary western that
features—can it be?—Sacheen Littlefeather, the woman who
once turned down Marlon Brando's Oscar. On the evidence of
this talkaholic turkey, she's never likely to get that close to the
magic statuette again.

Landis' joint is authentically beat Tenth Street weed, but
at least it dulls the senses before this onslaught of ennui. As he
passes it to his partner, Jimmy McDonough, a ribbon of smoke
curls up through the fetid air to join the sour stink of spilled
wine, bad breath and bodies not lately bathed. The crowd,
Landis decides, after boldly surveying the rows behind us, is actually an admixture of Popeyes and Blockheads, another

Sleazoid archetype: overbuilt physical-culture fetishists with too tight clothes, no necks and perpetually intense, sweat-sheened features—helpless compulsives in the grip of obsessions they only dimly comprehend. The Blockheads are here for the main feature, no doubt; the Popeyes are here out of habit.

The sight of Meeker's blood, however, has stirred some activity. Stumbling gingerly around the faintly repugnant puddles that pock the raw concrete floor, a line of agitated patrons is suddenly streaming toward the door of the men's toilet, which is conspicuously situated right next to the big screen before us. Landis studies them with sharpened interest as they converge on the john, and a crowd begins to form around the door to the toilet. Some of the men, prepared, produce dimes and enter. The rest are left to shuffle and scowl outside. Whenever the door opens, some slip in with their Popeye bags to join the milling throng inside. In all of his many visits to the Variety, Landis has never yet worked up sufficient journalistic zeal to actually enter the john and ascertain the exact nature of the activities inside.

"It could be a blow-job factory," he muses. "Or it could be they just stand in there and hang out and watch things, which Popeyes love to do."

Most of them are back in their seats by the time the main feature starts. It's *The Black Room*, a bizarre obscurity that, by any prevailing critical standard, completely lives up to its plot line's utter lack of promise. A husband, seeking to spice up his dull sex life, rents a candle-lit love nest in the Hollywood Hills, to which he takes teenage pickups. Their carnal romps are secretly photographed by the proprietors of the place, a Blockhead brother and sister. ("Just like a Blockhead to be taking pictures," says Jimmy McDonough with a derisive snigger.) After each R-rated sex interlude, the girls are subdued by injections from an eighteen-inch hypodermic and spirited off by the malevolent siblings to a basement surgery, where the blood is drained from their bodies and into the arm of the Blockhead brother. He requires three transfusions a day. Eventually, both husband and wife are imprisoned in the evil house, along with their two children and a baby-sitter. But disaster is averted when the husband strangles the brother and dumps him in a blood-filled tub, and the wife offs the sister with a twisted wire coat hanger in the neck. The family escapes, but the closing shot shows the Blockheads rising again, unkillable.

By normal standards, *The Black Room* is an inert and inscrutably obsessive film. But Landis is impressed. Obviously, he explains, sex is not the real subject of interest here—it's tossed off, dully done. Nor is the central turn-on the element of Blockhead implacability—the unstoppable zombie menace common to so many slasher and body-count movies. *The Black Room* is really fixated on the images of blood pumping through plastic tubes and into the veins of the erotically receptive brother. "It's a movie about getting high," Landis says, and its intended audience is not this theater full of poleaxed Popeyes, but the more motley and exotic denizens of Times Square, where *The Black Room* recently had a four-day run. Another low-budget wonder—and directed by a woman yet, one Elly Kenner. Landis sighs. Most moviegoers will never even hear about this strange Blockhead masterpiece.

Me, I'm wondering how big the blood-transfusion market can possibly be. What sort of people seek this stuff out? Did they start off as harmless trashophiles hooked on late-night TV screenings of *Attack of the 50-Foot Woman* and *The Brain That Wouldn't Die* and then move on, goggle-eyed and gagging, through the hardcore gore classics of Herschell Gordon Lewis. (*The Blood Feast, Two Thousand Maniacs* and others of that ilk), finally descending into the pit of perdition to which mainstream society consigns the really brutal and misanthropic stuff: *Ilsa—She Wolf of the SS*, the hideous 1977 version of *I Spit on Your Grave*, the transsexual upchuck epic *Let Me Die a Woman*? Is there an insidious chain of addiction here? Why do bad movies—badly made and, in the view of many a censorious citizen, bad for society—suddenly appeal to so many people? Fan mags devoted to the new sleaze-film aesthetic are flourishing: in addition to Landis' pioneering *Sleazoid Express*, there is *Trashola*, from San Francisco; *Gore Gazette* and *Confessions of a Trash Fiend*, from New Jersey; *The Splatter Times*, from Tennessee; *Chicago Shivers*, from Illinois; *Scareaphanalia* and *Fangoria*, from New York; and many more both here and, increasingly, abroad. Books on the trash tradition also abound, from the seminal *Sinema* and *Blue Money* to the Medved brothers' latest, *The Hollywood Hall of Shame*, and Michael Weldon's compulsively readable *Psychotronic Encyclopedia of Film*. Video buffs can also find most of their favorite sleazy flicks on cassette these days, and *Classic Gore*, a compilation of highlights from such genre hits as *Driller Killer, The Texas Chainsaw*

Massacre and the infamous *Snuff,* has been advertised for a mere $44.95.

This growing vogue for vile movies has excited the ire of the morally upright—most vocally, right-wing Bible beaters, as well as militant feminists allied under the banner of Women against Pornography. One can imagine how they must feel—a lot of this stuff is indefensible on any level. Maybe prolonged exposure to, say, *Meat Cleaver Massacre* or *The Tool Box Murders* (recently featured on "60 Minutes") or the legendary 1971 double bill of *I Drink Your Blood* and *I Eat Your Skin* really will rot the brain, leaving addicts awash in moral ambiguity. Slunking out of the Variety, past clumps of spittle-flecked Popeyes, brooding Blockheads and bag-wielding winos, I was reminded of the words of the notorious lunatic Popeye, Edward Kemper. Kemper, the subject of an incredulous mention in *Sleazoid* a few months back, was the "Coed Killer" of the early Seventies. According to *Sleazoid,* Kemper not only decapitated his mother and stuffed her vocal cords down the garbage disposal, but also hacked up a series of female hitchhikers and had sex with various parts of their bodies. When asked by a reporter for *Front Page Detective* magazine what he thought when he saw a pretty woman walk by, Kemper was thoughtful: "One side of me says, 'Wow, what an attractive chick. I'd sure like to talk to her, date her.'

"The other side says, 'I wonder how her head would look on a stick?'"

This is the abyss into which one must inevitably stare while tottering about out on the frontiers of sleaze.

What we're talking about here is simply exploitation movies. And exploitation movies—movies that exploit a perceived public interest or obsession—have been with us almost as long as cinema itself. Universal Pictures made a bundle on a white-slavery exposé called *Traffic in Souls* back in 1913, and pornographic films—perhaps the most abiding exploitation genre—date back as early as 1908. Today, the determined buff may delve into more than seven decades' worth of cinematic dreck: Thirties drug-scare melodramas, such as *Reefer Madness* and *Cocaine Fiends;* Forties baby-birth documentaries (often shown to sexually segregated audiences to boost the hype), such as William Beaudine's immortal *Mom and Dad;* a rich strain of Fifties horror movies (from frightening staples like *Invasion of the*

Body Snatchers to such zipper-up-the-back monster hoots as the 1953 *Invaders from Mars*) and Sixties teen-cult drive-in quickies (remember "Dynasty"'s Linda Evans in *Beach Blanket Bingo?*); and the generally unplumbed mass of product that came out in the Seventies. There's no end to the stuff.

A good overview of all this is provided by *The Psychotronic Encyclopedia of Film,* published last year by Ballantine Books. Michael Weldon, who edited and wrote many of its more than 3000 reviews, has a lively eye for detail. Did you know that Cristina De Lorean played a lesbian vampire in the 1975 Mexican film *Mary, Mary, Bloody Mary*? Or that fledgling *auteur* Francis Ford Coppola filmed the 3-D color inserts of the otherwise black-and-white 1962 German sex comedy *The Playgirls and the Bellboy*? Or that the underwear fetishist in the 1968 Hammer film *The Anniversary* inspired the early Pink Floyd single "Arnold Layne"? (Bette Davis played his malignant mother in a black eyepatch.) Memories—not all of them fond, but most quite funny—come flooding back. Who could ever forget white Ray Milland and black Rosey Grier sharing the same set of shoulders in the indescribable 1972 AIP epic *The Thing with Two Heads*? Or drag-queen director Edward D. Wood Jr.'s tatty transsex classic, *Glen or Glenda*? Weldon chronicles all this and more, from the Herschell Gordon Lewis gorefests and the surreal *oeuvre* of indy icon Ted V. Mikels to such cinematic sports as monster musicals *(The Incredibly Strange Creatures Who Stopped Living and Became Crazy Mixed-Up Zombies)*, tasteless memorials *(The Wild, Wild World of Jayne Mansfield)* and such stomach-turning anomalies as *The Worm Eaters*. To come across Weldon's review of something like *The Vulture*—a 1966 Paramount misfire that featured not only a killer vulture with the head of Akim Tamiroff, but also Broderick Crawford playing *an English squire*—is suddenly to realize how sedate one's life has been.

But while *Psychotronic* is catholic in its coverage, its heart is in fun trash. Weldon, a thirty-two-year-old native of Cleveland, Ohio, and the son of a professional magician, grew up glued to the tube, where he reveled in old films from the Thirties and Forties. In the late Fifties, he became captivated by imports: cheap Mexican creature features, fleshy biblical epics and, particularly, the lushly produced horror classics of England's Hammer Films (*The Curse of Frankenstein, Horror of Dracula*), most starring Peter Cushing and Christopher Lee.

"Foreign films always had a little bit more sex and violence than American films," Weldon says in his soft, scholarly voice. "You'd see spears go right through somebody, which was a big deal at that time, and people'd get real excited. And the biblical movies would always have women in thin robes, and they always seemed to be getting wet, so they were good for really mild sex scenes."

Forrest J. Ackerman's *Famous Monsters of Filmland* became a touchstone for Weldon's nascent trash aesthetic, and he also came under the sway of a local late-night film-show host named Ghoulardi, who spewed out Roger Corman and AIP teen films, biker movies, the whole wondrous wasteland of low-rent Americana. Weldon also haunted the local grind houses, and by 1968, when the MPAA ratings system was inaugurated, he was starting to see early X-rated sex-and-horror films by such European directors as Jesus "Jesse" Franco (*Succubus*), now-innocuous Scandinavian sex opuses and, later, a deluge of black-exploitation films. "And all these things were playing mixed on double bills in inner-city theaters."

Following his graduation from high school in 1970, Weldon held down "depressing menial jobs, took a lot of drugs and totally wasted several years." By 1977, a strong punk-rock scene had flowered in Cleveland. Weldon worked at a punk record store called the Drome and wrote a column of TV-movie reviews for a local magazine called *Cle* (which also employed Pere Ubu vocalist David Thomas). Weldon had found his calling. In 1979, he moved to New York City, and in the summer of 1980, he began publishing a weekly, hand-lettered TV-movie tip sheet called *Psychotronic*. (The name is derived from a 1980 obscurity called *The Psychotronic Man*.) Xeroxed on a painfully low budget, *Psychotronic* was nonetheless a godsend for warped TV-movie addicts who'd grown infuriated by the *New York Times'* smug dismissal of obscure films in its listings—"Not reviewed by us." Weldon flaunted his aesthetic allegiances: *Psychotronic* covers featured lovably lurid photos from Weldon's collection of vintage promotional art—*The Phantom Planet, Night of the Blood Beast, Horror of Party Beach,* diminutive Deborah Walley flying across the credits of *It's a Bikini World*. It was fun, but after fifty-three issues, Weldon was frazzled. He was also being courted by several book publishers, and he finally decided to close down the magazine and begin work on *The Psychotronic Encyclopedia*. Today, he sits in his small Lower East

Side apartment, located above a witches' supply store called Enchantments, and plots a sequel.

But Weldon also worries. Because New York's tatty Times Square district—the whole legendary Forty-second Street strip—is under unremitting attack by the forces of municipal morality and urban "progress." The city is determined to clean out all the hookers, hustlers and other local lowlifes who inhabit "the Deuce" (as it's romantically called) and replace all the porn shops, sex palaces and grunge-pit exploitation theaters with more upscale architecture and, subsequently, more upscale people. All this under the dubious assumption that simply to uproot urban blight is to eradicate it.

But Times Square and its lurid environs are no mere canker on the cultural landscape—they are a mecca for Z-movie buffs. At theaters like the Apollo, the Lyric, the Liberty, the Selwyn, anything is likely to turn up. On the charged and sometimes violent strip, a movie like the current *Mardi Gras Massacre* is almost a critical event, and even the most gruesome torture epics—*Make Them Die Slowly,* for instance, which had a marathon run at the Liberty—will likely find the twisted audience for which they were intended. To bulldoze this rich cultural mulch would distress trash-film aficionados more than it would the Popeyes, Blockheads and slumming tourists who'll be physically displaced. But it's inevitable, says Weldon. Already the twenty-four-hour action on the strip has dimmed a bit— some theaters are dark by midnight now—and he gives the whole area two more years at most before the big real-estate scam goes down for good.

"The developers are all gonna profit," Weldon says. "But their plans sound so dull and unappealing. Now they want to tear down the Times Square tower, too. And they probably will."

Bill Landis is also appalled at the thought of losing the Deuce. It is a rain-soaked night in late May, and we are walking through the Port Authority Bus Terminal at Forty-second and Eighth Avenue—the once wildly beating heart of the strip. The terminal's not what it used to be, Landis says almost wistfully. Cops all over the place now, and the boy-prostitution scene that once flourished inside has apparently moved out into the parking lots. Across Forty-second Street is the screaming red-white-and-yellow neon of Show World, a four-story hive of porno-loop booths, look-but-don't-touch nude displays and live sex shows. Landis once saw an aged Popeye drop dead in Show World. What a way to go. Over there is the Barking Fish, Landis' favorite fast-food place. And there, a gay strip club announcing HERE'S THE BEEF! Teenage hustlers scurry after johns. Young men moan in darkened doorways. Really, Landis wonders—how could they bulldoze all of this?

Bill Landis and his *Sleazoid* staff—McDonough plus a mysterious third character known only as "Buggin' Out"—are situated at the opposite end of the trash spectrum from Michael Weldon. Whereas Weldon maintains at least a modicum of detachment from some of the movies covered in *The Psychotronic Encyclopedia,* Landis seems to have disappeared into them. As McDonough says, he is a man "who was shaped by exploitation."

An air-force brat who grew up in France, England, Louisiana and, ultimately, New York, Landis remembers being transfixed at the age of nine by a garish ad for *Guttertrash,* a film by director Andy Milligan. (Milligan is notorious for a series of particularly hateful, ultra-low-budget medieval splatter movies filmed on Staten Island—little-seen wonders with such titles as *Torture Dungeon* and *The Ghastly Ones.*) The *Guttertrash* ad was Landis' first intimation that there might exist a whole netherworld of extremely weird human behavior, a world of strange, brutal beauty. It was the beginning of an obsession.

Landis whizzed through school and had a master's degree in finance by the time he was twenty. After a few disastrous stints of corporate employment, however, he came to the conclusion that "higher education is worthless," and succumbed to the call of the Deuce. He has worked as a projectionist at porno theaters and at gay cruise dives where toilet muggings were the norm and wallets were lifted from pants pockets with the slash of a knife, often leaving the victim with a gouged and bloody behind. He has written exploitation scripts, and he actually worked on the crew of an Andy Milligan film, bringing his obsession full circle. Now twenty-five, he could easily pass for sixteen. At least until he starts talking.

To chronicle the rancid ambiance of life on the Deuce, Landis started *Sleazoid Express* in the summer of 1980, shortly before Weldon founded *Psychotronic.* At first, he mostly reported on the incredible film fare of Forty-second Street, but when McDonough, a film-obsessed college dropout from Indiana, joined the enterprise, he encouraged Landis to branch out—to write about the things that *really* interested him. To Landis, most of the mainstream trash-film crowd is composed of Nerds, another archetype—list makers, fact hoarders, middle-class voyeurs and trivia fetishists. *Sleazoid* has taken for its turf a cinematic no-man's-land bordered on one side by gore and torture epics and on the other by the most reprehensible sort of hardcore porn—and all around by greed, stupidity and ineptitude. Although Landis doesn't condone torture, mutilation or half the other things he covers ("S&M," he recently wrote, "becomes addictive and destructive"), he does endeavor to look this stuff straight in the face. Not surprisingly, it's everything you've always imagined it to be. Nothing showing on the strip is too despicable for acknowledgment in *Sleazoid,* which has now grown to sixteen pages. Those curious about such films as *Shriek of the Mutilated* or *Elevator Girls in Bondage* or the ghastly *Blood-Sucking Freaks* are sure to have their curiosity sated in *Sleazoid.*

"It's more interesting than Nerds clucking about pictures of monsters," says McDonough. "At *Sleazoid,* we try to re-create going to an exploitation movie, to bring that feeling back. We try to get to the heart of what we see. Mainstream movies are just dullsville. These movies, even if they're moronic, have a soul—it may be twisted, but it *is* a soul. A lot of it *is* ugly; but we're trying to comment on what this stuff does without becoming Siskel and Ebert. I think there's a lot of good in these movies, too. I don't see anything more offensive about exploitation movies than mainstream movies—or ninety percent of MTV. We're not saying that these movies espouse any great viewpoint or anything. I mean, a lot of times, men stink, and there's more evidence of that in these movies than anywhere else. Men are Blockheads. Men do hate themselves. Men run amok."

Which brings us to the rampant misanthropy—and, more particularly, misogyny—that seems to run through many of the more extreme trash films, particularly slasher epics. The usual focus of opprobrium in this regard is a widely reviled but rarely seen film called *Snuff,* which is said to include footage of a woman actually being hacked apart and killed onscreen. In fact, *Snuff,* released in 1976, is a classic exploitation hoax, made to cash in on the alarm caused by the then-unverified snuff-film scare.

"I didn't see *Snuff* until last year," says Michael Weldon, "and I'm still greatly amused by the fact that people continue to cite it as an example of the most reprehensible movie possible. And women's groups are continuing to help its reputation by protesting the videotape sales, and I still don't think most people have seen it. It is a fairly disturbing movie, but everything in it is faked. Ninety-five percent of it was filmed in Argentina. It has some Nazis in exile, a Charles Manson type, a hippie commune, some women who kill people and some very nonexplicit sex scenes. A few fairly disturbing violent scenes, too, but none of them even comes close to the things that Herschell Gordon Lewis was doing in the early Sixties. It's really not that big of a deal. And then the American distributors filmed a brief sequence in New York City, in somebody's *apartment,* that has none of the same people and is almost entirely unrelated to the rest of the movie. In this sequence, an actress is supposedly killed onscreen. But anyone with any brains who's seen this movie can tell that it's not only faked, but *badly* faked. You can tell there's an actress with her head through a hole in the table, with a fake body with probably some animal guts, and the people hold 'em up to the camera, you know? That's shocking, if you've never seen something like that before. But it's not convincing, and it doesn't make it a real snuff movie."

Well, so women aren't actually being carved up for the cameras in these movies—nevertheless, what could be going on in the minds of the men who make them? What, one wonders, does Herschell Gordon Lewis have to say for himself these days?

At fifty-seven, Lewis is the granddaddy of gore. Back in the early Sixties, when the cycle of softcore nudie exploitation films pioneered by Russ Meyer was coming to an end, Lewis, a former teacher and freelance filmmaker who did government films, industrials and occasional nudies himself, was in Florida doing an inconsequential contract film and decided to use the cast and crew he was working with to make a commercial exploitation movie of his own. He needed a subject that the major studios wouldn't touch, and, with his producer, David Friedman, he decided to do the first hardcore gore movie. The result, *The Blood Feast,* made for less than $30,000 and released in 1963, was a boundary-breaking sensation. Lewis went beyond merely poking his characters with spears: in *The Blood Feast,* tongues are slashed out, brains splatter and limbs are hacked off in blood-drenched color. More than twenty years later, many people still can't stand to look at it.

"We catered to a certain category of anticipation," says Lewis, who now lives near Fort Lauderdale. "Not taste—there is no such thing as taste in this kind of film. Just an anticipation. And we *satisfied* that anticipation. Nobody who wanted to see that kind of film felt cheated. We made *The Blood Feast* almost as a specialty film, for the sort of people who go to a midnight show on Halloween."

Lewis is contemptuous of charges that in *The Blood Feast* and the later *Two Thousand Maniacs* he glorified violence against women.

"'Socially redeeming value' is a legal term that has been superimposed on this industry by people who want to censor films," says Lewis. "Our films were designed to entertain in a true Aristotelian fashion. When that guy cuts off the thumb in *Two Thousand Maniacs,* people leap out of their *seats.* Yes, we mutilated women, but we didn't degrade them. Nor was there any applause for the people who did it. I mutilated women in our pictures because I felt it was better box office. If that group of fanatics [Women against Pornography] would promise to go see a movie if I disemboweled a man, I'd do it. There is nothing more deleterious to the civilized society in which we live than dogmatic morality."

So maybe he's not a misogynist. As Bill Landis says, "The whole point of Lewis' movies is that he hates *people.*"

Michael Weldon isn't inclined to be overly judgmental about blood and guts either, or about the depiction of women in so many S&M-tinged trash epics.

"Sure, some of it's morally objectionable," he says. "It's real sick, no doubt about it: indefensible, deplorable—but often entertaining. What can I say? It's a real personal thing. Some splatter movies can be interesting and mindless at the same time. I've always thought they're a really good release of aggression and pent-up hostilities. Anyway, people can complain about them till they're blue in the face, but it's not gonna stop their popularity."

The slasher cycle may soon come to a natural end, though. "We've almost seen it all," says Weldon. "People are gonna get bored."

I was thinking about this as Landis and I made our way

down the Deuce that rainy night. Goodbye, Forty-second Street? Goodbye, gore and depravity? Then we looked up into the teeming sky, at a billboard perched high above the strip. Screaming letters, eye-popping art—a new attraction, due next week: *Trap Them and Kill Them*! Sleaze springs eternal!

Coming soon to a trash pit near you.

Sixteen

The Story of Blondie

(1986)

Written in 1986, this is one of those pieces that was not published—in part because I became bogged down in over-researching it, in part because Rockbird, *the Deborah Harry album that occasioned its assignment, expired pretty much upon release. A similar fate awaited her end-of-the-decade follow-up,* Def, Dumb and Blonde. *But Debbie remains an instantly recognizable pop icon, and an emblem of one of New York's greatest scenes. She and Chris Stein toured with some fellow CBGB alumni (including the Ramones) in the summer of 1990, and they are still very much together—no small accomplishment in itself, and one that more consistently successful stars might well envy.*

On the sidewalk outside of CBGB, a cluster of punks in full ripped-leather regalia rubs grubby shoulders with the area's indigenous derelicts. It is early in the day, but already a few of the local homeless have collapsed in discrete heaps along the street, composing a familiar Bowery tableau. Grunge blossoms unconquerably in every concrete cranny; a faint tang of sewage enlivens the sinuses. All these years later, and nothing has changed.

The inside of CBGB is like some hyperrealist museum installation on the theme of Urban Squalor. The same dank walls, the same beer-logged planking underfoot; the dead air, the dump-truck decor, the merciful lack of light—all is exactly as it was. Low-cal wine coolers are proffered at the long wooden bar now, and three different brands of non-beer—a nod to the abstemious Eighties. But essentially, CB's is still the same lovable scum-pit in which bands like Television, Blondie, the Ramones and the Talking Heads helped launch a pop revolution, of a sort, back in 1975. And on Sunday afternoons such as this, when the club's weekly "hardcore matinees" draw the latest crop of leather-clad kids down to the Lower East Side to jitter and twitch to the latest loud-and-fast combos, the years seem almost to melt away. There are more mohawks now, maybe, and the T-shirts champion different bands—Motorhead, CroMags, Suicidal Tendencies. But there's the same cramped stage down at the end of the alley-shaped room, and huddled upon it at this particular moment, a group of spindly youths affecting the still-fashionable chewed-by-wild-dingos look of a decade ago. A whip-thin guitarist is announcing the next song. It's called "Kill Your Family."

Deborah Harry, her pale, inscrutable face glimmering like some gorgeous anemone in the ambient murk, doesn't bat an eye. Glib nihilism is the oldest wheeze in the boho game, an easy pose for those upon whom life has yet to unload any real woe. Debbie, just back from several seasons in Hell herself, is unimpressed.

She is sitting unobtrusively with her partner, Chris Stein, at a table back near the bar, checking the scene. It's been years since Debbie and Chris last set foot in CB's. For a while, back around the dawn of the Eighties, they had been too busy topping the charts and touring the world with Blondie, the band they put together on these very premises. Life was rich then: In the course of just two years, from 1979 to 1981, Blondie lobbed six singles into the pop Top Thirty. Four of them went to Number One. Blondie albums—*Parallel Lines, Eat to the Beat, Autoamerican*—sold in the multimillions.

Then came the payback. Blondie's seventh album stiffed, and in the midst of an ill-starred 1982 tour designed to support it, the group fell apart. At the same time, Chris came down with a rare and loathesome skin disease that left him looking like a special effect in a David Cronenberg movie. ("For a long time I looked like that guy in *The Fly*," he says.) He was out of commission for the better part of four years, unable even to walk, let alone work. Blondie loot, which had been considerable, quickly dwindled. Debbie and Chris lost their house, their savings, just about everything they had—except each other. Yes, this is a love story.

Bandless, Debbie might have pursued the solo career she had tentatively launched in 1981 with an album called *KooKoo*. She might have made more movies. But Chris' affliction was potentially fatal, and Debbie's devotion, after nine years by his side, was apparently total. She walked away from show business and committed herself entirely to nursing him back to health.

Now they are on the scene once more—starting anew, and not all that far from square one, but still together. This year, they celebrate the thirteenth anniversary of their first encounter—that mist-tinged moment when their hearts first thrummed in unison across a crowded downtown barroom (or however else one might care to imagine the scene). Chris' hair is raked with gray now, but he's back on his feet, at least. He's even developed a lively interest in hardcore, as the punk rock of the Eighties is called. In fact, that's what brought him and Debbie back to CBGB this afternoon.

"Hardcore reminds me of the Ramones," Debbie says, as the band onstage concludes its set with a familiar seismic thwang. "Remember that chord?"

A gumcracking grin, seldom captured by cameras, lights up her face, and her green eyes glitter impishly behind a half-parted curtain of appealingly disheveled blond hair. Up onstage, the next band of the afternoon is arraying its guitar artillery. "DRI," they're called—short for Dirty Rotten Imbeciles. Too predictable. Debbie and Chris are out the door before the din begins.

"We don't do everything for money," Debbie had told Stanley Arkin when they first started working together. "You've got to understand that."

Arkin, who is now Debbie and Chris' manager, understood. He'd already made plenty of money as a top New York corporate lawyer. Now he felt free to follow his more elevated interests without having to calculate mere financial profit. Two years ago, when Debbie and Chris were pretty much on the rocks—their income eviscerated, Chris' medical bills pouring in, the IRS demanding payment of massive back taxes—Arkin was recommended to them by a mutual art-scene acquaintance. Arkin liked Debbie immediately—"She struck me as a woman of powerful poetry," he says—and agreed to help straighten out the couple's tangled business affairs, to get their career back on track.

They say he was a godsend. First, he oversaw the sale of the building they were living in up on 72nd Street—a pricey piece of real estate they'd bought in better days—and utilized the proceeds to negotiate an agreement with the IRS. He stabilized what cash flow there was and became their personal bursar, dispensing incidental funds to them as necessary. He renegotiated Debbie's still-extant contract with Chrysalis Records, the label that released most of the Blondie albums as well as Debbie's *KooKoo,* and managed to get all future Harry products in North America transferred to Geffen Records. The result: a new solo album—a comeback, she hopes—called *Rockbird.*

In addition, Debbie signed to CAA, the hottest talent agency in the country. She resumed the intermittent movie career that she'd begun in New York underground films back in the Seventies, and had pursued through such diverse flicks as *Roadie, Union City* and, most memorably, David Cronenberg's 1983 fantasy classic, *Videodrome.* She plays the elusive title character (opposite Hannah Schygulla) in Israeli director Amos Kollek's forthcoming cocaine-caper film, *Forever Lulu.* On a more modest level, she also stars in "The Moth," an upcoming episode of *Tales from the Darkside,* horror director George Romero's syndicated TV series.

So things are looking up, as Debbie happily acknowledged one day during a visit to Arkin's East Side offices. Still sporting the gray sweats and running shoes she wears to her regular workouts these days, she looked radiant—no lipstick, as usual, just a touch of blue at the eyes, crinkling with her occasional wisecracks into that unexpected smile. She had put on some weight during the years of Chris' illness, and while she liked the fact that the extra poundage added heft to her voice as well, she knew it would have to come off if she intended to tour again, which she does—with a real band again, too, she hopes.

"The idea of going out and doing the Debbie Harry Show with a bunch of really great musicians could be fun," she said. "But I'm basically a band kind of person. I mean, I didn't come into this business as a solo artist. I came in with a *band.*"

*   *   *

Blondie was more than just Debbie and Chris, but their relationship is all that remains of it. A dozen years ago, Blondie seemed the unlikeliest of punk candidates for mainstream success—as unlikely as the oddly matched couple at the core of the group. Debbie was a Polish-blooded blonde from the Jersey 'burbs; Chris, five years her junior, the city-bred son of classic Jewish lefties.

She was born on July 1, 1945, in Miami, Florida, to an unknown woman who gave her up for adoption. She was taken in by Richard and Catherine Harry, who named her Deborah Ann and raised her, along with a subsequent sister, in tranquil Hawthorne, New Jersey. There, she grew up feeling arty and out of it—longed to be a painter, wore a lot of black, that sort of thing. She dabbed early in the mysteries of hair-bleaching, discovered both pot and sex at age sixteen, and by 1965—after giving higher-ed a two-year shot—she decamped for Manhattan, the Mecca of boho authenticity. There she hung out at jazz clubs like the Five Spot and the Dom, and began singing with various little nothing groups, one of which included an escaped convict among its members. She worked in a headshop, went to concerts by the Doors, the Velvet Underground, Jimi Hendrix, and by 1967 had joined the Wind in the Willows, a limp folk-rock octet, which recorded two albums for Capitol, only one of which was released. It went nowhere.

In 1968 and 1969, she worked at Max's Kansas City, the hippest nightspot in town ("Ragni and Rado wrote *Hair* in the back room there," Debbie notes). Max's was a carnival of twisted hipness. She saw the Jefferson Airplane there. She saw Alice Cooper. She saw a guy in a bad wig named Andy Warhol.

By 1969, she had begun a nine-month stint as a Playboy bunny. In August of that year, she went to Woodstock, and sat in the mud along with half a million of her peers—one of whom, although she didn't know it at the time, was Chris Stein.

Like other hippies of the period, Debbie cultivated an interest in drugs, and it led her to heroin. This was hardly a luminous episode in her life, but she feels it's been overplayed—a flirtation, more than anything else. "I think you outgrow these things if you're lucky," she muses. "If you *live* through them."

Around that same time, Chris Stein was, in vintage Sixties fashion, flipping out. Chris was born in Harlem Hospital on January 5, 1950, and raised in Brooklyn. His father was a labor organizer in the Thirties; his mother was a window dresser and a painter. They bought him a guitar in 1962, and before long he was into folk music, traipsing into Manhattan to play in folkie-infested Washington Square Park. "But when the Beatles came out," he says, "I went the route that everybody else did."

Chris' father died in 1965, and he began to drift. He played very briefly—once in a barber shop—with a group called the Morticians, which subsequently evolved into the Left Banke, a band that had a 1966 hit with "Walk Away, Renee." In the middle of his junior year at Brooklyn's Midwood High School, he was expelled for having long hair. ("I hated fucking high school with a passion," he says.) He finished off at an inexpensive private school in Manhattan, then proceeded, in 1967, to the School of Visual Arts, where he studied painting and photography. But not for long.

When he was nineteen, Chris explains, "I sorta went nuts—from taking too much acid, and as a sort of delayed reaction to my father's death. It was just the general sort of adolescent craziness that everybody goes through, but I wound up going to Beth Israel Hospital for a couple of months, which was the standard procedure at the time."

Chris' mental muddle got him out of the draft and onto welfare—"I had credentials!"—and also enabled him to acquire a welfare apartment on First Street and First Avenue on the Lower East Side.

By 1972, a new craze was sweeping the downtown scene—glitter rock. Chief among its proponents was a group called the New York Dolls. With their campy makeup, tatty boas and clattering Stones-styled music, the Dolls—holding forth at such venues as the Mercer Arts Center and the Club 82—united the New York rock scene in an exciting new way. Judging by how *they* went about being a rock band, it really did seem as if anybody could do it. All that was required, apparently, was passion and attitude . . . and maybe a few truckloads of illicit stimulants. Before he actually saw the band, Chris says, "I thought they were a drag act. But they were really oriented toward girls. They were almost like the Stones with no audience."

Debbie, by this point, was a rabid Dolls fan herself ("I was almost a groupie!"), and in fact dated the band's lead singer, David Johansen. Marty Thau, who became the Dolls' manager that summer, remembers first meeting her.

"I was married then, and had a house upstate," Thau recalls. "So I invited them up one summer day, and they arrived in Debbie's Camaro. Debbie was so spectacularly beautiful, I did a double-take when I saw her. It was embarrassing—my wife was standing right next to me. Unbeknownst to me, they had all taken mescalin—well, maybe not Debbie, but some of the Dolls had. It was a great day."

By 1973, Chris had dropped out of school, just shy of graduation, and was playing guitar with a group called the Magic Tramps. Debbie was living in Jersey again, working at a beauty parlor in some godforsaken mall by day and rehearsing by night with a trash-rock girl trio called the Stilettoes, which she fronted with two other singers, Elda Gentile and Rosie Ross. The Stilettoes played their first gig—standing on a platform atop a pool table—at a bar on 24th Street called the Boburn Tavern. It was late September 1973. On the group's second night there, Chris Stein showed up, heavily into his high-heels-and-makeup glitter period, brought along by Elda's boyfriend, a singer named Eric Emerson. As Debbie later recalled: "We had a psychic connection right away. I couldn't see his face, only the outline of his head in the audience, but I could feel him looking at me . . . I delivered a lot of songs to him."

"I thought Debbie was amazing," Chris recalls. "She had short brown hair, her natual color, in a crewcut almost. I was totally taken with her, and did the best I could to win her over."

Chris quickly insinuated himself into the trio's backup group. Neither he nor Debbie was meaningfully involved with anyone else at the time ("Debbie had this boyfriend who used to chase her around with a shotgun," Chris recalls, "but she basically was single"), and within a few months they were an item. Dee Dee Ramone, whose own band, the Ramones, was just taking shape around then, remembers seeing Debbie for the first time at the Club 82. "She was with Chris," Dee Dee says, "but I couldn't tell if he was her boyfriend or not, you know? They were very mysterious. So I was tryin' to put the make on her. We danced a few times, but then she put somethin' into my drink. I remember babbling 'I'm crazy about you' or 'Gimme your number' or something—and then I passed out under the table. When I woke up the next morning, they were sweeping the floor, and they grabbed me by the cuff of my coat and threw me out the door.

Chris soon moved Debbie and her three cats out of New

Jersey and into an apartment on Thompson Street, in what is now SoHo. Chris and Debbie began writing songs—"In the Flesh," which would later become Blondie's first hit single, was a product of the Stilettoes period—and the group started drawing notice. Money was another thing: none of the new bands sprouting up was seeing much cash. Two of the Ramones—Dee Dee and drummer Tommy Erdlyi—rented quarters in Chris' welfare suite on First Avenue for a while, and Dee Dee remembers times frequently being tight. "Tommy would buy a potato and a hamburger patty every day, and cook that—that was all he had," says the bassist. "With my money, I would buy a bottle of brandy."

"Everybody just did it to be doing it," Debbie says. "There was no money involved, but it was really fun. There was a sort of community atmosphere."

The Stilettoes' band lineup solidified into Chris on guitar, Fred Smith on bass and Billy O'Conner on drums. One day, Elda Gentile was approached by Terry Ork, a scenester who wrote for Warhol's *Interview* magazine. Ork was managing a new band called Television, fronted by two private-school rejects, Tom Verlaine and Richard Hell. Television was playing Sundays at a derelict bar on the Bowery called CBGB, and they needed an opening act. Would the Stilettoes be interested?

CBGB was the brainchild of a music nut and self-described "Jersey farm boy" named Hilly Kristal—a furniture-mover by day and a club entrepreneur in his every spare moment. He had started out in the late Fifties managing the Village Vanguard, a celebrated jazz club—this was back in the days when Woody Allen still did standup, and Eric Dolphy still played with John Coltrane. Hilly also sang in stage shows at Radio City Music Hall. In 1969, he bought a wino dive at 315 Bowery and began promoting it as a jazz club for artists. This worked out pretty well, and he opened another club, a country-music place, on 13th Street. Unfortunately, with his attention thus divided, he was unable to adequately oversee the pot-smoking jazzbos at his Bowery locale. And so, in 1972, he closed the place down. He reopened it in December 1973, however, as CBGB & OMFUG—an ungainly acronym for Country, Blue Grass, Blues and Other Music from Under Ground. Television was one of the first young bands he booked. As he recalls, they were terrible. Their manager, Terry Ork, kept bringing in other bands to boost their appeal. The Stilettoes were but one.

The group quickly began falling apart. Essentially, Debbie and Chris departed, taking the band with them and leaving Elda high and dry. For a very brief period, they operated as Angel and the Snake. Then Blondie and the Banzai Babies. "Blondie" was Debbie's idea. "I would walk down Houston Street," she says, "and all these truck drivers were always yelling out, 'Hey, Blondie!' So I said, shit, that's great, you know? *Poi-fect!*"

By early 1975, Blondie and the Banzai Babies were in need of a new drummer. Chris placed an ad in the *Village Voice* and got an eighteen-year-old from Bayonne, New Jersey, called Clem Burke. Burke's first night with the group was a disaster. Between sets, bassist Fred Smith informed his bandmates that he was leaving the group to join Television. "Debbie was like in tears," Clem remembers. "We actually canceled the second night."

Fortunately, Clem had a replacement for Smith, a Jersey pal named Gary Valentine, whose only drawback, as Burke recalls, was that he "couldn't play at all." After auditioning with one of his own songs, on piano, Valentine was moved forthwith into Chris' Lower East Side commune. The addition of Clem and Gary to the group introduced a useful element of "crazy teenage energy." "I was like twenty-five," Chris says, "and Debbie was a little older. We had been around. So this was a whole new dimension. We hung around with them and all their friends—they had this whole crew of teenage miscreants from New Jersey, who were all pretty stoned. Several of them were carted off to the loony bin."

By the spring of 1975, the band was simply called Blondie. No one took them very seriously. There was something going on on the Lower East Side—something to do with back-to-basics music and a sort of sartorial recession-chic that maybe reflected the oil shortages and general economic recession of the mid-Seventies.

"The whole glitter scene, like at the Club 82, was dying down," Debbie says, "and there was this other thing happening. Everybody that was wearing glitter was also wearing ripped-up stuff. It wasn't focused yet, like 'new wave' or 'punk rock.' I think everybody regarded it as something that was *theirs,* you know? It wasn't just another business."

To the artier participants in this scene, Blondie seemed only incidentally a part of it. One of the group's modest number of admirers was Alan Betrock, who ran a record-collectors'

magazine called *Rock Marketplace,* for which he also wrote articles about Sixties rock and pop. Blondie was right up Betrock's
alley, and he became, on a very informal basis, their manager.
"I was just trying to get them gigs and press," Betrock says. "At
the time, they were really untogether as a live group. They
didn't have the right equipment, they'd change members, they'd
break guitar strings and have nothing to replace them with. I
thought they'd come across better on record, 'cause it was kind
of a disaster live."

That spring, Betrock took Blondie into a pathetic little
eight-track studio in somebody's basement in Queens and
cut five of the band's songs—one cover (of the Shangri-Las'
"Out in the Streets") and four originals: "Puerto Rico," "Plati-
num Blonde," "Thin Line" and a number called "The Disco
Song."

"We did it in one day," Betrock says. "I brought the tape
around to a couple of people, but at that time, no one was interested in new music at all. I'd say, 'Her voice is really original,'
and they'd say, 'Oh, she can't sing,' or, 'The songs aren't good,'
or, 'What *is* this?' I got kind of discouraged."

The nascent punk scene was gathering steam, though.
The Talking Heads appeared, and in the summer of 1975, CB's
put on a month-long "Festival of Unrecorded Rock & Roll
Bands" that drew even mainstream media coverage. Patti
Smith became the first of the "punk" artists to release an album on a major label. And Malcolm McLaren, a British
cultural entrepreneur who briefly managed the now-floundering
New York Dolls in the wake of their two commercially disastrous albums, became so inspired by the ripped-to-shreds artistic milieu of the downtown bands that he rigged up his own
version of such a group—the Sex Pistols—in London before
the year was out.

As for Blondie: "They drew the least," says Martin Rev
of Suicide, another pioneering group of the period. "And they
got the hardest time from the club owners and the booking people, because they were fronted by a girl. They used to tell Debbie, 'Why don't you go home and cook dinner?' Stuff like that,
you know? Because guy bands would draw girls, and the girls
would bring their boyfriends, so there'd be a bigger crowd. A
band with a girl leader wasn't gonna bring the girls as much. So
Blondie didn't seem to be creating much excitement on a local
level. But ironically, they became the biggest of them all as soon

as they started making records. I guess people needed something they could relate to in punk, something they could understand, as opposed to the stuff they felt scared of."

By the end of 1975, Blondie had rounded out its lineup
with a keyboard player: Jimmy Destri, a Brooklyn kid who,
like Chris, had attended the School of Visual Arts. Destri's instrument was a Farfisa—the greatest of all garage-band organs.
After one rehearsal with the Blondies, he was signed aboard
and invited to chip in to rent a loft at 266 Bowery, across the
street from CBGB's, where the band would live. "The commitment to join Blondie was: 'Are you willing to spend money?'"
Destri recalls with a laugh. "I was the only one working at the
time."

With the group complete at last, Clem Burke departed
for a few months in the winter of 1976 to visit a girlfriend in
London and to check out the scene there. The Blondies were
urged to practice and tighten up in his absence. Whether or not
they achieved this is in some dispute.

"Chris and the other guys in the band were kind of
crazy," says Hilly Kristal. "They didn't care about how they
played. They were raw, but not raw like Television was raw, and
got better and better. Blondie didn't get better until they started
to record. They started caring, I guess. But Debbie always had a
nice sound to her voice, and her lyrics were interesting—not
punk, but kinda punky. They were about what she felt, her way
of life. And she had—whether she likes to hear it or not—the
most magnificent face. The group had a certain flavor, and with
her voice, and that face, you knew they had to make it.

"Everybody was very proud of her," Hilly says. "I don't
know if she ever knew that, but we always were quite happy
about what they did."

The turning point for Blondie came one night in 1976 when they
encountered producer Richard Gottehrer at CBGB. Gottehrer
had been a founding partner in Sire Records, a label that had
just released the first Ramones album. Now hooked up with
Marty Thau, the former Dolls manager, and Craig Leon (who'd
produced the Ramones' LP), Gottehrer had formed a small production company called Instant Records, and was looking for
some groups to produce. Gottehrer had had hits in the Sixties
with the Angels, the McCoys and with his own group, the
Strangeloves, and he related strongly to the new punk sound.

His initial idea was to do a compilation album featuring several of the CBGB bands. Then he met Debbie.

"She said, 'Can we be on your album?'" Gottehrer recalls. "I had seen them maybe six months before, and I really hadn't thought they were very good. But I went to one of their rehearsals, and by the time I left, I was converted. It was absolutely amazing. I mean, their ideas were *far* ahead of their ability to execute them, but they were just *great.* Their sense of humor was fantastic, the songs were fantastic. Oh, I know it was Debbie . . . but it was *all* of them, you know? They all had something *together.*"

Gottehrer decided to cut a single with Blondie first: a song called "Sex Offender," written by Gary Valentine (who also played surf guitar on the track) and Debbie; the flip would be "In the Sun," a Chris Stein composition. The single was offered to Private Stock, a small, disco-oriented record company whose president, Larry Uttal, liked the record but balked at releasing a song called "Sex Offender." Gottehrer's wife, Judy, suggested altering the title to "X Offender," and the deal was struck.

"X Offender," with Destri's careening, roller-rink Farfisa, was a fabulous single. It did nothing commercially, but created enough of a stir on the scene that Private Stock agreed to shell out for a full Blondie album. This debut LP, *Blondie,* was released late in 1976, and while it made not a ripple in the U.S. pop charts, it created a sensation among those predisposed toward inventive, garage-style rock & roll—both here and, especially, abroad. There were songs about boy-girl love and beaches and monster movies; there was Destri's squealing Farfisa (bolstered with synthesizers now) and Clem's world-class pummeling. The lyrics were big-city smart, the melodies fresh and captivating. And Debbie, fronting the group in the cover shot, seemed a perfect punk angel. One track off the album, "In the Flesh" (Chris and Debbie's haunting ballad from their Stilettoes days), went to Number One in Australia—an early indication that foreign markets were where the new musical action was.

Blondie hired a manager—Peter Leeds, who'd managed Wind in the Willows. Leeds decided the first thing that had to be done was to get the band onto a more internationally oriented label. He raised $500,000 to buy them away from Private Stock and Gottehrer (to whom they were signed through Instant Records), and place them with Chrysalis. They played L.A., where everyone was still wearing bell-bottoms and flowered shirts. They went on a low-budget, five-month world tour—Europe, Asia, Australia.

"We were always fighting," Debbie says. "Me and Chris were together, but the guys were young, and everybody was always smashing or throwing things, going crazy because they wanted to go home."

They toured the States with Iggy Pop and David Bowie, who had heard their album in Berlin and loved it. The punk scene was exploding. In New York, Debbie was all over the pages of *New York Rocker,* Alan Betrock's latest enterprise. She was also a familiar face in *Punk* magazine, another new periodical. A big breakthrough seemed imminent.

Gottehrer produced one more album for Blondie, the half-great 1978 LP, *Plastic Letters.* It spawned the group's biggest European hit to that point, "Denis," a clever reworking of a 1963 single by Randy and the Rainbows. But strains within the group were already becoming apparent. Gary Valentine "made the mistake of telling us that he was gonna leave the group after we recorded the second album," Clem Burke says. Not surprisingly, Valentine was asked instead to leave forthwith. (According to Gottehrer, Valentine, a fine songwriter, didn't fit in with the group's live show: "He used to jump around onstage, pogo-style. It upset Debbie's routine, and it also put the synthesizers out of tune.")

To record *Plastic Letters,* Clem brought in another of his New Jersey pals, Frank Infante, to take up bass-and-guitar slack in the studio. "It seemed like I spent half my time either trying to keep certain people in the group or trying to convince Debbie and Chris to get other ones in," says Burke. "Somebody was always on the outs with somebody else."

Gottehrer, for his part, was essentially content to move along—he was already working with another of his punk-scene protégés, singer Robert Gordon. But he felt he'd accomplished something pure with Blondie, and he would miss it. "I got paid a substantial amount of money for my interest in their contract," he acknowledges. "My wife and I had just had a baby, and the money came in handy. But when I got home with the check that night, we both stayed up and cried about it, you know? That that period had come to an end."

Gottehrer's place was taken by Michael Chapman, a

onetime glitter-rock producer who'd already scored other hits for Chrysalis. Chapman had loved Blondie ever since he first saw them playing at the Whiskey in L.A. So had Nigel Harrison, a bassist then working with ex-Door Ray Manzarek's band, Night City. Harrison, an Englishman who in his own youth had actually seen the Beatles play the Cavern Club, was recruited to finally replace Gary Valentine. Chapman took the augmented band into the studio and got them a number-one record right out of the box. "Heart of Glass"—"The Disco Song," which they'd first recorded with Betrock in a basement in Queens four years earlier—topped the charts early in 1979, and was followed by another Top Thirty hit off the LP, "One Way or Another." Blondie had made it.

For two years, the hits kept coming: "Dreaming," "Call Me," "The Tide Is High," "Rapture." By 1981, they had amassed enough smashes to put out a greatest-hits album. That same year, Debbie released *KooKoo,* her solo debut and an augury of the band's end.

"The record company didn't want me to go solo," Debbie says. "They didn't push the record—as a matter of fact, they buried it. So when that happened, I thought, 'I can't be this "Blondie" anymore.' It was, like, *long enough,* already. Bowie couldn't be Ziggy forever, you know?"

With *The Hunter,* Blondie's 1982 offering, "We knew we were making the last Blondie album," says Chapman. "We were all at each other's throats. The entire relationship between each member of the band was breaking down. Personalities were changing, people were growing up, moving in different directions. It was a very depressing time for all of us. And then to see Blondie finally die was almost unbelievable.

"Island of Lost Souls," the first single off *The Hunter,* barely scraped into the Top Forty. Nevertheless, an elaborate world tour had been booked—complete with horns and other hired studio hands. Since Blondie hadn't toured in two and a half years, rehearsals would be essential. But Chris, who was suddenly having trouble breathing, would not be attending them.

"We thought he had asthma at first," Debbie says. "So he didn't go to any of the rehearsals for that tour. And everybody in the band sort of got . . . well, the people that could handle it were cool and supportive, and the ones that couldn't handle it, couldn't handle it. It was like, *This is the situation,* you know?

Either you're supportive and we do it, or you're not supportive and we don't. And it didn't work out.

"We were in a really great place," she reflects. "But it wasn't a cooperative effort anymore. There was this fear and paranoia. The band had just become so *valuable*—like, beyond a couple of the members' wildest dreams. They couldn't really handle it."

The 1982 tour, which started off in the States, was a disaster. The concert market was soft, the group's album wasn't doing well, they were overbooked. Oxygen tanks had to be brought along for Chris, whose breathing problems were getting worse, and who had also lost an alarming amount of weight, due to a mysterious and increasing painfulness in his throat. The group made it as far as Philadelphia's John F. Kennedy Stadium, and collapsed.

"It was a horrible gig," Clem Burke remembers. "A miserable day."

"We'd see Chris come offstage and go directly to oxygen," Jimmy Destri recalls. "He just couldn't do it anymore."

"It's funny to meet people who say, 'What the fuck happened?'" Burke says. "There were a lot of weird management things that happened. And I think our whole success was just like a progression of coincidences and mistakes—Jimmy's havin' a Farfisa organ was just a mistake. So we were never big on makin' decisions. I'd say that was one of the big reasons the band broke up, because no one was really business-minded. Maybe we were too much of a leftover of the Sixties ideology. In the Eighties, *all* things are businesses."

Chris Stein is lying across a double bed surrounded by a squadron of fuzzy stuffed creatures, souvenirs accumulated over the course of his and Debbie's career. There's Antonio the ant, Minkey the monkey, a rock lobster, a cuddly bat, a pet sushi from Japan. Chris chucks them about affectionately. Debbie is in L.A., and the bedroom is in bohemian disarray, as is the rest of their apartment—actually, the rented upper level of a Chelsea townhouse owned by Michael Keaton, the actor, who lives below. "I recommend that *everybody* come close to death," Chris says, dismissing the clutter. "You don't worry about anything after that."

When Blondie's 1982 tour stumbled to a halt in Philadelphia, forcing cancellation of all overseas dates, the band simply dissolved. ("It was like, 'I'll call you when we've got something to do,'" says Destri. "But we never called each other.") By February 1983, Chris was interned in New York's Lenox Hill Hospital, where his worsening illness was finally diagnosed as pemphigus vulgaris, one of the rarest and most debilitating of skin diseases.

Typically, pemphigus begins in the throat and mouth, as it had with Chris. The victim becomes unable to eat, loses weight, teeth begin to rot. As pemphigus spreads through the body, the epidermal layer of skin loses its cohesion—it can be sloughed off in sheets—and the skin ceases to act as a barrier against infection. Pemphigus is not contagious, but its cause remains unknown, and up until the mid-Fifties, when steroids were discovered to be an effective therapy, the disease was almost always fatal.

"I was completely hallucinogenic in the hospital," Chris says. "They had me on really high doses of steroids, and you get sort of psychotic. I was totally out-there. There was even one night when I barely knew who Debbie was. She was there watching over me, and I knew we were vaguely connected, but I wasn't quite sure how. I was completely out of it for a week, and then I came to my senses."

Debbie slept on a cot in Chris' hospital room. What few visitors they encouraged had to wear masks and gloves to avoid infecting him. It was a scary period. At one point, Chris had to submit to a bone-marrow tap—"I mean, they drill into your *bone,*" he says, wincing. "That was fuckin' horrendous." When he was finally released three months later, his skin was a ripped, blistery mess and his weight, thanks to the steroids, had ballooned to 200 pounds.

"I was very lethargic—sluggish and spaced-out—for quite a while," he says. "It was like being in a sort of gray mist. My skin was all open, so I had to stay in the house. I was totally bedridden. My muscles all atrophied. Debbie did everything. She gave up everything else and just took care of me. It really blows your mind when somebody actually does that. She was fantastic."

Chris has only been fully mobile since May. He's taking low, maintenance doses of the steroids now, and hopes to be off them altogether soon. He's been getting around a bit. In fact, he just got back from Lawrence, Kansas, where he visited William Burroughs, the writer, an old Bowery neighbor. (Both men are weapons freaks: old Bill's into guns and Chris collects exotic cutlery—antique martial-arts swords, mainly. There are dozens of them scattered around the apartment.)

There's even a hardcore scene in Lawrence, Chris says. It's young and fresh and unaffected—just like CBGB's in the old days. How far away they seem. David Johansen does a cabaret character called Buster Poindexter on *Saturday Night Live* now, and Robert Gordon does Budweiser commercials. Television is gone, and Fred Smith, the bassist, now plays with a country-rock group called Kristi Rose and the Midnight Walkers. Jimmy Destri says it took him "maybe two and a half years just to wake up" after Blondie; but he's back now, and producing a new group himself. As for Gary Valentine, Chris says he saw him in L.A. not long ago—says he's managing a video store, working toward a degree in philosohy, and has "no interest in pop culture." How times change. Chris already misses the prairie punks of Kansas.

"All I wanna do now," he says dreamily, "is play in a hardcore band."

"Chris is a fascinating person, you know? He really is. He's so intelligent, so interested in so many things. It's really cool."

Debbie is attempting, unsuccessfully, to catalog the attractions that have led to such a lengthy relationship. A song on *Rockbird,* is perhaps more eloquent. It's called "Secret Life," and describes two lovers, their "lives entwined like vines, man and wife . . . still the same two parallel lines":

> We come together
> Our story's told as one
> We come together
> After all is said and done

"I think that having success together really made it easy for Chris and me," Debbie says. "A lot of relationships break up over money problems. And over ego problems. We sort of had our ego problems out of the way before any money came into the picture. We worked together for years before anything happened, and we did that because we enjoyed it."

Debbie and Chris have never formally married ("We like

to be able to call each other girlfriend and boyfriend," as Chris puts it), but, yes, they have thought about children.

"They're better than pets," Debbie says with a chortle. "I mean, I had pets, and I was treating *them* like *people,* you know what I mean? Then I realized: These things have the brains of *squirrels.* They're never gonna get any *better.* Why not just have a child and stop fooling around?"

That smile again.

"People," she says, "get better."

Courtesy Michael Ochs Archives

SEVENTEEN
David Byrne, Brian Eno and Talking Heads
(1981)

*Talking Heads arose out of the clamorous
CBGB scene to become one of the biggest
experimentally inclined bands of the Eighties—a
status the group attained with considerable help from
producer and collaborator Brian Eno. At the time of
the story that follows, Eno and Heads leader David
Byrne had slipped off to concoct an album on their
own, leaving the rest of the band . . . kind of peeved.*

*The group rebounded, however; Byrne went on to
discover a new sideline in Brazilian music, and Eno
apparently made enough money producing U2 to
finance his own little English record label, Opal. We
surely haven't heard the last of any of them yet.*

Not all ghosts confine themselves to midnight moaning sessions
in abandoned mansions. Some are quite modern and speak
through their attorneys. Such is the style of Kathryn Kuhlman, a
noted radio evangelist recently returned to her sender. Kuhlman
is survived by her sermonettes, and David Byrne, leader of the
Talking Heads, heard one of these spectral addresses in Los Angeles early last year and taped it off the air. A person of Pres-
byterian reserve, Byrne was transfixed by Kuhlman's fervor. It

seemed the perfect vocal element for a record he was working on, so he went ahead and used it. Unfortunately, he failed to take into consideration Kathryn Kuhlman's estate, which retains a litigious life of its own. Approached some months later for permission to incorporate the sainted founder's taped declamations into what was faintly understood to be an avant-garde Afro-funk album called *My Life in the Bush of Ghosts*, the estate was not amused. Clearly, this Byrne fellow and his associate, a Mr. Eno, could only have an irreverent intent. Permission was then and forever denied.

Thus was one of the more fascinating musical projects of 1980 blown clear out of the water. By the time the Kuhlman estate's displeasure became known, Byrne and Brian Eno—the producer of three of the four Talking Heads albums—had already completed *My Life in the Bush of Ghosts*, their first independent collaboration. The album covers had been printed, and Kuhlman's posthumous contribution was duly credited on the sleeve, alongside a Lebanese mountain girl, whooping radio preachers and an unsuspecting Egyptian pop singer, Samira Tewfik. Each of these voices had been electronically stripped of its original context and set slithering through a dense thicket of peculiar percussive effects and wild, mimetic guitars. It was a strange and haunting record, and—in rebuke to some of the disembodied orthodoxies being spouted—quite danceable, too. But in September, after a stint of recording with the Talking Heads in the Bahamas, Byrne and Eno returned to New York and reluctantly removed Kuhlman's "vocal" from their album. Then, since they were in the studio anyway, they started tinkering and adding new material. The record's release date was pushed back six months (it's now due out in March).

In October, the new Talking Heads album, *Remain in Light*, preceded the Byrne-Eno LP into the marketplace. Radically influenced by the harmonic and compositional ideas developed on *Bush of Ghosts*, and with Eno listed for the first time as a full creative member, the album was a great hit. But it also raised certain questions. Would *Bush of Ghosts*—which Eno described as "a laboratory for the Talking Heads record"—be misperceived as a mere sequel? And in view of the fact that Byrne and Eno had virtually taken over Talking Heads for their own experimental purposes on *Remain in Light*, was the inscrutable Eno exerting a malign influence on Byrne, alienating him from the band? Rumors in New York and Los Angeles suggested that tensions within the group had been festering ever since the Nassau sessions. It was even said that the Heads might never record again.

The band did perform in the fall, both here and in Europe, but with a heavily augmented lineup that included former David Bowie guitarist Adrian Belew, Parliament-Funkadelic keyboardist Bernie Worrell, ex–LaBelle singer Nona Hendryx, bassist Busta Cherry Jones and percussionist Steven Scales. Byrne explained that this expanded aggregation was necessary in order to do justice to the Heads' complex new music, but fans wondered what was going on. Adding to the ambiguity of the situation was the absence of comment from the other three Talking Heads—bassist Tina Weymouth; her husband, drummer Chris Frantz; and keyboardist-guitarist Jerry Harrison. Weymouth briefly unburdened herself in the January issue of *The Face,* a new English music magazine, where her irritation with the Byrne-Eno infatuation was evident. "They're like two fourteen-year-old boys making an impression on each other," she said. "By the time they finished working together for three months, they were dressing like one another. It looked like they'd switched shoes. Eno was now wearing Thom McAn slip-ons. I can see them when they're eighty years old and all alone. There'll be David Bowie, David Byrne and Brian Eno, and they'll just talk to each other."

Eno is not unaware of the antipathies he's stirred up within Talking Heads. One night early in December, just before departing for his first trip to Africa (at the invitation of Ghana's Ministry of Culture), the thirty-two-year-old producer-composer sat sipping tea at a long table in his spacious New York loft and tried to explain his relationship to the group. A modest array of unexceptional stereo equipment lined one white wall, and there was a tidy stack of records: *Les Liturgies de l'Orient, Music of Bulgaria, Actual Voices of Ex-Slaves,* Parliament's *The Clones of Dr. Funkenstein.* . . . On a far couch were the central components of the "Eno sound," long in demand by the likes of David Bowie and Robert Fripp: two small Korg and Minimoog synthesizers, a black Fender bass and a Stratocaster tuned to an open chord. A Panasonic video camera pointed out the eleventh-floor window, and two upended TV sets stood side by side nearby, silently playing back the slowly darkening Manhattan skyline.

Eno explained that he had first been attracted to Talking

Heads after hearing their debut album, *Talking Heads: 77,* and realizing that they alone among the bands associated with the New York punk explosion retained a strong allegiance to the rhythmic conventions of black funk and soul. Yet there was something new happening, too—an angular, jangling intelligence behind the material that fascinated him. He signed on to produce the group's second album, *More Songs about Buildings and Food,* and stayed aboard for their third, *Fear of Music.* By then, he and Byrne had become intrigued by the possibilities of African music, and they came away from recording *Fear of Music* particularly excited about one track, the dense, tribal-sounding—and, for Talking Heads, quite uncharacteristic—"I Zimbra."

"That track was generated from a group improvisation," Eno said. "It was a step forward in a lot of ways. And we suddenly thought, 'This is really quite close to what we've been listening to.' We realized that we were nearly there, in some sense. It was an interesting piece, but it presented a real dilemma for the Talking Heads in that it was a new format for them. And I really wanted to encourage that."

With *Fear of Music* finished, Eno entered a New York studio in August 1979 and began recording with a large group of bassists and percussionists, including Chris Frantz. Byrne also played on those sessions, and some of the basic tracks on *Bush of Ghosts* date from that period. Eno took these tapes to Los Angeles a short while later. He wasn't sure whether this new material would amount to anything, but while staying at the Sunset Marquis, he encountered three members of the Tubes and, after playing the tracks for them, was greatly encouraged by their enthusiasm. "So I rung David up in New York and asked if he would be interested in coming to Los Angeles to do some work on a new record, which would be a collaboration between the two of us." Byrne arrived in L.A. in February 1980; the original version of *Bush of Ghosts* was finished (in San Francisco) by May.

Although several bassists and percussionists drift in and out of the album's eleven tracks, the bulk of the music was created by Byrne and Eno. A major marvel of *My Life in the Bush of Ghosts* is the way percussion and melody have been melded into a single, unifying force. Eno credits much of the album's thick, steamy percussion sound to engineer Dave Jerdan, another Talking Heads alumnus, who he says "had a real talent for making cardboard boxes sound great. We were using all sorts of weird ashtrays, film canisters, pipes, trash cans, lamp shades, pieces of the floor, anything that was around." Layering their "found" vocals over these exotic tracks—an exhortatory preacher on "Help Me Somebody," a group of Georgia Sea Island singers on "Moonlight in Glory," an unintelligible but superb Lebanese mountain singer named Dunya Yusin on "Regiment"—Byrne and Eno were able to create the most compelling example to date of what might truly be called one-world music.

Bush of Ghosts was completed just in time for the beginning of rehearsals for *Remain in Light*. By this time, however, Eno had no interest in producing the group again. "I wanted to do some work of my own, because I had been forming this idea—the African-psychedelic collision, or whatever—more and more strongly. And that was all I wanted to do. I wasn't interested in doing something that wasn't at the frontier of my ideas, if you see what I mean."

Eno said the Talking Heads still wanted him to participate, so as a compromise, he agreed to join them in the Bahamas as a musician and help work on the basic tracks. Once in Nassau, however, he became excited by the group's new approach. They had been rehearsing for three weeks with Byrne—fresh from the *Bush of Ghosts* sessions—and Eno noted that "they had been developing this groove-atmosphere style of work, rather than the traditional song format, and they had been working quite a lot in that direction. I thought, 'Yeah, this is really going somewhere interesting now.' And so I said, 'Well, as I've explained before, I've got strong ideas about what I want to do. What I think now is that you, too, share this idea. And if this is the direction the thing's going to go in, then I would be happy to produce.'"

That happiness was soon clouded by feelings of resentment as Eno and Byrne, writing almost all of the material, bent the rest of the band in their direction. "There was a sort of uneasy feeling about what exactly my role was," Eno admitted. "Things got pretty difficult at various times; there were all sorts of levels of *angst* going on. Some of them were for personality reasons, and others were for accidental reasons. But the group has been together six or seven years, and one of the things that affected *Remain in Light* a lot was this history of frictions within the group. And of course, they started manifesting themselves,

quite inappropriately, on this record, and they weren't particularly things that I wanted to deal with. But I had to.

"I had a number of feelings at the end of the Talking
Heads record," Eno concluded, running a hand through his
thinning blond hair. "One of them was elation—I mean, I
thought it was good. But the other was frustration. I felt, 'God,
it could have gone further.' Particularly in terms of vocalization.
To be honest, I really thought that if, at a certain point, I had
had those tracks and had carte blanche to write whatever I
wanted, songwise, over the top . . . I think that I could have
explored this intricate song form that I was getting into more
thoroughly. But I didn't feel comfortable about usurping the
compositional role any more than I had done already. So what
I'm doing next is stretching my wings in that direction."

As in Brian Eno's loft, a single table was the centerpiece of
David Byrne's sixth-floor walkup in lower Manhattan. On it was
a small glass of apple juice, a pack of low-tar cigarettes and a
book, *My Life in the Bush of Ghosts,* by Nigerian novelist Amos
Tutuola. Like the young protagonist in that tale, Byrne had ventured out beyond his native village—in his case, for the sake of
simile, the Talking Heads—and traveled extensively through the
mysterious musical bush, where he encountered all manner of
strange things. Whether or not he, like Tutuola's hero, will ever
return to the security of his village remains to be seen. It was a
January afternoon, and snow was floating down softly outside.
In a quiet, careful voice, Byrne tried to explain why he had become so obsessed with African modes of music, and why he was
so proud of what he and Eno had achieved on their album.

"There are a lot of similarities between music from West
Africa, the Yoruba area, and black music in the States," he said.
"For instance, it's just as important to know when *not* to play,
when to leave holes for the other players. In a lot of African
music, each individual's part has almost no meaning on its own,
and in many cases a musician physically couldn't play his part
without playing with other musicians. It would be like having
the guitar player on a Michael Jackson record or a Funkadelic
record just play his part—you'd have no idea what the song
sounded like.

The whole implication of that kind of playing is that a
group of people can do something together that they can't do
individually. And that they can achieve something that's much

greater than the sum of their individual parts. And I think that goes against the whole Protestant-capitalist sort of ethic here, this emphasis of individuality. You have to limit what you do and play less, but you get more in the end. And you get excitement as a result of that. The nature of the playing is that you give up a part of your ego, and if everyone's playing together and listening to one another, you get this sort of surge of—I don't know what you'd call it—psychic energy, or whatever. A real sort of spiritual, uplifting feeling. It's just thrilling. And it's not an experience, I think, that happens in rock music."

After experiencing these new sensations with the nine-member version of Talking Heads, Byrne did not seem inclined to return to the group's original quartet structure. "It's possible, but I think if we did that, we'd return playing together in a very different way. It wouldn't just be the four of us going back to being a rock band."

With two major albums finally completed, Byrne hopes to diversify his interests. He was involved in a video project with choreographer Toni Basil (an original member of L.A.'s Lockers dance troupe), and he has recently been approached about working with gamelan musicians on Bali.

It was apparent that Byrne intended to continue beating around in the bush of ethno-experimentation as long as there remained lessons to be learned from it. But if he sought a larger communality in this area of music, what was to become of the smaller but still vital community that is Talking Heads? Byrne thought about that for a moment. He really didn't seem to know the answer. "There is some dissension, on and off, but there is with every group. We'll probably start working again in the not-too-distant future, and we'll see what happens then." He crushed out his cigarette and took a sip of apple juice. Then, suddenly, he smiled. "I think we'll work out our differences," he decided. "Yeah, I think we'll keep going."

EIGHTEEN

Cyndi Lauper

(1984)

*Cyndi Lauper came on like a New York
cartoon, which blinded a lot of people to the power
and expressiveness of her inimitable pipes. Her
reinvention of the Robert Hazard song "Girls Just
Want to Have Fun" turned her into an overnight
video queen—and then, inevitably, into an
overexposed one. Her venture into movies (Vibes,
with Jeff Goldblum) was an experience that can best
be described as "educational." By the end of the
Eighties, her career seemed somewhat adrift, but if
her endearing talent doesn't pull her through, her
abundant resilience surely will.*

Even amid the exhilarating visuals of the Imperial Dragon, a
Manhattan restaurant squirreled away in the city's midtown
music-biz district, Cyndi Lauper is a riveting presence. The decor here, definitive of a style known to devotees as Screaming
Asiatic, elaborates upon vast paneled expanses of seething red-
and-gold dragons, with similar mythic reptiles writhing down
gilded pillars. Yet it might as well be Bauhaus the minute
Lauper walks in, sporting a look that would drop drawers at a
clown convention.

Tonight, she is turned out in blazing orange pants and a satin bomber jacket, under which she wears a white-beaded fringe vest pulled over an already assertive red-and-yellow shirt. Many bracelets ring her wrists, and pendulous earrings clatter about her lobes. Her eyes are shadowed with scarlet, the left lid divided by a bright gold stripe, and atop her head is a tartan cap—worn backward—from under which her hair erupts in a haystack of howling fuchsia. She pauses to survey the room, where seveal diners sit popeyed over their chopsticks. Not in shock, you understand, but in recognition. Acceptance. Some are even smiling. Lauper, for so long a laughingstock in both her personal and professional lives, is still not completely accustomed to such benign consideration.

"People used to *throw rocks* at me for my clothes," she says in her appealing Queens-side wheeze. "Now they wanna know where I *buy* them, right? Doesn't that seem *weird* to you?"

At the rustling of a kimono, she turns to greet a familiar waitress. Their conversation is brief but animated, and unpretentiously affectionate. Cyndi has friends everywhere. Many of them turn up in the videos with which she currently chronicles her existence. Few are of the standard glamour-puss variety, but she treasures them nonetheless.

"People are really somethin'," she says as we search for seats. "They're walking books, all of them. Sometimes you'll only meet them once, but you'll never forget them. So you try to enjoy them. That's why, even if you're in the ladies' room, you should always talk to the woman next to you. Even if you're in the stall, you can say, uh, *'Hey! No toilet paper! I guess it's drip-dry tonight!'"*

She's still yukking as we take a table. The manager—another pal—approaches. "Life," Cyndi says, before turning the full wattage of her winsomeness upon him, "is a great joy."

Her happiness becomes her. Although she considers herself something of an ugly duckling, she has the radiance of true talent and, nowadays, the beauty of that talent fulfilled. Not long ago, though, Lauper's life was nowhere near so swell. A long-struggling singer with one lone album to her credit—and that an expensive commercial flop—she had lost the band she'd dreamed of leading to pop stardom and had, in fact, been left without an official penny to her name. (In a dispute with the group's former manager, she'd felt compelled to declare bankruptcy in a New York court.) No one who'd heard her sing doubted the brilliance of her freakish, four-octave voice, and her songwriting ability was apparent even on the flop album. But less than two years ago, she was reduced to singing Little Peggy March tunes in a Japanese piano bar. She seemed a pop character without a context: a never-was, and edging toward thirty.

Then an astonishing thing happened—astonishing to everyone, that is, except Lauper and her circle of long-haul supporters. At the very nadir of her career, the dream finally came true. Her first solo album, *She's So Unusual,* turned into a platinum-bound Top Ten hit. And its first single, "Girls Just Want to Have Fun"—which went to Number Two and spawned a rollicking video that's made her an international celebrity—is now yielding to the bulleted followup "Time after Time." Suddenly, Cyndi Lauper, with her vivid New York yawp and Vegematic clothes sense, is the queen of the nation's TV screens: cracking up Johnny Carson on "The Tonight Show," trading Big Apple brays with Rodney Dangerfield at the Grammy Awards. And, of course, she's all over MTV, the music channel, which has used her as a kind of corporate mascot.

And there lies what even some admirers already see as a problem. With her professional pinnacle as a singer finally in sight, is Cyndi Lauper now being turned into a mere cartoon, another inflatable zany for the MTV/talk-show circuit? Is the mouth overshadowing the music? Will she soon be angled off toward Broadway—or, worse yet, Hollywood? In the end, might she really prove to be nothing more than a pop-rock novelty, a passer-through? Some of this speculation has not been without a certain amount of malice, typical in the biz.

Cyndi's heard this talk, of course. She knows who these people are. "They've always laughed at me," she says, toughening, reflexively. "People have always said I couldn't sing, always tried to label me. I ain't worried about them, because the minute I open my mouth and sing, I can blow them right offa their chairs. They can't take your talent away from ya. I am not a Broadway singer, and I am not a movie-TV person. I ain't into that shit. I'm no dummy. I'm not a puppet. And all the people that make fun of me, or call me a cartoon . . ."

She pauses to pour some hot sake from a porcelain flask, dismissing the subject with a sweet scowl. "They're talkin' outta their ass," she says.

* * *

Cyndi Lauper was born in a Queens hospital not far from her parents' home in the rough Williamsburg section of Brooklyn. Although Cyndi is sensitive to questions about her age—"What am I, a car?" is her standard riposte—an old band bio indicates her natal date to be June 20th, 1953. Her father was a shipping clerk, an unusual man. At home, his interests ranged from archaeology to playing the xylophone. Her mother had her hands full, tending Cynthia and her elder sister, Elen, and younger brother, Butch. Glittery Manhattan was just over the Williamsburg Bridge, but cultures away.

Cyndi's parents divorced when she was five, and her mother moved with the three kids to a neighborhood in Queens called Ozone Park. In the pantheon of New York City boroughs, Manhattan—the *real* New York—is to Queens as Hollywood is to the San Fernando Valley, or, perhaps more evocatively, as Fred Astaire is to Cheech and Chong.

At least, that's how Manhattanites see it. Or *hear* it: something about the way the typical Queens native talks, in a sort of throttled yowl that partakes equally of Arnold Stang and Francis the Talking Mule.

"My speaking voice," Cyndi admits, "is ridiculous."

Growing up in Ozone Park was—well, the name says it all. "Pretty spaced out," Cyndi quips. "I didn't belong there." She was tossed out of a local Catholic school—"because my mother was divorced," she says—and was subsequently sent to a convent type of Catholic boarding school in upstate New York. It was not a happy experience.

"That's when I realized that nuns and God could not have anything to do with each other," she says. "These women were trained by Nazis, I think. They were into torture; it was a torture chamber for kids. If you talked to a boy, they'd slap you as hard as they could in the face. I remember one time I scratched this girl's back in the middle of the night—I was, you know, nine, and she was twelve, and she asked me to scratch her back. A nun ran in, ripped me off her back, threw me against the lockers, beat the shit out of me and called me a lesbian. I didn't know what a lesbian was." Two decades later, she is still fuming.

"See," she says, "my mother didn't know about this stuff—you never think a nun is lying. It was all traditional: the church, the family, the government. And you know what I learned? Those are the three biggest oppressors of women that will ever come along."

So, at an early age, Cyndi decided that the straight life was "really bullshit. I withdrew, into music, records. I was different, and I was . . . you know, kids are cruel to each other. Now," she says, toughening again, "it doesn't bother me. I don't give a shit what anybody says about me. You don't like it, too fuckin' bad. Because the truth is, you can't stamp out individuality—there's too many of us."

Cyndi escaped from the convent school after six ugly months ("I asked the nuns if they menstruated, and that was it") and returned to Ozone Park. There she went to public school and happily discovered the existence of blacks and Jews, and started getting musical. The first records she ever heard were her mother's, which ranged from Eileen Farrell singing "Madame Butterfly" to Louis Armstrong croaking "All That Meat and No Potatoes."

But the major event of her young musical life was the arrival of the Beatles. "I was really fascinated by John Lennon's lower harmony, the way it moved. I would copy that when my sister and I harmonized as we did the dishes. Sometimes I'd wash and she'd wipe, or if we really wanted to get funky, I would just wipe and she'd put away, see? Anyway, my voice didn't sound like the Beatles'. I was so disappointed, I stopped singing."

Having inherited an acoustic guitar from her sister, however, she learned to play "Greensleeves" and launched herself as a typical folkette of the time. At this point, her musical endeavors—mostly singing in parks and at local hootnights with an early songwriting partner—were more successful than her educational efforts. Lauper was sure she had an affinity for music and art, but she couldn't seem to demonstrate it to anyone's satisfaction. "I got zero in art, and I went to an art school, Fashion Industries. Then they put me in this genius class—for geniuses that are nonachievers—and I failed that, too. And that was it. I figured, 'Oh, you thought you were a genius, just a genius who couldn't achieve. But really you're a dummy.' I got left back so many times I finally just quit and got my GED [General Equivalency Diploma]."

By then, she felt alienated and afraid—what would become of her? Her mother, who had married and then divorced again, worked fourteen-hour days in local diners to support her children, a situation Cyndi found horrifying.

"It was really the pits," she says. "She looked like she was killing herself. She always tried to be happy, and it wasn't a conventional thing then for women to be really happy. I think that the reason I am the way I am comes from watching my mother and my grandmother and the women in my family and in the neighborhood. It's funny, in a neighborhood, you see the women as teenagers, and then you see them grown with children—all in the span of your being five to ten. And you see them take on the same look in their faces that you saw on your mother's. And this is the life of women, you know?"

It was not for her. At seventeen, she left Ozone Park with no regrets. "I was packin' since I was fourteen, so it was about time, you know?"

Lauper worked odd jobs, and she took walks, long ones. "I used to walk and walk and walk," she remembers. "I felt like I was going to walk off the end of the earth. I felt really in a different world from everybody else."

She met an artist, a man in his sixties named Bob Barrell, with whom she studied for a while. He introduced her to poets and politics (although she'd already been a peace marcher in high school) and to such writers as Thoreau. Inspired, Cyndi set off with her dog, a mutt named Sparkle, for Canada, where she spent two weeks in the woods north of Toronto, sleeping in a tent and sketching trees. She got homesick for New York, though, and wended her way back by way of Vermont, where she stopped to take classes at an art school near Stowe, supporting herself by working as a waitress, a painting-class model, a race-track warmup attendant and a peddler of karate and judo lessons, about which she knew not the first thing.

"Sometimes I felt so *crumbled*," she says. "I thought, 'How will I live?' I used to pray all the time that I would change into this or that. But you can't. You can never run away from yourself. And I tried so hard."

Finally, somewhat demoralized but still determined to escape the traditional woman's lot, Lauper returned home to Ozone Park.

"I came back to do what I know how to do, and that is sing. *Nobody* has to teach me how to sing."

This assumption later proved technically inaccurate, but

it was the right attitude. In 1974, she landed a job as a backup singer and dancer in a Long Island copy band called Doc West. "It was disco," she says distastefully. "Cover, cover, cover. I used to sing Chaka Khan things, and LaBelle. I used to sing 'I've Got the Music in Me,' which I really hated. I didn't know much then, and I couldn't understand why on some days I could hit the notes and some days I couldn't. I'd be standing onstage going, 'I got the *muuu* . . . , I got the *muuu* . . . ,' and wondering what happened. Finally, I figured out why it was stuck: I had it *in* me, but it couldn't *come out* because I was doing covers. It was always someone else's *muuu.*"

The group also featured Cyndi in a typically tacky "tribute" to Janis Joplan. "I did that really good, until my friends started saying things like, 'When you sing, it's *almost like her.*' And I thought, 'That's right: I'm living in her body.' Onstage, I would feel her all around me. Finally, I just said, 'I can't do this anymore.' It wasn't me. I was wearing platform shoes, and I had pin curls in my hair. I looked like Isaac Newton."

Next, she started a band called Flyer, a more rock & roll–oriented outfit that played all the predictable hits by Rod Stewart, the Rolling Stones, et cetera—the Long Island bar circuit not being known for its love of originality. "It was always, 'Why does she run around so much?' And 'What's the matter with her voice? It sounds so weird and different.' And 'Why does she talk like that?' It was, like, give me a *break,* you know?"

In 1977, after some three years of mimicking Joplin, Stewart and Jagger, Lauper caved in. Her voice was shot, and when she called in a friend to replace her in the group, the friend recommended that she see Katie Agresta, a classically trained Manhattan voice coach.

"When she came to my studio seven years ago," Agresta recalls, "she could no longer speak. She was whispering. She had been told by three doctors that she would never sing again. I think she had one foot off the Brooklyn Bridge, to tell you the truth."

Agresta taught her new student about vocal exercises and warmups, proper diet and the damage that drugs and alcohol can do—not that Lauper was a serious abuser in either category. And slowly but surely, over the course of a year, Cyndi started singing again.

"I knew the day I met her she was going to be a star,"

Agresta enthuses. "She's a phenomenal singer, and what she's doing now is not even using a lot of what she really *can* do; it's a marvelous instrument she has. She always makes me cry. I've watched her go through the tortures of the damned. She came from nowhere, from nothing, and she had no help from anybody. She had so many opportunities to just give up, and she didn't."

After rebuilding her voice, Lauper got a gig singing at Trude Heller's nightclub—in Manhattan, at last. Ted Rosenblatt, her manager at the time, came to see her one night and brought along a songwriter named John Turi, who also played keyboards and saxophone. Turi and Lauper hit it off and soon were collaborating on tunes. By 1978, they had put together a Fifties-style band called Blue Angel.

In the spring of 1979, a tape of Blue Angel demos found its way into the hands of Steve Massarsky, an attorney who at the time managed the Allman Brothers Band. Massarsky was not impressed. "The tape was terrible," he says. "The songs were bad, the playing was bad. There was something interesting about the singer's voice, but that was all."

Massarsky was nevertheless inveigled into checking out the band in performance at an uptown club called Trax. "Cyndi walked in," he recalls, shifting his voice up into a register reminiscent of Daffy Duck's, "and she said to me: 'So you're Steve, huh? I'm surprised you showed up. Nobody ever shows up when we want 'em to; they just show up when we don't expect it, and we don't play good.'" Massarsky resumes his normal speaking voice. "I thought, oh, great. But she got onstage, and she opened her mouth to sing, and it was magic. I'd never heard anything like it. I fell in love. Of course, she was doing things like tripping over the other players and knocking things down as she walked—as klutzy as you can possibly be on a stage. But she was magnificent."

Massarsky was so impressed by Lauper's potential that he paid some $5000 to buy her management contract from Rosenblatt. Massarsky set up a showcase for Blue Angel and invited all his industry contacts to come see the band. The reaction, he recalls, was unanimous: "The singer's wonderful, get rid of the band."

Cyndi wouldn't hear of such a thing, though, and she held her ground until, six months later, Polygram Records offered a recording contract for the whole group. But the band's debut album, *Blue Angel,* released in 1980, was a stiff. Critics liked it, but not for the rockabilly stylings the band felt to be its specialty. It was Lauper's spectacular, octave-vaulting vocals on such doo-wopish tunes as "Maybe He'll Know" that caught the few ears that ever heard the LP. Lauper was angered by the whole experience. "She even thought the photos on the album made her look like Big Bird," Massarsky recalls.

Still, Cyndi resisted all efforts to lure her from the band and into a solo career. Massarsky remembers the time, before the first album was recorded, when Polygram flew him and his protégée to L.A. to meet with the renowned Italian disco producer Giorgio Moroder, whom Polygram originally wanted to produce Blue Angel. The premise for their meeting was that Lauper was to take a crack at singing the theme song for a teen-exploitation movie called *Roadie,* which starred Meat Loaf and Deborah Harry of Blondie. Moroder was a big gun in the biz, but Cyndi wasn't impressed.

"She was convinced that she was not gonna do this, and she set about to fuck it up," Massarsky remembers. "At one point, we were all in a coffee shop across the street from the studio, and she looked at Moroder and said, 'So, *George,* what kind of music do you listen to?' And Moroder said, 'Well, ah, what do you mean?' She said, 'Well, I mean, are you into Buddy Holly? Ya like Elvis? Whaddya think of Eddie Cochran?' And Moroder's going: 'Who *are* these people?' She goes, '*George,* these are the roots of rock & roll. You wanna produce me, you've gotta understand this stuff. Who're yer influences?' And Moroder goes: 'I am an original. I only listen to Giorgio Moroder.'

"Cyndi," Massarsky says, "was a star before her time."

It was Roy Halee, best known for producing Simon and Garfunkel in the Sixties, who eventually wound up producing the first Blue Angel album—and, as it turned out, the last. A new executive regime had taken over at Polygram and was demanding dynamite tunes before it would let the band back in the studio. Blue Angel had a falling-out with Massarsky, and when they dismissed him as their manager, he responded by filing suit against the group for $80,000 he claimed they owed him. Cyndi was among the members who decided to file for bankruptcy, which was granted, in her case, in the winter of 1983.

"That was the last time I saw her," Massarsky says, "at the settlement. I walked up to her, kissed her on the cheek and said, 'Hey, now go make all the money we all thought you could make to begin with. Go become a star.'"

"And the judge," Cyndi recalls with a giggle, "the judge said, 'Let the canary sing!'"

With Blue Angel effectively demolished by its first tilt toward success, Lauper was finally ready to go solo. But she wasn't about to rush into it. If stardom was to be hers, it would have to be on her own terms. So, before she'd jump for a new record deal, Cyndi waited and did what she could to make ends meet. She sang oldies at a Japanese piano bar called Miho, and she worked for a while at an Upper West Side vintage-clothing shop called Screaming Mimi's, whence came several of her more eye-catching ideas about clothing. A little bit earlier, she had met David Wolff, a manager whose own Connecticut-based band, ArcAngel, was signed to Portrait Records, a subsidiary of CBS.

Wolff, who has since become Lauper's manager and boyfriend, put her together with CBS executive producer Lennie Petze, who in turn arranged a meeting for her with producer Rick Chertoff. Soon a solo album started taking shape, with Chertoff calling in two friends, Eric Bazilian and Rob Hyman of Philadelphia's Hooters, to help out with the music. Songwriter Jules Shear also took part, as did drummer Anton Fig and bassist Neil Jason, two crack sessionmen. The resulting album, *She's So Unusual*, was probably the most exuberant vocal debut of 1983. And some of its better tunes were cowritten by Lauper, including the clever little masturbation ditty "She Bop."

The most immediately impressive performances on the record, however, were three inspired covers: the Brains' "Money Changes Everything," Prince's "When You Were Mine" and Philly rocker Robert Hazard's previously unrecorded "Girls Just Want to Have Fun," which Lauper couldn't identify with when she first heard Hazard perform it.

"I changed the words," Cyndi says. "It was originally about how fortunate he was 'cause he was a guy around these girls that wanted to have 'fun'—with *him—down there*, of which we do not speak lest we go blind. I tore it apart."

But it was the video for "Girls" that really made Cyndi Lauper a star. In it, she told the story of her own repressed childhood, her yearning for freedom and her mother's unhappy entrapment in the female status quo. She even persuaded her mother to play herself, and recruited a party load of friends and family to participate, including her brother, Butch, and her dog, Sparkle. "My mother was wonderful," Cyndi says. "Now it's gone to her head. She's picked out a stage name—Katreen Dominique—and she wears sunglasses whenever she walks Sparkle. As a matter of fact, Sparkle wears sunglasses now, too."

The video for her new single, "Time after Time," is equally autobiographical, recalling the time Cyndi once ran away from home. Her mom's in this one, too, as is David Wolff, typecast as her boyfriend. "Art should reflect life," Cyndi says, "not art. This video's about two people in a small town—small towns are great, if you choose that. Nowadays, there's more and more choices in the world, there really are. But no matter what you wanna be, you gotta break yer ass, you gotta work hard. Do what's in your heart and don't take no for an answer.

"Me, I always wanted to make world music—to say something that's worth sayin' and really touch humanity. That's why I'm here. There's a wonderful place that you go when you sing, there's a really good feeling. And it's wonderful to reach out and touch someone with it, because they touch you back. And sometimes that's worth the price of beans."

Courtesy Michael Ochs Archives

NINETEEN

Laurie Anderson

(1982)

Laurie Anderson, a downtown performance artist by trade, never positioned herself as a pop star. But the records she began making in the early Eighties—first the haunting single, "O Superman," and then the ravishing Big Science *album— demonstrated a major talent for sound collage and an apparent acquaintance with previous modes of music ranging from Pink Floyd art-wash to the patented squonk cataclysms of Captain Beefheart. Unaware of the record-making rules, Anderson made records that sounded unlike any others—which is how rock & roll was supposed to work in the first place.* Strange Angels, *her last LP to date, didn't fare too well in the pop marketplace—but then that's how rock works sometimes, too. Stand by for further communications.*

A coyote's howl wells up in the dark of the Palladium theater in New York City. A synthesizer begins to billow and drone as a fat, full moon floats gently across an enormous projection screen. Laurie Anderson, a small, Chaplinesque figure in a plain black suit, stands poised center stage at an Oberheim keyboard, gazing up toward the balconies.

"You know," she says, "I think we should put some mountains here. Otherwise, what are the characters going to fall off of?

"And what about stairs?" she asks, as the music shivers and shifts around her.

"Yodellayheehoo."

Laurie Anderson calls herself a performance artist, but she's really a new kind of pop star, with a whole new way of—literally—looking at music. Her professional persona is so open-ended that any number of futures seems possible. The Palladium show, which climaxed her month-long U.S. tour, was unlike anything seen in this country since Pink Floyd mounted an elaborate stage version of *The Wall,* their multiplatinum concept album, in New York and Los Angeles in 1980.

For ninety minutes, Anderson sang, joked, punned, played and talk-talk-talked—and she *talks* more eloquently than many singers *sing.* She sawed soulfully at a violin and squeezed strange, poignant tunes from a toy accordion. She donned a pair of custom-amplified spectacles and knuckled out a novelty beat on her spiky-blond noggin. She saluted the ecological engagement of Buckminster Fuller ("Have you ever thought about how much your buildings actually *weigh?*") and sang a song derived from William Burroughs, called "Language Is a Virus." ("Hearing your name," she muttered, "is better than seeing your face.") At one point, a black man in dreadlocks and a kilt marched out of the wings and blew a long, skirling jazz bagpipe solo. A quote from Ludwig Wittgenstein slid onto the screen: "If you can't talk about it, point to it."

What is going on here? It's not rock, really—although the Burroughs tune, among others, could pass for the authentic item. It's not jazz (despite the presence of veteran Philadelphia reedman Rufus Harley, the aforementioned Afro-Highlander). And it's not exactly theater, either. What Laurie Anderson attempts is something rather new—a conceptual circus of slides, films, tapes and parlor tricks that makes most big-bucks rock concerts seem constipated by comparison.

Those who missed Anderson on tour can contemplate the musical component of her complex message on *Big Science,* a brilliant debut album that also serves as a preview of *United States I–IV,* an eight-hour performance piece she plans to premiere next October at the Brooklyn Academy of Music in New

York. Although not outright rock or pop, *Big Science* offers some useful aesthetic strategies for more mainstream music-makers. Consider the recording process: ninety-five percent of *Big Science* was done in the Lobby, a small, sixteen-track studio in Anderson's big, busy loft in Manhattan's Soho district. (The Lobby is where she recorded the eight-minute-plus "O Superman" last year—a single version of which became a smash hit in Europe, expediting Anderson's subsequent signing by Warner Bros. Records to an eight-album deal.) *Big Science* also suggests ways in which ostensibly nonpop artists can connect with elements of the large pop-music audience (particularly those of the Captain Beefheart or Pink Floyd persuasion) without condescending. The record is a model of noncodified, nonelitist artistic communication. In short, good news all around.

This is important to Anderson, probably more so than the imminence of quasi-pop stardom. At thirty-five, she is an artist who has long been distressed by the American art establishment's seeming disinclination to reach out to ordinary people, and its preoccupation, particularly in the postwar period, with cold, bloodless theory to the sometimes total exclusion of content. This is reflected in her work. Take *Duets on Ice,* one of her early performance pieces. Characteristically, its props were minimal: a pair of ice skates and a violin. The violin was rigged with a built-in speaker, which allowed playback of a previously recorded violin solo. The blades of the skates were embedded in blocks of ice. Standing on a street corner, Anderson would lace on the skates and proceed to play a duet with herself until the ice melted, the blades clanked on the pavement and the concert came to a sudden, wobbly halt. "In between," she said, "I talked about the parallels between skating and violin playing—blades over a surface—and about balancing, and what it means to play a duet with yourself."

Anderson felt that performance art—which partakes of the belief that ideas develop interesting spins when you jostle them together—could be used to address questions that more academic artists didn't seem interested in answering. Like: Why do people *make* art? Sitting cross-legged on the floor of her studio one night, Anderson tried to explain.

"Maybe in the past, artists did work that incorporated certain social-political-religious ideas as a kind of propaganda, to convince other people. But when the need to convince other people in that way dropped off, there was still an enormous number of people left making art—kind of *in the habit* of making art. But . . . for what?" Anderson, who's wearing a pair of black trousers and a nondescript sport shirt, blinks her big eyes and runs a hand through her trademark mop. She lights an unfiltered cigarette.

"That's where *aesthetics* comes in and says, 'Look at this white square. Look at the proportions of this square and look how very straight this line is.' There can only be a small elite who understand why that line is straight and why that square is important. To everybody else, it looks like their bathroom tile. They don't know *why* they're looking at it."

To demonstrate the cultural conundrum posed by ultra-abstraction, Anderson created one of her first pieces for tape-bow, a violin with a tape-playback head installed at the bridge and a bow adapted to accommodate a length of prerecorded tape instead of horsehair. For this piece, she taped a quote from Lenin—"Ethics is the aesthetics of the future," which sounded like a typical art-party cliché—strung it onto her tape-bow and drew it *almost all the way* across the violin's playback head. The result: "Ethics is the aesthetics of the fu . . . the fu . . . the fu . . ."

Anderson may be a populist of sorts, but she knew she wouldn't be staying in the small town outside of Chicago where she grew up in the late Fifties. The second of eight children born to a well-to-do paint dealer and his wife, Laurie studied classical violin, played with the Chicago Youth Symphony and seemed likely to pursue a career as an international virtuoso.

"But I stopped playing, cold turkey, when I was sixteen," she said, leaning back and lighting another cigarette. "I realized that if I wanted to do that, that was *all* I could do for the rest of my life, be this kind of technocrat. I was pretty good, but I wasn't good enough to have a career like that. And I was horrified by the people who *were*, you know?"

In the mid-Sixties, she moved to Manhattan and studied art history at Barnard College. It was an exciting time. "I had one professor whose specialty was Chardin, who did these peaches. And this professor would go up to the wall and say, 'Look at those *peaches!*' And she'd start stroking the wall—'You can *feel* them!' Everybody got really excited—a roomful of girls going, '*Oh, my God!*' And then, after she'd hooked you sensually, she'd analyze it. I really liked that approach."

Anderson graduated in 1969, did some teaching and started writing articles for such magazines as *Artforum* and *ARTnews*. "I took it real seriously. More to just . . . go over to an artist's house, you know: meet a real artist and kind of spook around, see what was in his refrigerator. Probably the most interesting was Sol De Witt, but I don't think I ever really . . . well, yeah, I did get in his refrigerator, but I didn't actually *write* anything."

She did eventually wrest a master's degree in sculpture from Columbia University and soon started soliciting her first grants, a subject about which she's ambivalent ("O Superman" may have been the first hit single ever to carry a thank-you to the National Endowment for the Arts).

"Grants have helped me a lot," Anderson said. "But in Europe, you can almost get a grant for life. Dutch artists are designated artists, and they're turning out absolutely *horrible* stuff. Two times a month they give something to the state, and that's all they have to do. They're given a house and a monthly sort of middle-class salary. But they're not required to be there, so they're not interested. They *all* live in Spain."

Anderson lives less luxuriously on the sparsely furnished top floor of a loft building overlooking the Hudson River. She pursues her interests in many directions: venturing out to shoot random location footage for her shows and staying up all night working on new material in her studio.

The current, multimedia phase of her career began to take shape in 1975, when as an artist in residence, she went to work on a "talking novel" at ZBS Media, an audio facility in upstate New York. There she not only fell in love with recording, she fell in love *while* recording (for a time, at least) with her engineer. "It was extremely romantic up there. And, like, the engineer is behind this big plate glass, and you put on these headphones and he's *right inside your head,* whispering to you. It was just too much."

Even her sculpture took on audio overtones. She built a "stereo table," for example, that was ingeniously outfitted with concealed tape recorders and seventeen layers of alternating rubber and lead insulation. Its music could only be heard when a listener sat resting his elbows in two depressions and holding his head in his hands, absorbing the sound solely through bone conduction. (This table was a hit at the prestigious Für Ohren Und Augen media showcase in Berlin, where it vied for attention with a mechanical bird from the fifteenth century that not only flew around but sang.)

Anderson was also intrigued by such performance artists as Vito Acconci, a Brooklyn poet and sculptor noted for his live piece, *Seedbed,* in which he lay under a ramp in a New York gallery for weeks, intermittently masturbating and fantasizing lewdly into a microphone about the people strolling above him. Anderson admired Acconci's verve, especially in the context of the cool formalism then prevalent in art.

"That was the thing that was most resented when I started doing performance stuff," she said. "I put in things that I thought were funny, and humor was really considered very low-grade—a disguise for banality. But the flip side of that is that seriousness can also be a disguise for banality."

Laurie Anderson is now having the last laugh. But the uninitiated may wonder: Is she doing something new, or is she, in fact, simply an extension of that same old high formalism— works that cannot stand on their apparent substance and require explanations from their creators?

"In a sense, I feel like an extension of that attitude," she acknowledged. "Because I stand there, *too,* next to the images, and *talk.* It's a work in which language is the most important thing. It's really words more than anything else."

Lately, though, visuals have taken on an increasing importance for her. Appalled by the political and cultural state of the world, she hopes to come up with some new, positive images to countervail the current inventory of viciousness and dread that confronts us daily on the streets and in the media. She admits it's difficult to make good seem as metabolically exciting as evil, but she's looking around.

TWENTY

Andy Warhol

(1987)

For nearly thirty years, Andy Warhol defined the collective sensibility of New York's downtown art scene. He didn't seem to be saying anything (and by his own admission, he didn't actually do very much, either), but his influence—on music, on film, on both art and the business of art—was pervasive. Warhol invented a new attitude. He didn't celebrate sleaze and banality, exactly; he simply presented them to us unretouched—quivering little slices of contemporary experience unmediated by aesthetic judgments or moral strongarming. For reasons that still resist concise analysis, this was revolutionary.

Warhol's influence on rock was perhaps not as widely known as his Campbell's soup cans, but anyone who reveres the Velvet Underground will know that it was real. His death seemed to mark the closure of a tumultuously productive period in American art and popular culture.

Andy Warhol liked to watch. Anything: flowers, cows, stacked-up soup cans. Pop stars, comic strips, tabloid corpses. Society girls shooting up, drag queens flipping out, young hustlers engaged in fellation. His gaze was relentless, and awesome in its detachment. "A whole day of life," he said, "is like a whole day of television." Warhol demonstrated the seductive anesthetic effect of the image—of reality at one manageable remove. Secondhand life could be reviewed and savored, or simply switched off. All things really *were* equal. Andy looked at life and shrugged. "Gee," he said.

In the Sixties, we watched with him, of course. There was no choice: Andy was everywhere. Who among us has not stared in wonder or befuddlement at his deadpan Campbell's soup cans, his silk-screened Marilyns, his endlessly unreeling underground movies and thought, "Who is this guy?" Warhol, of course, had no comment.

"If you want to know all about Andy Warhol," he said, "just look at the surface of my paintings and films and me, and there I am. There's nothing behind it."

He positioned himself as an emotional void around which all manner of bizarre events flapped and fluttered. He was merely the ticket taker. And yet, when all the Warhol "superstars" are forgotten, when the shock of even his most shocking work has long receded, it is Warhol himself—the ultimate introvert—who will perhaps be remembered as the crucial figure in that most extrovert of eras.

Andy casually brought previously forbidden "underground" material into the cultural mainstream, desensitizing both it and us (even the most scabrous image becomes boring if stared at long enough). With his mixed-media shows and his unflagging penchant for the new and the experimental, he helped invent the Sixties. As an indefatigable party archivist, he practically defined the celebrity-addled Seventies. And by the end, he'd become the grand old man of the American avant-garde, at home at last in a world he'd largely refurbished.

"He was the person who created Attitude," said Tom Wolfe a few days after Andy's death on February 22nd. "Before Warhol, in artistic circles, there was Ideology—you took a stance against the crassness of American life. Andy Warhol turned that on its head, and created an attitude. And the attitude was 'It's so awful, it's wonderful. It's so tacky, let's wallow in it.' That still put you *above* it, because it was so *knowing*. It placed you above the crassness of American life, but at the same time you could *enjoy* it."

Before Warhol, art in New York was a capital-*A* affair, a

largely inscrutable ritual carried out among iron-browed god-artists, the critics who lauded them in little art magazines and a carefully cultivated circle of key dealers and well-heeled collectors. The public—the "sloboisie," as it were—played no part in this rarified minuet. The public, corrupted by the hateful consumerism of popular culture, was thought to be incapable of Taste. People would stand and look at this stuff—a Barnett Newman canvas, say: totally blue, save for a single fat stripe of darker blue running down one side—and they wouldn't get it. Or, for that matter, want it.

Back in the Forties, abstract expressionism—the rubric under which such various painters as Newman, Arshile Gorky, Adolph Gottlieb, Jackson Pollock, Willem de Kooning, Franz Kline and Mark Rothko came to be lumped—had been the first American style to reap international acclaim. The art-scene action had shifted from Paris to New York, where most of the ab-ex painters lived and drank (they were a very manly bunch), and this New York School still held sway at the dawn of the Fifties, when Warhol arrived on the scene. He must have realized instinctively that there was no place in it for him.

The youngest of three sons born to an immigrant Czech coal miner, Warhol had grown up in and around Pittsburgh. He took a degree in pictorial design from the Carnegie Institute of Technology in 1949 and lit out that summer to make his name as a commercial artist in Manhattan. In those days, setting up as a *commercial* artist in New York was tantamount to announcing oneself a traitor to the True Call. Serious young artists who found themselves reduced to taking commercial assignments to pay the rent did so under pseudonyms. Warhol not only worked under his own name but actually accepted *awards*—the ultimate depravity in ab-ex terms.

The ab-ex crowd created a tough-talking, two-fisted milieu—hard men doing a hard job, tending their muses in the wasteland of American culture. Three childhood bouts with chorea, a nervous disorder, weakened Warhol. He was left pallid and balding, and with his bad wig and fey manner, he was a made-to-order target for macho hostility. ("I certainly wasn't a butch kind of guy by nature," he once admitted.)

But the bell was already tolling for abstract expressionism. The style had grown remote and bloodless, a private communion among its purveyors. A groundbreaking exhibition at the Whitechapel Art Gallery, in London, in 1956 introduced a new group of artists who took as their subject all of the effluvia of consumerism—lollipops, comic books, body-building ads, bad furniture—that the ab-ex crowd so hated. This new art drew visual juice from television and advertising; it was fresh, tough and funny. A British critic, Lawrence Alloway, dubbed it Pop Art.

Around this same time, Jasper Johns began doing his first target and flag paintings in New York. An American Pop Art ethos was in the air. Warhol, who had prospered in commercial art, was by then living with his long-widowed mother, Julia Warhola (Andy had dropped the final *a* from the family name), in a town house on the Upper East Side. Andy admired Johns and longed to be recognized as a "real" artist, too. He had shown some whimsical little ink drawings around town, but to scant notice. Finally, encouraged by a friend, he began in 1960 to pursue a bold new style, painting pictures based on such comic-strip characters as Superman, Dick Tracy and Popeye and on such supposed visual clichés as Coca-Cola bottles. These unlikely subjects *spoke* to him. "What's great about this country," he later said, "[is that] the richest consumers buy essentially the same things as the poorest. You can be watching TV and see Coca-Cola, and you can know the president drinks Coke, Liz Taylor drinks Coke, and, just think, you can drink Coke, too."

When Andy subsequently discovered that another artist, Roy Lichtenstein, was also doing comic-strip art, he was encouraged. Something was happening, and maybe he could be a part of it. But it wasn't until 1962 that Andy had his first one-man show, at the Ferus Gallery, in Los Angeles, where local reaction to his first Campbell's soup cans was subdued. That all changed in the fall, however, when his new work was finally accorded its own exhibition in New York, at the Stable Gallery. The show, with its *Gold Marilyn,* its *Red Elvis,* its paintings of two-dollar bills, launched Warhol's reputation. Pop—like surrealism four decades earlier—made art seem fun again, exciting and subversive. Warhol, Lichtenstein and other artists of their ilk found themselves feted by the mass media. Andy was not amazed.

"The Pop artists did images that anyone . . . could recognize in a split second," he said, "all the great modern things that the abstract expressionists tried so hard not to notice at all."

By the time he began, in 1962, his Death and Disaster series—harsh black-and-white treatments of straight news photos depicting dead car-crash victims and leaping suicides—Warhol was drifting away from brush-on-canvas painting and into silk screening, a commercial process in which paint is screened onto the canvas, resulting in hard, bright, untouched-by-human-hands prints. In fact, the artist, after selecting whatever image it was that he wanted enlarged and reproduced, didn't even have to participate in the screening process: an assistant could apply the paint just as well. Andy liked that. "I wanted something . . . that gave more of an assembly-line effect," he said.

"What was radical in Warhol," art critic Robert Hughes later wrote, "was that he adapted the means of production of soup cans to the way he produced paintings, turning them out *en masse*—consumer art mimicking the process as well as the look of consumer culture."

In November 1963, Warhol and his assistant Gerard Malanga moved into a new studio, a loft in a decrepit factory building on East Forty-seventh Street. Inevitably, given Andy's methods, it came to be called the Factory. A new recruit called Billy Name moved into the place and covered the walls with silver foil. Billy's speed-freak friends began dropping by, people with names like Rotten Rita, the Duchess and Pope Ondine. Warhol found these extreme characters to be ideal subjects for the films he'd begun making—unstructured *vérité* exercises with titles like *Kiss, Eat, Sleep*. (The titles defined the content of these opuses precisely: *Sleep* simply showed a man sleeping for eight hours.)

Soap Opera, made in 1964, introduced one of Warhol's earliest superstars—Baby Jane Holzer, a rich, young Park Avenue matron with the perfect Sixties look and attitude. She was the Girl of the Year—why not? "In the future," Andy said, "everyone will be world famous for fifteen minutes." This was the perfect Pop notion. Like Claes Oldenburg's sculpted cheeseburgers and Lichtenstein's comic-strip machine guns ("BRA-TATATATA!"), it suggested that art could be produced from the lowliest materials, and by the unlikeliest people. In the future, everyone could be famous because, after all, it would only be for fifteen minutes, and then the next person would get a shot. Imagine the possibilities!

Other superstars would follow Baby Jane: the doomed Edie Sedgwick, Mario Montez, Ultra Violet, Viva, Candy Darling. The films in which they were featured over the years—nonacted, stream-of-footage epics—presented visual banality as a raw new style.

By January 1966, Warhol had brought a band into the Factory, a group called the Velvet Underground. He'd caught the Velvets at the Café Bizarre—two nights before they were canned for antisocial music making—and put them together with a German actress-model called Nico. The Velvets' Lou Reed wrote some songs for her, and Warhol put the group into the Cinematheque, an underground theater, for a week-long mixed-media show of his own. As Reed recalls it, "He said, 'Gee, I've got this week to do a show, and I was gonna show my movies, but why don't you play, and I'll show my movies on *you*?'

"He created multimedia in New York," Reed says. "All these clubs now with their lights and everything—they owe that mixed-media thing directly to Andy. The way people dress was affected by it, everything was affected by it. The whole complexion of the city changed, probably of the country. Nothing remained the same after that."

By March, the Velvets were on the road with a touring mixed-media rock circus Warhol called the Exploding Plastic Inevitable. The EPI had flashing strobes, light shows, film projections—all the things that would soon become rock theater. With the help of Tom Wilson, a producer who worked with Bob Dylan, Warhol produced the Velvets' classic first album and designed its famous cover, which featured a peelable banana. That same year Warhol produced his cow wallpaper and his split-screen epic *The Chelsea Girls* and added to his iconic *Jackie* series—screen prints of newspaper photos of President Kennedy's widow. His energies seemed endless. "He had a very intense work ethic that he was always drumming into us," says Lou Reed. "If I wrote a song, he'd say, 'Why didn't you write five songs?' He said, 'Work is everything. Work is the entire thing.'"

In 1967, Andy helped launch a discotheque called the Gymnasium and pulled off a startling bit of nonperformance art by retaining a Factory actor, Allen Midgette, to spray his hair silver and impersonate Warhol for a series of lecture dates—one of the great Sixties put-ons. In the space of five years, Warhol had largely created a whole new multimedia avant-garde—one with vast commercial as well as artistic potential. As Andy later said, "Being good in business is the most fascinating kind of art."

By this time, the Factory had become a magnet for all who aspired to be with-it—a place where Judy Garland might dance the twist with Rudolph Nureyev and still be outshone by the resident Warhol superstars. But the Factory's open-door policy was flooding the place with freaks. Baby Jane Holzer had dropped out, complaining about "too many crazy people" and "too many drugs." In 1968, Warhol moved the Factory into more elegant quarters downtown, at 33 Union Square West, not far from Max's Kansas City, the rock-and-art bar where Andy and his entourage held court in a fabled back room. ("He paid for all the food," recalls Iggy Pop, who first met David Bowie there.) Warhol was at the height of his fame when, on June 3rd, a disturbed woman named Valerie Solanis walked into the new Factory, pulled out a gun, fired two bullets into Warhol's stomach and nearly killed him. At one point, he was pronounced dead on the operating table. He lived, but it was the end of an era.

Warhol spent the rest of the year—the rest of the Sixties, in fact—recovering from massive internal injuries, and from a sudden mortal fear. New locks and security measures were installed at the Factory. Warhol started no new films or major paintings. (After 1968, he largely limited his film involvement to the role of producer.) In the fall of 1969, with the Seventies impending, he unveiled *Interview,* a magazine inspired, he said, by *Rolling Stone*, but devoted entirely to the arts, gossip and taped ramblings by this or that month's reigning celebrity—essentially more gossip. The magazine had undeniable zing. In the Seventies, as Andy may have suspected, gossip itself would become an art form—most notably in the work of his friend Truman Capote, whom he interviewed for *Rolling Stone* in 1973.

The Andy Warhol of the Seventies was himself a full-fledged celebrity. The Rolling Stones asked him to do the cover of their 1971 album *Sticky Fingers* (the celebrated crotch-and-zipper concoction). Bianca Jagger became his pal. So did Halston, the celebrity designer, and Diana Vreeland, the celebrity editor of *Vogue*. Andy became a fixture at Studio 54. He hung out with Liz Taylor, Liza Minnelli, all the usual fabsters. "I have Social Disease," Andy quipped. "I have to go out every night." ("But I think he went home a lot very early, too," says his designer friend Diane Von Furstenberg.)

Susan Blond, an early *Interview* staffer and latter-day Factory actress, remembers introducing Andy one night to Michael Jackson, who became an early *Interview* cover subject. "He asked Michael if he had saved all his performance clothes from when he was a kid," Blond recalls, "and Michael *had.* Andy really liked that—both of them collected *everything,* right? We ate at Regine's, and I asked Michael to dance, and he said, 'Oh, no, I don't dance. That's work.' The both of them had weird, interesting views on what was work and what wasn't, you know? They really hit it off immediately. Oh—and Michael asked Andy if he had children. Michael has always asked that question. Andy said no."

Embarking on his nightly celebrity wallows, Warhol always brought along his Polaroid camera and his little tape machine to document the fun, or whatever. "He was absolutely crazy about collecting images," says Mick Jagger with a fond laugh. "He would take millions of pictures—which is very *annoying* when you're eating your soup and you've just blurped a piece of minestrone down your chin. And he always had a tape recorder on the table to collect the inanities of the night."

For Warhol, tape *vérité* offered a peculiar conceptual comfort. "In the late Fifties," he once wrote, "I started an affair with my television which has continued to the present. . . . But I didn't get married until 1964 when I got my first tape recorder. My wife. . .

"The acquisition of my tape recorder," he explained, "really finished whatever emotional life I might have had, but I was glad to see it go. Nothing was ever a problem again, because a problem just meant a good tape. . . . An interesting problem was an interesting tape. Everybody knew that and performed for the tape. You couldn't tell which problems were real and which problems were exaggerated for the tape. Better yet, the people telling you the problems couldn't decide anymore if they were really having the problems or if they were just performing."

For his own part, the world's most famous artist continued to claim to have nothing to say. Andy did, however, have a standard line of advice for the lovelorn. "When I used to have boyfriend problems," Susan Blond recalls, "he would say, 'Oh, just work really hard and then you'll have all the money and all the fame and then you can choose whoever you want.'"

By the end of the Seventies, Warhol was beginning to seem his own greatest work of art. His paintings had grown richer, more painterly—particularly the outsize Mao canvases he'd begun in 1972—and his delicately muted 1974 portrait of his mother had suggested a new emotional forthrightness. He could still be prophetic, too—his raggedy 1975 portraits of Mick Jagger had anticipated the cut-and-paste punk graphic style that would erupt out of England the following year.

But as the Eighties got under way, Andy Warhol no longer seemed shocking—a tribute, perhaps, to the prevalence of his vision. In his fifties now, he accepted portrait commissions from the rich and famous, oversaw the burgeoning success of *Interview* and became a model for and mentor to a new generation of New York artists, among them Keith Haring, Kenny Scharf and Jean-Michel Basquiat. He launched his own cable-TV show, "Andy Warhol's T.V.," and later, on MTV, "Andy Warhol's Fifteen Minutes." He appeared in commercials, in rock videos, on "The Love Boat." He drew up plans for a fast-food restaurant—Andymat!—to be located next door to the Whitney Museum, in New York. And with a new expansiveness, he turned his attention to such subjects as Franz Kafka and Sarah Bernhardt (for a series called *Ten Portraits of Jews of the Twentieth Century*); to paintings for children (hung at kid height); and to paintings of endangered animal species. He most recently completed a version of Leonardo da Vinci's *Last Supper,* which was to be exhibited in Milan while the original was being restored.

Warhol's endless enthusiasm for the young and the new obscured a dread of sickness and death. He worked out, he popped vitamins. But finally he had to enter New York Hospital–Cornell Medical Center for gallbladder surgery on February 21st. The surgery was counted a success, but at five-thirty the following morning, he suffered a heart attack, and an hour later he was dead.

Warhol was buried in Pittsburgh on February 26th, laid alongside his mother (who had died in the Seventies) and his father. He left behind an estate valued at between $10 million and $15 million, an enormous body of paintings, drawings, sculptures, tapes, films and several books—documentation galore. And yet, the questions persist. Who was Andy Warhol? What did he do, and why?

As it turned out, the silver-haired eminence behind all those wild sex-and-drug scenes at the original Factory was a devout Catholic who attended church every week. He apparently was not a druggie and, in sexual matters, not a natural participant. He liked to watch—it was the fundamental stance of his art, just as his obsession with celebrity was a key theme. But he was an artist first, and the sincerity of his dedication was made clear in the terms of his will, which directed that the bulk of his estate be used to establish a foundation in his name for visual artists. (The will also leaves $500,000 to be divided between his elder brothers, Paul and John, and $250,000 to his longtime business partner, Fred Hughes.)

Warhol is missed in many quarters. Lou Reed calls him "one of the few people I've met in the business who never tried to screw anybody. People don't know what a good guy he was."

"The thing that he seemed to be able to do," says Mick Jagger, "was to capture society, whatever part of it he wanted to portray, pretty accurately. That's one of the things that artists do, is show people later on what it was like. If you want to be reminded of a certain period, you can look at what Andy was doing then. He was very much in tune with what was going on. Of course, he was criticized for that, for being sort of trendy. But I think that some people's great forte is being so in touch."

"He had tremendous wit," says Tom Wolfe. "But everything was stood on its head. His wit came not in saying witty things, but in *not saying anything*. It was a matter of timing, like Jack Benny.

"To me, there was great verve in his anesthetic approach to life. You know, today there are young novelists who write what I call the anesthetic novel. They are really putting into literary form something that Warhol originated, which is the idea of immersing yourself in a very exciting life—the life of the clubs and the discos—and *feeling nothing*. Which is again an inversion of the expected. And then the greatest piece of wit of all was that, of his acclaimed and widely shown work, none of it was actually *by him*. And he never said it *was*. The Campbell's soup cans and the Brillo boxes were, of course, somebody else's images. The cow wallpaper, the famous flower series from the Burpee seed catalog—these were all things, pieces of art, that had been created by someone else, often a commercial artist.

Then he took it and did something with it and often wouldn't sign it. People would say, 'But Mr. Warhol, you didn't sign this.' And he'd say, 'Oh, I didn't do it.'"

Andy Warhol may have been Pop's truest democrat, ever eager to spread the fame around.

"He always made everyone else feel like a star," says Susan Blond, "even though he was the biggest, brightest, greatest star of all."

FOREIGN C

PART THREE

RESPONDENCE

One of the great ancillary benefits of writing for magazines is the opportunity it affords to traipse the globe at other people's expense. Foreign locales also tend to reveal unexpected aspects of whatever celebrated character one is dogging around. Seasoned media pros such as David Bowie, Mel Gibson, and Tina Turner are likely to be a little looser in the sweltering outback of Australia than they would be munching crumpets at the Connaught. And even an interview with Sean Connery—a man who counts as a special blessing every moment not spent in the company of prying press people—gains a certain richness, I think, from being conducted in the little Spanish town of Marbella, where he lives.

England, of course, always has some sort of semi-hysterical pop scene going—it's the country's most reliable export. The English, as Malcolm McLaren has noted, are great packagers and presenters; and it was this that intrigued me about the "New Romantic" hubbub of the early Eighties: A whole herd of earnest young poseurs packaging and presenting *themselves*. Some of these people actually had talent. Others. . . well, you surely know who you are by now.

Ted Hawkins, a gifted performer given one of life's worst bad deals, hasn't yet managed to translate his British success into a Stateside breakthrough—but his records *are* still out there, and still highly recommended. (You can also catch him in a brief sort of man-in-the-street role in Diane Keaton's 1986 pop-philosophical documentary, *Heaven*.)

As for the nonexistent Max Headroom—here is the very embodiment of smug and meaningless celebrity (as opposed to stardom) in our time. May his reruns flourish.

Greg Gorman/Courtesy Isoiar

TWENTY-ONE

David Bowie

(Australia, 1983)

By the early Eighties, David Bowie had decided to abandon the succession of theatrical characters upon which he'd constructed his stardom over the preceding decade and to just be himself. He also decided to shoot videos for two songs off his new album, Let's Dance, *in Australia—which was where I came in.*

Bowie is a terrifically engaging character, always newly enthused about this or that painter or book or old record he's just discovered. He's also a very funny man who's not at all reluctant to share a laugh at his own expense. Peripatetic by nature, he proved the perfect guide to the sunbaked wonders of the Australian outback, a region he'd visited before and knew quite well.

Let's Dance *became Bowie's biggest album in years, and while he spent the rest of the Eighties in search of a similarly successful followup, his Seventies renown was such that he could continue to mount major tours in the absence of any massive hits. In 1989, Rykodisc began reissuing all of Bowie's old RCA albums on compact discs, and their renewed availability seemed likely to extend the influence of his early work, which has already been considerable.*

In Australia, David Bowie was a man without masks. Open, jokey, very . . . *warm* is the only word. Back home—which for Bowie these days is Switzerland—March is an unmistakably wintry month, but halfway round the world in Sydney, even as autumn arrived, a brilliant sun still bathed the beaches at Bondi and Manly, and in the clear, caressing night air, the stars seemed like so many crushed diamonds strewn across the antipodean sky. It was a paradise perfectly suited to Bowie's new *menschlich* mood, his gathering thaw.

"It's not hip to be cool," he said one day, sipping a beer. "It really isn't. I had a heyday with the whole iceman-cometh bit. I'm *cooled out,* man. I've seen so much cool, it's just left me *cold.*"

He ran a long hand through his bright blond hair, and his laugh was warm and wonderfully out of character. Or characters.

Bowie is thirty-six now. He made his first record—with a boyhood band called the King Bees—in 1964, and has been at it ever since. The past, of course, plagues him. All those masks he no longer needs, the old poses—they keep popping up anew. "The biggest mistake I ever made," he said one night after a couple of cans of Foster's Lager, "was telling that *Melody Maker* writer that I was bisexual. Christ, I was so *young* then. I was *experimenting. . . .*"

So: he is not gay, whatever he may have blurted out in 1972. Nor was he ever a transvestite, thank you. Still, American TV—for want of any more-recent product, it's true—has kept running his 1979 "Boys Keep Swinging" video, and so total strangers still breathily inquire whether he's doing drag onstage again. ("I've *never* done drag onstage," he huffs.) Then there were England's New Romantics, who were very big on his cocktail-zombie look for a while, and you wouldn't believe how many Ziggy and Aladdin Sane clones continue to abound. Even in Sydney, the earnest girls who patiently hovered outside the Sebel Town House, where Bowie was known to be staying, invariably included among their daily number at least one copper-shock hairdo from his *Pin-Ups* period. It was something to see, first thing in the morning.

He's put all that behind him now. Well, all but Ziggy. After a decade in mothballs, Ziggy still refuses to die. So this year, for a laugh, Bowie is bringing him back. He's remixed the soundtrack to the never-released Ziggy concert film ("I don't know what I was on when I mixed it the first time") and will finally unveil it later this year. The movie—which features Bowie in full glam-rock flower, backed for the last time by his classic band, the Spiders from Mars—was shot by documentarian D. A. Pennebaker at London's Hammersmith Odeon in 1973, and has been gathering dust in Bowie's archives ever since.

"That's something I couldn't look at for years," he says of this near-legendary Ziggy artifact. "I was so fed up with him . . . it—all that. But I dragged it out last year and had a look, and I thought: This is a *funny film*! This boy used to dress like that for a living? My *God* this is funny! Incredible! Wait till my *son* sees this!"

As it turned out, Joey liked it. But then Joey likes Captain Sensible, too, and as his dad says, a lot of the new British bands these days "make Ziggy look like a bank clerk." Joey—dubbed "Zowie" back in the glitter days, when David was still married to Joey's mother, Angela—is eleven now, a great-looking kid with soft, fair hair and a face full of freckles. Bowie takes him everywhere, and so here he is, nanny in tow, in Australia. Actually, *right* now he's down the block at a video arcade, pumping away at the ponging consoles while Daddy attends to his art.

Outside, it's another balmy day under the big Australian sun, and up and down the cobbled street, wind chimes tinkle gently in the warm coastal breeze. In the shadow of the great green-and-red pagoda gate that spans the entrance to Sydney's tiny Chinatown district, a camera crew is setting up a dolly shot in front of the well-regarded Ming Wah Restaurant. It is midday, *yum cha* time, and inside, waitresses wheel among bustling tables with steaming bamboo baskets of dim sum specialties, proffering pork-filled buns, translucent noodles, savory chicken feet and mysterious meats wrapped in large, green lotus leaves. David Bowie leans over his lunch with an oh-lucky-man grin and confides above the clamor, "Isn't this the greatest profession in the world?"

It's quite a life, all right. Just weeks ago, EMI Records parted with something in the neighborhood of $10 million for the privilege of putting out Bowie's next five albums; when he informed his happy new label that he wanted to film two promotional videos for the first of those LPs (the just-released *Let's Dance*) in *Australia,* of all budget-raping places, EMI—in a bit of a daze, perhaps—said sure. "It's an unbelievably wonderful way to live," says Bowie, who loves to travel. "The hardest thing is not to feel guilty about it."

He knows he's one of the lucky ones, flitting from concert stages and recording studios to feature films and straight theater work. In the pop business, he realizes, life at the top can be a trap. Look at poor Mick Jagger.

"Mick really wanted to do something different a few years ago," he says with a sympathetic cluck. "I remember him *crying,* 'Am I gonna be saddled with the Rolling Stones for the rest of my life?' But I don't know what he'll ever do now. I think you've got to make a move, just do something different. If you miss your chance, then . . . you settle for what you've got."

Bowie has never settled, never stopped making moves. Metamorphosis has been his métier. But a few years ago, he began wondering: What did it all *mean*? "I've had a considerable amount of success," he allows, "but some of it left me feeling quite empty. It didn't fill me up again with anything."

In fact, some of it was only a blur. Like those coke-stoked disco-lizard days in Los Angeles in the mid-Seventies—that whole era's pretty vague. "Incredible losses of memory," he says, hand slapping head. "Whole *chunks* of my life. I can't remember, for instance, any—*any*—of 1975. Not one minute!" Even the Grammy Awards show—the night he turned up in wing collar and white tie, looking bloodlessly sleek, and posed cadaverlike for the press with John Lennon, Yoko Ono, Simon and Garfunkel—*nada*.

"I didn't realize I'd done that until somebody called the office the other day and wanted to run a film clip of it. I said, are you *serious*? And then I looked back at it and . . . I mean, I knew I'd worn an evening suit *somewhere,* but I didn't know it was there.

"Actually," he says, stubbing out a cigarette, "I was amazed I was standing up."

Escaping from L.A. probably saved his life, he says. Another turning point came in December 1980, three months after he released his last album, *Scary Monsters (and Super Creeps)*.

He was in New York at the time, on Broadway, winding up his well-received tour with *The Elephant Man*. He still remembers the night—it was very late—that he got the awful news from May Pang, John Lennon's former secretary. Lennon had been murdered.

"The handful of performances after that," Bowie says, "were absolutely awful. Just *awful*. A whole piece of my life seemed to have been taken away; a whole *reason* for being a singer and songwriter seemed to be removed from me. It was almost like a warning. It was saying: we've got to do something about our situation on earth."

Bowie put his musical persona on low-profile and set about making a real home for himself and Joey in the pristine countryside near Geneva. He grew reflective. "Having a child to care for points up one's purpose, it really does. To see him grow, and be excited about the future—and then you think: 'Oh, shit, the future, yes. I'd forgotten about that, old son. Um . . . I'll see what I can do. . . .'"

It is this sea change, of sorts, that has brought Bowie back to Australia. He first came here in 1978, on his last concert tour, and at each city where he did a show, he would rent a Land Rover or some similarly rugged vehicle and clatter off into the outback, the parched and haunting bush. He was hypnotized: here was a country the size of the United States with a population of some 15 million people. Culturally, it had the upbeat, can-do character of America in the Fifties, before so much went so wrong there, but physically—with its idyllic coasts and endless, arid plains, and its singular wildlife—it was unlike anyplace else on earth.

But, like America, Australia had an ugly racial secret: the policies adopted toward the native Aborigines by the European settlers who began arriving on the continent in the late eighteenth century—many of them convicts and their keepers—could most gently be described as genocidal. On what is now the island state of Tasmania, Bowie learned, the indigenous Aboriginal population had been utterly extinguished.

"As much as I love this country," he says, "it's probably one of the most racially intolerant in the world, well in line with South Africa. I mean, in the north, there's unbelievable intolerance. The Aborigines can't even buy their drinks in the same bars—they have to go round the back and get them through what's called a 'dog hatch.' And then they're forbidden from drinking them on the same side of the *street* as the bar; they have to go to the other side of the road."

So Australia was ideal for what Bowie now had in mind. "It occurred to me that one doesn't have much *time* on the planet, you know? And that I could do something more useful in terms of . . . I know this is very *cliché,* but I feel that now that I'm thirty-six years old, and I've got a certain position, I want to start utilizing that position to the benefit of my . . . brotherhood and sisterhood." He winces, but continues. "I've found it's very easy to be successful in other terms, but I think you can't keep on being an artist without actually saying anything more than, 'Well, this is an interesting way of looking at things.'

"There is also a *right* way of looking at things: there's a lot of injustice. So let's, you know, *say* something about it. However naff it comes off."

In February, Bowie brought David Mallet, the London-based director with whom he collaborates, to Switzerland to help work up storyboards for the two videos he wanted to do: "Let's Dance," the title track from his new album, and another song on the LP called "China Girl" (which Bowie had written with his friend Iggy Pop in 1977, and which had previously appeared on Pop's album *The Idiot*). In less than a week, they were in Sydney with an English producer and cameraman, and an Australian crew numbering about a dozen people. Bowie had also secured the services of two students from Sydney's Aboriginal-Islanders Dance Theatre and a young Chinese woman from New Zealand named Geeling, and soon had them racing all over town. One morning, he'd have the Aboriginal pair—a boy named Terry Roberts and a girl named Joelene King—clambering up a hand-built "hilltop" on a promontory overlooking Shark Island in Sydney's spectacular harbor; in the afternoon, the whole company would tear across town to a machine shop in the sweltering suburb of Guildford, where Terry would be filmed toiling at a big steel milling machine amid stifling clouds of artificial smoke. (A few days earlier, Bowie'd had Terry actually pulling the machine down a major Sydney thoroughfare while Joelene, on her hands and knees, scrubbed down the intersection with soap brush and water—much to the audible dismay of an army of Saturday drivers.)

Geeling was also exotically occupied, one day "making

love" with Bowie on the beach, another romping through Chinatown in a gray silk Mao uniform and red-star cap. Aside from Bowie and Mallet, no one could figure out what the hell was going on.

Both videos, of course, were about racism and oppression. "Very simple, very direct," Bowie explained one afternoon. "They're almost like Russian social realism, very naive. And the message that they have is very simple—it's wrong to be racist!" He can't help laughing at the sentiment so baldly stated. "But I see no reason to fuck about with that message, you see? I thought, 'Let's try to use the video format as a platform for some kind of social observation, and not just waste it on trotting out and trying to enhance the public image of the singer involved. I mean, these *are* little movies, and some movies can have a point, so why not try to *make* some point. This stuff goes out all over the world; it's played on all kinds of programs. I mean—you get *free point time!*"

It is, as Bowie says, a place of "frankly brute character." Town of Carinda, a close-to-the-ground sheep-country settlement some 400 miles out over the Blue Mountains and down into the sun-baked bush west of Sydney. There's been no useful rainfall in these parts for four years, and the sun beats down with an incendiary power. At ten-thirty in the morning, crew members are already estimating the temperature at around 120 degrees Fahrenheit.

As a hard-scrub fantasy of a frontier outpost, Carinda might seem overdrawn even to Sergio Leone. There's no one on the main street except a fly-bitten dog and a town drunk, and at any moment, one expects to see Clint Eastwood stepping out into the glare with a bulge in his poncho, gunning for Lee Van Cleef. Inside the one-room pub in the Carinda Hotel, several large-bellied locals are already lined up at the bar, swatting down schooners of Tooths beer—leathery men in the bush shorts, T-shirt and sweat-stained slouch hats that are a kind of uniform among the good old boys of the outback. There isn't much to do out here beyond drinking and fighting, and these geezers, apparently, are getting an early start.

No one pays too much attention when Bowie walks in. He's wearing his usual gray shorts, bush boots, short-sleeve shirt and a kind of semisoft fedora known locally as a Snowy River. Even though he lacks the pendulous gut that makes for authenticity in these matters, he's not conspicuous. He looks around at the linoleum floor, the dart board and pool table, the overhead fan, the dust-caked cricket trophies above the bar, the wallboard menu offering chicko rolls and meat pies, and he smothers a chuckle. "I love this place," he says in a discreet whisper.

The locals soon realize that something's up: a lot of impossibly pale-looking people are starting to haul in Arriflex cameras and klieg lights and stun-size audio speakers. They're tacking glare netting over the open doorway, and one of them's starting to squirt smoke around, which is really stinking the place up. They've also brought a pair of Abos with them, which must be some kind of unwished-for first. "Where'd you get the dark couple?" asks one tippler in a flat, chilly tone.

By this point, the entire adult population of Carinda seems to have squeezed into the pub, along with several wild boys who are in town for the feral-pig hunts. (Wall posters offer fifty cents a kilo for boar meat, but according to one well-oiled sport, it's "pretty rank" stuff, given what the beasts are forced to feed on these days; what the hell, though—it's mostly shipped to Germany anyway.)

As the smoke thickens and the temperature inside the pub hits ninety-four degrees, a walloping funk beat comes leaping out of the speakers. It's "Let's Dance," the first single off Bowie's new album. Coproduced by Nile Rodgers of Chic, and featuring various Chic members in the band, the song and the rest of the album are not exactly what fans might have expected from the man who helped inaugurate the current wave of synthesizer-based dance pop. At least Bowie hopes not.

"I think that's what this record came out of. I was sort of disappointed with the way synthesizers have *bullied* music into a kind of cold place. So much of the music that's being made at the moment is very *earnest*. It doesn't have that quality of *necessity* that music used to have; it's become style over content. So in a natural progression, I just went back to the kinds of music that really excited me when I started. I was listening to people like Buddy Guy, Red Prysock, Alan Freed big bands. Stuff like that has such a dynamic, enthusiastic quality; it's the enthusiasm that I actually was looking for."

The album was recorded in three weeks ("I must try to better that next time," Bowie cackles), and simplicity was the keynote all the way. "John Lennon once said to me, 'Look, it's *very* simple—say what you mean, make it rhyme and put a backbeat to it.' And he was right: 'Instant karma's gonna get you,' *boom*. I keep comin' back to that these days. He was right, man. There is no more than that. There *is no more*."

Simplicity and directness of expression have become a passion for him now, he says. "I've never admitted this before—because it's never been true before—but this album is kind of tentative. I mean, I only kind of touched the edge of what I really·want to do. I want to go further, much further, with the next one."

And what will that be, then?

"A protest album, I suppose."

As the camera pans past Terry and Joelene, who are dancing across the smoke-filled floor, and then sweeps down the bar for a panorama of sweat-plastered faces, Bowie, wearing freshly pressed cream slacks, a lightly striped shirt and green tie, a pair of delicate white gloves rolled at the wrists, and carrying a cherry-red Stratocaster, takes his place against the front wall, next to an extra who's thumping away on a stand-up bass. By now, some of the locals, seized by the beat, are rolling around on their bar stools, and the owner of the place has waded in to actually take a stab at dancing with the two Aboriginal kids. Smoke is swirling all around, beers are scudding across the bar at a record rate, and not five feet from where Bowie stands mouthing something about "this serious moonlight," the wild-pig boys are wondering what to make of it all. Is it a toothpaste commercial? An advert for little white gloves? Or could it be . . . some kind of celebrity?

"'Ere," says one of the boar stalkers, jerking a thumb over his shoulder at Bowie and the prop bassist, an idea dawning in his sun-soaked brain. "'Ere, who's the group?"

On the final day of shooting, the crew sets out from its motel base in Coonabarabran, on the banks of the Castlereagh River, for the Warrumbungle range, a national preserve located thirty-odd kilometers away. It is a place of surrealistically spectacular sights: rock-topped hills rising in eccentric formations against the enormous blue sky, heat-shattered gum trees clawing the air or keeled over in droves on the arid plains, puff mushrooms bigger than baseballs, meat ants the size of termites and march flies that can chew right through your clothes to the flesh and blood below. There is much rendering of the "Australian salute" in an effort to fend off flying pests, and the heat is an autonomous and oppressive presence.

"What a *ridiculous bird!*" Bowie shouts delightedly, as an emu—a kind of bizarre, humpbacked turkey—goes trotting off through some nearby scrub.

There've been stranger sights out here in the bush, though: Aborigines carried off in helicopters; Geeling in her little Mao suit running back and forth across the dusty plain with a big red banner; Bowie standing tall in a black top hat and tails, muttering in the heat, "I feel like a well-dressed Arab." It's almost a wrap now.

Bowie could be forgiven for feeling beat by this point, but if he is, he doesn't show it. He's in great shape—and after all, this is only the beginning of what could well be his biggest year ever. His first tour in five years kicks off in Germany on May 20th (arriving in the U.S. for July and August, with a preview performance at the Us Festival in California on May 30th), and he says it will be "a lot warmer than most of the high-powered concerts are these days. It won't have the circus appeal of the Stones or the monolithic value of the Who. It'll be kind of . . . well, as *romantic* as you can get in a large-scale arena."

The tour will take up a good six months of his life, but in the interim, he'll also be highly visible at the movies. Apart from the Ziggy Stardust film, there will be *The Hunger,* a loony rendition of Whitley Strieber's erotic vampire novel, in which Bowie costars with Catherine Deneuve and Susan Sarandon; and *Merry Christmas, Mr. Lawrence,* a World War II prison-camp drama by the controversial Japanese director Nagisa Oshima, which costars Tom Conti, Jack Thompson (of *Breaker Morant*) and Riuichi Sakamoto (of Tokyo's Yellow Magic Orchestra), and will première at the Cannes International Film Festival in May.

Bowie is a bit ambivalent about *The Hunger.* He was drawn to the project because of the chance to work with first-time feature-film director Tony Scott (who is the brother of Ridley Scott, the director of *Alien* and *Blade Runner*) and by the opportunity to interact with Sarandon, whom he characterizes, most emphatically, as "pure dynamite." The end result, though, gives him pause. "I must say, there's nothing that *looks* like it on the market. But I'm a bit worried that it's just perversely bloody at some points. I'm not sure I can take any of that anymore," he sighs, waving the whole thing away.

The Oshima film is something else again. The director, best known in America for his startling 1976 sexual odyssey, *In the Realm of the Senses,* offered Bowie the part of Jack Celliers—a British soldier imprisoned in a brutal Japanese POW camp on Java in 1942—because, after flying to New York to see him in *The Elephant Man,* Oshima realized that Bowie had the perfect quality for the role: "an inner spirit that is indestructible."

The film was shot on the very remote Polynesian island of Rarotonga (the director had heard it was "the second most beautiful place on earth"), and Oshima's technique, according to Bowie, was as unorthodox as his preparations. "He built maybe two or three acres of camp—*enormous,* it was—which he *never shot.* And it was beautifully built with vine and bamboo and leaves; there were guard turrets that weren't *touched,* that nobody ever stood in. He only shot tiny little bits at the corners. I kind of thought it was a waste, but when I saw the movie, it was just so potent—you could *feel* the camp there, quite definitely."

That Bowie actually got to *see* a finished film must have been a happy surprise, given Oshima's methods. "He shot in the camera, in sequence, so it was ready to edit when it came out the other end. And he didn't have any rushes done—there were *no rushes!*—and the stuff was being shipped off from Rarotonga with no safety prints, either. It was all going out of the camera and down to the post office and being wrapped up in brown paper and sent off to Japan. He said, 'There's my film.' And the editor at the other end—this old man—would take it out, process it, cut it up, put it together—and by the time Oshima got back to Japan, he had a rough print within four days! I mean, I thought, 'Hey, baby, *that's* makin' a *movie,*' you know? *Say* what you mean, *make* it rhyme and *put* it to a backbeat—no fuckin' about! It was just glorious. And I think it's the most credible performance I've done in a film."

As with his previous feature-film projects—Nicolas Roeg's enigmatic 1976 opus, *The Man Who Fell to Earth* ("I'm so pleased I made that, but I didn't really know what was being made at all") and the ludicrous *Just a Gigolo,* in 1979—Bowie looks upon these latest outings as educational experiences as much as anything else. He noses around, picks up tips and hopes one day to do some directing himself. God knows he gets enough scripts in the mail. "Continually—and absolutely awful.

Real *shockers,* exploiting every known perversity of mankind. *Hundreds* of treatments of Ziggy have come my way, all co-lossally awful. And I've got more Martians-who-play-guitar scripts in my house than you'd believe."

His hapless sigh just sort of slips out. "I mean, you wouldn't think that many people *wrote* about Martians who play guitars, would you?"

The bright red fever ball of the sun has finally set behind the craggy hills, leaving galahs and ground parrots to flap about the gum trees, and the night-loving kangaroos to hop forth in search of food. Seen up close—and in the gathering dark you can get within three or four feet of them in a car—the kangaroo would seem to be among the world's gentlest creatures. To the totemistic Aborigines, it was always a kindred spirit, but to the sheep men who now occupy the ancient tribal lands, the 'roos are just another unwelcome mouth to feed in a time of brush fires and browning grass. At night, the wild boys sometimes come in their clapped-out bush buggies, roaring up alongside the startled creatures and lopping off their heads with axes, all for the simple sport of watching the great bloody beasts stagger off, spurting, into the scrub.

Filming has wrapped. It'll be good to get back to Sydney, now, back by the sea. Bowie calls it "the great sparkling city of the New World."

Wherever you go, chances are Bowie's been there first. When the New Romantics arrived on the English music scene four years ago, they were merely moving into artistic premises that Bowie had already vacated. "It's still a bit Me Generation for me," he says. "The whole thing still smacks a bit of 'I'm so important, I've gotta write a song about *me,* to describe how incredibly precious my feelings are, and I want to impart this to you—in three minutes and forty-five seconds.'

"But listen, I'll tell you what," he says, so as not to sound callous, "there's some good songwriting around."

He's already moved on, though. He's agreed to play the role of Abraham Lincoln in *The Civil War,* an avant-garde opera by Robert Wilson that will be performed during the 1984 Olympics in Los Angeles. This has given him some good ideas. He told Wilson he didn't have time to write any music for the show himself, but suggested that he either get David Byrne, of Talking Heads, to compose some material or "put Iggy Pop together with Philip Glass and see what comes up." Wilson is apparently working on this, and Bowie feels it could be the start of something.

"I think there's another format for music onstage," he says. "Usually, you have a Twyla Tharp who pulls in people like David Byrne. But I think maybe if it started from the rock & roll side, and it pulled in the Twyla Tharps, maybe something interesting could come of it. It's always come from the intellectual side first, and I don't think it should for rock & roll. I think it should come from the meaty bit first, and then try to conceptualize it for the stage."

And what about Wilson's original proposal, playing Abraham Lincoln? What exactly will that entail?

"Oh, fallin' out of a balcony, I suspect."

It's quite a life, all right. He is able to do things, go places—to Africa, to Europe, to Asia. He goes because he can afford it— or arrange it—and because there's no one to tie him down. He's arranged that, too. Corinne Schwab—"Coco," his invaluable aide-de-camp—has traveled with him for ten years now, but their relationship, while affectionate, is professional and purely platonic, he says. No great loves?

"My son, I think. I don't have any great attachments to anybody. Um . . . I've got a number of girlfriends that I see around the world—I'm a bit sailorlike, I suppose. But I wasn't happy with marriage; I went into it wrong. I think I just find it hard to live with anybody. I'm a very solitary person, actually, kind of selfish that way. I like my own company. I like thinking on my own, I like writing on my own. I find it hard to be perpetually enthusiastic about somebody else's life all the time. And rather than inflict that on someone, I'd just as soon see them more casually."

Mr. Self-Contained! But hey: for him it works, right? So who's to complain? Bowie whips out a bit of wisdom.

"There was one famous old Zen monk who regarded his house as his clothes," he says. "And somebody knocked on his door once, and he wasn't wearing anything. And they said, 'Why aren't you wearing anything?' And he said, 'What're you doing in my trousers?'"

Gary Gershoff/Retna Ltd.

Twenty-Two

Dress Right!

(London, 1981)

David Bowie had been nearing the end of his man-of-many-faces phase at the dawn of the Eighties when a whole new tribe of lipsticked and hair-slicked disciples suddenly popped up in his native London. They called themselves "New Romantics," and, yes, they seemed more than a little ridiculous at first— although not much more ridiculous than the first brocade- and bead-laden hippies must have seemed about fifteen years earlier. The idea of flying over to London to cover this scene was not an easy sell, as I recall, but by the time this story appeared, the windows of various high-toned Fifth Avenue department stores were already cluttered with fey little harem hats and fantasy pirate gear.

New romanticism, as I'm afraid we'll have to call it, never really took root at the street level in this country, as it had in Britain. But the music associated with the style—a sometimes chilly blend of big-beat Eurodisco, German synthesizer minimalism and straightforward dance-floor R&B—set the tone for much of Western pop for the rest of the decade. It also gave us such groups as Duran Duran and Spandau Ballet, and of course the actually talented Boy George. In case you were wondering whom to thank.

Woe, Britannia: civil war impending in Ulster; race riots in Brixton; a roaring inflation fanned by two years of Tory ineptitude. All this and lousy weather, primitive heating and the expensive silliness of a royal family, too. Britain is *hurting*. No future? Maybe the punks were right.

And yet, here tonight at Langan's Brasserie in Covent Garden, where waiters glide by bearing trays full of fat, pink prawns and *artichauts farcis*—here the apparently irreversible crumbling of Britain's postwar political order is not a subject that springs spontaneously to mind. At Langan's, one sinks into a sea of sleek chat and rippling piano music, and as the chilled, glistening bottles of pricey Bordeaux and Alsatian Riesling go bobbling by, somehow the no-hope-and-welcome-to-it world of punk seems very far away. The Blitz crowd, an enterprising in-group of disaffected musicians, dance-club DJs, upstart designers and aspiring entrepreneurs, owns the moment in London now.

Most of these people are in their early twenties, and many were initially inspired by the explosion of punk style in 1976. But they ultimately rejected punk's downbeat political prognosis as a dreary dead end. Why be down when you can be up? Why look terminal when you can look terrific? New attitudes were required for the Eighties. New sounds, new clothes—a whole new pose. Whereas the punks raged against the undignified decline of once-mighty Britain, these new kids see only possibilities. In a trendy and imperfect way, Blitz is about optimism. And, of course, fun. "Rock & roll has never been and never will be the end of the world," says Robert Elms, a young writer and scenemaker in the Blitz circle. "If you forget that, you can enjoy it."

Naturally, these upstart trendies titter and whine when the press labels them "New Romantics," or worse yet, "Blitz Kids" (after the Covent Garden club where their Day-glo-retro lifestyle first went public two years ago). If the music papers and fashion rags must have a handle, they prefer the clunky "Cult with No Name"—a term impossible to utter with a straight face.

It's a moot concern. This latest British subcultural sprawl defies concise designation. What musical tag, for instance, could adequately encompass the tribal drums and pirate drag of Bow Wow Wow and Adam and the Ants; the gilded rockabilly revivalism of the Stray Cats, Polecats and Shakin' Pyramids; the semiridiculous preening of the music-for-clothes crew—Spandau Ballet, Duran Duran, Classix Nouveaux, Depeche Mode; the beatnik flash of Blue Rondo à la Turk; and the vivid electronic impressionism of such veteran Cold Wave synthesizer bands as Ultravox, Landscape, even the arid Gary Numan? For purposes of pigeonholing all of this, "Blitz"—as in Zap! Pow! Look at us!—will have to serve.

Three key members of this new pop elite of Swinging London 1981 are here tonight. Midge Ure and Billy Currie, both of the formerly scorned but now ascendant Ultravox, are sipping cocktails in the lounge. Midge is wearing—one notes these things nowadays—a generously draped, dun-colored suit, rather in the manner of Robert Donat in *The Thirty-nine Steps*. He sports a neat pencil mustache, a discreetly sculptured pompadour and long sideburns that slice down to perfect points at midcheek. Billy is casually shapeless in a pair of roomy, high-waisted trousers and a quaint, short-sleeved blue shirt with a sort of Peter Pan collar; if it wasn't for the thin gold hoop in his ear, he'd pass for a busboy at a Brighton resort. At a nearby table sits Rusty Egan, nursing an orange juice as he talks with a visiting fellow DJ from New York. Rusty, a producer, drummer and record-spinner at such seminal new night-life clubs as Billy's, the Blitz and Hell, is a striking exponent of the Young Winston look—big, smartly cut blue pin-stripe suiting, natty red tie cinched in with a collar pin, wavy reddish hair cut short and slickly brushed back. Rusty and Midge and Billy are all participants in an independent and highly successful musical project called Visage, and at any moment now they're expecting their lead singer, a bizarre young—but wait: judging by the sudden outbreak of stifled gasps and dropped jaws, he's obviously just arrived.

Even in Langan's, heads still spin shamelessly when Steve Strange makes his entrance, accompanied by a small entourage. Steve is the centerpiece of the Blitz phenomenon, its purest expression—a man who lives to get dressed up and go out at night. And tonight, as always, he looks great. He is wearing—how to describe it?—a kind of Piccadilly Pasha get-up: a billowing red blouson ensemble with an ornate black-and-gold Moroccan vest and ballooning pants legs tucked into soft, suede midcalf boots.

There's a string of small gold coins around his neck, and his fingers are aglitter with rings. His rather full face bears a dusky stubble of beard and is exotically darkened with a rich bronze makeup. His eyes are drawn with mascara and further set off by green eye shadow, and his tinted hair erupts like a mutant haystack, a good twelve inches above a broad Oriental headband, from either side of which dangle long, ornamental tassles. It's the ultimate in drop-dead dressing. Steve calls this latest look "Moroccan Indian," and it's not something you can just slip into for a quick trip to the greengrocer.

"Getting ready in the morning is not easy," he confides, beckoning the rest of the party toward a favored table at the back of the long dining room. "I can't just *go out.* I have to put the face on. It only takes me about five minutes to pick an outfit, because I know I've got it sussed what's good-looking. But I mean, I can't get up and do my *face* in five minutes, because to me, makeup is an important part of an outfit."

Steve has a how's-the-weather way of saying such things that's instantly disarming. One can almost picture him padding about his flat wondering where that damned emerald eye shadow got to, or perhaps prying the mascara away from the cat. But in the beery, bedrock Britain of football clubs and workingmen's pubs, not everyone appreciates all those hours he puts in at the vanity table. Someone's always cracking off—like the time Steve climbed out of a taxi to pay his fare and the cabbie, running a rheumy eye down whatever orchidaceous outfit he was wearing that day, sourly inquired, "Excuse me, but you *are* from another planet, aren't you?"

Steve is unfazed by such witless drool. So typical, you know? So mean. As a born extrovert, he's had to deal with this sort of Cro-Magnon mentality ever since the age of fourteen, when he got bounced out of school in his native Wales for dyeing his hair orange. That was at the height of his infatuation with David Bowie. Now, he says, as we all sit down to sup, his chief problem—much as one expects Bowie's must be—is keeping ahead of his fans and imitators. Blitz isn't about imitation, it's about total warp-five individuality. But what's to be done? With his various images—Regency fop, windblown Robin Hood, chalk-faced fantasy creature, black-robed priest of Byzantium—plastered all over the Sunday papers and adorning such upmarket magazines as *Vogue, Queen, Harper's* and *Der Stern,* he's been hard pressed to stay one step ahead of his own publicity pics. So now, as soon as a new set of photos is taken, he immediately dumps the look and completely alters his act. Such a time, he tells me, is once again at hand. In fact, his friend Helen Robinson at PX, the influential Covent Garden boutique, is at this very moment executing a new outfit he's designed.

"It's trousers and shirt, with sash on the waist and a sash for the neck. It's all elephant print, with hummingbirds."

"Elephants?" I ask, not quite sure I've got this right.

"With *hummingbirds*," Steve enthuses. "All on a print."

"I think the King's Road is more exciting now than it has been for a long time," says Steve, peering out the window as we taxi down London's famous fashion alley the following afternoon. "It's funny to see the photographers here again, and the tourists takin' pictures of their kids." He gestures toward two little girls posing glumly in freshly purchased Union Jack derbies. The street is certainly jumping, and no wonder. Blitz is big business now, and whatever Blitzed-out look one has in mind (the options are limitless) can be put together right here. Robin Hood boots at Sacha International, gypsy silks and pastel mohairs at Downtown, camouflage and glitter moccasins at Meducci, Bryan Ferry–style silk shirts and class leathers at Take Six, sailor suits and seersuckers at Chopra. There's even a boutique called Mini-rock for Blitz nymphets.

More wonders await inside the Great Gear Market arcade, a dizzy conglomeration of clothes stalls, coffee bars and junk bins selling knee-length sweat shirts, Mary Quant sparkle tights, Johnny Rotten box-plaid suits, Thalonia makeup kits ("Wildcat," "Clown," "American Indian"), red suede winkle-pickers, tubes of lime-green hair dye—you name it. Overhead, king-size speakers boom out Roxy Music's majestic "A Song for Europe." Rusty Egan's Eurofunk record shop, the Cage, is here, and so's the Axiom design group—John Baker's outlet for such leading young designers as Melissa Caplan and Simon Withers (who creates clothes for Spandau Ballet). These and other like-minded fashion-school refugees—Willie Brown, Judith Franklin, Chris Sullivan—were launched by the Blitz club scene and have already made their ideas about shape and drape felt in Paris and New York. When critics dismiss the whole Blitz phenomenon as empty and inconsequential, these are the people Steve points to.

"I think what we've done with the club life and night

scene—with photographers, designers, artists, milliners, the shops, giving people jobs—is much more creative than just sitting in front of the telly and complaining about the state of the world. We've given more opportunity to young kids to do things, and we've put London back onto a *very* fuckin' dreary map. People thought London was a *dead city*. They thought it was *finished*. Nothing from here had influenced Paris designers since 1976." Steve pauses to swat a tassle off his nose and watches bemusedly as a gaggle of psychopunks stumbles by in screaming pastel Mohawks and Bauhaus and Theatre of Hate band-fan jackets.

"I'm not just speaking about fashion," he continues, "because fashion can't make a record, and fashion can't sell a record. You need good musicianship as well."

Steve is talking—rather defensively—about Visage, a group that has never played a gig but whose self-titled debut album, like Ultravox's superb *Vienna* LP of last year, provides a stirring soundtrack for the new state of mind. The cool, high-tech production (by Midge Ure and the rest of the group) leaves plenty of room for Rusty's fat, visceral disco wallop, and the ten tracks bristle with ideas and atmospheres—from the grand, sweeping art-rock anthem of the title track and the loopy synthesizer line of "Tar" to the charging martial beat and Duane Eddy–ish guitar on "Malpaso Man" and the epic groove of a lone instrumental called, *most* appropriately, "The Dancer." Detractors may grump and wheeze about the recherché aspects of all this, but *Visage* has obviously struck a timely cultural chord in Europe. Released last November, the album sold a very solid 120,000 copies in Britain and lodged in the Top Twenty for three months. In Germany, it was Top Five for three months, and it's also gone Top Five in France, Belgium, Denmark and Australia. Two singles off the LP, the haunting "Fade to Grey" and "Mind of a Toy," were smash hits on both sides of the Channel.

The roots of both the Blitz phenomenon and the Visage project go back to the King's Road, where, in 1976, Rusty Egan first met Steve Strange (né Harrington) outside a café. Steve had dyed blond hair then, and he was wearing jackboots and a full-length, green-leather German officer's trench coat. Rusty, who appreciates panache, thought he looked great, and they started hanging out together. Neither of them was doing much at the time. Rusty, a fast-talking, Irish-born drummer from a family of professional musicians, was getting nowhere auditioning for the Clash. Steve, who until recently had lived in Wales with his divorced mother and younger sister, had come to London after witnessing an early Sex Pistols gig near his hometown of Newbridge. For money, he cleaned toilets at the Roxy, London's legendary punk palace. Punk was king, and Steve was looking for a way to fit his skills—which at that point consisted largely of looking sharp on a next-to-nothing budget—into the scene. Both he and Rusty were interested in fashion, but at the moment, aside from the ever-inventive David Bowie, nothing very fashionable was going on.

Eventually, Steve drifted into a notorious scam called the Moors Murderers, a band organized by Sex Pistols manager Malcolm McLaren and named after a particularly vicious pair of British mass murderers—much to the scandalized delight of the English tabloids. Steve was badly burned by the sleazy publicity, but still game. At night, he and Rusty would hook up and go out to clubs like the Speakeasy, where Rusty would badger the dozing DJ into letting him spin some records. As it turned out, he was very adept at programming dance music, and soon was filling in whenever the DJ took a night off.

Rusty finally scored a job with the Rich Kids, the band formed by original Sex Pistols bassist Glen Matlock. Musically, it was a very dodgy proposition until Matlock called in guitarist James "Midge" Ure, a diminutive Scot who had just emerged from the wreckage of a hit pop group called Slik with nothing to show for the experience but an enormous debt. Midge helped whip the Rich Kids into shape, but soon discovered that their main problem—given the Matlock-Pistols connection—was that they were not punks. "We didn't have the leather jackets and the spiky hair," he recalls. "We were quite a smart wee outfit that wanted to do good-quality pop songs. Unfortunately, nobody liked it. I mean, loads of people used to come to our gigs, but mainly to throw things at me."

The Rich Kids fell apart about the time that Midge bought a synthesizer and, to Matlock's dismay, attempted to introduce it into the group. Punks hated synthesizers, associating them with the mushy, overwrought music of people like Keith Emerson and Rick Wakeman. And, of course, disco.

As the Rich Kids wound down, Rusty Egan was getting fed up with the whole gigging scene. Steve had moved in with

Rusty, and together they started going out to clubs; mainly gay clubs like Bangs and Billy's—the latter a Soho hangout particularly favored by transvestites. It was an eye-opening experience for both of them: in contrast to the punk clubs, the gay clubs were classy, nonviolent and very much into funky, rhythmic music. They were also extremely tolerant of the most bizarre individual dress and behavior. After a few weeks of checking out the scene at Billy's, Rusty approached the owners and proposed taking over the club for one night a week—a standard way of breaking into the club business in England. Tuesdays were slow, and so a deal was struck.

Rusty's first decision was not to advertise his new "club" in any traditional way. Instead, he handed out flyers with a picture of David Bowie, announcing:

FAME, FAME, WHAT'S YOUR NAME
A CLUB FOR HEROES
DISCO ON THE TRANS-EUROPE EXPRESS

The flyers bore no address, but word of mouth spread quickly, and soon the place was packed every Tuesday night. "A lot of people who were fed up with punk," Steve says, "were waitin' for somewhere to go."

At Billy's, Steve and Rusty gave them "Bowie Night," and habitués turned up wearing personalized versions of Bowie's greatest looks. There were lots to choose from—the androgynous glitter mode of his Ziggy Stardust period, the Fifties bopsuit cool displayed on the *Pin Ups* album, the futuristic *Aladdin Sane* gear, the disco spiff of *Young Americans* and the Euroartiste image favored by the latter-day Bowie. But if Bowie always seemed to have taken a style as far as it could go, the kids at Billy's used his images as stepping-off points. And while Rusty spun records appropriate to his nascent concept of "electro-disco"—lots of synthesized European stuff like Kraftwerk, Ultravox, some Magazine sides, singles by Telex, the Normal and Human League, the occasional track by Brian Eno, lots of vintage Roxy Music and, of course, Bowie faves—Steve, done up in his best duds, would stand at the door and attempt to keep out drunks, slumming football fans, people who wanted to run home and slip into their scuba gear so they could frolic with the freaks—anyone who seemed unlikely to, ahem, *participate.*

Meanwhile, inside, a new style was being born: men in bright-colored military uniforms, medals, forage caps, Cossack outfits; women on a *Breakfast at Tiffany's* trip with pillbox hats, veils and long cigarette holders. No black leather. No T-shirts. And not a shred of denim.

The apparent elitism of the door policy bothered a lot of people, particularly the press, which couldn't get in. "Nobody understood," says Rusty, "but there were enough people who looked great—who enjoyed it—that you couldn't fit anybody else in. Unless you looked *exceptionally good,* then of course you got in. But it was so bloomin' crowded."

Where Rusty saw crowds, the owners of Billy's saw a fortune to be made. Why keep *anybody* out? they wondered. Rusty and Steve could see what was coming—zoo world. And so after a few months, they moved their little scene over to Covent Garden, to a club called the Blitz, on Great Queen Street.

By this time, Steve had also started singing with a short-lived band called the Photons (whose lineup included future members of the Psychedelic Furs and Adam and the Ants). The Photons rehearsed in a room underneath the PX boutique, and one day Helen Robinson, the designer, asked Steve if he'd like to work in the shop during the day. With this gold mine of fine threads at his disposal, Steve was soon on his way to becoming the Beau Brummel of postpunk London.

Because by 1979, punk was definitely dead. Something new was in the air, something not yet quite defined—but you could see it at the Blitz, which became a magnet for all those kids who were sick of black leather and no future and strong-arm bouncers and long waits for lame bands and the whole squalid late-punk scene. "You could see the transition," says Rusty. "Like, you'd see a girl and you'd think, 'Wow, she looks really great,' you know? But she's a little bit punky. And you'd sit down and she'd say, 'Fuck off! I hate ya!' They didn't know what to do; they didn't know how to react. Because they'd been goin' around for two years tellin' everybody they hate everything, and then they're sittin' in a club and they *love* it. And probably for the first time in two years, they actually fancied some bloke, you know? Somebody who didn't have a pin through his face and blackheads everywhere. And then they'd get really annoyed because the bloke was gay—and he was probably only gay because the women looked *so awful* for the last few years."

Midge Ure seconds that emotion. *"God,* you'd wake up next to one of those things in the morning. . . ." He shudders. "But then you'd go to the Blitz," he says, brightening, "and you'd sit and talk to some girl who looked like Lollobrigida or Marilyn Monroe. And it's like a *big difference* when you wake up next to Marilyn Monroe. It's like, 'Hey! Hello!'"

The changes that the Blitz kids soon wrought in the pop-rock social hierarchy were never more apparent than on the night Mick Jagger showed up. "He came to the club and he was *completely* pissed out of his head," says Steve, who was of course running the door. "He was shouting over the queue, 'You don't know who the fuck I am! I don't know why I should bother to queue up for this fucking place—I should just walk through the door!' The people he was with were so embarrassed. I said, 'Look, Mick, you're just making a fool of yourself. I think you shouldn't bother to come in; you should go home.' Because the kids in the queue didn't give a fuck about the Rolling Stones. I mean, I don't knock the Rolling Stones, but I don't know much *about* them. I've never really listened to them, to be quite honest."

The original purpose of Visage, Midge Ure is telling me in his broad Scottish accent, was to create some new music for the Blitz cub. When the Rich Kids folded, Midge and Rusty realized that the group still had some studio time booked; they decided to take advantage of it. Steve wanted to sing, so the three of them went into the studio and Midge produced three totally synthesized tracks—an original tune called "All the King's Horses" and unlikely cover versions of the 1969 Zager and Evans hit, "In the Year 2525," and Barry McGuire's primordial "Eve of Destruction." Midge took these to his record company, EMI, which "couldn't make head or tail of it." Midge, Rusty and Steve weren't discouraged; they had already hatched a plan to recruit some of their favorite musicians from other bands and record a whole album of electro-disco tracks. Fortunately, the musicians they had in mind—violinist and keyboardist Billy Currie of Ultravox and keyboardist Dave Formula, bassist Barry Adamson and guitarist and sax player John McGeoch, all of Magazine—agreed to the project. Then Martin Rushent, producer of the Stranglers and Buzzcocks, invited them to record the album at his home studio in Reading and offered to release it on Radar Records, with which he had an independent production deal. Rushent's home studio was literally that—the group actually had to go into the kitchen to capture certain otherwise unobtainable sounds. A single from these early sessions, "Tar," was released late in 1979 but sank without a trace after Radar Records suddenly folded.

The band kept plugging away at an album, though, and Midge and Billy Currie developed a strong musical rapport. Currie, a gifted, classically trained musician, was at loose ends. Ultravox had just lost its lead singer and stylistic figurehead, John Foxx, and the band's future seemed bleak. Midge, a big Ultravox fan, offered himself as a replacement for Foxx, and in order to raise some money to help resuscitate the group, he accepted a job as a guitarist for hard-rockers Thin Lizzy. Currie, for his part, signed on for a short tour with Gary Numan—whose one-note futurism owed much of what little substance it had to Ultravox. With these complications, the Visage album took nearly a year to complete.

Meanwhile, London's new night life was exploding at clubs like Le Kilt, St. Moritz and the Beat Route. Electro-dancemania had even spread to the provinces—places like the Rum Runner in Birmingham, Tips in Manchester, Tanzschau in Cardiff. One person who had been keeping a close eye on all this was the godfather of Blitz himself, David Bowie. One night early last year, Bowie walked into the Blitz club and selected several of the more photogenic poseurs on hand, including Steve Strange, to appear in a video for a song called "Ashes to Ashes," from Bowie's latest album, *Scary Monsters*. That video, with Bowie and the Blitz kids pursued down a deserted beach by an enormous bulldozer, was shown all over the world, and even though the eighteen-foot train of the ecclesiastical gown Steve wore for the occasion kept getting bollixed up with the bulldozer, he looks back on the experience of actually working with his all-time idol as quite an honor. "I admire Bowie," he says. "He's the only major performer, I'd say, who has got enough suss to know what's going on in every major territory. He's *there*. He'd walk into the Blitz because he knew it was the most happening club in London—and he'd check it out."

After two years at the club, though, Steve and Rusty were ready to pack it in. Eager for fresh challenges, they moved on to an eight-month residency at a club called Hell. Next, they tried working with live bands at London's Venue. Finally, they decided that a complete change of attack was called for. Last

Valentine's Day, as a gesture of fond farewell to the original Blitz era, Steve and Rusty threw a party at the Rainbow Theatre for some 3000 fans from all over Britain. They had done their job—the Blitz lifestyle of do-it-yourself elegance was definitely going international. Several of the leading bands—Spandau Ballet, Landscape, Classix Nouveaux, Duran Duran—had been signed in America.

As for Visage, Polydor Records is determined to break their album as big in the U.S. as it's been abroad and plans to fly Steve over for an extended stay. (Rusty has other projects to occupy him, and Midge is busy working on the next Ultravox album.) The company is also cooking up a series of Blitz "events" in July in New York, Boston, Los Angeles, Chicago, San Francisco and—this sounds interesting—Atlanta. Blitz-style clothes have already arrived. New York boasts both an Axiom outlet and an offshoot of London's World's End shop run by pioneering punk designer Vivienne Westwood (also *couturier* to Bow Wow Wow). Bloomingdale's and Macy's both snatched up the "pirate look," and you can even buy the stuff in L.A.

Some Americans may look askance at all this and see Visage and the other Blitz bands as a hideous rehash of all they loved least about Eurodisco and early-Seventies art rock. As for the clothes, well, weren't the Kinks doing a Regency lace-and-velvet look seventeen years ago? And haven't we seen Adam Ant's brocade "pirate" jacket before—on Jimi Hendrix? In fact, what's so new and shocking about the whole space-face brigade? Doesn't anyone remember psychedelia?

Steve is sanguine about such aspersions. "I was on this interview show with John Entwistle of the Who last week," he recounts. "And I said over the air that David Bowie is a very clever thief—and the producer was going, *'Sssshhh! You can't say that on the air!'* But then, when they played a record, John Entwistle turned to me and said, 'You know, you're right, Steve. But everybody does it.'"

The Bettman Archive

TWENTY-THREE

Sean Connery

(Marbella, Spain, 1983)

Sean Connery's monumental contempt for showbiz pretension, and the concept of stardom in general, is a positive tonic in this age of rampant smarm and self-absorption. His sheer, screen-filling physical presence once tended to obscure his shrewdly deployed gifts as an actor, but by 1983, he had become something of an international film treasure—a man confident enough in his talents to agree to take one last pass at the role he'd already walked away from twice before: that most celebrated of secret agents, James Bond.

Never Say Never Again was—I now realize— nowhere near as interesting a movie as I'm afraid I made it sound in the following piece. It did, however, serve to coax Connery out of his customary between-films seclusion and actually sit down for an interview one day—an experience I'm sure he enjoyed not at all, but one that made this Bond fan's year.

It was on April 4th, 1958, that Lana Turner's teenage daughter shoved a carving knife into the unsuspecting stomach of one

John Stompanato, her mother's menacing boyfriend, thus not only ending Stompanato's unpleasant career on what seemed an altogether appropriate note but setting off a succulent Hollywood scandal (*Aging Actress Whipped Like Dog by Hoodlum Lover!*) and also causing no end of inconvenience for young Sean Connery, who was in town at the time working for Disney.

Connery remembered Stompanato, of course. He had paid a brief, disruptive visit to Turner in London the year before, when she was starring in *Another Time, Another Place,* a wheezing screen vehicle for which Connery had been chosen by Turner, who was ten years his senior, to play the love interest. Stompanato was a flashy L.A. thug who wore lime-green suits and little pistols for cuff links, and he was known to guard the body of Mickey Cohen, the noted racketeer. A nasty customer, Connery had decided at the time. Something of a sentimentalist, too, as it turned out: he had saved Turner's love-and-hate letters from London, and in the wake of his death, choice passages from them were splashed all over the local press. Some of the letters were innocent, some intimate. Some detailed the after-work excursions of Turner and her daughter to London vaudeville shows in Connery's company. Some of Stompanato's friends didn't like the sound of this.

One day, Connery got a phone call in his room at the Hollywood Roosevelt Hotel. It was Mickey Cohen. He came right to the point. "Get your ass outta town," he said.

Connery did not need this. At twenty-seven, his movie career—studded so far with stiffs like *Hell Drivers* and *Action of the Tiger*—was just beginning, however tentatively, to blossom. He was under a seven-year contract to Twentieth Century–Fox, at whose behest he was in California in the first place, having been rented out for a Disney opus called *Darby O'Gill and the Little People.* He was *working,* damn it.

Under the circumstances, however, Cohen's advice had a certain attraction. Connery packed his bags and disappeared into the San Fernando Valley, holing up at an inelegant oasis called the Bel Air Palms Motel. It was probably a prudent move. As he says, "I didn't know what I was dealing with, and I didn't see any point in discussing it."

And that, for the record, is the last known time that anybody pushed Sean Connery around.

And got away with it, that is.

A quarter of a century later, I am sitting in the private, palm-coddled garden of the Marbella Club, where the whitewashed walls are acrawl with colorful flowers and the fat Mediterranean sun is just cresting over the sloping, red-tiled roof of the indoor restaurant. Connery has lived in Marbella, an inordinately gorgeous resort situated on Spain's Costa del Sol—midway between the teeming tourist middens of Torremolinos to the east and Algeciras, gateway to Morocco, a quick seventy kilometers to the south—for the last twenty years. He has a beachfront villa nearby, abutting the glittering Puerto Banús—a rambling Andalusian affair he acquired for what one is tempted to assume was a song at the time. The villa is not without distinction—a mosaic by Jean Cocteau is embedded in one wall—but there is no swimming pool, and one would hardly describe the place as a pleasure dome. It is, however, home to Connery—at least on those rare occasions when he isn't off traipsing through the Sahara, climbing about in the Alps or splashing around (as he was for his latest movie) in the Caribbean—and to his spirited second wife of eight years, Micheline, who is a painter and, like her husband, a golf nut. There are, perhaps not coincidentally, more than a half-dozen golf courses in the Marbella area.

Home is an important concept to Connery. A sign out front, near the small fountain in the drive, announces PRO-PIEDAD PRIVADA, and means it. Connery will not have journalists in the house, writing up the furnishings and sniffing in the fridge. He will meet them, when he must, at the Marbella Club, and he will meet them early. Except for the sparrows that flit and skitter among the empty tables, the garden is practically deserted. Not a ripple disturbs the surface of the nearby swimming pool, where a prominently posted message from the management discourages female toplessness in four different languages. It is nine-thirty on the dot when Connery comes gliding across the patio, heavy with presence, and pulls up a chair.

He is dressed casually, in light blue slacks, loafers and a pink knit shirt bearing the small but celebrated crest of the Sunningdale Golf Club. A thin gold chain around his neck sets off his clear brown eyes and deeply tanned features. His hair is long on the sides and frankly graying. He is, of course, not wearing his working toupee. A dapper mustache droops down over the corners of his mouth, and his occasional smile is craggy and rather magnificent. Yesterday, August 25th, Sean Connery turned fifty-three. He looks great.

Enough of this small talk, though. Connery slides the keys to his Mercedes—an economical diesel turbo he bought in honor of the oil crisis in 1978—onto the table and summons a waiter. His thistly Scottish accent seems less pronounced now than it was twenty-one years ago when *Dr. No,* the first installment of the long-running James Bond series, suddenly rocketed him to international stardom.

Café con leche arrives in two porcelain pots, and Connery pours. He is cordial, but hardly effusive. This is as expected. His enthusiasm for personal publicity may be gauged by the fact that he has never in his life employed a press agent. One understands: this is work.

We are here because James Bond is back. The real James Bond. *Not* Roger Moore, the foppish pretender who usurped the role when Connery last walked out on it, after *Diamonds Are Forever* in 1971. And certainly not George Lazenby, the Australian male model who briefly desecrated the part (in the little-loved *On Her Majesty's Secret Service*) after Connery defected the first time, following *You Only Live Twice,* in 1967. At that point, the recalcitrant Scot had been heard to rumble, "Never again." But now he's back in his seventh outing as 007, and its title, *Never Say Never Again,* is one of the film's several engaging ironies. What's the story?

Connery's official line on this return to the Bond role is simply that he "reconsidered." But was it the $5 million, plus percentage, that he is reportedly receiving for his performance that swayed him? Or was it the rare, promised chance to exert quality control over everything from the script to the casting? Was commerciality a consideration? Did Connery long for one more major popular success in his advancing years?

The personal possibilities are complex, considering the caved-in state Connery was in by the time he made his fifth Bond film, *You Only Live Twice,* in 1967. He was more than bored. He was sick—sick of his circuslike celebrity, the pointless public clamor, the ever-intruding press. "At the highest time of the Bond films," he says, "like when I was doin' *Thunderball* in the Bahamas . . . fifteen consecutive nights, shooting from six-thirty until six in the morning. Long nights, long days. And then I'd go back and try to have some free time to sleep, but the hotel was full of journalists and photographers who had been promised all sorts of things by . . . I don't know who. I'd get messages, telephone calls. And I was left to handle it, you know?"

Staying with the series, lucrative as it was, could only lead to artistic suicide. "I'd been an actor since I was twenty-five," he says, "but the image that the press put out was that I just fell into this tuxedo and started mixing vodka martinis. And, of course, it was nothin' like that at all. I'd done television, theater, a whole slew of things. But it was more dramatic to present me as someone who had just stepped in off the street."

James Bond had become, as Connery later observed, "a Frankenstein monster."

So what is he doing in *Never Say Never Again*? Connery peers off into some private middle distance. He is a man of deep and abiding reserve, and thus reluctant to elaborate on the reasoning behind this latest contradictory comeback—starring in the movie they said would never be made, in the role he'd sworn he would never play again. "Back in Bondage," as the fan press puts it. Why, exactly? Connery says, simply, "I was curious."

Hmmm. Three thousand miles from New York to Spain, and he was "curious"? One had been warned, of course: Connery is a notoriously tight-lipped interview. All of his friends testify to his self-containment, his monumental passion for privacy. He recently sued one unauthorized biographer for bringing out a book that Connery contested as inaccurate. He won that suit, he says (a thousand pounds plus court costs, which he donated to charity), and is now closely scrutinizing a second biography out of Britain.

"You cannot stop anybody if he wants to write a book about you," says Connery, frowning at the injustice of it all. "That's the law. But anybody who takes it upon himself to write one should know that I'm not interested in giving any kind of assistance." And, of course, be aware that he may sue your ass. Connery wants to be known for what he does onscreen; his off-screen life is nobody's business.

"He really is the anti–James Bond in private," says one longtime friend, Parisian film rep Denise Breton. "I remember that when we were filming *Five Days One Summer* in Switzerland, he wanted to see a movie one night with his son. He got in line but couldn't get tickets; they were sold out. Nobody recognized him, and he refused to go to the manager and

say, 'I'm Sean Connery, could I get in?' He wouldn't use his
name. So they went to dinner instead."

Obviously, the man revels in anonymity. Not for him the
game of idle gossip or the presumptuous probing of his private
life. Sex, you say? Has he ever succumbed to carnal temptation,
especially back in the halcyon Bond days?

"Well," says Connery, very evenly, "if I had, I certainly
would never reveal it."

Right, none of my business. What about religion? Has he
pondered life's great questions?

"I get very few answers when I try," he says. "If one has
any kind of philosophy, it's just to leave the world a better place
than you found it—or at least no worse."

Okay. Politics, then: Does he vote in Britain?

"No, I'm not involved in that scene at all. I follow it, as I
follow what's going on in the United States. It's a sort of hobby
of mine, geopolitics."

What *is* going on, then, in his view?

"Well, I've never seen the situation in the world so pro-
nouncedly right and left. It seems everybody's pushing to their
frontiers: Zia in Pakistan, Thatcher in England, Marcos in the
Philippines, Mitterrand. . . . You know, it's ironic that Mitterrand is attacking Reagan for being a warmonger, and here *he* is
in Chad with more troops than the Americans have in the whole
of Central America. The lesson there is, keep your mouth shut
and your front door clean."

Connery, of course, learned that lesson long ago. So what
are we to make of his serendipitous career: a working-class Scot
from the slums of Edinburgh who came to symbolize all the
gleaming values of well-off Western society; a ferocious patriot
who's opted for exile rather than pay the queen's taxes; a profoundly private man who makes normalcy seem enigmatic. Connery is a conundrum. So let us, then, attempt to unravel his
roots.

Connery is disinclined to romanticize the deprivation of his
childhood, but it was real enough. Born Thomas Connery in Edinburgh in 1930, the eldest of two sons of Joseph Connery, a
Scots-Irish truck driver, and his wife, Euphamia, Sean grew up
in a cold-water tenement flat with no bathroom and began earning his keep at age eight, delivering milk. Times were tough,
and they got tougher when Britain went to war with Germany in

1939. Connery quit school when he was thirteen and scuffled hard for jobs. "The war was on, so my whole education time was a wipeout," he says. "I had no qualifications at all for any job, and unemployment has always been very high in Scotland anyway, so you take what you get. I was a milkman, laborer, steel bender, cement mixer—virtually anything."

He was a fighter, and so the Royal Navy must have seemed a good way out of all that. Connery signed up for a lengthy hitch, picked up two now-faded tattoos on his right forearm (MUM AND DAD and SCOTLAND FOREVER), developed an ulcer and was given a medical discharge after three years' service. Back home in Edinburgh, he used his navy disability grant to learn the wood-polishing trade and soon was buffing coffins, sideboards and all sorts of furniture for a living.

But he would also begin paying more attention to his imposing, six-foot-two-inch physique, working out and lifting weights as if his life depended on it—which, in a way, it did. He worked as a lifeguard at the Portobello swimming pool in the summer, and in the winter, he says, "I worked as a model at the art college in Edinburgh, for which I used to get . . . I don't know, one pound something an hour. You posed for forty-five minutes. It wasn't nude; you wore a pouch thing, but that was it. It was very arduous—quite a good discipline."

At this point in his life, Connery's career seemed to be bordering on beefcake. Advised that a competition for Mr. Universe was being held in London, he headed south to participate. He didn't win, but his ticket turned out to be worth the investment. While in London, he heard about auditions for a roadshow company of *South Pacific*. He somehow landed a job in the chorus and toured with the company for eighteen months.

Connery doesn't recall where the nickname "Sean" came from; as a child, he'd been "Big Tammy." But Sean was the handle he answered to when he joined *South Pacific,* and when asked how he wanted to be billed, he decided on Thomas Sean Connery. "They said it was too long. I didn't know if I was gonna stay an actor, so I used Sean—Sean Connery. And it's stayed."

He soon decided he loved the theatrical life, but realized that his new artistic enthusiasm considerably outstripped his cultural education. "When I decided to be an actor," he says, "I spent all the time on the tour going to the library in whichever town we were in—'cause one was always staying in pretty lousy digs, you know? So it was the theater and the library. I had a motorcycle with me, so I'd usually go to the theater in the morning to collect the mail and whatever I needed, and then go from there to the library or the repertory or the cinema in the afternoon. And that's how I turned it all around and gave myself an education."

He read Stanislavsky. He worked on his diction. He began getting jobs in television and in 1956 even landed his first movie role, a minor bit in a forgotten film called *No Road Back*. In 1957, however, he appeared far more memorably in a British TV production of Rod Serling's *Requiem for a Heavyweight,* in which he played the over-the-hill protagonist, Mountain McClintock, to considerable critical acclaim. Film offers poured in. Connery appeared with Claire Bloom in a BBC-TV production of *Anna Karenina,* and his big-screen billing improved when he made a potboiler called *Hell Drivers* with Stanley Baker, Herbert Lom and Patrick McGoohan. Soon, he signed to do a similarly awful movie called *Action of the Tiger,* which starred Van Johnson and Martine Carol and was directed by Terence Young. It turned out to be a fortuitous film.

"He was a rough diamond," Young remembers. "But already he had a sort of crude animal force, you know? Like a younger Burt Lancaster or Kirk Douglas. The interesting thing is that Martine Carol, who was a very famous French actress at the time, said, 'This boy should be playing the lead instead of Van Johnson. This man has big star quality.'"

The movie was a dud. "A *terrible* film," says Young, "very badly directed, very badly acted—it was not a good picture. But Sean was impressive in it, and when it was all over, he came to me and said, in a very strong Scottish accent, 'Sir, am I going to be a success?' I said, 'Not after this picture, you're not. But,' I asked him, 'can you swim?' He looked rather blank and said, yes, he could swim—what's that got to do with it? I said, 'Well, you'd better keep swimming until I can get you a proper job, and I'll make up for what I did this time.' And four years later, we came up with *Dr. No.*"

It was producer Albert "Cubby" Broccoli who cabled Young about the possibility of directing the first James Bond movie. Broccoli and his partners sensed that a James Bond film could be very big. It was 1961, and Ian Fleming's books were slowly creating a buzz: John Kennedy was a big booster (and so, it turned out, was Lee Harvey Oswald, who borrowed Bond novels from the library); CIA chief Allen Dulles was a fan, and so was England's Prince Philip. Sean Connery, a thirty-one-year-old former coffin polisher from an Edinburgh tenement—who had only recently asked for and received a release from his seven-year Fox contract—seemed an unlikely choice to play the Dom Pérignon–drinking sophisticate of Fleming's novels. But after a no-nonsense interview—during which Connery declined to test for the role—the producers signed him up. Next came his grooming for the part, which was undertaken by Terence Young, a man of assiduously cultivated tastes.

"I had a very clear idea of what an old Etonian should be," says Young. "I was a [Royal] Guards officer during the war, and I thought I knew how Bond should behave. So I took Sean to my shirtmaker, my tailor and my shoemaker, and we filled him out.

"He knew this was a big chance, and he made no mistake about it. But don't forget—he was a damn good actor by then. He'd had stage success; he'd appeared in *Macbeth,* and he'd been *brilliant* in a Jean Giraudoux play called *Judith,* which played in the West End for about six months. Besides, four or five years had elapsed since *Action of the Tiger.* He'd matured, he'd become a better actor—and when the chance came, he was ready for it."

Dr. No was shot in Jamaica on a shoestring budget of $1 million. Bernard Lee played M, the crusty old secret-service chief, and Lois Maxwell played his lovelorn secretary, Moneypenny (a part she's reprised in all of the Bond films to date). Also on hand were television's Jack Lord as Felix Leiter, James Bond's CIA buddy; Joseph Wiseman as Dr. Julius No; and—oh, yes—Ursula Andress, who made one of the most stunning bikini debuts in screen history.

"The thing that looked great right when it was being filmed was that scene with Ursula Andress coming out of the water," says Island Records head Chris Blackwell, a young friend of Ian Fleming's who worked on *Dr. No* as a location scout. "When that scene was done, everybody applauded."

Another scene, in which Connery—who likes to do his own stunts—was required to drive a small sports car between the giant tires of a construction crane, was nowhere near as pleasurable. "He's very lucky to be alive," says Young. "We damn near killed him. When we rehearsed it, he drove about five or ten miles an hour, just to see if he could go under it, and he cleared it by about four inches. But as we were shooting it, he was coming at forty, fifty miles an hour—and he suddenly realized the car was bouncing two feet up in the air, and there he was with his head sticking out. It so happened that the last bounce came just before he reached the thing, and he went down and under—or he would've been killed."

Says Connery: "If I remember correctly, going under the crane was Cubby Broccoli's idea. Maybe," he says, with a mordant chuckle, "he'd paid very heavy insurance beforehand."

Cubby Broccoli, who has grown extraordinarily rich as the moneyman behind the purveyor of James Bond films, is inexorably linked to Sean Connery's career. If he thought he had made Sean Connery and, thus, could break him, he'd likely forgotten the rough-and-tumble roots of his star.

His relationship with Connery has been tempestuous. There were regular disagreements about pay (mostly won by Connery). There were long negotiations about Connery buying his way out of the Bond bind after *Live and Let Die,* which resulted in the actor making that film for less than he would normally have attempted to negotiate. There was the successful attempt by Broccoli to lure Connery back in 1971 to make *Diamonds Are Forever* for the then astronomical sum of $1.25 million, plus a percentage. Connery promptly donated his salary to charity, the Scottish International Educational Trust, an organization he'd founded in hopes of reversing the sort of emigration that had earlier carried him away from his homeland.

Whether Connery's action was, in part, a way of showing Broccoli—and the movie industry—that he didn't really need James Bond money anymore is another issue. That Broccoli has had huge success with Bond films without Connery, and that Connery, without Bond, hasn't done nearly as well, is indisputable. Yet it is also indisputable that Broccoli has gone to extraordinary lengths to block *Never Say Never Again* from being released—in essence, to prevent Connery from being Bond without Broccoli's blessing. And this tale illustrates well the intrigue that has surrounded the Bond opus from the start.

The new film is technically a remake of *Thunderball,* the 1965 Bond epic in which Connery also starred. Ian Fleming, who began writing the Bond novels in 1952, had conceived the initial setting for the *Thunderball* story during a rehabilitative visit to a health clinic in Surrey in 1956. In 1959, stuck for a follow-up to the seventh Bond book, *Goldfinger,* Fleming was persuaded by Irish movie entrepreneur Kevin McClory to turn the *Thunderball* idea into a screenplay for a James Bond film.

Together with another writer named Jack Whittingham, McClory and Fleming turned out a script called *James Bond of the Secret Service.* According to McClory, it was he who introduced SPECTRE—the Special Executive for Counterintelligence, Terrorism, Revenge and Extortion—into the Bond canon as a substitute for Fleming's outdated Soviet *apparat,* Smersh.

Fleming eventually drifted away from this collaboration, returning to Goldeneye, the Jamaican retreat where he wrote all of the Bond novels, and churning out *Thunderball.* McClory decided that the book derived in large part from the screenplay he and Whittingham had helped write, and he took Fleming to court. After much legal wrangling, it was agreed, in 1963, that Fleming would be allowed to retain the literary rights to *Thunderball* (with credit for his collaborators appended to subsequent editions of the novel), but that McClory would get the screen rights.

The legal impasse over *Thunderball* halted plans for it to become the first Bond novel to be brought to the screen. Cubby Broccoli and Harry Saltzman, co-owners of Eon Productions and a Swiss-based holding company, Danjacq S.A., thought they had bought all the Fleming movie rights. When McClory won the film rights in court, Eon had no choice but to bring him in as executive producer of the 1966 version of *Thunderball.* As part of their deal, McClory contends, he had signed a contract allowing him remake rights to *Thunderball* after ten years had elapsed. But by 1976, when McClory attempted to implement this option, Eon was still raking in bucks from the Bond films and wanted no competition from a rival production—especially one in which McClory hoped to feature Sean Connery. McClory was taken to court.

Connery, who knew Fleming in the years before he died in 1964, and liked him ("A terrific snob, but very good company—tremendous knowledge, spoke German and French, got an interview with Stalin one time when he was working for Reuters"), had always been amused by McClory's upset victory over the influential author and his obtaining the *Thunderball* film rights. "With all of Fleming's connections—Eton, Sandhurst, naval intelligence, all that—everyone figured McClory, an

Irishman in an English court, didn't have a chance. But never underestimate Kevin McClory."

Connery initially became involved in McClory's remake project not as an actor, however, but as a writer. McClory suggested that he and Connery team up with espionage author Len Deighton (*The Ipcress File*) to confect a new screenplay based on the old *James Bond of the Secret Service*. According to Connery, they came up with quite a bizarre tale.

"We had all sorts of exotic events," he says, sipping his coffee. "You know those airplanes that were disappearing over the Bermuda Triangle? We had SPECTRE doing that. There was this fantastic fleet of planes under the sea—a whole world of stuff had been brought down. They were going to attack the financial nerve center of the United States by going in through the sewers of New York—which you can do—right into Wall Street. They'd have mechanical sharks in the bay and take over the Statue of Liberty, which is quite easy, and have the main line of troops on Ellis Island. That sort of thing."

As time passed, though, and the legal challenges to the McClory project proliferated, Connery finally bowed out. McClory persevered in court, however, and eventually, abetted by Micheline Connery, persuaded Connery to take another crack at acting the role he'd originated on the screen two decades earlier. A fiftyish James Bond? Could be fun, Connery figured. And Micheline provided the title: *Never Say Never Again*.

The movie began filming late last year, but even after it had been completed, legal objections continued to accumulate. Broccoli was unavailable for comment on the case, but Connery is well acquainted with the efforts to halt the new film.

"There was a time when I had tremendous loathing for [Broccoli and Saltzman]," he admits. "But I don't see that much of them now. Cubby and United Artists have been quite relentless with the lawyers; they haven't won a round, but there's been an enormous amount of money and time spent. I think the next hearing is in November—but then, the intention really was to stop the film *coming*. Now that they've had their innings, as it were, with *Octopussy* [the latest Roger Moore movie], I can't imagine why they persist."

Well, actually, yes he can. In the mean streets of Edinburgh, where Connery grew up, people pushed you around with their fists; in the movie business, they use lawyers. Either way, the result is essentially the same. Connery's pal, actor Michael

Caine, has an interesting way of putting it. "In Japan," says Caine, "if you have a son who is a ne'er-do-well, you make him a lawyer. Because in Japan, being a lawyer is an extremely dishonorable profession. The Japanese are men of their word, so what do they need lawyers for? People who break their word in Japan kill themselves. People who break their word here kill *you.*"

The Bond career quickly brought with it massive changes in Connery's life. Shortly after *Dr. No* opened in 1962, Sean Connery and Australian actress Diane Cilento slipped away to Gibraltar, where they were married in a quick civil ceremony—he for the first time, she for the second. They honeymooned on the Costa del Sol. Cilento, who brought a five-year-old daughter to the marriage, was a woman of considerable talent (she was later nominated for an Academy Award for her performance as the trollop in *Tom Jones*) and a volatile temperament. The marriage officially lasted eleven years—not bad, considering the strains of their dual careers—and was, by all accounts, a loving one. At times, it was also quite tempestuous.

"I remember once I was with them in Nassau," says Michael Caine. "Diane was cooking lunch, and Sean and I went out. Of course, we got out and one thing led to another, you know, and we got back for lunch two hours later. Well, we opened the door and Sean said, 'Darling, we're home'—and all the food she'd cooked came flying through the air at us. I remember the two of us standin' there, covered in gravy and green beans."

In most respects, however, Connery and Cilento seemed well matched. Both were pros, and before their marriage, they had studied movement theory together in London. Connery was fascinated by all the new notions of time and motion and "inner attitudes in action" that he learned during that time, and you can still see the results in the way he walks through a scene today.

"He has a whole thing about the physical part of acting that's real interesting," says Brooke Adams, who worked with Connery on the Richard Lester film *Cuba* in 1979. "It's about how much space a character needs around his head and how centered he is and how much weight he has. Sean is intuitive, but he's also very trained."

In 1963, his training was put directly back into the service

of the second James Bond movie, *From Russia with Love,* which
was filmed on location in Turkey with a splendid cast that included Robert Shaw as the chilly blond SPECTRE assassin and,
perhaps most memorably, Lotte Lenya as the crypto-lesbian
Rosa Klebb. *From Russia* also featured one of the most hyper-
kinetic fight scenes ever filmed, a breathtaking bash-out aboard
the Orient Express between Connery and Shaw that was scheduled for several days' shooting but was wrapped in a single day
when the actors decided to forgo their doubles and do the fight
themselves.

"I had $2 million for *From Russia With Love,*" says
Terence Young, who once again directed. "That was a good
budget, and it was, in my opinion, the best of all the Bond
films—because it was the best of the Bond books."

Connery agrees with this assessment—he has striven in
Never Say Never Again to retrieve some of the humanity that so
distinguished that second Bond epic. But at the time, he was
already getting restless with the role. Broccoli and Saltzman
were cleaning up, and Connery felt he deserved a bigger piece
of the action. He also had certain artistic ambitions—non-Bond-
ian ones. In 1964, he appeared in *Woman of Straw* with Gina
Lollobrigida, and with Tippi Hedren in Alfred Hitchcock's
Marnie—a movie that, as detailed in Donald Spoto's recent
Hitchcock biography, *The Dark Side of Genius,* was unpleas-
antly disrupted when Hitchcock made a blatant sexual overture
to Hedren. Connery was unaware of the incident at the time, he
says, and he doesn't much care to hear about it twenty years
later, either. He dislikes armchair analysis and any sort of
breach of personal privacy.

"I know that Hitch was intrigued by that blond, Grace
Kelly–type of woman," he says, "but I find it kind of sad to be
looking for something like that against somebody as special as
Hitch was. I'm not mad about that sort of Sherlock Holmes bit,
you know?"

Hedren, who today lives on a California ranch, was engaged at the time of *Marnie* but not unaware of Connery's mag-
netism. "It was interesting doing *Marnie,*" she says, "because
Sean Connery is a very, very attractive man, and here I was
playing the part of a woman who *screamed* every time he came
near her. But he was marvelous. He practiced golf a lot. In his
free time, he always had his golf shoes and clubs out. I guess if I
hadn't been interested in somebody else at the time, *I* probably
would've played golf."

*   *   *

It is sometimes hard to remember, but in the wake of *Goldfinger*'s release there erupted a James Bond craze that made such recent rages as *E.T.* seem like mere publicity stunts. Shows like "The Man from U.N.C.L.E." and "Secret Agent" filled the TV screen, commercials began featuring such characters as "James Bread from Bond" and "Goldnoodle," and novelty stores were filled with toy versions of the latest futuristic James Bond gadgets.

But surely that sort of Bond hysteria has died out now, right?

Meet Richard Schenkman. Richard is twenty-five, works for MTV in New York City and is, in every outward respect, a rational, responsible person. He is also president of the James Bond 007 Fan Club, which caters to the connoisseur of 007 minutiae.

Schenkman hatched the idea for a James Bond fan club with a friend in the summer of 1972. "We realized that we should create a fan club for the fictional character of James Bond," he explains. Good point: after all, actors come and go, but there's nothing like the real thing.

"Bond is a traditional hero in the sense of Robin Hood," says Richard, "and an intellectual adventure hero. He's very contemporary, in that he touches on cold-war politics, hot-war politics, science-fiction-tinged espionage capers. And there's the travelogue aspect, too. The detail! Fleming's books are so underrated. He was such a good writer."

And Sean Connery? Richard is grateful to him for being the best of all possible Bonds and wishes him well in whatever he may undertake. "He's always good," Richard says, even in a bad film like *The Red Tent*. "He's taken his money and bought his privacy and freedom."

James Bond has made Sean Connery a very wealthy man. But Connery has refused to be held hostage to such profit. He's continually struck out in search of new films to make, new chances to take. Some of these movies, like the Russian-Italian production of *The Red Tent,* Richard Lester's *Cuba* and Richard Brooks' *Wrong Is Right,* have been fairly awful—and yet Connery has always managed to emerge from them with his class intact. And when the films are good—like John Huston's *The Man Who Would Be King*—Connery reminds you anew what star quality is all about. A good deal of that quality is on display in *Never Say Never Again,* a carefully crafted and quite lively addition to the lately listless Bond series. Connery actually seems in better shape now than he did in *Diamonds Are Forever* back in 1971, and he occupies the movie with effortless ease. Whether blowing away a host of bad guys in the early scenes or unexpectedly dancing a courtly tango with Kim Basinger in the casino at Monte Carlo, Connery's Bond seems wittier and altogether more human than ever before. At fifty-three, he may just be reaching the peak of his career.

So this is life at the top with the lion of Marbella: quiet, sunny days spent far from the gaudy bazaars of the film business and the prying scribes who infest them. Golf, tennis, tranquility, freedom. Connery is a man who grabbed his main chance and rode it to freedom—and never stopped to kiss anybody's ass along the way. Back in the mid-Sixties, against the imprecations of his advisers, he sued Jack Warner for a relatively minor amount of money owed him from the film *A Fine Madness.* Warner might have squashed him like a bug, blackballed him—but thought better of it and paid up. A decade later, when Allied Artists failed to come forth with $180,000 he said it owed him from *The Man Who Would Be King,* Connery sued again, and Allied went toppling into bankruptcy. He will not be bullied, will not tolerate injustice in any form.

Michael Caine recalls the night he and Connery went to a comedy club in Los Angeles and were confronted with a decidedly unfunny novice comic. Connery endured the routine quietly, as did Caine. "But there was a group of English guys behind us who were heckling him, and he couldn't handle it. Finally, Sean got up, lifted the leader off his chair and said, 'One more word out of you lot and I'll smack you through the fuckin' wall! *Now give the kid a chance!*'"

That's Sean Connery. As Terence Young says, "With the exception of Lassie, he is the only person I know who's never been spoiled by success."

And so there we close the Connery case. He is exactly what he appears to be, and he lives, according to John Huston, calling one day from Cuernavaca, "a very stable, steady, conservative life—no cavorting, no *deep coughing,* no nonsense." If we've unearthed no answers about the man, perhaps it's because there are no questions.

Well, there is one: Will he ever find a professional life beyond Bond?

Huston on the horn again: he's got the answer to that one, too. "May I say that as long as actors are going into politics, I wish, for Christ's sake, that Sean Connery would become king of Scotland."

Courtesy Lorimar/Telepictures

TWENTY-FOUR

Max Headroom

(London, 1986)

*Max Headroom, the ultra-unctuous parody
talk-show host, was one of those bizarre but brilliant
creations that made total and perfect sense the very
first time you saw it. Of course—the ultimate
expression of video soul. The inventive Brits who
created Max (actually actor Matt Frewer in prosthetic
makeup, his televised image electronically modified)
had dreams of world conquest—and, indeed, they
did make quite a bit of money off him. But his show
was strictly a cult item in the States, and a short-lived
one at that. Appropriately enough, he was too hip
for TV.*

Multiple images of Max Headroom—the familiar self-absorbed smirk, the sculpted blond hair, the zitless artificial skin—suddenly blip into being on a small galaxy of video monitors arrayed above a crowded sound stage at Ewart Television Studios, a private production facility in London's Wandsworth district. The audience, a hundred-odd mostly young Maxheads, breaks into cheers. Max is back.

The "computer generated" talk-show host is taping his second series of half-hour programs, ten in all, for broadcast in the U.S. on HBO's Cinemax service starting August 1st; they will air on England's Channel Four (which launched Max last year) in the fall and eventually on TV outlets in Finland, Japan and at least a half-dozen other eager foreign markets. "Max mania" is a growth industry: it's generated two books in Britain so far (both to be published in the U.S. in October), a pair of lucrative product-endorsement campaigns (including the $25 million ad blitz mounted by Coca-Cola) and a dance-rock video and single recorded with the English disco-tech group Art of Noise. There are Max T-shirts, Max posters, Max computer games; even a line of Max cosmetics is in the offing. A one-hour adventure pilot for ABC is also in the works, and if successful it will lead to a weekly network series. In short, there is every indication that before the year is out, Max Headroom, the world's most deeply superficial media star, will have conquered the globe, or at least those parts of it plugged into the great electronic subconscious of television.

The studio crowd's applause for this wildly successful (if technically nonexistent) native son is prolonged. Max, in characteristic fashion, acknowledges their clamor as no more than his due, and quite possibly less.

"Am I on?" he asks with transparent coyness, the celebrated smirk echoing across the studio's battery of video screens, the transatlantic accent cranked up to full smarm.

"Y-y-yes," come the shouted replies—an affectionate aping of Max's occasional staticky stutter. Max announces that, tonight, he is in—Italy! In a flash, the ever-shifting pattern of computer-graphic pin stripes that provides his usual backdrop is replaced by tacky travelogue footage of *la bella Italia*. "A nation of Ferrari drivers," Max cracks, "trapped inside Fiats . . . How they love tourists here—if you stay long enough, they make you prime minister!" And so on: a rim-shot litany of ethnic abuse. Max tells a fart joke in German. He introduces a video. He brings on guest artists: the Broomstick Men, a sort of avant-pratfall act, and a mime called Les Bubb, who appears with a rubber glove pulled over his head. Then Max reappears on the monitors, and a minicrane supporting one of the video units slowly rolls forward and dips into the studio bleachers, bringing Max tube to face with his fans. He is strangely taken with one young woman's nose. "Tell me," he asks, craning for a closer look, "do you ever use a wire-brush attachment on it?" He admires another woman's fashionably padded jacket. "I like a girl who wears ashtrays on her shoulders." Swooping down on yet another hapless female, his smirk blossoms into a dazzling display of expensive dental enhancement. "I think you could make my floppy disc stiff," he informs her, in an oily purr that makes it clear this is *her* lucky day, not necessarily his.

Appalling stuff, this: cheap-shot one-liners, ancient dialect slurs, dorky double-entendres, the whole of it a-quiver in the monumental aspic of Max's self-regard. A half-hour in his presence is like being accosted by every slick, grinning, vapid personality in the TV industry—every talk-show twit, every curdled game-show host, every last blow-dried newsbot—all at once. And the audience laps it up. Because Max so overwhelmingly exudes the preening egotism and hollow mock empathy that are hallmarks to the TV host, his salutary effect is to utterly deflate the medium's most tiresome and inbred pretensions. Even his incorporeity subtly points up the satire: as the world's first computer-generated celebrity, Max Headroom is not merely *on* television, he *is* television.

The roots of this knowing lampoon lie, appropriately enough, in advertising, that fertile nether world where art and commerce find common cause. Peter Wagg, producer of "The Max Headroom Show," was head of creative services at Chrysalis Records in London five years ago when Andrew Park, a commissioning editor at the then-new Channel Four, suggested he develop a half-hour show devoted to rock videos. Wagg and Park had previously launched the first of what has since become an annual British video-awards show, and both felt that a weekly music-video program would also fly.

Chrysalis came up with development money for such a series, but who should host it? "I didn't want a human being," says Wagg, "because the only point in doing this was if it was international, and I felt that an individual presenter wouldn't travel." The project proceeded slowly. Wagg approached George Stone, an advertising copywriter and former colleague, for input. Stone suggested a computer-oriented format. He also came up with an evocative name for the proposed program: "The Max Headroom Show," suggested by a common abbreviation of the "maximum headroom" vehicular warnings familiar to British motorists from highway underpasses and parking garages. "It was just out of his head," says Wagg, "but it seemed to feel right. It was like . . . sound and vision—what videos were all about."

It was 1983 by the time Wagg commissioned the well-regarded video team of Rocky Morton and Annabel Jankel to help bring this nebulous concept into reality. "Originally, what Chrysalis wanted was just graphics and effects and animation to link pop videos," Jankel recalls. "We didn't think this idea was particularly inspiring. We decided Max should be a character—a computer-generated TV host." And to make clear the origins of that computer-generated character, the Max team—Jankel and Morton, George Stone and Peter Wagg—eventually realized that their video show would require an extensive prologue of some sort. "We decided," says Jankel, "that what we really wanted was to make a paranoid-conspiracy movie."

As 1984 dawned, Peter Wagg saw his modest idea ballooning into a veritable saga. He and his colleagues were flush with ideas but almost entirely lacking a script, a visual concept and, of course, money. Channel Four would shell out for the original video series but couldn't fully fund the one-hour TV film that Wagg's team was proposing. Wagg was advised to take his case to the States. In late February he made his pitch to Bridget Potter, head of original programming at HBO and Cinemax in New York. "I talked her through this stupid story about this investigative journalist who hits his head on a crash barrier," Wagg recalls. "We had no script, we had no image of Max, didn't know what he was gonna look like." But within forty-eight hours, Potter agreed to lay out half a million HBO bucks for joint production of Wagg's TV movie, "Max Headroom: Twenty Minutes into the Future."

By the summer of 1984, George Stone had dropped out of the project, leaving behind a screenplay that in the words of Steve Roberts, the writer recruited to replace him on the team, "was a series of brilliantly connected brilliant notions, but unmakable as a movie." The script told the story of a star TV reporter of the future who unearths a scandal—something to do with "blipverts," a highly condensed form of subliminal advertising that is causing death by spontaneous combustion among passive TV viewers. The reporter is captured and nearly killed by minions of his own employer, the gigantic Network 23, which has secretly been airing the blipverts. Afraid that the popular reporter's absence from the airwaves will stir unwanted inquiries, network execs allow a malign computer genius in their employ to feed the reporter's cranial specifications into corporate data banks, thus creating Max Headroom, the computer-generated generic TV star.

Easing into a writer-director slot, Roberts retired with the rest of the Max team to "a very bad hotel in Cornwall," where they beat the screenplay into shape. Meanwhile, Wagg was attempting to produce his original project, the Max Headroom video show, and had signed on the comedy-writing team of Paul Owen and David Hansen—veterans of such satirical British TV shows as "Not the Nine O'Clock News"—to fashion material for Max. From the beginning, says Hansen, the pair saw Max as more than just an electronic simulation of a video-show host. "He was supposed to be an all-round personality—Mr. TV."

"We tried to give him a persona that crossed all the aspects of 'light entertainment,'" adds Owen, "and took the piss out of it."

Wagg had also taken considerable pains to locate an actor suitable to play both Edison Carter, the reporter protagonist of the movie prologue, and the video-borne Max himself. British accents were out, Wagg decided; they "wouldn't travel." After innumerable auditions in England and the U.S., he finally arrived at Matt Frewer, a twenty-eight-year-old Canadian who'd had bit parts in such films as *Supergirl* and *Monty Python's The Meaning of Life* ("Remember in the beginning, the guy that jumps out the window and yells, 'Shit!'?").

Wagg was impressed with Frewer's wild ad-libbing ability, and with his smart but sexy presence. "Max and I have a very symbiotic relationship," Frewer says, deadpan. "I use his hair occasionally; he uses my legs. In the beginning, I played him as kind of a hybrid of the goofy charm of Ted Baxter and the slickness of Johnny Carson. The cool thing about playing Max is that you can say virtually anything, because theoretically the guy's not real, right? Can't sue a computer, goddamnit!"

By October 1st, 1984, the Max team had knocked together a shooting script, and filming began on November 14th at studios in Wembley and at an abandoned gasworks. Morton and Jankel finally devised a convincing computer-generated visual treatment for Max. Ultravox leader Midge Ure, up to his ears in the approaching British Band Aid recording benefit, was somehow persuaded to score the movie. And at the same time, production of the thirteen-show video series was proceeding apace.

"Max" the movie was delivered in early 1985, debuted on

Channel Four in the spring and was enthusiastically reviewed. The video shows began running in April, on Saturday nights at six, and they were wild from the outset. The first show opened without titles or fanfare, only an unexplained image of Max Headroom—speaking in German. Then came a video, also in German. Then the show cut to—commercials. At the end of thirty minutes, Max simply disappeared from the screen. There were no credits of any kind. This is not generally the way TV is done in Britain.

Computer magazines were the first to start calling, curious about the computer-generated aspects of Max's persona. How was it done? they wondered—a computer-conjured image that seemed not just spontaneous, but downright interactive. Then the kids started paying attention: Max seemed blandly affable on the surface, but when they listened closely they heard him tossing off such irreverent mots as "The thing about politicians is, you always know when they're lying—their lips move." Soon *Smash Hits* and other teeny pop mags started ringing up for interviews with the burgeoning star. They were followed in short order by the Sunday papers and mainstream magazines. *The Sunday Times Magazine* ran a Max "interview" on its celebrity-profile page, "A Life in the Day of"; scripted by Owen and Hansen, it was an eviscerating parody of the whole celebrity-profile genre, with Max asserting that he, too, like all good celebrities, rose early each day, ate a healthy breakfast and jogged. The only vanity he admitted to was "reverse tinted" windows in his limousine—to spare him the tiresome sight of "ordinary people getting wet in the rain."

By the fall, when the Max movie and video show began running on Cinemax in the States, all kinds of interesting possibilities were becoming apparent. For one, there was a book market for what had become Max mania: Steve Roberts whammed out a picture-book novelization of his film script, and Owen and Hansen came up with *Max Headroom's Guide to Life* (the most suitably pompous title they could concoct), and both sold well. It was also discovered that Max conducted great interviews. Sting was his first subject, and their encounter produced a definitive Max moment: when the singer let slip that he owned a personal tennis court, Max, his computer-perfect face filled with an eerie mixture of envy and obsequiousness, purred through his bogus grin, "*Stiiing,* I'm im*pressed.*" Subsequent guests have ranged from Roger Daltrey, Boy George and members of Duran

Duran to Vidal Sassoon and actors Michael Caine and Oliver Reed.

The question now, of course, is whether Max is more than just a gimmick, more than just a computer-generated geek good for a few fat seasons and then off to rerunville. In fact, *is* he actually generated by a computer? Matt Frewer says, "I don't think any of the techniques we're using are revolutionary, but I think the way we blend them is probably new." Whatever the technical reality behind Max, the *effect* is of a computerized human, and that effect is convincing. The Max team's tricks will be unraveled in due course and will then seem obvious. But by then, the saga of this video star will have moved beyond such trivial considerations.

"In the process of generating this character," says Roberts, "we generated something much, much bigger than any of us anticipated. We suffer from the biological inconvenience of mortality—of being incapable of really traveling in our next chosen medium, which is space. We die too easily. But Max is immortal. And once you put him into a computer, he's as world-wide as the telephone network, which means he is infinite. And that's the magic of Max. I think that through humor, and without being heavy about it, Max can actually make understandable many bizarre and fascinating concepts. The Max we've had so far is nothing compared to what we're going to do with him."

Courtesy Michael Ochs Archives

TWENTY-**F**IVE

Mel Gibson
and Tina Turner

(Australia, 1985)

*Like Sean Connery, the Australian-American
actor Mel Gibson has had to fight an ongoing battle
to overcome the public's perception of him as a mere
hunk. Like Connery, too, he dislikes the trappings of
celebrity, especially long, probing interviews. And
like the erstwhile James Bond, Gibson, at the time I
talked to him, was returning to a role he'd previously
determined to quit—the road warrior of the
postnuclear wastelands, Mad Max.*

The making of Mad Max Beyond Thunderdome
*was thus already enough of an event to warrant yet
another trip to Australia; the addition of Tina Turner
to the cast offered the supplementary possibility of
inter-iconic heat—Rock Bombshell Meets the
Incredible Hunk. And then there was the director,
George Miller . . . but read on for yourself.*

Mel Gibson wants a beer. Maybe several beers. He is sitting at
a table in the canopy-shaded area adjacent to a small catering
van, and he is sweltering. A thermometer in the van's cramped
kitchen reads 118 degrees, but that is only because it goes no
higher. According to a sweat-dappled cook, who is deftly crop-

ping string beans for a salad, the actual temperature—out *there,*
that is, under the brain-sizzling sun of South Australia—has
got to be a good 125. Gibson, unseasonably attired in dusty
road leathers and mismatched biker boots, sips glumly from a
cup of tepid apple juice. He bums a smoke. He runs a hand
through his brown hair, now streaked with blond along the
sides. A trickle of blood is painted down his left temple, and a
similarly fake abrasion adorns his right cheek. He checks the
time: almost an hour till his next camera call. In this distance the
desert horizon dances madly in the midday heat. *God,* a beer
would be good.

But George Miller, the director of *Mad Max Beyond
Thunderdome,* has decreed this a dry set—nothing stronger than
fruit juice. It is a cruel but probably necessary deprivation. Alcohol dehydrates the body, an unwise thing in such a sunbaked
locus as this. It is late November—summer in Australia—and
the heat out here, 400 miles north of Adelaide and the nearest
balmy coastline, is homicidal. So far today eight crew members
have dropped from sunstroke and dehydration, and last night
another camel died, joining two previously deceased beasts.
Nine of the surreal, custom-sculpted hot rods that populate the
picture have blown out under the broiling sun, and it's a struggle
just keeping the others gassed up (the fuel tends to vaporize
before it can reach the tanks). Staffers with spray bottles circu-
late among the cast of discreetly gasping, black-leather-clad actors, spritzing their reddened extremities with a cooling mixture
of cold water and cologne. A unit nurse, ministering to new ar-
rivals at the remote site, dispenses vitamins for the depleted and
lozenges for parched and swollen throats. "Don't worry," she
says brightly, "everyone gets it. You'll start spitting blood
soon."

Gibson smiles—a dewy, blue-eyed grin that's been
known to induce lewd musings among the soberest of female
moviegoers. He stubs out his cigarette and sighs. *Thunderdome*
is the fourth movie Mel has made in the last year, and frankly,
he's a bit frazzled. He needs a break—some time back at the
beach house in Sydney with his wife, Robyn, and their four kids.
And yet, here he is, roasting once more in the lunar scrublands,
playing again the part to which he'd previously determined
never to return.

The role of Max, warrior of the wasteland, has confirmed
Gibson as the most charismatic slam-bang action hero to emerge

since Clint Eastwood snarled into view twenty years ago in the Sergio Leone spaghetti westerns. But after making two hugely successful Max movies with Miller, Gibson felt there was nowhere left to go with the material. He had subsequently won a more elevated sort of critical approval for his performance in Peter Weir's film *The Year of Living Dangerously* (1983), and after starring with Sissy Spacek in *The River* and Diane Keaton in *Mrs. Soffel,* he could take his pick of more dignified projects (at a reported per-picture fee of more than $1 million). Miller and Terry Hayes, who wrote *Thunderdome* together, won Gibson back with a more humanized approach to the Max character and his apocalyptic world.

"There *would* have been no point in doing it again if it was gonna be the same thing," Mel allows. "However, it isn't. I think George and Terry are getting better as they go along. They've actually taken the whole Max concept a step further. They're traveling, making more of a journey with it. I thought the first film was quite relentless in its violence. The second one was much more stylized, more clownish. Oh, it had that hard feeling—so will this one. But now it's going from that toward . . . well, something perhaps a bit more hopeful."

Like many Max fans, Gibson sees the Miller movies as "a sort of cinematic equivalent to rock music. It's something to do with the nihilistic sentiments of the music of the Eighties—which can't continue. I say, let's get back to romanticism. And this film is actually doing that. It's using that nihilism as a vehicle, I think, to get back to romance."

Over the last six years the saga of Max Rockatansky, a decent highway-patrol cop driven berserk by the bike-gang murder of his wife and child and fated to roam a squalid postholocaust landscape in search of Redemption (and the precious gasoline required to keep seeking it), has become a cult epic of imposing international proportions. The mutant look of the movies—with elements lifted gleefully from punk rock, professional wrestling and S&M pornography—reverberates in everything from Amoco commercials and Billy Idol videos to a slew of inferior wasteland wheelers. And Miller's headlong editing style and affinity for the mythic have become touchstones of the action genre. You could feel some of the influence of Miller's furious autokineticism in the truck-chase sequence of Steven Spielberg's 1981 action hit *Raiders of the Lost Ark.* (Spielberg later hired

Miller—they are mutual admirers—to direct a segment of his thriller anthology *Twilight Zone: The Movie.*) James Cameron's brilliant 1984 film *The Terminator,* with its motivating messiah myth and its sense of embattled humanity amid postnuclear desolation, likewise struck a Millerian tone.

The kernel of the story was presented in *Mad Max,* released (over the grave doubts of its first-time director) in 1979. Filmed around Melbourne in nine weeks, *Mad Max* cost $400,000 to make. In two years it grossed more than $100 million. The Japanese saw it as a samurai movie. To Scandinavians it was a Viking bike flick. In stripping the action tradition down to archetypes and setting them amid flat, unsignifying Australian expanses, *Mad Max* unwittingly tapped into a near-universal crash-and-burn consciousness.

At the time Miller was a hippie M.D. whose only formal cinematic training had been a summer university film course of one month's duration. ("I learned the best way there is," he says, "by going to the movies.") His film-course pal and production partner, Byron Kennedy, was a self-educated entrepreneur, a car nut, film buff, airplane pilot and the builder of his own rockets, robots and cameras. This unlikely pair suddenly found themselves handsomely established as independent filmmakers— a toy store for the taking!

Miller had met Terry Hayes, a gregarious Australian journalist, while the movie was still being edited and had hired Hayes to write a quickie novelization. Hayes remembers Miller then as "this funny Greek doctor. I thought he had to have talent—who'd give up medicine to go into movies unless they did? He showed me a very rough black-and-white video of the work print. Whole chunks of it were missing. He tried to explain what was happening in the story—I didn't understand any of it. But I wrote the book—very, very quickly—and George liked some of the things in it. He asked how I'd like to write a script with him. I said I didn't know anything about script writing. He said that was okay. Later I realized *he* didn't know anything about it, either—he didn't have the first idea!"

Miller had spent so much time poring over *Mad Max* in the editing process that he'd come to hate the film. It was not at all what he'd seen in his head while making it. For his next project he decided to do a rock & roll movie, to be called *Roxanne.* He and Hayes would write the script in Los Angeles, affording themselves an opportunity to observe how *real* movies were made. This proved an unenlightening experience.

"Hollywood," says Hayes, "is an institutionalized form of conflict. The writer fights to defend his work against the director; the director fights the producer; and the producer fights the studio." By contrast, the younger Australian film industry seemed open and wholeheartedly collaborative. "In Australia," Hayes says, "you get a chance not just to be a writer or a director. You get a chance to be a filmmaker."

Work on the *Roxanne* script proceeded fitfully before being shelved indefinitely. Miller was still puzzling over the widespread success of *Mad Max,* and still frustrated by its failure to depict his vision. Reading Carl Jung and a book by Joseph Campbell called *The Hero with a Thousand Faces,* he became intrigued by the deep and resonant commonality underlying the world's mythologies. He went back to the films of favorite directors, to John Ford and Alfred Hitchcock, and he became fascinated with the work of such Japanese masters as Akira Kurosawa. They, too, he realized, had had to surmount the sort of creative stymies he had encountered in making *Mad Max.* Reassured, and convinced he was onto something with this mythological tack, Miller returned his attention to the Max material.

Kennedy-Miller (as George and his partner had incorporated themselves) took nine weeks and $4 million to shoot 1981's *Mad Max II*—released in the United States and some other markets the following year as *The Road Warrior.* The film far outstripped its predecessor. Whereas *Mad Max* had been a dark and sometimes unpleasant picture to watch—a straight revenge fantasy with interludes of unusual emotional brutality—*The Road Warrior* took wing. Norma Moriceau, a London-based Australian designer, contributed punk-conscious costumes and a bent satirical approach to the macho posturings of the action genre. And Miller, working with Hayes, lightened up on the sadism. At the end, as the settlers Max has reluctantly saved drive off across the wasteland to reinvent civilization anew, the receding image of Max, standing in the wreckage-strewn roadway, suggests semi-Redemption. Half barbarian himself, Max has nonetheless assisted the survival of humanistic values with which he long ago lost touch.

No one really wanted to make a third Mad Max movie. Kennedy-Miller had purchased an old art-deco theater on Orwell Street in King's Cross, the red-light district of Sydney, and had begun producing a series of highly successful TV miniseries there. The peripatetic Hayes had been away in Europe. In early 1983 he and Miller rendezvoused in Los Angeles.

"George was sitting and talking to me about . . . quantum mechanics, I think," Hayes recalls. "The theory of the oscillating universe. You could say he's got a broad range of interests. And I said something about 'Well, if there was ever a *Mad Max III* . . .' And he said, 'Well, if there *was* . . .'"

In ninety minutes the two men came up with a concept: a tribe of wild children. They live at the bottom of an idyllic tropical crevice called the Crack in the Earth and revere tribal memories of a Captain Walker—the pilot of the crashed 747 that had left their like stranded in the desert many years before. Walker had set off in search of help and never returned, but his memory was venerated in the churchlike hulk of the now long-dune-bogged aircraft. As the kids grew beyond, say, Peter Pan age, they would propagate, then eventually set out across the surrounding wasteland on their own quest for the skyscraping cities of which Walker had once spoken—cities long since reduced to rubble, along with everything else, by the oil-sparked superpower conflagration that is prologue to the action of the Max movies. When Max himself is discovered perishing in the desert—a victim of the harsh justice of Aunty Entity, the ruler of far-off Bartertown—the kids decide he must be Captain Walker returned to rescue them. They implore him to take them back to the nonexistent cities. Max, however, weary from his years on the road, would prefer that they all remain at the Crack in the Earth, which appears to him a paradise. The kids prevail, and soon they are all entangled with the formidable Entity.

Thunderdome was to be a tale of human renewal amid the gaping realities of death and decay. It would be codirected by Miller and George Ogilvie, a well-known Australian stage director who'd worked in the past with both Miller and Gibson. (Byron Kennedy died in a helicopter crash in July 1983.) Gibson liked the new Max story enough to agree to star in it. Angry Anderson, leader of the Sydney-based hard-rock band Rose Tattoo, was recruited to play Ironbar Bassey, Entity's pugnacious majordomo. And Angelo Rossitto, a dwarf actor who appeared in the 1932 cult film *Freaks,* would portray the Master, the scientific brain behind (or, actually, beneath) Entity's Bartertown: a primitive economic community powered by methane gas extracted from the subterranean excretions of 400 pigs. An elaborate, neomedieval set for this settlement would be built in the Sydney brick pits: there Entity would rule, consigning the luckless to Thunderdome, an arena for hand-to-hand murder conceived as part hard-rock show and part pro-wrestling match.

But who would play Entity? Miller is said to have casually considered such actresses as Jane Fonda and Lindsay Wagner. While in London, Miller had seen Tina Turner on TV discussing her desire to act. In developing the *Thunderdome* script with Hayes, he began to refer to Entity as "the Tina Turner character." Finally, with production nearing, he flew to Los Angeles to test Tina Turner herself.

A real Miller moment this afternoon: burning piles of tires, noxious fumes and billowing black smoke, a truck-mounted wind machine whipping up a hot sirocco of blinding dust. Tina Turner, in a chain-mail minidress and a flaring blond wig, is sitting at the wheel of one of the film's fantastic wasteland vehicles—in this case, a two-ton truck that has been stripped to its chassis and rebuilt with two Ford V-8 motors, a serpentine array of pipes and hoses and an actual jet engine attached at the back. As the dust and smoke swirl around Entity's bizarre automobile, a crewman in the rear, out of camera range, manipulates a long pole wedged under the bumper, causing the mighty machine to buck and rumble as though it were actually clattering across the flatlands on some unmerciful mission. "Simulated travel," George Miller calls it. It's one of his favorite old-time techniques.

Miller sits off to one side of the action, peering into a laughably low-tech black-and-white monitor housed in a crude pine box. In his voluminous desert whites, blue-tinted wind goggles and safari helmet with a little solar-powered face fan built into the brim, he looks like some silent-screen eccentric beamed in off a Biograph back lot. This is appropriate: Miller edits his images without sound and feels that "silent movies are the pure film language." He re-cues the wind machine, and his shoulder-length hair begins flapping in the squall.

When a break is called, Tina climbs down from her car to talk to Norma Moriceau, the costume designer. A Sydney native, Moriceau moved to England in 1964, working as a photographer and teen-mag fashion editor amid the heady pop clamor of Swinging London. A decade later she was in on the birth of punk. In 1975, while living around the corner from Malcolm McLaren, she began shooting ad photos of the strange new clothes he and his partner, Vivienne Westwood, were selling in their protopunk boutique, Sex. When McLaren concocted the Sex Pistols, Moriceau was on hand at their earliest rehearsals, shooting crude Super-8 footage that later turned up in the Pistols movie, *The Great Rock and Roll Swindle*. Moriceau subsequently met Miller during a brief return to Australia and saw his then-current hit film, *Mad Max*.

"I thought it was great," she says, "the essence of moviemaking."

She and Miller kept in touch, and he later invited her to work on *The Road Warrior*. She characterizes the slyly unsavory style of her wasteland costumes as Male Trouble.

"It's all to do with male sports and the medals men give each other in clubs and things," she says. A pack of passing Mohawked warriors illustrates her approach: shoulders bulked out with black-sprayed football pads; leathers accessorized with bike reflectors, rearview mirrors and metal automotive logos; butts a-swish with horsehair tails. "Big Butch Business," Norma chuckles.

Moriceau has had wardrobing offers from Billy Idol, Duran Duran and other rockers aspiring to her fashionable wasteland look, but has turned them down. ("Too much trouble," she says dismissively.) Now Tina wants her, too. The dress Moriceau concocted for Entity is an expressionist classic: a seventy-pound soldered amalgam of dog muzzles, coat hangers and chicken wire, the whole overlaid with gleaming chain-mail butcher aprons and accesorized with pendulant auto-spring earrings. The accompanying wig, styled to echo the movie's male plumage, required Tina to shave her head for proper fitting. She offered no protest.

"This is the best possible movie I could've done," she says, popping a catered strawberry into her mouth. "It follows up on my stage image, and it'll show the world that I can act. I'm not *terrific*, but I'm good enough for this part. And the training I'm getting from George is opening me up. I know that this is the brink—this is what I want to do."

Tina thought she had blown the initial audition. "I speak very fast," she says. "I've been a singer all my life, not an actress. And I *knew* I was speaking fast, so I wasn't pleased with the reading."

But Miller was willing to take a chance. "Ostensibly," the director says, "Entity is the bad guy of the movie. If she were dark and one-dimensional, she would be a very clichéd character. But Entity is a survivor; she isn't one-dimensional. And that's what struck me about Tina, that her persona is very strong, very good. Very positive. And that was the main thing. We recognized that it was going to be difficult for her—as difficult as an actor singing a rock concert. So we insisted that she come over for some workshops. And one of the most exciting things for us was to see her intense *learning*. She just sucked it all up."

Now Tina's talking about doing her own stunts, too, but Miller's not buying that yet. So when Entity is required to lead a charge of Bartertown war wagons down a plunging desert slope, Tina must watch from the sidelines as a stunt double climbs into her imperial machine. But Tina is herself a major *Road Warrior* fan, and as the growling sand buggies go barreling over the lip of the incline and screaming down the hill, she can't suppress an excited whoop. "Was that great?" she says. *"Shit!"*

Each evening at dusk, a caravan of *Thunderdome* workers rattles back into Coober Pedy, the isolated opal-mining town where the company bunks. Coober Pedy is a strange place—a sort of Dodge City down under. Its attractions are quickly enumerated: two Greek restaurants—one "full of hookers," according to Tina—and, of all things, a disco: Porky's. A sign on the wall at Porky's sets the tone for the town: PATRONS, CHECK GUNS AND EXPLOSIVES AT THE BAR. The crowd is mostly opal miners, a curious breed.

According to George Mannix, Miller's location manager, the distribution of opals in the earth is too scattered to be of interest to large mining concerns. The business attracts loners and outlanders—Yugoslavs, Greeks, Italians—who, to avoid the vicious summer heat, must make their homes in windowless underground burrows into which sunlight never reaches. After a while they may start acting rather strangely. About a year ago, says Mannix, a miner decided to blow up his girlfriend. He came running up to her residence with six sticks of gelignite, and then, being seriously drunk, he tripped. The local cop who related this story had been laughing when he recalled how they found the man's backbone a block away. "Coober Pedy," says Mannix, "is the perfect place for a Mad Max movie."

The heat and the boredom conspire to lure restless *Thunderdome*rs to Porky's, Mel Gibson among them. Rather late one night he is still stretched out in a dark booth, knocking back beers and contemplating the future. Eight months hence, when *Thunderdome* is released, he will again be importuned to embark upon a promotional press slog, and the thought does not flood his heart with warm feelings. *"Gene . . . Shalit,"* he says, savoring the name of the "Today" show's movie maven as if it were some sort of turnip-flavored breath mint. "What is that guy *on?*" He dislikes the avidity of the American media for celebrity revelation. "You can't live up to what people expect," he says. "Nobody can. But I guess that's my problem, not theirs."

When Porky's closes, Mel heads somewhat unsteadily up the street toward his motel room, stopping en route at the more high-toned of the two Greek restaurants to pick up a box of gyros—greasy chunks of spit-roasted lamb—and a container of black olives and feta cheese. It's so hot on location during the days that he finds it impossible to eat. Back in his room he goes straight to the refrigerator and extracts its sole contents: two bottles of beer. One is open and half-empty, the other fresh. With an ambiguous snicker he offers the flat one to a visitor.

"Reclusive?" he says, in response to an inquiry. "I'm not reclusive. I'm a guy that dances on tables, puts lampshades on his head, sticks his dick out in crowds. But I'm married now, got kids. I figure, stay healthy, live longer."

Certainly there's little time for dissolution in Gibson's heavily booked film schedule. In the years since his *Mad Max* breakthrough, he has stiven assiduously to enhance his born-hunk physical equipment—160 pounds appealingly arranged on a five-foot-ten-inch frame, topped with the sort of guileless good looks that can make women whimper in appreciation while at the same time striking men as matey and unaffected—with an acting style so subtly naturalistic as to sometimes seem transparent. Off the set, Gibson, who'll be thirty next January, exhibits little interest in his abiding, poster-boy perfection.

"The camera likes some people," he says simply. "Some people it doesn't. The most beautiful woman in the world can look like dogshit on camera. Fortunately for me, it also works the other way round."

One of Gibson's most intriguing qualities as an actor is his ambiguous accent, a product of his divided nationality, which adds an understated tension to many of his performances. Born in Peekskill, New York, the son of a railroad brakeman, he's lived in Australia since 1968, when his parents decided to emigrate there rather than lose any of their eleven children to the Vietnam War. He has maintained U.S. citizenship, but also a decided cultural ambivalence.

"There's an element of the hybrid nature in me," he says, swigging some beer. "I'm aware of it, but I don't really have any burning desire to identify myself one way or the other. If you're a hybrid, you're a hybrid, you know? You're pieces of this and that. I like it because you can really be a lot more objective, more of an observer. To be uprooted from one place and put into another, you really have to watch stuff. You observe, and then you begin to adapt—and that sounds like an actor to me."

Acting, Mel suggests, is the art of "lying convincingly."

He kills the beer and stuffs several chunks of lamb into his mouth. The talk turns to Miller and the raw vitality of his style, particularly compared with Spielberg's more polished Hollywood approach.

"Yeah," says Mel, "and Spielberg knows that."

Obviously, says his visitor—meaning, just look at the Indiana Jones movies. But Gibson's red-rimmed eyes swell paranoically.

"Whatta you mean, obviously?" he rasps. "Has Spielberg got money in this? I heard he had! It's hard to find out with George. But I don't care anyway—as long as I've got my cut!"

He cackles maniacally, then slumps back in his chair. "I didn't realize I was so intoxicated," he says, suddenly looking very tired. He cups his face in his hands. "I've been out here for ten fucking weeks."

Will *Thunderdome* be the last of the Max movies? Don't bet on it. Commercial pressures to extend the saga will certainly be strong; while Miller would love to do a comedy, the Max chronicle, he admits, seems to have a life of its own.

As for Gibson's continued participation, the actor—in a less wired moment—is also unsure. "If they could come up with an even better story than this one," he says, "I might be in on it. But I think they should leave it alone; they've done their dash."

And so has he. "It can be pretty tough saving the world sometimes," Gibson says, smiling again. "It's a special branch of work, isn't it?"

David Peabody/Retna Ltd.

TWENTY-SIX

Ted Hawkins

(London, 1987)

Blues history is filled with the names of remarkable artists who never got the breaks they deserved, who were ground down by hard times or bad luck or personal demons too deeply rooted to resist. Or, like Ted Hawkins, by all three.

It is late afternoon in London, and a gray April sky is spitting rain. Ted Hawkins raises one large brown hand to his brow and runs it down over his face and his clipped white beard, wiping away the wet. He is sitting on a damp granite stair step in a darkening, deserted side street not far from Oxford Circus, strumming his guitar and smiling patiently as a Japanese photographer flits about him, clicking off some final shots before the light dies. It is cold and windy, but Hawkins does not complain. He has waited fifty years for the world to look his way, to lend an ear, to spare him anything more than a kick or a curse or an occasional quarter. He's happy to grin in the drizzle for this nice little man with the Nikon.

Hawkins lifts his fretting hand, enclosed in a trademark leather work glove, to the neck of his guitar. Barring an open chord, he tilts back his head and begins to sing. His radiant baritone rumbles out into the street and resonates mightily between the stone façades of the bordering buildings. It is a voice of hypnotic sweetness, primitive in its raw power yet instinctively polished and emotionally affecting beyond any particularity of lyric or theme. For a transported moment, one almost expects the skies to clear and the sun to pop out. The photographer snaps off his final frames with renewed fervor as the burly singer winds up his song—which happens to be "There Stands the Glass," a Webb Pierce country classic. Ted Hawkins does not sing the blues, exactly, although God knows he'd be entitled.

The photos for which Hawkins is posing will appear in a Japanese music magazine. The Japanese, like the British, are fanatical archivists of neglected American musical idioms, and Ted Hawkins—who is an idiom unto himself—is about as neglected as one can get. By any traditional arithmetic of American life, he ought to be pushing up weeds in some forgotten potter's field. His bio, if not his repertoire, is truly the blues—a harrowing chronicle of wino camps, work-gang whippings and aimless boxcar rambles; of hunger and homelessness so abject that the singer's frequent stints in prison came to seem like sylvan interludes in a never-ending travelogue of hell itself.

All that's behind him now, though not far. Only a year ago, Hawkins was singing for tips on the boardwalk back in Venice Beach, California. Then, just last fall, a few weeks before his fiftieth birthday, a sudden wave of transatlantic acclaim swept him up off the streets and beaches of Los Angeles and transported him to London, where a crusading DJ had been playing the bejesus out of an obscure American album Hawkins had recorded fifteen years earlier. Listeners across Britain were flipping. The singer, financed by an inexperienced but enthusiastic young manager, settled in. He began to perform in places with ceilings, and his concerts were sellouts. Two of his albums, rush released, topped the British independent-label charts. His brutal life was poked over in periodicals ranging from *The Face* to the London *Sunday Times,* its dismal litany of loserdom made all the more appalling by the fact that, despite the man's incandescent voice and the heart-piercing personal detail of his best songs, Ted Hawkins was still totally unknown to the vast majority of his fellow Americans.

That situation will surely change. Hawkins is a magical artist whose appeal obliterates all piddling boundaries of age and race and commercial style. Even though the unique blend of country, folk and soul elements in his music makes him impossi-

ble to pigeonhole within the cramped gamut of contemporary
cookie-cutter American pop, room will simply have to be
cleared for him. He's that good. Until then, Hawkins—who has
spent a lifetime watching his fondest dreams wither—is happy
enough just to have found an audience in Britain.

"I ain't never had it so good," he says, rising to stretch
his six-foot-five-inch frame as the photographer rewinds his film.
"People really respect me here, just me and the guitar. My God,
man, I *sure* don't want this to stop."

That seems a remote possibility. He has already toured
Holland and Belgium and will soon perform in Japan (where
cultists speak knowledgeably of his obscure *oeuvre*). *Happy
Hour,* his superb third album, is a British hit, and Harry Bela-
fonte has already put out feelers for the movie rights to
Hawkins' life story. Slowly, Americans seem to be getting the
word, and this makes Hawkins especially happy.

"Until they know who I am, I'm *nothin',*" he says. "I
want *especially* them to know." His eyes focus on some middle
distance, as if picturing the glorious day. "They'll see me car-
ryin' myself in a dignified and respectable manner," he says with
a slight quaver in his voice. "They'll see that I'm not like they
may think."

If ever a man seemed born to lose, it was Theodore Hawkins
Jr., who was delivered into abysmal poverty on October 28th,
1936, in the hamlet of Lakeshore, Mississippi. His mother, Ce-
lestine Henderson, was a prostitute and an alcoholic. His father
disappeared early, leaving behind only his name, which Henderson bestowed upon her son. By the time Hawkins was five, he
and his mother had drifted down to Biloxi, on the Gulf Coast.
There, Henderson's drinking and trysting continued, and her
son was left almost entirely to his own devices. He was un-
washed, ill clothed, frequently hungry—and repeatedly a victim
of sexual abuse.

"My mother couldn't even look after herself in the state
she was in," says Hawkins. "I got food the best I could—go
behind the stores, take my finger and dig out the rind of an
orange, the rot of an apple; lick the scraps and stuff. Chewin' on
candy behind dresses in Woolworth's—that's why I ain't got no
teeth today. I coulda died. I came up *wild,* you see. I was a little
guy, and barefooted—they used to call me Dirty Junior, you

know? The other children didn't want me. And I was molested about twenty-five times by different adults, men and women."

His first scrape with the law occurred when he was only eight. Down South in those days, Hawkins says, "a guy might have went to jail for stealin' a loaf of bread, you know? Tryin' to keep body and soul together." At age twelve he was sent to a reform school outside of Jackson. Up until that point, although he'd been exposed to gospel singing during occasional visits to a Baptist church in Biloxi, music had played little part in his generally miserable existence. At reform school, however, he heard a recording by the white country singer Red Foley of the yearning hymn "Peace in the Valley"—"the first music that really made me feel something." He learned to play an open-tuned guitar, and encouraged by the school superintendent's wife, he made his performing debut at a talent show in Jackson, singing a gospel song.

"I went out there, scared to death—and tore the house *down,*" Hawkins recalls with a rich chuckle. "It made me feel good, the way people ran to me after the show—kissin' me and huggin' me, all them people. I wanted *more!* But," he says with a sigh, "I didn't know how to go about gettin' more."

Released from reform school at age fifteen, Hawkins resumed his wild ways. Attracted by the black leather jackets displayed in a Harley-Davidson motorcycle dealership, he broke into the place, walked out wearing one—and was immediately nabbed by the police. This time, without benefit of a lawyer, he says, he was sent to the Mississippi State Penitentiary at Parchman—the notorious Parchman Farm—where he dug up rocks on road gangs and endured the whippings of a particularly sadistic guard who "got his jollies from whuppin' black butts."

By the time he got out of Parchman, he was eighteen, and his mother, he discovered, had died of cirrhosis. Alone in the world, he decided to hop a freight train and head north. He eventually arrived in Chicago and from there hoboed his way to Philadelphia—"the City of Brotherly Love," he says with grim irony. "It was *cold* there, and it wasn't only the weather. The people's *hearts* was cold." He hung out with the bums who congregated around Sixth and Vine, huddling near trash-can bonfires and passing bottles of cheap whiskey to keep warm. Before long, he was back on a boxcar again—unfortunately, one that was headed even farther north. When he hopped out, he found himself in Buffalo, and it was freezing. He was actually happy to see a police hobo patrol parked nearby.

"I thought, 'I can get some sleep now and eat some breakfast.'" Hawkins remembers. "They were goin', 'Halt! Halt!' I said, 'Aw, man, ain't nobody runnin'.'"

Back out on the streets of Buffalo the next day, he made his way to a local Pentecostal church and was befriended by a female parishioner who took pity on him and invited him to come live with her family. Soon he was singing in the church choir and attracting admirers. One of these was a young woman named Celeste, with whom he began keeping company. When she became pregnant and gave birth to a daughter, Hawkins married the woman, but Celeste's mother disapproved ("I was poor and couldn't support nobody," he acknowledges) and had the marriage annulled. Glumly, he bummed his way to Newark, New Jersey, where he took up with another woman, named Ola. Their relationship was rocky, and when Ola acquired another boyfriend, Hawkins almost threw the new suitor out a third-story window ("I caught myself," he says). In turn, the man—bolstered by his knife-wielding brothers—beat Hawkins bloody with a club. Enraged, he borrowed an automatic pistol from a restaurant where he'd been washing dishes and went to seek vengeance. He had no idea how to fire the gun, though, and only narrowly avoided a one-way shoot-out with the police before escaping over a fence. Making his way downtown, he saw a group of winos being herded onto a bus and joined them. Once under way, he learned that they were destined for a remote spot in the countryside to dig potatoes out of the ground. At least it was work, Hawkins figured—until he discovered that the winos were paid only in wine. After two weeks of sore knees and depressing nights in a vomit-spattered flophouse provided by the potato people, Hawkins walked away.

He hitchhiked as far as he could—which turned out to be the small town of Geneva, New York. Here, at last, his life took a modest turn for the better. At a local church, as usual, he met Liza Simpson, a respectable practical nurse with a young daughter. They married, but before long Liza fell sick. It wasn't until he went to visit her in the hospital and found her dead, Hawkins says, that he learned she had had cancer. Her daughter was taken in by relatives, and Hawkins received a check from his wife's estate for $5000. The check said, "Cash immediately," which he did.

"I never seen so much money in all my life," Hawkins says. "I went back to the house, locked all the doors, took the telephone off the hook and tried to count it. It was too much to count. Big ol' stack of money. So I put some in this pocket and filled it up and put some in that pocket—and I went out. And everybody I saw, I'd give 'em a fifty. They said, 'Oh, my God—for *me?*' I said, 'Yes, for *you.*' I saw some children goin' into a store; I handed 'em twenty, twenty, twenty—'Oh, *wow!*' Then I went to the train station. The snow was knee-deep at the time. I went to the ticket office and said, 'Where on earth can I go where it don't get cold?' The woman said, 'Los Angeles, California.' I said, 'Give me a one-way ticket.'"

When Hawkins arrived in L.A., he decided to try to become a professional singer. His idol was Sam Cooke, whom he'd followed since the singer's days with the renowned gospel group the Soul Stirrers. Cooke had managed to cross over from gospel to white pop, and Hawkins thought he might be able to do the same. His voice, although huskier than Cooke's, bore a haunting stylistic resemblance to the famous singer's. Cooke, however, had been shot dead in an L.A. motel in 1964, two years before Hawkins got to town. So he went to RCA, Cooke's label, searching for his manager, J. W. Alexander. Instead, he encountered a man named Alexander Scott, a noted black DJ who ran a radio show out of a local record store called Dolphin's of Hollywood. Scott encouraged Hawkins to write some songs, and he decided to give it a try. A street acquaintance introduced him to marijuana, rolling it up in a cardboard joint and blowing the smoke into Hawkins' mouth. Artificially inspired, he stayed up all night writing a song called "Baby," and Alexander arranged for him to record it for Money Records, a label that also operated out of Dolphin's record shop. The single—credited to Ted "Soul" Hawkins—got some airplay around L.A., but Hawkins says, he never saw a dime from it. Deeply depressed, and by now broke again, Hawkins flipped out.

"I had a nervous breakdown," he says. "Listenin' to my song on the radio, then askin', 'Where's my money?'—and they say, 'You ain't got nothin' comin'.' Next thing I knew, I wound up in Vacaville, screamin' and hollerin'. I don't know what I did."

The California Medical Facility in Vacaville—the nation's largest prison—was to become Hawkins' intermittent home over the next sixteen years. He had apparently become unhinged by the accumulated miseries of his life. Kept afloat by occasional welfare money, he was drinking heavily and smoking cocaine when he could get it. He wandered the streets, sometimes shoeless, singing songs for whatever loose change passersby might toss at his feet. And when the street life began to crowd in on him, he'd pull some nonviolent caper—a botched burglary, a bungled drug deal—and get shipped back to Vacaville, where he could rest and write.

There were brief flashes of hope. The year he had arrived in L.A., he had met and married a supportive woman—his sometime singing partner, Elizabeth—and they had set up a home with her three young daughters; their son, Theodore Hawkins III, was born later. But Ted's real home remained the street. In 1971 he was discovered singing outside a liquor store by another black DJ, who connected Ted with Bruce Bromberg. Bromberg, a young, white blues producer (who has since recorded hit albums for Robert Cray), cut solo versions of several of Hawkins' original songs at a local radio studio and at a subsequent session added backup by guitarist Phillip Walker and his band. Two of these songs—"Watch Your Step" and "Sweet Baby"—were released as a single in early 1972 but didn't do much. When Hawkins drifted back into Vacaville again, Bromberg stored the other tapes he had made with the singer and gave him up as a lost cause—an assessment that was pretty much shared by Hawkins himself at that point.

The next eight years were a blur—wandering the streets, often in a haze of drink and drugs, singing for handouts; getting busted for various numskull infractions ranging from theft to indecent exposure. Much of the time, Hawkins says, he had little idea of what he was doing. The lowest point came in late 1980. Hawkins had a woman on the side, and the woman had a thirteen-year-old daughter. The woman, he says, still pained by the recollection, "was so fat she couldn't hardly get through the door." Her daughter, suffice it to say, was not. One day, when the mother was out, Ted and the daughter were home alone. "I don't know what happened," he says. "We was in each other's arms before I knew it." When the mother came home and found her daughter in midgrope with her wayward boyfriend, she turned him in.

In the white world of rock & roll, cavorting with underage nymphets is something of a tradition—Jerry Lee Lewis even married a thirteen-year-old. But Hawkins was essentially a black vagrant (in the tradition of such legendary blues hobos as Ragtime Texas) and an ex-con (in the tradition of the great folk singer Leadbelly—a convicted murderer). No force had been involved in the encounter, however, and it wasn't consummated, so the judge sent him back to Vacaville for only an eighteen-month stretch. Hawkins, nevertheless, felt he'd finally hit bottom.

Then, out of nowhere, he was contacted by Bruce Bromberg. In moving to new digs, Bromberg had come upon the tapes he'd cut with Hawkins nine years earlier. Struck by how good they still sounded, he had arranged a deal with Rounder Records, an independent label, to release them as an LP. Could Hawkins make himself available for a photographer to come to the prison and snap his picture for the album cover?

"I had just got there," says Hawkins, recalling his panic at the time. "I said, 'Will somebody *please* lend me a comb?' And they said, 'Whatcha mean, brother? You got three packs?' See, if you ain't got three packs of cigarettes in jail, you ain't got nothin' comin'. I said, 'No, man. I ain't got no cigarettes. I just got here. Help me!'"

Hawkins got his comb, and the cover photo for his first LP was shot in a Vacaville courtyard, with barred windows in the background. Released in 1982, the album, titled *Watch Your Step,* ranged from funky struts like the title track to luminous laments for unloved children ("The Lost Ones") and sonorous country ballads ("I Gave Up All I Had"). Critics who heard the record loved it. Unfortunately, not many real people heard it and fewer still bought it.

Nevertheless, this small surge of attention apparently helped Hawkins to turn a major corner in his life. In prison, he finally kicked his drug and alcohol problems and made a firm commitment to the religious beliefs he'd been circling musically for so many years. He also began writing songs nonstop.

Released from Vacaville in 1982, Hawkins started commuting to Venice Beach, where street entertainers—from run-of-the-mill buskers to a guy who juggled a chain saw—were a staple on the city's boardwalk. Setting up at the end of the promenade with his guitar and a milk crate to sit on, Hawkins began pumping out every song he knew—Sam Cooke tunes, country standards, soul ballads, folk numbers, pop ditties—for weekend strollers. One of these was a young white man from Columbus, Ohio, named H. Thorp Minister III. Minister had arrived in L.A. a few years earlier determined to become an actor. Soon disillusioned, however, he altered his goal to personal management. When he first spotted Hawkins on the Venice boardwalk, in the spring of 1985, hollering out tunes for hours on end and holding down open chords with a gloved hand to prevent string gashes, he knew immediately that this was the client he needed.

"He'd have at least 150 people there," Minister recalls. "They'd be young, they'd be old, they'd be rich and poor—it didn't matter. It didn't matter what race they were. Everybody loved him."

In August, Minister, very short on funds himself, swung a $5000 bank loan to take Hawkins to Nashville—where an old fraternity pal worked as a recording engineer—and cut a twenty-seven-song tape of Ted singing his beach numbers. Back in Venice, they hawked these cassettes, titled *On the Boardwalk,* for ten dollars a pop, well into the winter. A faint buzz could be heard developing.

By the following spring, a copy of Hawkins's LP, *Watch Your Step,* had made its way to England and into the hands of BBC Radio One DJ Andy Kershaw, who loved the album and began programming it heavily on his weekly late-night show.

"I just went crazy about it," Kershaw says. "And the listeners started to write in, in considerable quantities. I thought, 'Well, I'm not the only one. Somethin's goin' on here.'"

On a field trip to the U.S. in April 1986, Kershaw tracked Hawkins to his apartment in Inglewood, and with a small Sony cassette machine, he recorded four more songs. Back in London, he added these new cuts to his on-air inventory. By September, Kershaw had instigated a British release of *Watch Your Step;* subsequently, he also edited down the sprawling *On the Boardwalk* collection for a more compact U.K. release. The buzz was building into a roar, albeit 6000 miles away.

There were other hurdles to be overcome. Hawkins's years of shouting out songs on the boardwalk had resulted in a vocal-cord nodule that required immediate surgery. Minister borrowed another $5000 to pay for it—and then a further $5000 to finance the flight to England that now seemed requisite. And after they arrived (with less than $100 to their names), Hawkins was found to need yet another throat operation.

Since then, however, most of the news in Ted Hawkins' life has been good. As his wife, Elizabeth, says proudly, "I thought he was dynamic when I met him, and I still do. He was just hiding his light under a bush. Now he's pulled himself up by his own bootstraps." Temporarily residing in England to fulfill ever-accumulating concert commitments, Hawkins lives with the family of his English road manager in the tiny Yorkshire town of Bridlington, about five hours from London, and he relishes the isolation for his songwriting. His concerts continue to sell out, and *Happy Hour,* his latest LP for Rounder—recorded by Bromberg in 1983 and 1984 but released last April—certifies him as one of the most emotionally compelling artists in popular music right now. It's not just his quietly astonishing voice, either—that uncategorizable conflation of gospel roar, pop croon and any number of unexpected soul and country influences. It's the searing intimacy of his original songs: the bitterly autobiographical sense of romantic betrayal that suffuses "Bad Dog"; the ripe, hilarious sexiness of "You Pushed My Head Away" (with Robert Cray guesting under the handle Night Train Clemons); the quiet heartbreak of "Cold & Bitter Tears." In the latter, perhaps his most sublime song to date, he sings to a departed woman:

Wonderin' why you left me, after all I tried to do.
You know I miss you, baby, and the children miss you, too.
Tonight we done the dishes, just to keep your memory here.
I cooled the hot dishwater with my cold and bitter tears.

Anyone who can encapsulate a whole universe of everyday sorrow in four short lines like that is—one notices upon looking around—a rare and unique artist.

But is Hawkins himself still bitter about the brutal road he's traveled?

"If I'm bitter," he says with hard-won serenity, "I take that bitterness and channel it and make it my strength, and I work for a higher callin'. I've got peace of mind—there's no reason for me to be gettin' in trouble anymore, because I'm some*body* now." He laughs a big man's free-at-last laugh. "And," he says, "it feels *good.*"

PART FOUR
STATE OF
THE NATION

Pop star political pontification—a legacy of the Sixties that grew to epidemic proportions in the Eighties—is not something one usually seeks to encourage. But Frank Zappa isn't exactly a pop star, and his sociopolitical conclusions are so well-informed and diligently thought-out and, in general, so unlike the conventional-wisdom-plus-dash-of-Jung that passes for profundity in showbiz circles, as to make rationality seem a radical stance. He's really funny, too—no small thing in itself.

For the most part, I try not to add to all the political nattering that clutters up the music scene. But "Jingo Bells" is something I felt compelled to rattle off in 1985, in the face of a monumental misreading by election-happy Republicans of Bruce Springsteen's deeply ambivalent album, *Born in the U.S.A.* The spectacle of right-wing politicians attempting to appropriate this particular piece of work seemed to cry out for a dissenting screed. Here it is.

$\boldsymbol{T}$WENTY-$\boldsymbol{S}$EVEN

"Jingo Bells"
(1985)

I'm not exactly a doctrinaire liberal, but whenever America's worst inclinations toward moralistic hysteria and a sense of divine mission converge in a gathering swell of political purpose, I, too, get scared. Nineteen eighty-five was that kind of year. Unfortunately, as we have since seen, it was not the last of its kind, either.

In 1985 there was a new patriotism upon us, a great flexing of the national pecs. You could see it everywhere, from the Oval Office down to the local concert hall. Unlike the old patriotism—which, in the wake of Vietnam and Watergate, had become largely the concern of obscure talk-show cranks and crackpot fundamentalists—this new patriotic imperative played to a pop demographic. It was packaged for broad consumer appeal, as if the American spirit were simply an assemblage of marketable parts—of big cars and cold beers and other symbol-bedecked social accessories. It invited participation, this new fervor, rather than contemplation. Workaday burghers were encouraged to mutter darkly about devious foreigners (particularly those presumptuous enough to manufacture cars, clothing or other commodities that proved popular with the less stalwart legions of U.S. consumers). Rock stars did their part by re-discovering America (and finding it good, if troubled), and their fans waved flags and felt, well, kind of nice about being Americans, too. Small children conducted counterpane body counts with a new generation of G.I. Joe dolls, while their elder siblings—the cannon fodder of tomorrow in a country comfortably retrofitted with selective-service registration—flocked to cheer the commando-style commie-bashing epics of Sylvester Stallone, Chuck Norris and other can-do avengers. As for the cranks and crackpots who'd kept the old patriotic faith—Jerry Falwell, Jimmy Swaggart and presidential aspirant Pat Robertson among the professionally pious; broadcast buffoons such as Wally George out in right-wing lulu land—they were now paraded through the mainstream media as avatars and exegetes of a newly tumescent Americanism.

There had been earlier ripples of this renewal, of course. As the political pall of the Nixonian Seventies lifted, Americans grew weary of being bad-mouthed as scumbags of the earth—of being ritually reviled by foreigners who couldn't even field a decent phone system, for God's sake. They wanted to feel good about themselves again. And if invading Grenada wasn't quite the ticket, the 1984 Olympics in Los Angeles—slickly packaged by an American TV producer, and with the Soviets comfortably out of the running—really hit the spot. The ain't-we-great fervor attendant upon that event lingered and grew, and in 1985 the whole country seemed suddenly seized by a sort of purposeful wholesomeness. Pop musicians, nicking a concept from the British Band Aid benefit, mounted virtuous works on a massive, all-American scale—USA for Africa, Live Aid, Farm Aid, the *Sun City* album. This was can-do charity, not political education; the near est-ian "We Are the World" was presented without an inkling of irony, and little mention was made at Farm Aid of the government's extensive (and disastrous) subsidy of American farm programs. But these extraordinary benefits raised bucks and further burnished the national self-image. More and more advertisers detected the trend, and soon various corporate wares were being heralded as "An American Revolution" and "The Spirit of America." Unable to license Bruce Springsteen's "Born in the U.S.A." for an ad campaign, Chrysler, the most shameless of the auto makers, came up instead with its own dubious anthem, "Made in the U.S.A." The new patriotism turned out to be very good for business. As one Pepsi-Cola VP told

Newsweek, "Live Aid demonstrates that you can quickly develop marketing events that are good for companies, artists and the cause."

This is true—as Coca-Cola, which is sponsoring next year's Hands across America charity stunt, has quickly recognized. The mass charity projects of 1985 were marvels not so much of pure American beneficence (the fans, after all, got something in return for their money: a record, a concert, a sense of event) as they were of plain old capitalist merchandising. This was appropriate. In an earlier pop period, musicians were at pains to deplore the trappings of crass commercialism. But in the era of corporate tour support and lucrative product endorsements, such principled disdain would have seemed quaint. By 1985, rock & roll—once the music of rebellion and dissent—was neck-deep in the upwardly mobile mainstream of American life. And it felt *right.* In a sobering leap of logic, some rockers, such as Neil Young, have expressed support not only for Ronald Reagan, the author of this new abundance, but for his outwardly mobile foreign policy as well.

This dismaying political drift is everywhere apparent. Consider the alarming alliance of certain feminists with the anti-erotic right in the latest war on pornography. Or the sad sound of Smokey Robinson lending his classic voice to the rejuvenated jihad against pop-song lyrics. When Bruce Springsteen stomps out the opening chords of "Born in the U.S.A."—a song whose lyrical intent is anything but celebratory—before a crowd of clenched-fisted, flag-wagging fans, you can, if you close your eyes, almost hear them as easily exhorting Stallone's Rambo to blow away some more of those little yellow fellows.

In fact, Springsteen seems to be the focus of a substantial misunderstanding about the new patriotism—a misunderstanding on the part of both pop kids and politicians. In 1985, Springsteen embodied the American moment more compellingly than any public figure save Ronald Reagan. Like Reagan, Springsteen seemed to stand for something; casual rock fans—such as politicians—might vaguely surmise that they stood for the *same* thing. Springsteen's album *Born in the U.S.A.* has been at or near the top of the pop charts for the last year and a half. One can imagine some sharp politicos checking out its red-white-and-blue cover and eyeballing those evocative song titles—"My Hometown," "Glory Days," "Working on the Highway"—and thinking, "Well, *all right,* a whole new constituency available for the co-opting."

Some such addled perception must have impelled the speechwriter who persuaded Reagan, while stumping through New Jersey in last year's presidential campaign, to ludicrously allude to the state's most famous native son by name. And how was one to fathom the experience of George Will, the conservative columnist and TV oracle, who, after witnessing one of Springsteen's marathon concert sweatfests (with sensibly stoppered ears), came away from it hymning the return of the hardwork ethic? And if the politicos never perceived Springsteen's intent, one wonders if all of his cheering fans do, either. What makes their red-white-and-blue fervor so unseemly at times are the songs that spur it. Like its closely related predecessor, the 1982 Springsteen album *Nebraska, Born in the U.S.A.* is populated by Americans adrift in a land of dislocation: the laid-off protagonist of "Downbound Train," the desperate dead-enders of "Dancing in the Dark" and "My Hometown," the devastated Vietnam vet of the title song. These are people in pain, and Springsteen brings them hauntingly to life—not as subjects for a sermon but as recognizable characters. Springsteen doesn't go into political specifics, and he offers no glib solutions. And perhaps because of the emotional primacy of his writing—and the irresistible exhilaration of his music—it is easy to overlook Springsteen's intentions. Easy, for example, to forget the bitter irony of a title like "Born in the U.S.A."—almost a curse upon the character the song chronicles—and to perceive it in the beer-pumped heat of Springsteen's live show as a simple, house-rocking salute to the big country whose name it so ambivalently invokes. Easy enough to decide, as Max Weinberg's mighty drums kick in, that, yeah, this *is* a great country. Maybe—*urp!*—the greatest goddamn country in the world.

Surely most humans harbor in their viscera the conviction that their country—that fabled place where the tribe parks its tents—is somehow "the best," a spiritual geography of enveloping swellness. Americans seem peculiarly prone to public utterance on this subject—even, alas, abroad. But the cozy jingoism that passes for banter back in Dobro Falls, or wherever, tends to ring tinnily in foreign parts, where the chief awareness of America may be as a sower of missiles, subverter of sovereign governments or supporter of odious autocrats. Who knows where they get these ideas?

Americans, far removed, as always, from the impact of their government's foreign policies, seem to be slipping into a provincial self-satisfaction. Oblivious to the lyrical import of an artist as musically persuasive as Springsteen, and uplifted by the astonishing accomplishments, however politically limited, of the Live Aid phenomenon, a lot of people appear to have concluded that happy days *are* here again—and are likely to be puzzled (at first, then irritated) when the rest of the world fails to cheer along. And then they may suddenly find themselves rubbing homilies with the long-haul politicos and crackpot cranks of the far right—people whose blinkered conception of patriotic virtue remains a compost of exasperated nationalism, misconceived moral certitude and a kind of muscular evangelical can-doism (the whole proclaimed with flourishes of ritual flag humping and the usual biblical hoodoo). The ascendance of such values—the values of political domination and death—in that part of American culture heretofore shaped by rock & roll humanism can only seem ominous to those who remember the ocean of patriotic gush upon which we floated our Southeast Asian adventure back in the Sixties, who recall how short a step it is from "can do" to "will do," and how little connection there ever has been between loving one's country and dying for one's government.

*T*WENTY-*E*IGHT

Frank Zappa

(1988)

*F*rank Zappa has always had an unsparing eye
for nitwit social phenomena, from preening hippies
in the Sixties to the "Valley girl" culture of the
Eighties (not to mention "Trouble Coming Every
Day," on the first Mothers of Invention album, a
song that ranks with Bob Dylan's "Only a Pawn in
Their Game" as one of the most perceptive racial
takes of the civil-rights decade). Nowadays, he
focuses his scorn largely on politicians, an eternally
deserving target, and the authoritarian ideologues
with whom they are frequently in league.

I was talking to Zappa in Philadelphia one night
in February of 1988, when the conversation turned to
politics—in particular, to the Democrats' latest
debacle at the polls: a presidential rout occasioned by
the presence on the ballot of the party's classically
hapless nominee, Massachusetts Governor Michael
Dukakis. Back in New York a few nights later, we
pursued related topics. A distillation of this
peripatetic chat is what follows.

As a Democrat, what did you make of the Democratic party's dismal showing in the last election [1988]?

I think what the Democrats have to do is not only rethink what their issues are; they also have to rethink advertising. Because this election was decided, more than any other election in American history, based on advertising. In the middle of the campaign, I tried to get ahold of Dukakis' advertising people with some ideas for commercials that I had. But it was virtually impossible.

What ideas did you have?

I had storyboards for thirty-two spots.

What was their gist?

I thought the best way to start reducing the effect of the Republican disinformation campaign was to run a series of spots that called into question exactly who these fucking people think they are. So one of the spots had a guy—obviously a Republican—standing on a lawn in front of a mansion, saying, "I'm a Republican, and I *care* about the environment." He points to his house: "*My* environment."

And then there was another one made out of videotape of Manuel Noriega. He's ranting away in Spanish, and a Chyron comes on the screen saying, "A Message to the American People from Manuel Noriega." Then an interpreter comes on and tells the American people what Manuel's saying, and it's something like: "People of America: Panama is a small country, and most of our income is derived from the drug trade. We have a good working relationship with George Bush. *Don't blow it for us now!*" Then, scrawled across the screen in Noriega's big handwriting, it would say: "Thanks—Manny."

Are the Democrats ready for this?

Well, the problem is, they're *not* ready for it, and that's the reason why they keep losing elections. I mean, as long as they're gonna play footsy with the Republicans and let the Republicans get away with the type of spin-doctoring that they put on everything that comes out, they're always gonna chomp it. You've gotta go for the fuckin' *balls* with these guys.

What should have been the Democrats' approach to the federal deficit? Are higher taxes the answer, or should the emphasis be on spending cuts?

Well, the only place where spending really ought to be cut down is defense. The fact of the matter is that the money that's spent on defense is spent on toys. It's spent to keep the buddies of the administration—the defense contractors—rolling in bucks. I'd propose that if they're willing to spend a trillion dollars on Star Wars, they take the trillion dollars and divide it by the total population of the United States and pass out the result in cash—along with an Uzi and a box of ammo. *Then* let the Russians come over.

I mean, does anybody in this country really believe the Russians are gonna start shootin' missiles over here? Look at these fuckin' people—they're waitin' in line for some pumpernickel. They got enough problems.

Do you hold out any hope at all for the Bush-Quayle administration?

Bush-Quayle is a scandal waiting to happen. It would be better if they hadn't won, because I have a feeling that once the facts come out about Bush's trip to Paris on October 18th, 1980 [to meet with Iranian representatives and allegedly offer them a $5-billion weapons deal in return for delaying the release of U.S. hostages that Iran was holding until after Ronald Reagan could defeat Jimmy Carter in the November 1980 presidental election], we may be looking at impeachment time again here. And then you'll see the real reason for Dan Quayle being pasted onto the ticket: he's the lowest form of impeachment insurance. But there's just too much garbage. They've shoved so much stuff under the rug, you can't roll the furniture over it anymore. There's *lumps*. It looks like flocked cottage cheese.

Speaking of the Middle East, what did you think of the recent U.S. decision to deny entry to PLO leader Yasir Arafat when he wanted to come to New York to address the UN General Assembly?

I think that Arafat should be able to enter the United States. They let Shamir in, and that motherfucker is a terrorist, too, you know? I mean, both of these guys have engaged in what can literally be called *terror*-ism in the pursuit of whatever their individual nationalist goals were. One guy comes in and gets a White House reception; another guy, because he's wearin' a swami hat, they want to keep him out. It does make the United States look slightly laughable to the rest of the world.

Do you think the special relationship between the U.S. and Israel is endangered by the increasingly hard-line domestic policies being practiced by the Israeli government?

I think the special relationship between the U.S. and Israel, if it is to be practical, has to be reevaluated. U.S. politicians are living in fear of the Israeli lobby, and in Israel, the people who are moderates live in fear of the Israeli religious fundamentalists, who are just as crazy as the Hezbollah. I mean, once the human mind gets to the point where policy is determined by the theoretical wishes of an invisible alien being, who has supposedly written lifetime instructions in a book someplace, which are to be followed regardless of their consequences, you've got a problem. People who want to enact legislation based on religious dogma are a danger in any society.

You obviously take politics very seriously, and you're articulate about political issues. So why did you turn down an offer from the Libertarian party to make you its 1988 presidential candidate?

I went through their platform piece by piece, and it was obvious that I was not a doctrinaire Libertarian. There's some things the Libertarians say that I can agree with. "You own yourself; the government does not own you"—I think that's pretty basic. And the gold standard's a nice idea . . . but we're past that, you know? It ain't gonna work. I read the Libertarian platform and I said, "Basically, you guys are closet anarchists. If you could have your way, there wouldn't be any government at all." And perhaps, in an ideal world, after a thousand years of evolution, maybe that'd be terrific. But I don't see any way that you can do away with law and order. The human race just hasn't evolved to the point where you can say, "Yeah, we'll all each take care of ourselves. We'll each clean our own water, we'll each pick up our own garbage, and we'll each take care of our own foreign policy." You have to have somebody else who can do that.

Have you thought about running for political office under other circumstances?

You know, I think about running for office, and I go: "God, could I really stand to go out and *campaign*?" It's so nauseating. I think I might be just as effective by reminding people of what's going on.

Have you always been a Democrat?

I'm a *registered* Democrat, but only because you don't have any choice in California. You either have to register as a Republican or a Democrat, or you can't participate in the primaries. Otherwise, I would be an independent. Until the Republican party sees fit to regain control of its platform from the fundamentalists who purchased it in 1979, there's no way that I would ever register as a Republican. It's too embarrassing. It puts you in bed with some really odd creatures. But as far as the Democratic party goes, I don't know *what* the fuck they stand for, or what they *think* they stand for. It's *not* clear. I would say that I'm a conservative, in the old-fashioned sense of the word.

Like a nineteenth-century liberal?

Well, it's this corny old concept: smaller government and lower taxes, you know? That's basic, bedrock conservatism. All the stuff they talk about as conservatism now—prayer in school and all that—that's religious fanaticism. That's got nothin' to do with *governmental* conservatism.

You've been taking potshots at the religious right in your current work, both onstage and on record. What do you think accounts for the continuing appeal of Christian fundamentalism in this country?

Psychology Today ran an article saying that at no time since the Middle Ages have more people believed in the existence of the devil. And that's because of the growth of these religions that believe in the devil. Literal devil—literal horns, literal tail, literal monster, gonna getcha. And meanwhile, they're talking about the 900-foot Jesus and hearing voices and . . .

Talking in tongues . . .

Yeah. And, okay, you have the right to do that. You have the right to talk in tongues any time you want. You have the right to see the 900-foot Jesus, feel the 900-foot Jesus, give money to the 900-foot Jesus. But you do not have the right to transform superstition into legislation, thereby making life untenable for those of us in this country who happen to not believe there *is* a 900-foot Jesus.

Which seems to be the aim of this new right. . . .

Yeah, "the new right." Come on, let's call a spade a spade here. These fuckers are fascists. Fascists with a cross.

Do you think churches should be taxed?

Well, those parts of churches that deal with the ethereal—*certainly* do not tax them. But let's face it: every church is a business. And when a business is allowed to compete unfairly with other people who are in business, that's not the American way. If the Baptist church has cotton mills, what's that got to do with Jesus?

I heard a funny story about one of the California televangelists being questioned by the IRS about the car he drove and telling them, "That's not my Cadillac; that's Jesus' Cadillac."

Yeah? Well, the day I see Jesus *drivin'* it, I'll believe it. Besides, didn't Oral Roberts say the guy was 900 feet tall? That's a hell of a Cadillac.

You've also been in the forefront of the fight against another branch of the new right: the Parents' Music Resource Center. Do you disagree totally with their contention that children need to be protected from pornography—or, more to the PMRC's point, pornographic rock lyrics?

Well, I happen to think that the more sex you do, the better off you are, as long as you do it in such a way that you don't get a disease from it. And I think that science has moved the society forward at such a rate that, probably by about thirteen, kids are out there doin' it—and probably doing it better than their parents are.

What about, say, six-year-olds?

The idea of protecting kids below the age of thirteen from certain sexual concepts is ridiculous. I mean, you can say *blow job, blow job, blow job,* and a six-year-old ain't gonna know what a blow job is, you know? So why are we protecting the six-year-old from the blow job here?

What about the alleged connection between heavy metal and Satanism—a subject exploited rather gaudily on a recent Geraldo Rivera TV special? Did you see that—the one where he had two women on who claimed to have bred babies for Satanic rituals?

Yeah. Here's Geraldo sitting there treating them with all

this great deference—*because they found Jesus.* I mean, suppose you were interviewing a woman who had been *raising babies to be skinned alive for the devil*? How do you talk to a woman like that? I don't care whether she says she's born again. This doesn't make it okay. If she raised a baby to be skinned alive for the devil, there ought to be something we can do about this, you know?

People must like to watch this kind of stuff. That show got record-breaking ratings.

Yeah, they like it because it's so ridiculous. People who would be emotionally perturbed by it have already joined the PMRC anyway. The rest of the people who watch it sit there and think the same thing that you and I think: Geraldo is full of shit.

Did you catch his skinhead show?

You bet.

What do you think about the practice of putting people like that— admitted Nazis—on television?

Well, I think it depends on what you *do* with 'em when you get 'em on, okay? I think if you put them on and just give them a platform to deliver their spew, without countering them in some way, you're creating a problem. If I had a show like that, I wouldn't put 'em on.

You know, people like to join things. You show some guy in Middle America that there are such things as skinheads, and what they do is go after minority races and certain religions, and they dress a certain way and act a certain way and talk a certain way, and they have something going for them, and you're a kid with nothing to do, living in the middle of nowhere, and you go: "Well, shit, I'll be one of those. I never was cut out for the Spandex pants and heavy-metal hair." So here is an offering of an optional lifestyle for a person who might be looking for something to do.

Recent studies suggest that racism is on the rise among college students and that American youth in general has grown more conservative in the Eighties than would ever have been thought possible in the Sixties. Would you agree?

I think that there's some truth to that. But if you want to

place blame for it, you have to say, "As above, so below." The rise of this stuff was all during the Reagan administration.

Given your views, are you a permissive father? Have you had any difficulty bringing up your own children?

Well, it was not easy. Moon and Dweezil are very level-headed, but Ahmet is pretty much of an extrovert, and so is Diva. They're absolutely fearless. They'll say anything to anybody, any time. 'Cause they see *me* doing it. So that's hard. How do you tell them, "Ahmet, you're thirteen, you can't do that yet"?

What do you tell them, then?

I try and tell 'em about manners, which is one of those lost secrets of America, you know? Manners are great. The reason that they were invented is, they make things work better. They can be carried to an extreme, but I happen to think that manners are very useful. Especially in tense social situations, or places where too many people live together in the same small area, you *need* them in order to just get along.

You smoke a lot. Do you ever worry about your kids taking that up?

Well, I don't care. I happen to think that the risks of smoking are greatly exaggerated. And also, you have to consider the source for the complaints about smoking. I don't trust Dr. [C. Everett] Koop [surgeon general under President Reagan] any farther than I can throw him.

Yeah, that uniform he wears . . .

Dr. God! I want to know: you've seen surgeon generals before—did they ever dress like Dr. God? What the fuck *is* this shit, okay? And besides, he's a Reagan appointee. That's strike number one. Strike number two is the Dr. God suit—no explanation given. Why does he look like an admiral? Is he the Admiral of Health? And I question any medical advice given by a man who joins the PMRC onstage during their symposium and talks about anal sex while they talk about backward-masking. I got a problem with this guy, you know? I mean, what do you say about a guy who thinks it's a photo opportunity to pose with Mr. Potato Head on the day they take his pipe away? Have we been reduced to that?

I like tobacco; there it is. I've always liked it, since I was a kid. I had asthma as a child. My mother told me, "If you smoke, you'll die." She was wrong. I smoke about a pack and a half a day, and I enjoy it. I did a lecture once in San Francisco, and one of the questions from the audience was, "Well, if you don't like drugs, why do you smoke cigarettes?" And I turned to the guy and I said, "Because to me, a cigarette is food. I live my life eating these things and drinking this black water in this cup over here. Now, this may be a baffling concept to people in San Francisco who believe they're gonna live forever if they stamp out tobacco smoke, but there it is." Fuck 'em.

Don't nonsmokers have rights?

They do have rights. But they don't have the right to be weasels. Come on.

PART FIVE

CLASSIC ROCK

$\mathcal{I}'$ve never had much of an ear for (or much of an interest in) predicting what songs will become popular hits or which new strain of music will capture the national imagination. One shrewdly crafted pop tune is pretty much as likely as another to go zooming to the top of the charts. So what? Outside of the more unified pop scene of the mid-Sixties—a period that produced a phenomenal number of brilliant records by truly talented performers—much of the stuff that clutters up the pop charts in any era is fairly disposable. Really adventurous new music is, by its nature, a hard sell for people fond of hearing new music that sounds reassuringly similar to the old music they liked.

Thus, most of the classic records described in this section—their origins researched for a special 1987 issue of *Rolling Stone* devoted to the 100 best albums of the preceding two decades—were bombs by any rational sales measure. And yet, the epochal masterworks by Captain Beefheart and the Magic Band, Iggy and the Stooges, the Ramones, the Sex Pistols and—especially—the Velvet Underground have enchanted and inspired more adventurous young musicians than most mere chart-toppers could ever hope to reach.

Another of these records—*We're Only in It for the Money,* by the Mothers of Invention—stands today as one of the most resounding put-downs of pop pretension ever committed to grooves. As for the Beatles' White Album and David Bowie's art-rock masterpiece, *Ziggy Stardust*—well, you know all about them . . . or do you? I know I learned a few things while researching them.

In any event, I hope that those who may be unfamiliar with some of these astonishing records will perhaps be motivated to pick them up and give them a listen. Not that it'll help most of the artists at this late date. The Beatles, the Velvets, the Sex Pistols and the Mothers are all history— although various of their members continue to record. David Bowie and the Ramones have soldiered on, but Captain Beefheart has retired to northern California, to paint and sculpt and celebrate every waking moment in which he no longer has to deal with the American music industry. That most people have never seen him perform with one of his several brilliant Magic Bands (and now, more than likely, never will) is a melancholy thought. Only his records remain; get them while you can.

NEVER MIND THE BOLLOCKS HERE'S THE Sex Pistols

Courtesy Michael Ochs Archives

TWENTY-NINE

Never Mind the Bollocks Here's the Sex Pistols

The Sex Pistols
Warner Bros.
Released November 1977

Nothing in rock was ever quite the same after *Never Mind the Bollocks*. The Sex Pistols swept away the cozy corporate musical verities of the Seventies in a tidal wave of spit and derision. To the overcranked velocity of the Ramones (an American band they admired), the Pistols added a profound contempt for all things phony and overinflated in the established culture—from jet-set rock stars to the reigning monarch of their native Britain. As critic Paul Nelson remarked in a lead review of *Bollocks* in *Rolling Stone,* "The rock wars of the Seventies have begun, and the Sex Pistols, the most incendiary rock & roll band since the Rolling Stones and the Who, have just dropped the Big One." Today, ten years after its release, such critical acclaim for *Bollocks* (Nelson called it "just about the most exciting rock & roll record of the Seventies") still seems entirely on target.

The group came together via Sex, a bondage-chic boutique in London's ever-trendy King's Road run by pop gadfly Malcolm McLaren and his wife, clothes designer Vivienne Westwood. Glen Matlock, a young painter and guitarist who was also learning bass at the time, worked in the shop on Saturdays, endeavoring, among other things, to discourage potential shoplifters—among whom were two young men named Steve Jones and Paul Cook. Jones and Cook had been pals since grade-school days; by 1975, Jones was, as Matlock recalls, "a burglar, basically. He'd nicked all this band equipment and didn't know what to do with it."

"I was like addicted to stealin' bands' equipment," Jones acknowledges. "I used to steal tons of it. That wasn't the reason we got a band together, but it was definitely convenient havin' all that stuff."

Whatever the case, Jones and Cook were already rehearsing with two other more-or-less musicians: a bassist named Del Nunes (Cook's brother-in-law) and a guitarist named Wally. At first, Jones attempted to play drums but soon handed his sticks to Cook. Matlock was brought in to replace Nunes on bass, and Jones became the singer.

They plugged away at cover versions of old Who and Small Faces and Jonathan Richman tunes, and McLaren began dropping by to monitor their progress. What the nascent band most urgently required, McLaren noted, was a real singer, and the Pistols began tacking up notices inviting aspiring vocalists to present themselves at McLaren's shop. One day John Lydon walked in.

"He was really different," says Jones. "He had his hair green, and he had a Pink Floyd T-shirt, and he'd wrote above the name I HATE. That was pretty cool. And he had the safety pins goin'. He was just perfect for what we wanted to do." Noting the greenish tinge of Lydon's teeth, Jones dubbed him Johnny Rotten.

With the addition of Lydon and the repositioning of Jones as a guitarist, the band suddenly clicked. McLaren discerned a promise that he felt transcended mere rock stardom. He wanted to dress them in gear from his bondage shop, have them write the most scabrously offensive songs imaginable, market them as an affront to public decency—and make the public pay for the thrill of being scandalized.

"We thought it was ridiculous," says Jones. "Whenever McLaren butted in with the music, we'd tell him to piss off. 'Cause we knew he didn't have a fuckin' clue about music or what we wanted to do."

"I remember writing 'Sub-Mission' in a pub with Rotten," says Matlock. "Malcolm had said to write a song about submission, because his shop was like bondage and rubber wear and all that. And I remember sittin' in the pub and John goin', 'Oh, God, I don't really wanna do this.' I said, 'Well, what's the idea of this song? What's the name of it?' He goes, 'Submission.' I said, 'Okay, how 'bout "I'm on a submarine mission for you, baby"?' So we sat in the pub and wrote this song, right? It's got nothin' to do with submission. It was about takin' the piss out of Malcolm McLaren."

But McLaren's antisocial concepts were key to the Pistols' impact. "It was a five-way situation," says Matlock. "It wouldn't have worked without Malcolm, and it wouldn't have worked without us. We had this kind of Sex Pistols kibbutz, you know?"

The Pistols had been recording demos with their concert soundman, Dave Goodman, and also with guitarist Chris Spedding. McLaren took the Spedding tapes to Chris Thomas, a producer whose work with Roxy Music Jones and Cook had long admired. Thomas was impressed. "They just sounded like a fantastic rock & roll band," he says. "Anarchy in the U.K.," a roaring social broadside, was released at the end of 1976, and immediately banned from radio airplay by the BBC. The Pistols' maiden tour, in support of the single, was effectively scuttled by public uproar: they were prohibited from playing all but three of twenty-one scheduled gigs. EMI, their record company, was so shaken by the outcry that it dropped the group. A&M Records signed them, then had second thoughts and dumped them a week later. By this point certain internal frictions were also coming to a head.

"John really hated Glen," says Jones. "We all kinda hated Glen, really. 'Cause he liked the Beatles so much, you know? Knew all these fancy fuckin' chords. He was just not a Sex Pistol at heart."

So, although Matlock had cowritten almost an album's worth of songs with the group, he was history. To replace him, Lydon brought in an old school pal named John Ritchie, whose dissolute charisma overshadowed his complete lack of ability as a musician. Lydon dubbed him Sid Vicious.

The group signed with its third label, Virgin, and in May 1977 released a second single, the deliriously irreverent "God Save the Queen." The record went to Number One on the sales charts despite another airplay ban by the BBC.

In midsummer the Sex Pistols went into Wessex Studios, in Islington, to record more songs for their first album. Jones and Cook handled the rhythm tracks, to which Lydon added his snarling vocals. Ritchie, according to Jones, "didn't do anything. The guy was fuckin' never around. I played the bass on the bulk of it. Sid played on maybe 'God Save the Queen,' but it's got two basses on it—mine and his." Rumors that Chris Spedding actually played on the Pistols' records are, according to Thomas, totally untrue. "He had nothing to do with it," says the producer. "Steve Jones did everything."

Bollocks took about a month to record. The completed album was a sensation—it contained all three of the group's singles to date ("Anarchy," "God Save the Queen" and the recent "Pretty Vacant"), plus such withering blasts as "Bodies" (about an abortion), "EMI" (aimed at their first record company) and the self-explanatory "No Feelings." The group signed an American deal with Warner Bros. in October and launched a short, chaotic tour of the United States at the beginning of 1978. On January 14th, following their final date, at Winterland, in San Francisco, Lydon announced that the group had split up.

"I'm sure if we woulda stayed together, we could've been the biggest thing since sliced bread," says Jones. "But at the time the only thing I wanted to do was to fucking get out of it. It was drivin' me nuts. We wasn't writin' any songs. I didn't like John's attitudes toward music. Sid was gettin' more and more into junk and wasn't playin'. And all me and Paul really wanted to do was rock, you know?"

Lydon went on to form the audaciously abrasive Public Image Ltd. Ritchie died of a heroin overdose in New York in February 1979. Jones, now a member of Alcoholics Anonymous, has just released his first solo album. Cook drums for a British band called the Chiefs of Relief. Until last year, when the three surviving Pistols won a court case against McLaren and regained the rights to their songs, none of them had ever profited from album sales. Only Matlock, who had secured his song-publishing rights before leaving the group, has regularly received royalties from *Bollocks*.

"I'm waitin' on some now," he said recently. "I hope they come pretty soon, because I've only got half a bottle of vodka left."

Recorded at Wessex Studios, London, summer 1977. Producers: Chris Thomas and Bill Price. Engineer: Bill Price. Highest Chart Position: Number 106. Total U.S. Sales: 575,677.

Courtesy Michael Ochs Archives

THIRTY

The Rise and Fall of Ziggy Stardust and the Spiders from Mars

David Bowie
RCA
Released June 6th, 1972

"**I**'m going to be huge," David Bowie told a reporter toward the end of 1971. It was a typically outrageous comment by the former David Jones, who had been making records since 1964 but had only just released his fourth album, *Hunky Dory*. The followup to that LP, however, was already in the can—and this fifth album was the one that would break his career wide open, turning him overnight into the international pop presence he has managed to remain to this day.

Ziggy Stardust presented to the world rock's first completely prepackaged persona. It also defined the glitter-rock moment of the early Seventies and took rock theatrics and pansexuality to a new peak. Most of all, despite the calculated feyness of its presentation, *Ziggy Stardust* packed an exhilarating sonic wallop.

The keys to *Ziggy*'s success were several: eleven excellent songs, all but one composed, down to the last reverberating riff, by Bowie (the exception was Ron Davies' much-covered "It Ain't Easy"); an immaculate and unmannered production by Ken Scott; and explosive backup by the Spiders from Mars—in retrospect, clearly the most exciting band Bowie has ever had. Bowie met guitarist Mick Ronson in late 1969 and quickly recruited him to play in a short-lived group called Hype, which also included his then producer, Tony Visconti, on bass. Before long, Ronson brought in drummer Mick Woodmansey to help Bowie record a single version of "Memory of a Free Festival," a popular song from David's second album. Ronson and Woodmansey had worked together in their native Hull, in the north of England, in a blues band called the Rats, which had released two obscure singles. By the spring of 1971, Ronson and Woodmansey had been joined in London by yet another Rat, bassist Trevor Bolder, and the soon to be Spiders from Mars were complete.

The Spiders made their vinyl debut backing Bowie on a single, credited to Arnold Corns (a Bowie side project) that paired "Hang On to Yourself" and "Moonage Daydream," two songs that would later be recut for the *Ziggy* LP. For the *Hunky Dory* sessions they were joined by the future Yes keyboardist Rick Wakeman. Then, in June, Bowie took his trio into London's Trident Studios to begin work on *Ziggy Stardust*. Behind the board (a simple eight-track) was Ken Scott, who had started out as an engineer on two earlier Bowie LPs and had become his producer with *Hunky Dory*. Bowie, who had previously been a bit of a hippie, told Scott that *Ziggy* was going to be a real rock & roll album. Several of the songs he had written for it had already been tested before concert audiences, and on LP they were to be connected within a concept—the prefab legend of Ziggy Stardust, a dissolute, ambi-sexual "plastic rocker" whose fictive saga was loosely based on the career of an obscure American singer named Vince Taylor, whom Bowie had encountered on the streets of London some years earlier. The character's concocted surname was borrowed from the Legendary Stardust Cowboy, one of Bowie's label mates when he was with Mercury Records. And Ziggy, as Bowie later told *Rolling Stone,* "was one of the few Christian names I could find beginning with the letter *Z.*"

Ziggy was a very shrewd move: it presented Bowie, the fledgling artiste, as an established rock star. In early January 1972 he created an image to match the character, cropping his Garbo-length hair and dyeing it drop-dead yellow for the album cover, which was photographed in rain-soaked Heddon Street, just off London's Regent Street. He put the finishing touch on his new persona in the January 22nd edition of *Melody Maker,* telling writer Michael Watts, "I'm gay, and always have been." (Later Bowie would characterize that remark as "the biggest mistake I've ever made.")

If Bowie's Ziggy character provided the album's unifying concept—aligning apprehensions of personal doom ("Rock 'n' Roll Suicide") with more universal forebodings ("Five Years")—the music itself derived much of its startling power from Ronson's howling, Jeff Beck–influenced guitar: a Les Paul run through a 100-watt Marshall amp and, rather anachronistically, a wah-wah pedal. "I only used the wah-wah pedal for the tone," says Ronson, a classically trained musician who also wrote the album's string arrangements. "That's how come it had a very honkin', Midlands sort of sound, you know? And then I had a rotten little fuzz box that never used to work. But basically it was just guitar straight through an amp." The result, especially on "Suffragette City," the album's most ferocious track, was a whole new level of guitar-rock aggression.

Released on June 6th, 1972, *Ziggy* was immediately acclaimed a hit. "I wasn't at all surprised *Ziggy Stardust* made my career," Bowie subsequently said. "I packaged a totally credible plastic rock star—much better than any sort of Monkees fabrication. My plastic rocker was much more plastic than anybody's."

And, as the legion of Ziggy clones who still pop up at Bowie concerts confirms, more enduring as well.

Recorded at Trident Studios, London, December 1971 to January 1972. Producers: David Bowie and Ken Scott. Engineer: Ken Scott. Highest Chart Position: Number Seventy-five. Total U.S. Sales: 800,000.

Courtesy Michael Ochs Archives

THIRTY-ONE

The Beatles

The Beatles
Apple
Released November 22nd, 1968

By the spring of 1968—when they began recording what would be their most straightforward and eclectic collection of songs since *Rubber Soul*—the Beatles, as a unit, were clearly crumbling. The previous summer, while the boys were off in Wales pursuing an infatuation with a visiting Indian mystic, Maharishi Mahesh Yogi, their manager, Brian Epstein, had died. Paul McCartney had begun asserting his leadership within the group—engineering the *Magical Mystery Tour* film project, subsequently judged the Beatles' first bomb—and his mates were growing uneasy—especially John Lennon, whose passion for Yoko Ono was beginning to eclipse his interest in the group. In February, the Beatles had flown to India to meditate (along with such fellow pop figures as Mia Farrow and Donovan) with the maharishi at his ashram in Rishikesh. When the toadlike guru reportedly began coming on to some of his female disciples, however, the Beatles, disillusioned, split.

So on May 30th, when the group entered EMI's studios on Abbey Road to begin work on an album for year-end release, the atmosphere was anything but easygoing. Lennon, ignoring the customary Beatles ban on girlfriends in the studio, brought Ono along (she eventually wound up warbling on such tracks as "Birthday" and "The Continuing Story of Bungalow Bill"). Flaunting his avant-garde proclivities, Lennon went right to work on "Revolution 9," a raucous brew of thirty different tape loops that eventually clocked in at more than eight minutes—

the longest, and noisiest, Beatles track ever. There was a decided tension in the air. Over the next three months, with producer George Martin at the helm, the group managed to
complete only ten tracks.

"They attempted to be nice to each other when they were
laying basic tracks," says Ken Scott, who had worked as an engineer with the Beatles ever since *A Hard Day's Night*. "But there
was one time, when we were putting brass on one of Paul's
songs . . . Everything was going real well, and then John and
Ringo walked in—and for the half an hour they were there, you
could have cut the atmosphere with a knife. It was awful. At
one point Ringo quit the band for a couple of days—he had
reached that point, and he walked. When he came back, they
filled the entire studio with flowers and big WELCOME HOME
banners. They wanted him back."

Things improved somewhat when Martin decided to take
a three-week vacation and brought in his assistant, Chris
Thomas, to take his place. In those three weeks, the group managed to barrel through ten more tracks. And when Martin returned, the pace accelerated even further. But it would never
again be like the old days. Now each songwriter worked on his
own songs, using the others as backing musicians.

The album has no discernible center: it is a sprawling collection of songs, several of which were written in Rishikesh—
Paul's "Rocky Raccoon" (composed with help from Lennon and
Donovan), John's "Dear Prudence" (about Mia Farrow's sister,
who was along for the pilgrimage) and "Sexy Sadie" (a kiss-off
to the maharishi: "You made a fool of everyone"). And there is
no stylistic unity: the tracks range from Paul's folkish "Black-
bird" to John's doo-wop-flavored "Happiness Is a Warm Gun"
to Ringo's galumphing "Don't Pass Me By" (his songwriting debut) to George's stately "While My Guitar Gently Weeps"
(which featured Eric Clapton playing lead).

If group unity was in short supply, inspiration wasn't.
"The fastest track we did was 'Birthday,'" says Scott. "We
started it in the afternoon, then we all went round to Paul's
house to watch one of the old rock & roll movies, *The Girl Can't
Help It,* that was being shown on TV. That gave everyone a new
lease on life, and we went back in the studio and finished the
song that night."

By October, says Scott, "panic was beginning to set in.
We were trying to beat the time frame. Then, on the last night,

John comes in with a new song he wants to record. It was 'Julia.' And that was the last track we did."

Lennon persuaded Martin to release the tracks—all thirty of them—as a double album. McCartney had spoken to Richard Hamilton, the noted British Pop artist, about designing a cover composed of news clips and headlines, something splashy and garish. Hamilton suggested a different tack—to really stand out, he said, the cover should be absolutely white. The group agreed.

The Beatles was the first album to be released on Apple, the group's new label. It seemed an auspicious beginning, but it was actually the beginning of the end. Seventeen months later, the Beatles—the most magical phenomenon in the annals of rock music—would be history.

Recorded at Abbey Road, London, May 30th to October 17th, 1968. Producer: George Martin. Engineer: Geoff Emerick, Chris Thomas and Ken Scott. Highest Chart Position: Number One. Total U.S. Sales: 6 million.

PEEL SLOWLY AND SEE

Andy Warhol

Courtesy Michael Ochs Archives

Thirty-Two

The Velvet Underground and Nico

The Velvet Underground
MGM / Verve
Released March 1967

This sensational album—a monument of lyrical and musical innovation in rock and a record of continuing influence—was banged out, for the most part, in a crumbling four-track studio over two days at a cost of $1500. "We recorded at a place that was being torn apart," says John Cale, who played piano, bass and electric viola on the album, alongside lead guitarist, singer and main songwriter Lou Reed, guitarist Sterling Morrison, percussionist Maureen Tucker and—on three tracks—the fetchingly frog-toned German vocalist Nico (Reed's girlfriend at the time). Andy Warhol, who had discovered the Velvets at New York's Café Bizarre early in 1966, was credited as producer of the group's debut LP, but according to Cale, "This shoe salesman, Norman Dolph, put up the money, and he got a deal at Cameo-Parkway Studios, on Broadway. We went in there, and the floorboards were torn up, the walls were out, there were four mikes working. We set up the drums where there was enough floor, turned it all up and went from there."

Cale says Dolph ran the sessions—sort of. "He didn't understand the first fucking thing about recording. He'd say, 'Hold it, I think we've got a hot one here!' He didn't know what the hell he had on his hands." According to Dolph—a former Columbia Records sales executive, not a shoe sales-man—the sessions were held at the decrepit Scepter Records studio on Fifty-fourth Street. He agrees that he may not have been the most together of producers, "but nobody knew what they were doing." Dolph went on to write "Life Is a Rock (but the Radio Rolled Me)," a hit for the group Reunion in 1974.

Cale further recalls the New York sessions as being slightly tense. "Everybody was very nervous about it. Lou was paranoid, and eventually he made everybody paranoid." MGM staff producer Tom Wilson subsequently took the group into a Los Angeles studio to finish three tracks, among them the Nico feature "All Tomorrow's Parties." Nico's sudden appearance in the group (she'd previously been a model) was, according to Cale, "very funny. It was like the lead singer has a girlfriend, and she wants to sing, so let her. She took it very seriously. She really was determined not to be a model, a hunk of beauty. She was determined to make something of herself." The end result of all this was an electrifying collection of eleven songs with a startling new urban sensibility. Unfortunately, many listeners were apparently put off by the references to drugs ("Heroin," "I'm Waiting for the Man") and sadomasochism (the haunting "Venus in Furs"). They overlooked such complexly gorgeous odes to love and life as "Sunday Morning," "I'll Be Your Mirror," the much-covered "Femme Fatale" and the majestic "All Tomorrow's Parties"—the latter song available in a striking alternative take on the new CD edition of the album. MGM's promotional strategies didn't help, either. "Frank Zappa was on the label, too," says Cale. "So the promotion department decided, 'Zero bucks for VU, because they've got Andy Warhol; let's give all the bucks to Zappa.'"

Whatever the case, listening to this epochal LP twenty years later, one can still feel the thrill of new rock territory being opened up.

"We were really excited," says Cale. "We had this opportunity to do something revolutionary—to combine avant-garde and rock & roll, to do something symphonic. No matter how borderline destructive everything was, there was real excitement there for all of us. We just started playing and held it to the wall. I mean, we had a *good time.*"

Recorded at Scepter Studios, New York City, and T.T.G. Studios, Hollywood, California, April to May 1966. Producers: Andy Warhol and Tom Wilson. Engineers: Omi Haden

STEREO
STS 1053

TROUT MASK REPLICA

CAPTAIN BEEFHEART
& HIS MAGIC BAND

Courtesy Michael Ochs Archives

THIRTY-THREE

Trout Mask Replica

Captain Beefheart and His Magic Band
Straight
Released Spring 1969

Trout Mask Replica is rock's most visionary album, a true masterpiece. The breathtaking vocals of Captain Beefheart (his real name is Don Van Vliet) recalled the Delta yowl of Howlin' Wolf, but his music—lurching rhythms, car-crash guitars and wailing, free-form horns—resembled nothing that had ever been heard in rock (or perhaps on earth) before.

Van Vliet was a child-prodigy sculptor in his native Los Angeles. At thirteen he moved with his family to the desert town of Lancaster, California, where he taught himself saxophone and harmonica and met the young Frank Zappa, who dubbed him Captain Beefheart because, it's said, he seemed to have "a beef in his heart" against the world. Zappa eventually moved to L.A. and formed the Mothers of Invention. Van Vliet founded his first Magic Band in Lancaster in 1964. Drummer John French joined early on, and he subsequently recruited guitarist Jeff Cotton and bassist Mark Boston. Guitarist Bill Harkleroad completed the classic lineup, and each member assumed a stage monicker: Zoot Horn Rollo (for Harkleroad), Antennae Jimmy Semens (Cotton), Rockette Morton (Boston) and Drumbo (French).

By this time, Van Vliet and his band had relocated to a secluded house near L.A. Don had already recorded three albums for two baffled record companies. Fortunately, Zappa had established his own label, Straight, and he agreed to produce *Trout Mask*.

Van Vliet says he wrote all twenty-eight of the *Trout Mask* compositions on a piano in eight and a half hours and taught each of the players his part. But, says Zappa, "you'd have to give some credit to the musicians, because Don would ask them to do stuff that was, by normal standards, wrong. They had to really want to play his music a lot." According to French, it was he who taught the band how to play the tunes.

The group rehearsed for months. "We all had a lot of respect for what Don was doing," says French, "but he was always paranoid that somebody was trying to sabotage the music. So he would interrogate us. It was almost like being in a cult. But Don was just afraid—he'd been really ripped off when he was young."

Zappa initially recorded the band at its house but recut most of the tracks at a local studio, with Don's cousin, Victor Haydon, honking along on bass clarinet as the Mascara Snake. One number, "The Blimp," is actually a Mothers of Invention track with a Jeff Cotton vocal—taped over the telephone—laid on top.

Trout Mask was hardly a "hit," but its influence can be felt in rock and jazz to this day. Van Vliet hasn't made a record since 1982, and doesn't intend to. He lives in a remote part of California and passes his time painting, sculpting and cultivating an interest in basketball. "The best percussion of all," he says, "is done by the Lakers."

Recorded at the Magic Band's house, in Woodland Hills, California, and Whitney Studios, Glendale, California, spring 1968. Producer: Frank Zappa. Engineer: Dick Kunc. Total U.S. Sales: 75,000.

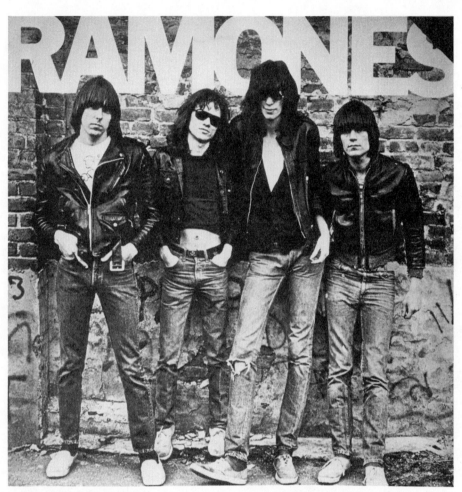

Courtesy Michael Ochs Archives

*T*HIRTY-*F*OUR

Ramones

The Ramones
Sire
Released May 1976

By 1976 rock & roll was twenty-one years old and—according to an increasingly vocal segment of hard-core fans—beginning to show its age. Disco pop reigned, and rock itself seemed to have gone soft (Wings), sappy (Peter Frampton) and stagnant (the increasingly lugubrious Led Zeppelin). The Ramones, four leather-jacketed reprobates from the glue-sniffing, acid-dropping teen milieu of Forest Hills, Queens, landed on this flabbed-out scene like a boulder on a box of sugar-cream doughnuts. Their debut album contained fourteen tracks, not one of which approached the three-minute mark (the shortest clocked in at a head-spinning 1:30). They played no ballads, no guitar solos. Their lyrics were ridiculous ("Beat on the brat / Beat on the brat / Beat on the brat with a baseball bat"), and their sound unvaryingly loud. In short, *Ramones,* recorded in one week at a total cost of $6400, was perhaps the purest expression of head-first rock velocity in the music's history.

The Ramones came together in 1974, with Johnny Ramone (John Cummings) on maxi-blast guitar, Dee Dee Ramone (Douglas Colvin) on rhythm guitar, Joey Ramone (Jeffrey Hyman) on drums and, briefly, one Richie Stern on bass. This lineup, however, proved unworkable. "Johnny wanted to be the fastest guitar player in the world," says Joey. "Everything kept gettin' faster and faster, and I couldn't keep up no more." When it was decided that Joey had the best voice of the three, he moved out front and was replaced by another pal, Tom Erdelyi, a Hungarian-born guitarist (and fledgling recording engineer: he had worked on Jimi Hendrix's *Band of Gypsys*), who had been functioning as the group's manager but had never played drums before in his life. (Erdelyi, of course, became Tommy Ramone—the fictive surname inspired by Paul Ramon, Paul McCartney's nom de hotel back in the Beatles' early touring days.)

The Ramones became stars of the burgeoning scene at CBGB, the Bowery punk mecca. "We would get on and do seven-minute *sets*," says Tommy. "Play like twenty songs. Those were really bizarre shows." By the time they recorded their first LP, they were able to buy big-league Marshall stacks to replace the dinky little battery-powered amps they had been using. Unfortunately, says Dee Dee, "we didn't know how to work the Marshalls, so we just turned everything up all the way."

"The studio engineers didn't know what the hell was going on," says Tommy of the resultant din. "They looked like they were into jazz a lot, you know? They really seemed confused by the whole thing." *Ramones* was greeted with derision in the pop mainstream. Every song was loud and fast, and the lyrics were cartoons—odes to punk girlfriends and sniffing glue and cult films like *The Texas Chainsaw Massacre*. (There were darker elements, too: according to Dee Dee, the song "53rd & 3rd" refers to the Manhattan intersection "where I used to go to hustle, to get money for heroin"—a habit he's been free of since 1980.) But *Ramones* recalled the glory days of the rock & roll single: every song was short, fast and—to those so disposed—unforgettable. "Even though they called it punk," says Joey, "we always considered ourselves rock & roll." Whatever one labeled it, *Ramones* took rock back to its teen-junk roots, a reminder to everyone that of all the music's possible conponents, fun may well be the most essential.

Recorded at Plaza Sound, Radio City Music Hall, New York City, February 1976. Producer: Craig Leon. Engineer: Rob Freeman. Highest Chart Position: Number 111. Total U.S. Sales: 123,860.

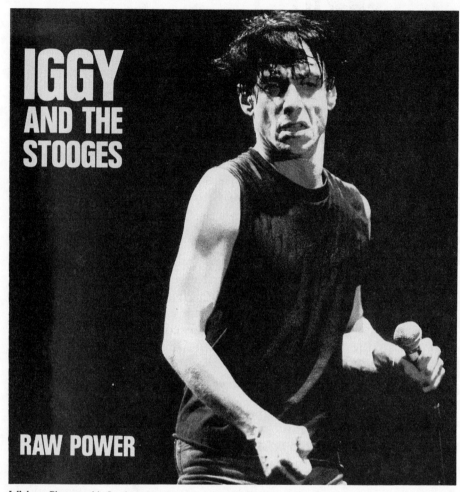

IGGY AND THE STOOGES

RAW POWER

Jellybean Photographic Services, Inc.

THIRTY-FIVE

Raw Power

Iggy and the Stooges
Columbia
Released February 1973

Raw Power was the first great punk-guitar album, a roaring, glorious mess of a record that—festooned as it was with such songs as "Gimme Danger," "Death Trip" and "Your Pretty Face Is Going to Hell"—helped set the emotional tone for the international punk explosion that followed three years later.

By the beginning of 1971, the Detroit-based Stooges—paragons of drug-gobbling rock excess—had worn out their welcome at Elektra, the label that had released their first two albums. The group had disbanded, and Iggy Pop, its scabrously charismatic leader, was at loose ends when, in the fall of that year, he met David Bowie and his manager, Tony DeFries, at Max's Kansas City, the celebrated New York rock club. Bowie, then in the midst of concocting his Ziggy Stardust persona, was an admirer. ("Iggy has natural theater," Bowie said. "It's his own . . . straight from the street.") He persuaded DeFries to sign Pop to his management firm, MainMan. Within a week, DeFries had engineered a deal for Iggy with CBS Records. (For his audition in the office of label chief Clive Davis, Iggy wore a tuxedo and sang "Shadow of Your Smile." "He signed me on the spot," Iggy says. "Just said, 'Call the lawyers, six figures, no problem.' I think he was pissed off that he'd missed out on David Bowie.")

By the summer of 1972, Iggy had relocated to London with guitarist James Williamson, a Detroit legend Iggy had recruited into the Stooges after the release of their second LP,

Fun House. Williamson was a maestro of the Marshall-amp stack and a perfect songwriting foil for Pop. DeFries had wanted to "get rid of those awful, dirty Stooges," as Iggy remembers it. But Iggy insisted on importing Stooge brothers Ron and Scott Asheton to play bass and drums on the new record. The reconstituted group holed up in a house DeFries rented for them—an elegant place that came complete with pricey pictures by painter Marc Chagall. (We said, 'What is this shit he's got on the walls?'" Iggy says. "We threw 'em in the backyard.")

The *Raw Power* sessions, conducted in late summer at CBS Studios in London, were predictably chaotic, according to Iggy. "The drugs we were taking," he says, "heightened what was already a sense of acute disrespect for the music industry and what we thought was the phony, shitty music it was churning out at the time." The group produced itself ("We didn't really understand multitracking or any of those concepts"), and Iggy—even more disastrously—mixed the resulting tapes. ("The treble was really pushed up and the compression was off all the way, and the stuff sort of barked at you, like a yelping dog.")

DeFries hated the tapes and in November prevailed on Bowie to take them into the Western Sound studios, in Los Angeles, and remix them. "He used some state-of-the-art gizmos that he wanted to experiment with," Iggy says. "One of 'em he called a Time Tube, which he put the guitar tracks through—it looked suspiciously like a large bong. The sound came out the other end sounding like the guy was playing in the Himalayas. And he wanted to get the drums . . . I don't know if he used the word *tribal,* but he wanted it to sound as if the drummer was beating on a log. David was interested in the primitive aspect of the Stooges. I think to him we were a bunch of Neanderthals. I see his point—especially compared to this guy from London who knew all this stuff about who painted which picture and what Anthony Newley song was on which opera or whatever. So I think he tried to bring out the sort of talking-drum aspect of Scott Asheton's playing."

Raw Power was the Stooges' swan song. Iggy went on to kick his drug and alcohol habits, tour with Bowie (who has produced three Pop solo albums to date) and generally clean up his act. But he has no regrets and looks back upon *Raw Power* for what it was, and remains: an out-of-control classic.

Recorded at CBS Studios, London, July and August 1972. Producer: Iggy Pop. Engineer: Mike Ross. Highest Chart Position: Number 182.

Courtesy Michael Ochs Archives

THIRTY-SIX

We're Only in It for the Money

The Mothers of Invention
Verve
Released Fall 1968

Nineteen sixty-seven's summer of love was kicked off with the June 2nd release of *Sgt. Pepper's Lonely Hearts Club Band.* In San Francisco hippies hailed the dawn of a new pop-based youth culture. But down in Los Angeles, Frank Zappa had his doubts.

"*Sgt. Pepper* was okay," Zappa allows, "but just the whole aroma of what the Beatles were was something that never really caught my fancy. I got the impression from what was going on at the time that they were only in it for the money—and that was a pretty unpopular view to hold."

The result of Zappa's skepticism was the third Mothers of Invention album, *We're Only in It for the Money*—perhaps the most mercilessly derisive raspberry ever flung at the rock scene by an actual participant therein. In Zappa's lyrics, San Francisco was populated by "phony hippies" cavorting in the "psychedelic dungeons popping up on every street," most of them hapless out-of-towners with no higher aspiration than to "stay a week and get the crabs and / Take a bus back home." He parodied the dippier lyrical tendencies of the day ("Diamonds on velvets on goldens on vixen / On comet and cupid on donner and blitzen"). He decried the hippies' irritating elitism ("Who cares if hair is long or short. . ."). And he summed up the situation with the doo-wop question "What's the Ugliest Part of Your Body?" (Answer: "I think it's your mind.")

Appropriately the album was recorded in New York City, far from the great West Coast flower-power fiesta. Zappa had relocated the Mothers to Manhattan following the Sunset Strip youth riots of 1967 and the subsequent shutdown of many Hollywood rock venues by the L.A. police. The group had begun a celebrated four-month residency at the Garrick Theater, in Greenwich Village, at Easter, playing two shows a day, six days a week. By summer's end, Zappa was attempting to entice his weary musicians into the local Mayfair Studios to begin work on *Money*. However, he says, only bassist Roy Estrada and multi-instrumentalist Ian Underwood "pretty much stuck with it. The rest of the guys didn't really like it. Most of them had quit at least five times. It was hard to get 'em to show up to sessions. That's why I did most of the stuff."

Money is also the first Mothers album that Zappa produced, and his tape-splicing compositional technique is boldly deployed on the instrumental track "The Chrome Plated Megaphone of Destiny." ("Before they started making dolls with sexual organs," he says, explaining that title, "the only data you could get from your doll was looking between its legs and seeing that little chrome nozzle—if you squeezed the doll, it made a kind of whistling sound. That was the chrome plated megaphone of destiny.") He also scattered aural collages throughout the record, including the voice of visiting pal Eric Clapton babbling, "It's God, I see God." (Clapton didn't play on the album, however, as was widely assumed, nor did Jimi Hendrix, another celebrity drop-in, who had jammed with the Mothers at the Garrick and was recruited to pose for the *Pepper*-parody jacket photo.)

In addition to lambasting hippie culture, Zappa also sought to immortalize some of his more bizarre childhood acquaintances—in particular, two brothers named Kenny and Ronnie, who featured in the song, "Let's Make the Water Turn Black."

"Ronnie had been busted for bootlegging," says Zappa. "He used to make raisin wine and sell it to kids in junior high school. Ronnie saved snot on a window in his room. He had gotten into this syndrome of flipping boogers. One day his mother went in there and started howling because she couldn't see through the window—it was all green. They had to use chisels and Ajax to scrape the stuff off. This is absolutely true."

Kenny, the other brother, lived in a garage in back of the house with Mothers sax man and roadie Jim "Motorhead" Sherwood. Since there was no plumbing in the garage, they began urinating in some Mason jars Kenny's mother kept for canning, then in the earthenware crocks that Ronnie had used to concoct his raisin wine. They covered the crocks with a board.

"One day," says Zappa, "just out of curiosity, Kenny lifted the board to see how the whiz was doing, and there were these *things* swimming in it—like some mutant tadpoles that had been brewing in there. The father found out and made them flush it all down the toilet. So whatever was living in the jars is now probably eleven feet long and living in the sewer system in California."

And the song's concluding line, "Wait till the fire turns green"?

"When they weren't pissing in jars and saving their snot on the windows," says Zappa, "they were lighting each other's farts. So there it is. It's like a folk song."

Recorded at Mayfair Studios and Apostolic Studios, New York City, August to September 1967. Producer: Frank Zappa. Engineers: Gary Kellgren and Dick Kunc. Highest Chart Position: Number Thirty.

ABOUT THE AUTHOR

A former senior editor at *Rolling Stone,* KURT LODER is the author of *I, Tina,* the 1986 autobiography of Tina Turner, and of several of the Q&A pieces collected in the 1989 compilation, *The Rolling Stone Interviews: The 1980s,* to which he also contributed an introductory essay. He currently works for MTV in New York City, where, at regular intervals throughout the year, he can be heard whining on about the merits of Howlin' Wolf and Jimmy Reed during meetings of the so-far unpersuaded Nominating Committee of the Rock & Roll Hall of Fame.